Studying Successfully

Ray Baxter

**Formerly Senior Lecturer in Education
Course Director Access to Higher Education Course
New College Durham**

ALDBROUGH ST JOHN PUBLICATIONS

Aldbrough St John Publications
Greencroft
Aldbrough St John
Richmond
North Yorkshire
DL11 7TJ

First published 1995

© Ray Baxter and
Aldbrough St John Publications, 1995
ISBN 0 9525393 0 6 softback

British Library Cataloguing-in-Publication Data.
A catalogue record for this book is
available from the British Library

Printed in Great Britain by
The Parkgate Press Ltd
Print House, Borough Road, Darlington,
Co Durham, DL1 1SW

The diagnostic tests,
examples of filing systems
and list learning programmes
are available from the publishers
on 3½" floppy disc for use on IBM compatible PC's.

A4 versions of diagnostic tests etc,
with photocopying license are
available for Tutors.

Please write for details.

Ray Baxter was born in North Yorkshire, obtained his degree in Leeds and taught in schools in Leeds and Bicester, then became Senior Lecturer in Education at Middleton St George College of Education. For the last 5 years he was Director of the Access to Higher Education Course at New College Durham. He is married and has 5 children.

CONTENTS

Acknowledgements

I am grateful to Norah Cohen, for permission to use her work on interview techniques, Penny Grennan for permission to use her work on assertiveness and communication skills, Daphne Williams for permission to use her work on examination preparation and careers guidance, and Alan Roebuck for permission to use his work on time-management. All of them have in fact contributed a great deal to the book in terms of advice and comment. Thanks to Cath John for her work on apostrophes! Thanks to Karen Greenwell, one of our students now at Suffolk University, for her advice and work on the cover of the book. Thanks to Alan Clifford, former Education Advisor to the City of Coventry for proof-reading the final manuscript and to Grace Buckle for her last minute efforts with checking for errors and omissions! Thanks to Colin Walker for his encouragement to go ahead! Thanks to Robert Postema of Management Books 2000 for permission to use material in section 4 pp 2-7 which I have adapted from "Building Your Own Rainbow" by Hopson and Scullie. Thanks to Andy Brown and Jim Jarvie of The Parkgate Press for their professional competence and enthusiasm.

Without my colleagues, this book would not have been written. I would like to thank Norah Cohen, Penny Grennan, Alan Roebuck and Daphne Williams for being the finest people with whom to work. Norah's commitment to the Access to Higher Education Course we ran at New College Durham and her imaginative, compassionate approach to her students has brought about real enlightenment and freedom in so many of her colleagues and students. Thanks to Penny, for your intelligence and wit and the ability to take everything in your stride - a creative thinker and a great shoulder to cry on! Thanks to Alan, who has always been the most enthusiastic and skilled of teachers, and the loyalest of friends. Thanks to Daphne, sensitive and informed counsellor and teacher of the highest qualities whose opinions are based on carefully thought through axioms. Thanks to all of you for the support and above all the friendship and love that has grown between us and made the 5 years we worked together a delight and pleasure. I am proud to have worked with you. To all the students who came on our Access to Higher Education Course, thanks for responding so well. I do hope all of you go on achieving as you did with us. To Mary my wife, thanks for all the encouragement and support you've given: without you it would not have been possible. To my children Paul and Philip, James and Thomas and Becky, thanks for being so patient!

I dedicate this book to all of you. I hope that the work you've all enabled me to do will be able to be passed on through this book to many more who want to benefit from education.

Foreword

by John McGuiness

Since meeting Ray Baxter, watching him teach and observing his effect on hundreds of students, I have come to place him in a venerated pantheon of teachers I have known, who contribute to what Postman and Weingartner described as the "continuing struggle against the veneration of crap". It is a powerful phrase for a powerful concept, and the activity it describes strikes terror into the hearts of those pseudo-educators who want students to be submissive, grateful, uncritical and regurgitative. Ray, on the contrary, revels in irreverence, search, unorthodoxy, creativity and challenge - and sees that his students would best contribute to the universities and colleges they go on to, by carrying on that tradition. In the most noble sense he stands side by side with Postman and Weingartner in seeing good teaching as a "subversive activity". That he was able to gather around him a team of like-minded teachers is a testament to his resilience, energy and vision. They see teaching as an exercise in liberation.

That said, he is also acutely aware of the skills needed by students to give credibility to their intellectual jousts with tutors, their forays into research literature and their critical analysis of the orthodoxies of the day. A vast array of skills are worked on - everything from spelling and grammar, through data assembly and analysis, on to structured argument, logic and persuasion, culminating in a real grasp of inferential values, conclusions and defensible positions.

Students from the Access Course at New College Durham came to realise that the exploratory adventure of education is much more complex and satisfying than a pub gripe or a club moan; they learned from Ray's course that it is a disciplined, skilled, descriptive, analytical, critical sifting of material, which permits creative, judicious, challenging positions to be assembled and defended. I know, because as an external examiner of the course for three years, I met the students and read their work.

I also saw the developmental power of the course modules. Students beginning hesitantly, almost apologetically, growing in confidence and skill as the course progressed, producing powerful and cogent dissertations as final pieces of work. Ray would be the first to acknowledge the powerful influence of his teaching colleagues on that student growth - and they would be equally eager to recognise that the clarity of the course materials he produced, the meticulous developmental sequences established and the skilful gradation of tasks asked of the students, created precisely the right balance of support and challenge to encourage the students to take the risks involved in learning.

I am consequently delighted that Ray has decided to crystallise a lifetime's work into this text. I am confident that it will be invaluable, both to course tutors and to students themselves. I am also honoured that he has invited me to make this introductory statement to his book.

In an article I wrote in 1993 about the so-called reforms of education initiated by the 1988 Education Act, I commented on the almost total absence of respect for persons that is involved in taking us away from the view of humans as intrinsically valuable, as being the driving force of education, towards that cold and implacable master, the market place, where human beings are seen as commodities with only consequential not intrinsic value. We are no longer to be educated because we have, every one of us, an inviolable core of worth and dignity; the state is now to invest in us to the extent that we look capable of offering a financial return on the investment. We have Darwin in the classroom - crude, insensitive pragmatism, survival of the fittest, and a criminally negligent waste of talent.

The teaching Ray Baxter offers celebrates the worth of every student he works with. (I write wondering whether Ray would get me to put that last preposition somewhere else - and I know that if he did, he would do it with the kind of gentle courtesy and respect that would leave me feeling not put down, but somehow enhanced. That is good teaching.) This book, too, is a statement of Ray's confidence in the ability of returners to education - they will find here a storehouse of helpful ideas, encouragement and guidance, as they embark on the adventure of education. Ray Baxter may have retired, but he is still an educator.

John McGuiness
University of Durham
May 1995

Introduction

Over the past few years I have been lucky enough to lead a team of people running an Access Course, which successfully helped several hundred adults to get into Universities and Colleges all over the country. Many of these adults had no qualifications whatsoever before they came on the course. Those who wanted to go on to Higher Education actually got places at universities after only 1 year of study with us. Not only that, but the vast majority (over 90% of those who started the course) succeeded in getting their degrees and I am now hearing of those going on to take MA.'s and Ph.D.'s.

Many of these former students have written to me to ask if I have any copies of handouts and lectures about studying, because they want to use them in their studies in the universities. Having retired, I decided that I would put together the hints and tips and guidelines and handouts and lectures into a coherent book which would be of use to any student.

The first part of this book helps you identify clearly where you are now, where you would like to get to in a few years time, and what you need to know and do in order to get there.

The second part is concerned with getting organised in order to learn, and helps you to acquire the skills, knowledge and confidence needed to succeed in 6th Forms, Further and Higher Education.

Please do not hesitate to write to me with comments about the book and with your queries and especially your stories of success. If you feel I can be of help then please contact me. I sincerely wish you the best of luck.

Ray Baxter
Greencroft
Aldbrough St John
Nr Richmond
North Yorkshire
Saturday 18th March 1995

ix

Studying Successfully

PART ONE

Getting in to study

How to start

This is a reference book. It is not a book that you read from cover to cover. It is designed to direct you to those parts of the book that are useful to you at the various stages of your progress through the education system.

Part One helps you to identify clearly:

where you are now,

where you would like to get to in a few years time, and

what you need to know and do in order to get there.

On the next two pages are descriptions of where you might be at present. I have tried to cover most of the situations in which most of the readers of this book are likely to find themselves. Read them through and decide which of them (there may be more than one) best describes your situation. Turn to the page(s) indicated and follow the instructions there.

Don't try and do everything at once. Break things down into easily manageable pieces.

You know exactly what career you want, what qualifications you need,
and you know how to set about getting all these.
Go to page 4 of this Introduction.

You know you would like a particular career but
you don't know how to set about getting into it.
Go to page 6 of this Introduction.

You really haven't the faintest idea what career you want.
Go to page 8 of this Introduction.

You are a student already in higher education.
You know where you are going to after you have finished your course
and you just need to have help with things like essays and note taking.
Go to page 10 of this Introduction.

You are just a housewife who wants to find out what's available for you.
Go to page 12 of this Introduction.

You are unqualified and feel you would like to return to study
in order get some qualification.
Go to page 14 of this Introduction.

You are retired and just want to do some studying.
Go to page 16 of this Introduction.

You want to go to a University, get a degree and then see what happens.
Go to page 18 of this Introduction.

You haven't the faintest idea about how to get back into education at all.
Go to page 20 of this Introduction.

You are a student already in a Sixth form, or equivalent,
and you want to know about how to apply to a University
and to improve your study skills, like essay writing and note taking.
Go to page 22 of this Introduction.

You are in a job now and want to improve your qualifications
so that you can get on in your present area of work.
Go to page 24 of this Introduction.

You are in a job now and want to improve your qualifications
so you can move to a different area of work.
Go to page 26 of this Introduction.

You feel you have a specific disability,
such as deafness, partial sightedness or mobility,
which affects your chances at further or higher education level.
Go to page 28 of this Introduction.

You feel you have problems with writing, spelling and/or reading,
which you feel will seriously affect your chances of succeeding
in further or higher education.
Go to page 30 of this Introduction.

You are not described here by any of these.
Go to page 32 of this Introduction.

> **You know exactly what career you want, what qualifications you need, and you know how to set about getting all these**

Well, Part One is probably not able to tell you a great deal, however, I suggest you skim read all the Sections in Part One, just to make sure that you really do have your ideas clear at this stage. It is very easy to start on a path towards your goal and then realise, when you have been travelling some time, that the destination is not going to be the one you expected, or one that you would rather not reach!

Far better to spend time now researching the specific long term goal that you have, than realise at a later stage that you'd really have preferred to do something different, or that the qualification you have been studying is actually not quite the right one for that destination.

Don't forget too that the structure of careers is rapidly changing and what once looked like a job for life has become much more insecure. For example, there have been many teachers made redundant. More people are being employed on short term contracts. I do urge you to make as certain as you can that your chosen long term goal is realistic and that you know precisely what qualifications are needed to attain that goal.

> I suggest that you skim through:
> Section 1 Education for adults now [ ]
> Section 2 How to get into higher education. [ ]
> Section 3 Long term planning [ ]
> Section 4 What career should you have? [ ]
> Section 5 What should you study? [ ]
> Section 6 What course should you take? [ ]
> Section 7 Where should you go? [ ]
> Section 8 Should you be Full Time or Part Time? [ ]
> Section 9 How will you pay? [ ]
> Section 10 How do you apply? [ ]
> Section 11 How do you cope with the interview(s)? [ ]

At the same time:

- get in touch with your local Further Education College and seek advice on the specific career route that you have planned, making sure that you check carefully the qualifications necessary to get there (e.g. do you need to have GCSE Maths and English before you start, as is the case with teaching?).   [ ]

- It's not easy to go to a College for the first time. They are big, rambling places and can be quite intimidating with everyone else seeming to know where they are going and what they are doing. I suggest that a first step would be to ring your local College of Further Education (phone number in book). Ask to talk to someone who can give you advice about your present qualifications and what you will need to become what you wish to become.

– If you don't know where the College is, then ask how you get to the College, and how you find the appropriate room.

- if you need to get to Higher Education and you haven't got the qualifications then ask about an Access Course at your local College of Further Education. That route will be quicker than taking all the GCSE and 'A' levels.

- contact any professional organisation connected with the career you have chosen and ascertain if there are any recent developments in the career structure which might affect your plans.   [ ]

- contact anyone already in the career you've chosen and talk to them about your plans: there may have been changes since you took the decision to follow that career.   [ ]

I suggest that you should look at:

Section 12 How should you prepare?   [ ]

just to check that you have covered all the possible areas which I think are essential for studying at further and Higher Education levels.

You should certainly attempt:

Section 13 Where are you now?   [ ]

which will allow you to step back and take stock of where you are now and where you are heading, then have a look at Part Two of this book for advice on developing the necessary study skills for the course you have chosen.   [ ]

If you feel that you lack confidence in your abilities to succeed with all this, then look at Section 15.   [ ]

You know you would like a particular career but you don't know how to set about getting into it

---

Before you set off on your route to your destination, please just take some time to reflect on the decision that you have already made about that destination.

I have known many students regret decisions they have made on entering Higher Education because they were unaware of other destinations open to them. For example, teachers who go straight to teaching degrees not realising that there other ways of entering the teaching profession which leave more opportunities available to them.

If you are determined to enter the career that you have chosen and you've already thought deeply about that and about alternatives, then fine, you don't really need to go through that process again. I do suggest that you should look **briefly** at the Sections indicated below.

But, if you have not thought about it a lot, or if you have a few doubts, then perhaps now is the time to re-examine your decision to become whatever it is you've decided and just re-think the possibilities. I suggest you examine thoroughly the Sections set out below.

Section 1 Education for adults now   [ ]
Section 2 How to get into Higher Education   [ ]
Section 3 Long term planning   [ ]
Section 4 What career should you have?   [ ]
Section 5 What should you study?   [ ]

After that I suggest that you:
- get in touch with your local Further Education College and seek advice on the specific career route that you have planned, making sure that you check carefully the qualifications necessary to get there (e.g. do you need to have GCSE Maths and English before you start, as is the case with teaching?).   [ ]
- if you need to get to Higher Education and you haven't got the qualifications then ask about an Access Course at your local College of Further Education. That route will be quicker than taking all the GCSE and 'A' levels.

- contact any professional organisation connected with the career you have chosen and ascertain if there are any recent developments in the career structure which might affect your plans.   [ ]

- contact anyone already doing the career you have chosen and talk to them about your plans: there may have been changes since you took the decision to follow that career.   [ ]

The other Sections in Part One may well be of use to you, whether you are sure or not about your career, and you should **certainly** check:

Section 11 How do you cope with the interview(s)?   [ ]

Section 12 How should you prepare?   [ ]
just to make sure that you have covered all the possible areas which I think are essential for studying at further and higher education levels.

You should also do
Section 13 Where are you now?   [ ]
which will enable you to take stock of where you are now and where you are planning to get to.

If you feel at any time that you lack confidence in your abilities to succeed with all this, then look at Section 15.   [ ]

You really haven't the faintest idea what career you want

Really you are the person for whom Part One is written! You don't have to rush to make up your mind what you want to become, but I do feel strongly that you need to gather information about the likely things that you will be happy and fulfilled doing in, say five years time, and set yourself a deadline by which you will make up your mind what your long term goal will be.

Your first step will be to find out a bit more about our education system and also about yourself and then gather information about those careers which seem to fit you best.

However, there does come a time when you have to say - right, in the light of all the evidence I have gathered, all the thinking and talking I've done, I will make a decision as to where I am aiming.
I suggest that you read all the Sections, carefully and systematically. You can tick them off here as you finish them and complete the activities suggested.

Section 1 Education for adults now	[ ]
Section 2 How to get into higher education	[ ]
Section 3 Long term planning	[ ]

After doing these Sections you may well want to get in touch with your local College or University to see exactly what is on offer and where you would best fit. Would you need to get extra qualifications before going on to a higher level of study?

Section 4 What career should you have?	[ ]
Section 5 What should you study?	[ ]
Section 6 What course should you take?	[ ]
Section 7 Where should you go?	[ ]
Section 8 Should you be Full Time or Part Time?	[ ]
Section 9 How will you pay?	[ ]
Section 10 How do you apply?	[ ]
Section 11 How do you cope with the interview(s)?	[ ]
Section 12 How should you prepare?	[ ]
Section 13 Where are you now?	[ ]

I must emphasise again that whilst reading the book can help, you do have to get face to face advice from those trained to help. If you work slowly through the Sections above and then, when you feel you have a broad idea of where you want to get to, get in touch with your local College.

If you feel that you lack confidence in your abilities to succeed with all this, then look at Section 15.   [ ]

> ### You are a student already in higher education. You know where you are going to after you have finished your course and you just need to have help with things like writing essays and note taking

Before you set off on Part Two of the book, which is concerned with the study skills that you need, please just take some time to reflect on the decision that you have already made.

I have known many students regret decisions they have made on entering HE because they were unaware of other possibilities open to them. For example, teachers who go straight to teaching degrees not realising that there are other ways of entering the profession which leave more opportunities available to them.

> I suggest that you should look briefly at the Sections here in Part One:
> Section 3 Long term planning [ ]
> Section 4 What career should you have? [ ]
> Section 5 What should you study? [ ]

After that I suggest that you:
- go to the Careers guidance section of your University and seek advice on the specific career route that you have planned, making sure that you check carefully the qualifications necessary to get there (e.g. do you need to have GCSE Maths and English before you start, as is the case with teaching?) [ ]

- contact any professional organisation connected with the career you have chosen and ascertain if there are any recent developments in the career structure which might affect your plans. [ ]

- contact anyone already doing the career you have chosen and talk to them about your plans. [ ]

When you have finished that then turn to Section 11:"Where are you now" and then go on to Part Two. [ ]

If you feel that you lack confidence in your abilities to succeed with all this, then look at Section 15. [ ]

It is perhaps worth while pointing out that there is a great deal of unemployment at present amongst graduates. You should keep an eye on the labour market whilst you are at University and begin to make contacts certainly by the last year of your course with people who may be in a position to get you employment in the career of your choice.

Watch out for advertisements in any of the journals, periodicals and/or newspapers connected with your career.

Many of the techniques implied by Section 11 How do you cope with the interview(s)? apply to job interviews.

You are just a housewife who wants to find out what's available for you

Firstly, please do not regard yourself as "just" a "housewife"! It is very easy to see oneself as not very important when all the glamorous images in advertisements seem to boost the image of everyone else except the person one is!

Over the last few years I have become increasingly aware that many people have been forced into staying at home and looking after the family and almost losing their own personality in planning and organising the lives of others. The fact that you have acquired this book and are reading this page indicates that you have decided at least to explore the possibility of developing the potential which is within you. I can assure you that your horizons will be extended and that you will become a more fulfilled person as a result of returning to learning.

It has been my experience that many people in your position do feel that they lack confidence to get on easily in education. I can assure you that you will very soon realise that you will feel at home in the environment of a College. More and more older people are returning to education and the Colleges and universities are realising just what a huge potential you have got. Many universities and Colleges run courses especially aimed at helping people return.

You may find it difficult to believe, but I can tell you as a matter of FACT that women (and men) who return to education after a gap of few years are successful students. I have taught them and I have taught people straight from school. Compared with young people coming straight from school the older students invariably do better.

This may be due to the young people having got used to the idea that they will be told all the time what to do and not being used to thinking for themselves, or something to do with their trying to find themselves, or perhaps suddenly being free from parental and school control and being unable to cope with this sudden "freedom" - well, I'm not too sure. What I do know is that people like yourself, who have returned because they WANT to, after having done something other than school, always seem to be able to cope with the demands of being a student far better, perhaps because of a wider frame of reference.

Secondly, you should make an appointment at your local College of Further Education. It's not easy to go to a College for the first time. They are big, rambling places and can be quite intimidating with everyone else seeming to know where they are going and what they are doing. I suggest that a first step would be to ring your local College of Further Education (phone number in book). Ask to talk to someone who can give you advice about where you are now. If you don't know how to find the College, then ask how you get to it, and how you find the appropriate room. All of the Colleges are very keen to welcome you into education. Almost all run introductory courses, some aimed specifically at women wanting to return to learning. They will give you information about what is available in your area for you.

Finally I suggest that you slowly and carefully make your way through each of the Sections below:

Section 1 Education for adults now	[ ]
Section 2 How to get into a Higher Education	[ ]
Section 3 Long term planning	[ ]
Section 4 What career should you have?	[ ]
Section 5 What should you study?	[ ]
Section 6 What course should you take?	[ ]
Section 7 Where should you go?	[ ]
Section 8 Should you be Full Time or Part Time?	[ ]
Section 9 How will you pay?	[ ]
Section 10 How do you apply?	[ ]
Section 11 How do you cope with the interview(s)?	[ ]
Section 12 How should you prepare?	[ ]
Section 13 Where are you now?	[ ]

If you do feel that you lack confidence in your abilities to succeed with all this, then look at Section 15.   [ ]

There are many books which may help too: the list below is what many women on our Access Course found useful. They should be available in your local library:

Equal Opportunities - A careers Guide	Alston	Penguin
Equal Opportunities for Women	HMSO	HMSO
Daycare for kids	Kozac	Daycare Institute
Rights and Wrongs of Women	Mitchell/Oakley	Penguin
Housewife	Oakley	Penguin
Women's Consciousness, Man's World	Rowbotham	Penguin
Women and depression	Sanders	Sheldon Press

The Women's Pack by the Scottish Community Education, from Atholl House, 2 Canning Street, Edinburgh, EH3 8EG

Just like a Girl	Sharpe	Penguin
Double Identity:Lives of Working Mothers	Sharpe	Penguin
Equal Opportunities		Penguin
Complete Woman's Reference Book		Penguin

You are unqualified and feel you would like to return to study in order get some qualification

---

Firstly, I suggest that you need to look at your long term plans in terms of what you would realistically like to be doing in five years time.

I suggest that you read the Sections:
Section 1 Education for adults now　　　　　　　　　　　　　　[ ]
Section 2 How to get into Higher Education.　　　　　　　　　[ ]
Section 3 Long term planning　　　　　　　　　　　　　　　　[ ]

Secondly, make sure you **are** in fact **unqualified!** Some of the experiences you have had since leaving school may be regarded as qualifications. Take a trip to your local College of Further Education and ask to have a chat with someone in their Careers and Guidance section. Many Colleges have the facilities to be able to help you to sort out what you are most suited for.

It's not easy to go to a College for the first time. They are big, rambling places and can be quite intimidating with everyone else seeming to know where they are going and what they are doing. I suggest that a first step would be to ring your local College of Further Education (phone number in book). Ask to talk to someone who can give you advice about where you are now. If you don't know how to find the College is, then ask how you get there, and how you find the appropriate room.

I must emphasise again that although reading these Sections can help you, you MUST get face to face advice from those trained to help. If you work through the Sections above and then, when you feel you have a broad idea of where you want to get to, get in touch with your local College.

You will need to find out at what level you are and the best place in the College to ask about this is the Adult Basic Education Unit or Learning Support Unit. The people there will be able to diagnose and prescribe for you after they have seen what you can do. Let me reassure you that they are trained to do this tactfully, and sensitively. There is no chance of you being turned away or told you are too old or that you haven't enough qualifications. It's a bit like a visit to a doctor - they will do a checkup of your strengths and weaknesses. You will be surprised at the level you can achieve.

I do know how difficult it is to go back into a College/School atmosphere, especially if you feel that you weren't all that good at school, or that you will be too old, or that you will be different. It may surprise you to know that in many Colleges now the older people outnumber the younger ones!

It is also my experience that older students in FACT perform better than those straight from school. Those who return to education after a gap of few years are successful students. I have taught them and I have taught people straight from school. Compared with young people coming straight from school the older students invariably do better.

This may be due to the young people having got used to the idea that they will be told all the time what to do and not being used to thinking for themselves, or something to do with their trying to find themselves, or perhaps suddenly being free from parental and school control and being unable to cope with this sudden "freedom" - well, I'm not too sure. What I do know is that people who have returned because they WANT to, after having done something other than school, always seem to be able to cope with the demands of being a student far better.

Enquire especially about Access Courses. They can be much quicker at getting you into higher education than taking GCSE's and A levels.

If you feel that you lack confidence in your abilities to succeed with all this, then look at Section 15.   [ ]

You are retired and just want to do some studying

Many more people are returning to learning after their working life has finished. On the course I ran we had at least 10% of our students over the age of 55. So don't feel that you will be the only older person in the College! It's not easy to go to a College for the first time. They are big, rambling places and can be quite intimidating with everyone else seeming to know where they are going and what they are doing. I suggest that a first step would be to ring your local College of Further Education (phone number in book). Ask to talk to someone who can give you advice about where you are now in terms of qualifications and skills and your ambitions with regard to a future career. You will find the reception you get very friendly and welcoming. Ring them up for an appointment with someone who can advise you. There is usually a careers and counselling service and there may be a short introductory course to help you find out what is going to be of use to you as an individual. If you don't know, then ask how you get to the College, and how you find the appropriate room. I would be very interested to know what your welcome is like and would welcome any comments you have.

I must assure you that the notion of students being between the age of 18 and 25 is not in line with the present situation. There is an increasing number of "wrinklies" (as mature students are often jokingly called!) returning to Colleges of Further Education and into universities. I remember Catherine, aged 56, who wrote to our students after she had gone on to Newcastle to study a BA. in History, saying:
"Make that first move: ask to see someone at the College and get onto a course to lead you to higher education. Dig in! The best is yet to come when you get to University, which is brill./ fab./ great/ super/ smashing/ hellish/ wunderbar and bloody hard work. So dig in there!".

I can recall Michael who went on to Newcastle to study a BA. in French & East Asian Studies, writing to the students to say :*"When (not if!) you:*
(a) feel that you can't cope with the workload
(b) wonder why on earth you ever decided to go to University/College
(c) become really depressed
(d) are frightened that you are going to fail
(e) begin to envy the "carefree life" of the man sweeping the street
(f) feel like giving it all up
DON'T WORRY! All these feelings are perfectly normal and natural. I haven't met any student, young or old, who doesn't have some or all of these feelings at some time or another.

1st: Don't panic or think that it's only you who feels that way, remember you weren't given a place because you have such a winning smile. You were given it because the selectors recognised that you have ability. So you must also recognise this.

2nd: PERSEVERE. Keep at it! Of course there will be times when you feel overwhelmed and wonder what on earth you are doing, but don't despair. Think positively. Mature students have a tendency to magnify negative feedback and minimise positive feedback, thus sustaining their low sense of learning competence."

I can recall Harry, born in 1926, whom I first met by accident whilst we were both shopping in a supermarket in Spennymoor, telling me that he felt purposeless and frustrated because life had passed him by. I persuaded him to join our Access to Higher Education Course and during the year of the course he was accepted to do Economics at 6 universities throughout the country. He chose York and felt thoroughly at home.

I could quote many other people over the age of 50[1], and some in their 70's for whom satisfaction and fulfilment came as a result of making that first difficult initial step of going and asking if they could give it a try by making an appointment for a chat at the local College of Further Education.

In the meantime, whilst you are waiting for that appointment, have a look at the pages in this book about finding out about the routes available through our education system.

Section 1 Education for adults now [ ]
Section 2 How to get into Higher Education [ ]
Section 3 Long term planning [ ]
When reading this and the following Sections remember that I am aware that you are not necessarily wanting to study in order to get into a career.
Section 5 What should you study? [ ]
Section 6 What course should you take? [ ]
Section 7 Where should you go? [ ]
Section 8 Should you be Full Time or Part Time? [ ]
Section 9 How will you pay? [ ]
Section 10 How do you apply? [ ]
Section 11 How should you prepare? [ ]
Section 12 Where are you now? [ ]

If you feel that you lack confidence in your abilities to succeed with all this, then look at Section 15. [ ]

---

[1]. *Have a look in Appendix I for other comments from students who took that first step of asking at their local College of Further Education and who never regretted it.*

> # You want to go to a University, get a degree and then see what happens

In my experience many people have this attitude towards entering a University. For whatever reason you feel that you don't want to make a decision about what you wish to do after leaving further study. This is fine and if you really have no reason for earning a living afterwards, or if you are absolutely decided that you need to make up your mind at a later stage, then that's fine.

However, I must point out that many people who have completed their degree course often regret they did not take a different degree in the light of their career ambitions. Certainly my experience leads me to urge people who are entering HE to think carefully at this stage about their long-term future goals since it is difficult to change courses once you have set out on study.

There are dangers in setting out on a course without thinking about what career you will have at the end of it:
- you may find that you have chosen the wrong course to get into the career you want to get into.

- You may find that you aren't too sure of your reasons for following the course that you have chosen and this could lead to a weakening of your motivation.

- There may be options within your course which may be difficult to select because you are not sure of their relevance to future career plans.

- I should also mention the fact that none of us get any younger! Do you have time to put off the decision about what you will be doing in 5 years time?!

However:
You may already have decided that you want to get a degree and then decide what job to do. That's fine.

You may have decided that you want to study a degree just for the sake of studying the degree! Please don't be tempted to skip the Sections in Part One yet...

...I suggest, even though you may have decided to continue without making any specific decisions about your future career, that you go to Section 1 "Education for adults now", which shows you the very broad range of opportunities available at present, and then have a look at the Sections on "Where do you want to be in 5 years?", and "What career should you have?". These Sections may help you clarify your purpose in studying.

You could then skim the Sections "What should you study?" and "What course should you take?", just to make sure you are choosing the right course for you.

You should certainly read "Where should you go?", "Should you be Full Time or Part Time?", "How will you pay?", "How do you apply?", "How do you cope with the interview(s)?" and "How should you prepare?", since these questions are relevant to your situation.

You should tackle "Where are you now?".

If you do select a broad area of interest then you should seek clear career guidance from your local College of Further Education, or from the University careers services at as early a stage as possible.

If you need to get into Higher Education and you haven't got the qualifications then ask about an Access Course at your local College of Further Education. That route will be quicker than taking all the GCSE and 'A' levels.

It's not easy to go to a College for the first time. They are big, rambling places and can be quite intimidating with everyone else seeming to know where they are going and what they are doing. I suggest that a first step would be to ring your local College of Further Education (phone number in your local telephone directory). Ask to talk to someone who can give you advice about where you are now. If you don't know how to find the College, then ask how you get to it, and how you find the appropriate room.

If you feel that you lack confidence in your abilities to succeed with all this, then look at Section 15.   [ ]

You haven't the faintest idea about how to get back into education at all

---

Well, in that case the first thing to do is to contact your local College of Further Education and ask their advice about where you are now in terms of qualifications and skills and your ambitions with regard to a future career. You will find the reception you get very friendly and welcoming.

Ring them up and ask for an appointment with someone who can advise you. There is usually a careers and counselling service and there may be a short introductory course to help you find out what is going to be of use to you as an individual. I would be very interested to know what your welcome was like and I would welcome any comments you have.

I must assure you that the notion of students being between the age of 18 and 25 is not in line with the present situation. There is an increasing number of "wrinklies" (as mature students are often jokingly called!) returning to Colleges of Further Education and universities.

I know how hard it is to take that first step and make contact with the College. You may find it useful to read what people who came on our Access to Higher education Course have said:

Female student Fiona aged 35, who went on to Durham University to study a B.A. in English Literature says: *"Stop saying "Yes, but what if?" I have found that I can do all that is required of me if I just concentrate on the one thing right in front of me rather than projecting about the next endless number of things - and if I do just that then I also enjoy the one thing so much more because I'm not wishing to get on to something else. My degree course is enjoyable, fascinating, exciting etc etc: so can yours be!"*

Timothy aged 20, who went on to Manchester Metropolitan University to study a B.A. in Social Science says: *"Get to that College and get on that course! Stick it out - it can be done, and the time goes incredibly fast - before you know it you've finished your exams and you're waiting to go to University, and be careful to hang on to the various bits and pieces you collect on the course, they can come in handy."*

Joyce aged 34, who went on to Sunderland to study a BA. in Social Science says: *"You just need to make that first step. Then plan your study, make timetables etc. But if you have any problems or worries ask your tutors: they are there to help. I'm proof that Ray's approach is successful - anyone can be successful at HE with careful planning - I learned how to learn and how to study. I was also able to combine study with a family life."*

Moira aged 38, who went on to Sunderland to study a B.A. in Combined Arts says:*"Make that first move and then stick in - it's well worth all the trials, tribulations and the tears!"*

Yvonne aged 35, who went on to Durham to study a B.A. in Anthropology says: *"Get through those College doors! You'll not regret it! When Ray tells you that FE/HE is like a drug - he is right: you become hooked. It's hard work. It's frustrating, but, above all, it's fun. Good Luck."*

I could quote many other people of all ages[2].

It's not easy to go to a College for the first time. They are big, rambling places and can be quite intimidating with everyone else seeming to know where they are going and what they are doing. I suggest that a first step would be to ring your local College of Further Education (phone number your local telephone directory). Ask to talk to someone who can give you advice about where you are now. If you don't know how to find the College, then ask how you get to it, and how you find the appropriate room.

In the meantime, whilst you are waiting for that appointment, have a look at all the Sections in Part One. Take it slowly and carefully, Section by Section. Don't try to rush. Go at your own pace.

Section 1 Education for adults now	[ ]
Section 2 How to get into Higher Education	[ ]
Section 3 Long term planning	[ ]
Section 4 What career should you have?	[ ]
Section 5 What should you study?	[ ]
Section 6 What course should you take?	[ ]
Section 7 Where should you go?	[ ]
Section 8 Should you be Full Time or Part Time?	[ ]
Section 9 How will you pay?	[ ]
Section 10 How do you apply?	[ ]
Section 11 How do you cope with the interview(s)?	[ ]
Section 12 How should you prepare?	[ ]
Section 13 Where are you now?	[ ]

If you feel that you lack confidence in your abilities to succeed with all this, then look at Section 15. [ ]

---

[2]. *Have a look in Appendix I for other comments from students who took that first step of asking at their local College of Further Education and who never regretted it.*

> # You are a student already in a Sixth form, or equivalent, and you want to know about how to apply to a University and you want to improve your study skills, like essay writing and note taking

You may or may not be receiving help in making your decisions about which course and which University you wish to go to. If you have not been able to make up your mind about what you will be studying at University, or which University you are going to then you need to start making decisions about that immediately.

You need to decide:
1. what sort of career you would like for yourself after higher education
2. what course you want to take in higher education
3. which universities you wish to apply to.
These are complex decisions
I advise you to have a look at the following Sections:

Section 3: Long term planning,   [ ]
Section 4. What career should you have?   [ ]
Section 5. What should you study?   [ ]
Section 6. What course should you take?   [ ]
Section 7. Where should you go?   [ ]

There should also be someone in your school with specific responsibility for helping sixth form students apply to the universities.

Ask for help.

The sooner you can get information the better.

If you don't get any satisfaction then look through Section 10 How to apply and Section 11 How do you cope with the interview(s)?

There are other possibilities to consider too. Rather than going on to University in your next year there is always the possibility of getting an acceptance to go, but not immediately. It is possible that you could benefit more in the long run by taking a year off before going on to University.

I do NOT advise taking a year off and then applying. I mean that you should get your acceptance and then ask for deferment for a year.[3]

- Some people feel that it is less stressful to apply AFTER the results are known, but it is unlikely that you will have the choice of places by going through Clearing. Some students, however, prefer to wait that year, knowing what their results are. It is not an easy choice.

Let me make it clear too that I don't mean have a year off to do nothing but lounge around and get bored and self-indulgent! I mean take off a year to do something with a specific purpose. Whatever you choose make sure that it has relevance to your future - wandering over Europe without any attempt to learn a language, get some form of income, or any point other than not going to University is pointless and you will regress rather than develop.

A further point you should consider is MONEY! It is an expensive business being a student. There are grants, but they are never enough to live on. You will almost certainly have to get some form of part time work. You can to some extent prepare for this by perhaps saving money before you get there and asking relatives and friends to give you book tokens, but perhaps more important acquiring some skill so that you wont be limited to the jobs which almost all students seek (and there are therefore not many of them in University towns and cities!) of baby-sitting, pub-work and labouring. We are rather hoping that, rather than washing up for about £2 an hour, our son Tom will be able to earn his way through University by teaching the flute at about £10 an hour!
There are some useful publications: "Summer Jobs in Britain" and "Summer Jobs Abroad" for about £8 each by Vacation Work, 9 Park End Street, Oxford, OX1 1HJ.

If you feel that you lack confidence in your abilities to succeed with all this, then look at Section 15.   [ ]

---

[3]. *Most institutions are prepared to consider you during the present year of application for deferred entry in the following year. You should have a clear and specific reason for doing so. Do NOT be vague and say what your HOPES are: your plans must be specific and firm, and you should give clear detail as to WHY this deferment is preferable to entering this year, and precisely how the year off will be relevant to your studies and future career. You MUST check with the University before filling in the UCAS form. You will need to present a good reason for asking for deferment. See the UCAS Handbook on these points.*

> # You are in a job now and want to improve your qualifications so that you can get on in your present area of work

You should approach your manager(s) and ask what are the best ways of improving your qualifications. If there is a clear career structure in your work then you should be able to obtain information very easily and quickly. There may even be opportunities for you to go on courses during work time and have your fees paid by your firm.

If there are problems in doing this then consult your Union, or Association. They may be able to provide you which information relevant to your position.

If you still find there is no joy from these two sources then contact your local College of Further Education and ask for their advice. Their careers service should be able to ascertain what would be an appropriate further qualification for someone in your position.

At the same time you could check if you really do want to stay in the same type of work and look at other possibilities. In which case you might like to follow the advice in the following Sections:

Section 1 Education for adults now	[ ]
Section 2 How to get into higher education	[ ]
Section 3 Long term planning	[ ]
Section 4 What career should you have?	[ ]
Section 5 What should you study?	[ ]
Section 6 What course should you take?	[ ]
Section 7 Where should you go?	[ ]
Section 8 Should you be Full Time or Part Time?	[ ]
Section 9 How will you pay?	[ ]
Section 10 How do you apply?	[ ]
Section 11 How do you cope with the interview(s)?	[ ]
Section 12 How should you prepare?	[ ]

If at the end of all this you find that you cannot work and do the course you want then you will be faced by a very unpleasant decision: give up work or give up the idea of getting that qualification. I'm afraid I cannot help you with that decision. You are really the only person who can, in conjunction with those with whom you live, decide what in the long run is going to bring most satisfaction and fulfilment to you all.

If you need to get into Higher Education and you haven't got the qualifications then ask about an Access Course at your local College of Further Education. That route will be quicker than taking all the GCSE and 'A' levels. However, you may not find one that fits in with your present work patterns. Some Colleges do run evening Access Courses and some have courses which are based on you dropping in when you can.

It's not easy to go to a College for the first time. They are big, rambling places and can be quite intimidating with everyone else seeming to know where they are going and what they are doing. I suggest that a first step would be to ring your local College of Further Education (phone number your local telephone directory). Ask to talk to someone who can give you advice about where you are now. If you don't know how to find the College, then ask how you get to it, and how you find the appropriate room.

One further Section which may help you is:

Section 13 Where are you now?   [ ]

This could help clarify some of your feelings about your present position. It won't provide easy answers, but it might raise important questions!

If you feel that you lack confidence in your abilities to succeed with all this, then look at Section 15.

> **You are in a job now and want to improve your qualifications so you can move to a different area of work.**

If you know what career you want then you can go straight to the experts in that career and ask them how to get into it. By experts I mean:
- anyone doing that career now
- your local Further Education careers service
- any Trades Union or professional association connected with the career
- your local library and ask for help from the librarian to find an up to date book about that career.

You should make contact with **all** of the above.

It may well be that you will then find that you have to take courses which you will be doing in evenings and spare time, since it is most unlikely that your present firm will pay for you to be trained so that you can go and work somewhere else!

If your desire for change is great and your finances will allow it then you might well want to give up your present work in order to train for your preferred career, but be wary of this as there all sorts of hazards in giving up a job. For example, you will probably not get any Unemployment Benefit, or Job-Seeker's Allowance, since you have given up the job voluntarily.

If you do know what you want then study the following Sections:

Section 1 Education for adults now   [ ]
Section 2 How to get into higher education   [ ]
Section 5 What should you study?   [ ]
Section 6 What course should you take?   [ ]
Section 7 Where should you go?   [ ]
Section 8 Should you be Full Time or Part Time?   [ ]
Section 9 How will you pay?   [ ]
Section 10 How do you apply?   [ ]
Section 11 How do you cope with the interview(s)?   [ ]
Section 12 How should you prepare?   [ ]
Section 13 Where are you now?   [ ]

If you feel that you lack confidence in your abilities to succeed with all this, then look at Section 15

If you need to get into Higher Education and you haven't got the qualifications then ask about an Access Course at your local College of Further Education. That route will be quicker than taking all the GCSE and 'A' levels. However, you may not find one that fits in with your present work patterns. Some Colleges do run evening Access Courses and some have courses which are based on you dropping in when you can.

It's not easy to go to a College for the first time. They are big, rambling places and can be quite intimidating with everyone else seeming to know where they are going and what they are doing. I suggest that a first step would be to ring your local College of Further Education (phone number in your local telephone directory). Ask to talk to someone who can give you advice about where you are now. If you don't know where the how to find the College, then ask how you get to it, and how you find the appropriate room.

If you are not sure about what you want to study then in addition to the above read Sections 3 and 4 which are about helping you to clarify your thoughts about possible alternative careers. Again you need professional help and I urge you to consult with your careers advisers at your local College of Further Education.

I have met people who have successfully moved from one career to another. One in particular Tracey, who moved from the Civil Service to Teaching and who wrote to me and said to pass on this advice to others:
"I've certainly had regrets about giving up a secure job in the Civil Service. But when I look back these are financial regrets. I still don't earn as much as would have had I stopped. But the rewards I get are not countable in money terms. I have to say be VERY VERY sure about your decision because you will be on the breadline. There isn't much money in being a student for 5 years, which is what it took me. But for me it was worth while."

Equally I have known people make the decision and then regret it because the stresses of finance and the pressure that puts on relationships makes the sacrifices not worth while at all.

It is a very difficult decision and must be made by all those whom it will affect. That should not put you off discussing it, informing yourself about the opportunities and talking it through with trained professional advisers who will help you clarify your thinking.

> **You feel you have a specific disability, such as deafness, partial sightedness or mobility, which affects your chances of performing well at further or Higher Education level**

A lot of progress has been made recently in making sure that those with disabilities are not disadvantaged in further and Higher Education. The provision is not uniform throughout the country.

If you have any disability and you wish to return to education or are already in it but feel you are being held back by the disability then you should consult with:

1. your doctor, who may be able to supply a written letter verifying and explaining the nature of the disability.

2. with the staff in charge of your studies, who may be able to supply direct advice as to where help may be available and may speak on your behalf, or write a letter explaining your needs.

You will probably get advice to consult with:

your local council.

take the information you have got from your doctor and/or your tutors so that you can explain clearly and with authority the nature of your disability and what you need to compensate for it. The council will tell you if there is any form of assistance for those with disabilities in education. The help is sometimes available from the Education department and other times available from Social Services.

Some authorities supply a wide range of help including computers, mobility allowances and professional help for those disadvantaged in ways that prevent them from learning easily. I must emphasise that the pattern is patchy and there is no guarantee that you will get anything. But you should ask. On our Access Course we had many cases where people were helped with computers for those with reading and writing difficulties, special equipment for the partially sighted to help them with reading.

If you are unemployed and you have a disability which prevents you from working then you should also ask to see the person responsible for those who are unemployed and who have disabilities.

Most Colleges have someone who is responsible for the needs of those who have disadvantages in terms of mobility and most, but not all, Colleges have a stated policy on meeting the needs of those who find access to the College difficult for whatever reason. For those with physical handicaps and who have to use a wheelchair some Colleges have fitted ramps and lifts. In some Colleges there are rooms fitted with amplification for those who have problems with hearing. You should be able to talk with someone who will give advice and encouragement to you in order to help you gain easy access to the College. A phone call in the first instance is fine.

It's not easy to go to a College for the first time. They are big, rambling places and can be quite intimidating with everyone else seeming to know where they are going and what they are doing. I suggest that a first step would be to ring your local College of Further Education (phone number in your local telephone directory). Ask to talk to someone who can give you advice about where you are now. If you don't know how to find the College, then ask how you get to it, and how you find the appropriate room.

The Royal National Institute for the Blind has produced Braille and cassette editions of the book about grants and loans for students. Copies are available free of charge from RNIB[4].

You may feel that you lack the confidence to seek assistance on your own. Perhaps you can find a friend who can give you support to begin with. Failing that I am sure that your College will be welcoming and friendly and may even be able to visit you at home and make introductions to other students who can help you.

I suggest that you turn back to page 2 of this Introduction and, if you haven't already done so, identify another description which fits you and follow that route.

[4]. _Royal National Institute for the Blind, PO Box 173, Peterborough PE2 6WS. Telephone 01345 023 153._

You feel you have problems with writing, spelling and/or reading, which you feel will seriously affect your chances of succeeding in further or Higher Education

---

A lot of progress has been made recently in making sure that those with disabilities are not disadvantaged in further and Higher Education. The provision is not uniform throughout the country.

If you feel you have problems with spelling or reading or writing then it may be that you are suffering from what is called "dyslexia". Dyslexia means without words and is a term used to describe people who have problems with words in whatever form. There are estimated to be over 2,500,000 people in Great Britain suffering from this. Dyslexia occurs irrespective of intelligence or background. It affects coding and sequencing generally, not only in reading and writing. It seems that abnormalities in nerve cell arrangements and the use of the two hemispheres of the brain can be detected in dyslexics. Dyslexia affects each individual in different ways and to differing degrees. Strategies can be learned to overcome it. Given the right tuition dyslexic people can and do succeed.

If you do have problems with the written word then you should have an assessment by an educational psychologist. If you are at school then contact the Schools Psychological Service or the Careers Service. If you are at College or University ask for help from the Special Needs tutor/department. The institutions themselves SHOULD be able to provide the help you need. There is also an organisation called the "Dyslexia Institute"[5] which exists to prevent people experiencing educational failure, provide educational assessment, which identifies abilities and difficulties, offers teaching in literacy, numeracy and learning skills to underpin work you might be doing in the ordinary class-room at College, and gives adult dyslexics a second educational chance. The Institute can be accessed directly, or via your school, College or work place.

Many people who are dyslexic are successful at school and at University. We have had experience of this with our Access Course where we found at least two people with serious dyslexia. Bruce, a 23 year old went on to get a degree in Sports Studies at the University of Northumbria and Anita, aged 32 went on to get a degree at Newcastle University in History.

Many people are unaware that they have a mild form of dyslexia. They have difficulties picking up reading, difficulties with spelling, reversing the order of letters and numbers, making "careless" reading errors on familiar words, missing

---

[5]. *The Training Office, The Dyslexia Institute, 17 Station Road, Stone, ST15 8JP.*
01785 818 783

---

off endings of words in reading and spelling, difficulty with timed written examinations. The difficulties may be seen in College work as having problems with note-taking, revision, reading for information or out loud, spelling, getting ideas down on paper, written number work, planning and organisation of work, meeting deadlines for written work, finding the right words to express thoughts and ideas verbally.

If you do suffer from these symptoms then you should ask for a psychologist to give you an assessment. You can sometimes do this through your school (if you are attending a school), or through the Special Needs Department of your local College of further education. It will probably be free. For a fee, which was about £165 in 1995[6], the Dyslexia Institute can arrange for an assessment by an independent professionally qualified psychologist who has specialist knowledge of dyslexia. It is helpful if s/he has information from your employer or College tutor, but you can get help direct without involving anyone else. No information which is gathered will be revealed to anyone except you. A psychological assessment takes about two hours, which includes time to discuss the findings and talk about ways of approaching any difficulties which may have been revealed. Testing is designed to investigate the profile of thinking and learning and problem solving skills to obtain indication of areas of strength and of difficulty. It examines attainments in reading, spelling, writing and mathematics. The psychologist then assesses whether there are areas which are not up to the expected level. If this is so then it usually indicates that there is a specific difficulty which has made it hard to develop certain skills. Further testing and discussion explore possible reasons for this. Following the assessment session the psychologist will give practical advice according to the severity of any difficulties and what educational/career goals are being sought. Typically advice and recommendations include: making others aware of the presence of the specific learning difficulty so that they do not constantly criticise the poor spelling and/or handwriting, a recommendation that time be allowed, or other special arrangements made in order that specific difficulties do not unduly affect performance in examinations, provision of computer support to minimise the impact of specific spelling difficulties, a short course designed to improve some or all of spelling, report writing, study-skills, revision and exam techniques and time-management and general organisation, an individualised learning programme designed to address difficulties in basic skills. If you have other disabilities which are holding you back then turn to page 28. I suggest that you turn back to page 2 of this Introduction and, if you haven't already done so, identify another description which fits you and follow that route.

---

[6]. _Assistance with tuition fees may be available for a short period in cases of extreme hardship, but funds are very limited. You should be able to get the same sort of assessment through your school or local College._

You are not described by any of these

If you do not fit into any of these categories please write to me and tell me how you would describe your interest in getting into education.

I think you can examine the contents of Part One and decide what is relevant for your particular case:

Section 1 Education for adults now   [ ]
Section 2 How to get into Higher Education   [ ]
Section 3 Long term planning   [ ]
Section 4 What career should you have?   [ ]
Section 5 What should you study?   [ ]
Section 6 What course should you take?   [ ]
Section 7 Where should you go?   [ ]
Section 8 Should you be Full Time or Part Time?   [ ]
Section 9 How will you pay?   [ ]
Section 10 How do you apply?   [ ]
Section 11 How do you cope with the interview(s)?   [ ]
Section 12 How should you prepare?   [ ]
Section 13 Where are you now?   [ ]

You should also contact your local College of Further Education. It's not easy to go to a College for the first time. They are big, rambling places and can be quite intimidating with everyone else seeming to know where they are going and what they are doing. I suggest that a first step would be to ring your local College of Further Education (phone number in your local telephone directory). Ask to talk to someone who can give you advice about where you are now. If you don't know how to find the College, then ask how you get it, and how you find the appropriate room.

If you feel that you lack confidence in your abilities to succeed with all this, then look at Section 15.   [ ]

Then examine the Introduction to Part Two which offers you a diagnostic test to find out for yourself if you have any weakness(es) in Study Skills which can then be practised in the appropriate Section(s) Part Two.

SECTION 1
EDUCATION FOR ADULTS NOW
Introduction

There are many opportunities available for adults in our education system. These opportunities range from help with basic subjects like English and Maths, through GCSE's and A levels, to diplomas and degrees in Higher Education. Whatever you need to get for a particular career or job, there'll be a course available!

In the next few pages I try to give you an over view of what's available. It might be worthwhile just checking through this rather tedious, but very vital information.

Overview of routes[1]

Attempts are being made to rationalise and simplify our education system's qualifications. In general terms there are three kinds of qualification:

1. General education:
   GCSE's: General Certificate of Secondary Education
   GCE A levels, AS level and S level
   Access Courses.
2. Vocational education
   GNVQ's: General National Vocational Qualifications at 3 levels:
   Foundation
   Intermediate
   Advanced
3. Training for jobs
   NVQ's: National Vocational Qualifications at 5 levels

1. General education

1.1 GCSE's: General Certificate of Secondary Education

Until 1987 there were GCE's, (the General Certificate of Education), and CSE's (the Certificate of Secondary Education). These qualifications are still valid, but have been superseded by a single system of examinations: GCSE's (the General Certificate of Secondary Education). These are available to anyone. They can be taken in a very wide range of subjects.

Results are graded on a 7 point scale, A-G.

   A-C = "O" level or CSE grade 1
   D-G = at least as high as CSE grades 1-5

All syllabuses, assessments and assessment procedures are monitored by the Schools Examination and Assessment Council to ensure they conform to national criteria.

---

[1]. See summary p.5.

Courses usually.last 1 year in Colleges of Further Education.
Students are usually tested in course work and examination at the end of the course.

1.2 Advanced level

Advanced level examinations are open to anyone who can indicate that they will benefit from studying. Normally you need 5 GCSE's at grades A-C for entry, but adults are often accepted with less than that and in some cases with no formal qualifications, provided that they can supply evidence that they will not be wasting the time of the Tutor. They can be taken in a very wide range of subjects.

Results are graded on a 7 point scale, A-G.

  A-E = Successful

   N = Narrow failure

   U = Unclassified (no certificate given)

All syllabuses, assessments and assessment procedures are monitored by the Schools Examination and Assessment Council to ensure they conform to national criteria.

Courses usually last 2 years, but there are 1 year courses. Students are tested mainly by examination at the end of the course. They have traditionally been the route to Higher Education. For adults they are not the only route.

1.3 AS level (Advanced supplementary level)

These are an alternative to and complement to A level examinations. They cover not less than half the amount covered by the corresponding A level syllabus and where possible are related to it. 2 AS level's are the equivalent of 1 A level.

Results are graded on a 5 point scale, A-E.

  A-E = Successful

Grade standards are related to A level grades.

All syllabuses, assessments and assessment procedures are monitored by the Schools Examination and Assessment Council to ensure they conform to national criteria.

1.4 S level (Special/Scholarship level)

Most examination boards allow an S level examination in most subjects. This is a paper of greater difficulty.

Results are graded on a 3 point scale, A(1),B(2), unclassified.

  A-B = Successful

   U = Unclassified (no certificate given)

All syllabuses, assessments and assessment procedures are monitored by the Schools Examination and Assessment Council to ensure they conform to national criteria.

1.5 Access Courses

These are run mainly in Colleges of Further Education and give the equivalent of 2 A levels and 5 GCSE's to usually mature students. Courses last 1 year and can be full time or part time. They are usually assessed on what is called a CATS scale. CATS stands for Credit Accumulation and Transfer System. You have to achieve Level 3 under this system in order to qualify for entry to a University (even then entry in not guaranteed since you have also to pass an interview). **Access Courses are at present the fastest route for mature students who have few or no qualifications.**

2. Vocational education

2.1 GNVQ's: General National Vocational Qualifications at 3 levels

They were introduced in September 1993. The long term aim is that half of all 16-17 year olds will take these qualifications. They are designed to lead to work and to Higher Education. They develop the knowledge skills and understanding needed in broad vocational areas such as Manufacturing, Business, Leisure and Tourism, Health and Social Care, Built Environment, Hospitality and Catering, Science, Engineering and Art and Design. Other areas are being developed in Information Technology, Media, Agriculture, Distribution and Management. They also develop core skills in communication, numeracy and information technology.

Foundation level

This is equivalent to four GCSE's at levels D-G. No qualifications are required to enter at this level.

Intermediate level

This is equivalent to four GCSE's at levels A-C. You probably need one or two GCSE's at grades A-E, or the Foundation level.

Advanced level

This is equivalent to two A levels. You probably need about four GCSE's at A-C level or an Intermediate GNVQ.

Results are graded on a 3 point scale:

> Distinction
>
> Merit
>
> Pass

GNVQ's can lead to work or further study at NVQ level (see below) or Higher Education level.

The courses usually last for two years. They are available as part time or full time courses.

Students are tested by regular short examinations and assessment of work done during the course. You can carry forward units you gave passed and re-take ones you've failed.

2.2 Training for jobs

NVQ's: National Vocational Qualifications at 5 levels

In the past it has been a problem to work out just what GCSE's to take for a particular job. The National Council for Vocational Qualifications has been set up to introduce a new flexible method of obtaining relevant qualifications. They are designed to run alongside GCSE's and A levels. They allow students to build up vocational general knowledge and skills relevant to a range of related occupations. There are now over 600 NVQ's available. They are designed by employers and show that you are competent to do the job. They can be taken unit by unit at a pace that suits the individual. NVQ's can be taken in school or College, but there must be work based experience.

They are made up of a series of units of competence. Each unit relates to specific activities within a job. Each unit is further broken down into elements which specify the skill, knowledge and understanding that you should demonstrate to prove that you are competent at that activity.

A particular unit of competence can be credited to more than one NVQ (e.g. a unit of health and safety applies to both bricklaying and carpentry).

NVQ students are assessed in workplace conditions and are also often tested by practical, oral or written examinations. Past achievements are recognised by a system called accreditation of prior learning. When you can prove to an assessor that you meet the standards laid down then you get the NVQ or a credit towards it.

There are 5 NVQ levels:

Level 1: indicates that a person is competent in the performance of work activities which are mainly routine and predictable.

Level 2: indicates that a person is competent in a broader and more demanding range of work activities. This reflects greater individual responsibility and autonomy than level 1.

Level 3: indicates that a person is competent in skilled areas which involve performance of a broad range of work activities. This includes many tasks which are complex and non-routine. This level may also indicate that a person is able to supervise others.

Level 4: indicates that a person is competent in a comprehensive range of complex, technical, specialised or professional activities. The tasks include design, planning or problem solving activities for which the person has a significant degree of responsibility. This level can also indicate competence in supervising or managing others.

Level 5: indicates that a person is competent in applying a significant range of fundamental principles and complex techniques across a wide variety of contexts. Main features include personal autonomy and often responsibility for the work of others and the allocation of resources.

Overview of qualification routes

via Access	via GNVQ	via NVQ	GCSE/A
Level 3 Student develops the capacity for sustained study using critical and evaluative skills and understanding.Study may prepare for entry to HE/ professional training	GNVQ Level 3 The Advanced GNVQ awarded for 12 units + 3 core skills units	NVQ Level 3 competence in a range of complex non-routine work activities with some autonomy and control and guidance of others	2 A Levels with + 5 GCSE's
Level 2 Student acquires or develops basic concepts and principles of enquiry Student can achieve functional competence in skill areas such as maths, language, creative and community based applications	GNVQ Level 2 The Intermediate GNVQ awarded for 6 units+ 3 core skills units	NVQ level 2 competence in varied work activities which may be complex and non-routine with some personal autonomy and control and guidance of others	4 GCSE's at Grade C and above
Level 1 builds on existing skills or introduces a range of new foundat- ion skills & subjects eg craft & artistic skills learning to learn skills language & maths & group skills	GNVQ level 1 The Foundation GNVQ designed for those not yet equipped to begin level 2	NVQ level 1 competence in a range of varied work activities most of which may be routine or predictable	Pre-GCSE
Introductory level is the foundation level skills necessary in everyday life:writing speaking, numeracy practical/coping skills			

4. Colleges of Further Education

The Education Reform Act 1988 defines Further Education as all provision of education up to and including A levels and its equivalent outside of schools to people over the age of 16. Since 1992 the Education Reform Act has removed all Colleges of Further Education and 6th Forms from control by Local Education Authorities and they are now funded directly from central government. There is a body called the Further Education Funding Council which controls the funds and is also responsible for assessment of the quality of the provision of education. The Colleges of Further Education are now independent corporations controlling their own budgets, owning their own assets and employing their own staff. The accountable governing body of each corporation is its board of governors and the Principal. Funding is determined in part by the number of students the College enrols.

Courses are taught in the Colleges, but also in Universities and adult education centres. The courses are broadly vocational in nature, ranging from lower-level technical and commercial courses through courses aiming at entry into higher level posts in industry, commerce and administration, to professional courses. They are increasingly delivering the courses described on pages 2-5 of this Section.

Whatever your age you can get initial advice and information from careers offices and you can consult a computer database called ECCTIS in a large number of secondary schools, Colleges, Universities, libraries and Training Access Points.

You can get a free copy of a booklet called "It's Your Choice" describing all the options at 16 from the Department for Education, Publications Centre, PO Box 2193, London E15 2EU. Telephone 0181-533-2000.

If you are 16-18 and want to study full time you are entitled to a place in a school or a College. If you are 16-18 and want to study part time, or if you are 19 or over and want to study part time or full time you can apply for a College place, but you may have to pay the fees.

Full time students aged 16-18 who are ordinarily resident in the European Community are entitled to free tuition. If you are 19 or over, or studying part-time at any age, you (or your employer) may be charged by the College their fee for the course. There may be reductions - this depends upon the policy of the individual College.

If you are studying for an NVQ at levels 1-4 or a GNVQ and pay your own course fees then you are entitled to tax relief. This means you will pay only 75% of the course fees.

There may be a discretionary award for you depending on the policy of the Local Education Authority . If you do not qualify for a discretionary award and are 19 or over and study a vocationally relevant training course then you may be eligible for a "career development loan". There is a Freephone for details: 0800 585 505

There may be help with transport costs too. Again this depends on the Local Education Authority .

You may be able to claim social security benefit if you are in one of the special groups, for example part-time students, students with disabilities and students who are single parents. Ring Freephone 0800 666 555 or your local social security benefits agency office.

The College will tell you if it has any "access funds" or other sources of financial aid for students.

There are 418 Further Education establishments in England and Wales and 2669 adult education centres. There are in the region of 450,000 full time and sandwich students and 800,000 part time students on Further Education courses.

5. Institutes of Higher Education

Higher Education is used to describe education above A level and Higher grade or their equivalent. It is provided in Universities and Colleges of Higher Education. There is no division between Universities and polytechnics, the latter have become Universities. They are funded by the Higher Education Funding Councils of England, Wales and Scotland.

To get into a University you need what is called "matriculation". This is essentially academic evidence that you will benefit from study at Higher Education level. In formal terms it is usually stated to be 5 GCSE's (or equivalent) and 2 A levels in relevant subjects. However, each University can accept or reject whomever they wish! There has been a 140% increase in the number of mature students entering Higher Education since 1979 and many of them have got there by taking 1 year Access courses run in Colleges of Further Education, rather than the longer route of GCSE's and 'A' levels.

Universities also run some "franchised" courses in Colleges of Further Education which are like an entry year to particular courses: they are sometimes called "year 0" courses. They are rather like the Access courses, but are designed for entry onto specific courses in specific Universities.

If you do get accepted by a University to do a degree then you will be able to apply for a grant from your Local Education Authority. The grant helps with living expenses and pays the course fees[2].

All Universities award their own degrees. When you go to a University it is usually as an under-graduate (i.e. you have not yet graduated by getting a degree). You will study for you first degree and that will be a "Bachelor"'s degree. A Bachelor of Arts B.A., and a Bachelor of Science, a B.Sc. are the most common. After you have graduated you become a "post-graduate" and, if you wish, you may study for a further qualification, usually a "Master"'s degree, a Master of Arts is an M.A., and a

---

[2]. *More detail of applying to Universities and how to pay for your course is given in Sections 9 and 10.*

Master of Science is an M.Sc. Beyond that is the Ph.D., a Doctor of Philosophy, which is awarded for very high levels of study.

Most under-graduate courses take three years, though some professional qualifications take longer e.g. medicine, dentistry. For details of entry and how you can pay for the courses see the following Sections.

However, many Universities run Part-Time courses which can take a flexible amount of time, some up to 6 years, for people who do not have time to attend lectures full time and who have other commitments. Many degrees are offered in this way and I suspect there will be an increasing number of such courses to meet the needs of people who would like to acquire their qualifications whilst, perhaps, bringing up the family.

You should also note that there are many opportunities to take your first degree or a part of it in European Union countries: Switzerland, Denmark, Norway, Sweden, Germany, Finland, Austria, France, Belgium, Holland, Luxembourg, Ireland, Italy, Spain, Greece, and Portugal. There is a booklet called "The European Choice" available from Department for Education, Publications Centre, PO Box 2193, London E15 2EU. Telephone 0181-533-2000. This lists all the available courses and gives details of financial arrangements.

There are 80 Universities in England and a further 50 Colleges of Higher Education. There are in the region of 700,000 full time and sandwich students.

6. Open University

The Open University was founded in 1970. There are no entry qualifications, no admission interviews, no barriers at all. The Open University teaches you at home with what they call supported open learning, via specially prepared packs of information, TV and radio broadcasts and there are short residential courses. You receive personal attention from a network of Tutors and counsellors. The Open University is flexible and can tailor studies to meet your individual needs. You don't have to take time off work or give up your social life completely!

They offer a wide variety of programmes, including professional training for managers, a nine month course in family history and, which is what is relevant to you, many undergraduate degree courses. These are in Arts, Social Science, Mathematics and computing, Technology, Education, Science, and Environment.

The main characteristic of the Open University is its teaching method. You stay at home and you are sent a set of specially written and professionally printed text books and or work-books. They have developed these materials extremely well since 1970. They use the BBC TV and radio to help keep you up to date as well as providing personal Tutorial support at their 13 regional centres.

You are placed in a small group attached to a Tutor/Counsellor whom you can meet at your local study centre. The Tutor's job is to help you with any personal and/or academic problems you may have throughout the course. You can join self-help, groups of other students in your area following the same course.

You are assessed by

- continuous assessment of your performance in written assignments. These can essays marked by your Tutor, or may be computer marked multiple choice questions.

- examination marks at the end of the course are combined with the continuous assessment to provide a final result.

6.1 The BA and B.Sc. degree programme

At present you must apply to do these by first doing one of the five Open University foundation courses. You can apply for exemption from this if you have already done some undergraduate-level work.

Most students feel they need on average between 12 and 15 hours a week to be set aside for study for one of the foundation courses. This lasts for nine months of the year, from February to October.

The shortest time taken for completion of a degree from scratch is three years, but that would mean studying 2 full courses every year and that would mean 24-30 hours of study a week, which is like being a full-time student. Most people spread the work over 5 or 6 years.

You can try out Open University study by doing one of the Foundation courses. You would get a preparatory pack in the Autumn, followed by your first two to three months on the course at an initial tuition fee of about £150. If after that you decide not to carry on you don't have to pay any more.

You are put in touch with your Tutor before the course begins who advises you on preparation. The Tutor arranges a series of optional tutorial sessions at the local study centre. The Tutor also gives you regular guidance on your progress by correspondence and is available for help on the phone. The Tutor also helps you plan your future studies.

6.2 Fees and financial support.

Detailed fees can be obtained from the Open University. The fee for a foundation course in the undergraduate programme for students in 1995 is £279, the undergraduate programme starts at £475, with an additional £187 if there is a residential course involved. You can pay by instalments. Unlike full-time students in Higher Education Open University students don't automatically get a mandatory grant. Some Local Education Authorities do provide a Discretionary grant. There is a leaflet available from the Open University called Financial Support for Open University study. General enquiries are dealt with at:Central Enquiry Service, The Open University, PO Box 200, Walton Hall, Milton Keynes, MK7 6YZ. Telephone: 01908 653 231

6. WEA

Founded in 1903 the Workers' Educational Association is a voluntary, democratic and nationwide organisation which welcomes the active participation of a membership drawn from its students.

It provides educational opportunities for adults who wish to continue learning throughout life. The WEA class provides a unique forum for learning. It follows a syllabus worked out in partnership by student and tutor.

There are academic and liberal studies, women's education, community education, Second Chance to Learn, post retirement education and seminars and study tours.

There are no entrance requirements and no examinations. The WEA works in conjunction with many organisations, Universities, local education authorities, community organisations and trade unions.

If you are looking to just "put your foot in the water" and are not anxious to get formal qualifications[3] then you may well find the WEA just the place for you.

I have listed their District Offices below. You will get good information from them.

WEA District Offices
Cheshire, Merseyside and
West Lancashire District
7/8 Bluecoat Chambers
School Lane
Liverpool
L1 3BX.
01517 080 046

WEA District Offices
Eastern District
Botolph House
17 Botolph Lane
Cambridge
CB2 3RE
01223 350 978

WEA District Offices
East Midland District
16 Shakespeare Street
Nottingham
NG1 4GF
01602 475 162

WEA District Offices
London District
44-66 Crowdale Street
London
NW1 1TR
01713 887 261/ 878 966

WEA District Offices
Northern District
51 Grainger Street
Newcastle upon Tyne
NE1 5JE
01912 323 957

WEA District Offices
North Western District
4th Floor
Crawford House
University Precinct Centre
Oxford Road
Manchester
01612 737 652

---

[3]. *You do usually need formal qualifications to progress into Higher Education.*

WEA District Offices
South Eastern District
4 Castle Hill
Rochester
Kent
ME1 1QQ
01634 842 140.

WEA District Offices
South Western District
Martin's Gate Annexe
Bretonside
Plymouth
PL4 0AT
01752 664 989

WEA District Offices
Thames and Solent District
6 Brewer Street
Oxford
OX1 1QN
01865 203 282.

WEA District Offices
Western District
40 Morse Road
Redfield
Bristol
BS5 9LB
01272 351 764

WEA District Offices
West Mercia District
78/80 Sherlock Street
Birmingham
B5 6LT
0121 6666 101

WEA District Offices
Yorkshire North District
6 Woodhouse Square
Leeds
LS3 1AD
01132 450 883

WEA District Offices
Yorkshire South District
Chantry Buildings
Corporation Street
Rotherham
S60 1NG
01709 837 001

Scottish Association:
Riddles Court
322 Lawnmarket
Edinburgh
EH1 3PG
01312 263 456

National Office:
WEA
Temple House
17 Victoria Park Square
London
E2 9PB
01819 831 515

7. Open Learning

There are a lot of terms used now to cover an increasing number of flexible ways of acquiring qualifications. There is "Open Learning", "Flexi-study", "Home Study", and many others. The courses described by these terms are usually designed to bring educational opportunities in forms which are attractive and useful to people who do not want to go to the traditional evening or day class. Many Colleges of Further Education run "Open Learning" courses. These are resource based learning workshops where the emphasis is on providing materials and assessment so that students can study at their own pace to gain academic qualifications. There is sometimes the opportunity to use "drop-in" facilities for students to sample a wide variety of subject materials.

"Flexi-study" is a term used for providing courses for "Home Study" where the student cannot get into College on a weekly basis. The system usually entails enrolling at a College in a particular subject, varying from GCSE to A level. You are given a personal subject tutor who is responsible for your progress through the course. The Tutor marks and comments on the assignments you do and assists you in general to pass the course. The courses are designed in a variety of ways, but usually involve working from specially written, easy to follow units which are written either commercially published or produced specially by College staff and used in conjunction with a text book. You are able to be in touch with the tutor by letter or at prearranged times by phone or by visiting.

Sometimes the term "Distance Learning" is used to cover similar methods.

These courses are extremely flexible: you can usually start them at any time of year, not just when the College year begins. You are not constrained by the speed of others in the class. If you are prepared to devote the time and effort then you can usually complete the course more quickly than in a traditional class. Equally you can take longer or take time out and then return to study[4]. The advantages are obvious for someone with limited time.

There are less obvious disadvantages in not being one of a crowd who can compare progress and learn from each other, and have regular on-going contact with the class tutor.

Cost is usually the cost of the materials and the cost of the normal course at the College.

---

[4]. *If the course is a nationally examined one such as GCSE or A level then you will have to take the exam at the same time as others.*

---

8. Private Correspondence Courses

I would advise against anyone taking on these unless the course is unavailable elsewhere. They are expensive and really are out to make money from you. If you are able to study only at home then go to a local College of Further Education in the first instance and enquire about their Open Learning opportunities described on the previous pages. The course you wish to study will probably be available from there and will have a much larger backup service than a small correspondence service. If you need a higher level then consider the Open University.

9. Some difficulties

9.1 Study and unemployment benefit

One of the main difficulties of taking advantage of all these opportunities is paying for them! There are constant changes in the provision of education for people who are over the age of 18. At present, 1995, there are some horrendous contradictions in the theory and practice which actually disadvantage many unemployed and unwaged adults who wish to return to education. A student who is in receipt of unemployment benefit must be available for work and be actively seeking work whilst attending a Part Time course. The student will lose benefit if attending a College for more than 21 hours per week[5] (in effect this is 18 hours per week since three hours is added for lunch times). Thus a student who wishes to keep benefit cannot follow Full Time Courses, but can take the Part Time Courses as long as they total less than 18 hours per week.

If you are a doing a Part Time course and you are signing on as available for work and actively seeking work, then a claim for unemployment benefit (where you must have the correct amount of NI contributions) or for income support **may** succeed. You must agree to give up the course if suitable employment or training is offered.

These regulations change frequently and the latest proposals are that unemployment benefit will be paid only to those who take on training or voluntary work. The benefit is called the Job Seeker's Allowance. I don't know how this will affect the unemployed person seeking to gain qualifications via education.

I hope that this situation will soon change and that those wanting to return to learning will find that that route is well funded and regarded.[6]

I must emphasise that all the detail listed above this is in a constant state of change and that you should consult with your local College of Further Education as to what is available in terms of courses and in terms of financial assistance.

---

[5]. *There are recent moves to make this 16 hours.*
[6]. *More detail about how you pay for your course is in Section 9.*

SECTION 2
HOW DO YOU GET IN?

1. Matriculation

To get into a University you need to convince the University that you will benefit from study there. The traditional method of entry has been what was called "matriculation", which was at least 2 "A" levels and 5 "O" levels and sometimes an interview.

2. Normal entry for school leavers

The normal method of entry to Higher Education for those in 6th forms and the equivalent is to apply through the UCAS system (which is explained in detail in Section 10). The entry qualifications are usually matriculation. All the requirements are set out in the UCAS handbook.

3. Concessionary entry for older students

By older people I mean those who have left school, had some experience and then decide to return to education. The average age of those coming to our Access course was 35, but the spread was from 19 to 71!

There has always been a direct way into many Universities for older students for whom concessions are made and many older students have gained access to the Universities without these traditional qualifications. Acceptance is on the basis of their previous experience, personality and commitment to study. This usually involved an interview and then a meeting of the University's Senate committee to consider the individual case. Thus it is always worth while approaching the University of your choice and asking for an interview. **I strongly advise you to be clear what course you wish to do and why you want to do it before you apply for such an interview.**

4. Access Courses

The usual response from a University to a mature student who does not posses "matriculation" is to advise going away and getting evidence of recent study. This has usually meant going and getting the 5 GCSE levels and the 2 "A" levels in evening classes or by correspondence course to be sufficiently qualified. This is changing. Older students are being encouraged to return to study. Over the past few years other qualifications have been accepted as "matriculation". Many Universities accept students from 1 year Access courses run mainly by Further Education Colleges.

These courses are usually very "user friendly". They are often part time and can be as short as 9 hours per week. They are run to meet the needs of older students with families who need to be free to see to their children in the morning and receive them from school in the afternoon. Many have facilities for looking after preschool children. There are also many which lamentably do not!

5. "Franchised" year 0 courses

Some Universities now run degree courses (sometimes called "franchised courses") in other institutions such as Further Education Colleges which have a year of preparatory work to enable the student to find out if s/he is fitted for the course. Do note that these courses do not prepare you for general acceptance in any Univerity for any course but are usually designed for entry to a specific course at a s[pecific University.

6. Important points for older students

I want you to be clear that as an older student (usually called mature student) you will be more than welcome in Universities and Colleges. There are three basic reasons why this is the case:

    - Higher Education institutions report that mature students perform significantly better than the younger students going straight from school. This is probably because while younger students are still "finding themselves", you, the mature student, have a clearer idea of what you want from your course, have more "invested" in the course in terms of money, time and effort, and are therefore better "motivated" to study rather than play!

    - You are cheaper than the younger students (!) who tend to want accommodation, whereas the older student usually has accommodation already nearby, since they have families and commitments to a local area!

    - The Government has wanted to get more adults to return to education.

All Universities welcome mature students. It is always worth while ringing up the University which is nearest to you and asking if you can visit to have a chat with some of the older students who usually have their own group within the University. The old idea of students being 18-21 year olds is fast disappearing as more and more older people return to the Universities.

The traditional route to HE has been either the sixth form or the "five years hard labour" through evening classes to gain the necessary GCSE and "A" levels. No special facilities were made available for these latter students. Many dropped out and exceptional motivation, resilience and determination were required. Now, with the Access Course route, older people are being empowered to realise their potential. If you don't believe it then read the comments of former Access students in Appendix I!

SECTION 3
WHERE DO YOU WANT TO BE
IN 5 YEARS?

Introduction

It is essential that you should have some long term objects in mind now that you have asked the rather dramatic question of "What do I want to do with the rest of my life?"! It really is as dramatic as that! What you have decided to do is not usual! Most people allow life to act upon them! They go to school, they sit exams, they go for interviews and they get, or don't get jobs! There seems to be a general trust that it will work out.

Another trap you may fall into is to rush and take the first course that you come across. Now is a time for careful reflection and careful planning.

In fact, what you have decided to do is to say: "No, I want to be in charge. I want to become something worthwhile, and having found out what I want to be I'll be able to do things today to start bringing that about."

1. The important questions to answer

1.1 Long term goals

One approach which some people find useful is to answer the following questions in the order in which they are asked below:

---

1. Where do you want to be in 5 years time?
2. What sort of qualifications do you need in order to get there?
3. Which HE course should you choose?
4. Which HE Institution should you choose?
5. What route will you have to follow in order to get there?

Don't worry if at this stage you can't answer question 1. There are people who go forward to Higher Education, especially in the Humanities, purely to widen their knowledge. Question 1 is important, however, if you need to bring home a wage packet at the end of your courses of study.

1.2 Practical questions

There are then practical questions to be answered such as:

---

1. Should you be Full Time or Part Time?
2. How will you pay for the course?
3. How should you prepare yourself and any people around you for entry to the course?

---

2. Answering the questions

In this and the following sections I will try to help you answer these questions. You must remember that it is YOU who must give the answers to these questions. You really ought to go to professional careers guidance people whom you will find at your local College of Further Education and hopefully they will give you information, support and guidance, but essentially it is your responsibility to yourself to make the decisions, based on the best information you can gather.

I suggest that you read through this section and get the idea of what is to be done and then settle down to answering some of the initial questions posed. Where you find yourself ignorant or unable to answer a question you may well find some guidance on the pages suggested.

3. Where do you want to be in 5 years time?

This is your starting point. You should be exploring NOW, BEFORE you start on any course, where you want to get to AFTER your preparation for Higher Education, even AFTER your Higher Education Course.

I suggest that you start with where you want to get to, and then work backwards from there to which course at Higher Education level you need to get to your destination, and what you need to do to qualify for that Higher Education level course.

In other words **gather information about your long term destination** so that you can be fairly sure that it is a place you want to be!

You can never be certain about that destination, but at some stage, you should be able to say that, in the light of the evidence you have considered, you are aiming at a particular destination in 4-5 years time!!

Thus your first task is to clarify, at least in broad terms, what you want to be doing in five years time.

You may already have decided. You may have only the thought you want to stop what you are doing now and try something else. You may be somewhere in between. Whatever your situation now, this is your starting point. You need to

---

begin the task of exploring where realistically you would like to be in five years time.

   - decide the broad area
   - begin to narrow it down, either by selecting something that appeals or by rejecting those that do not appeal. Try giving each a mark out of ten, and select the best one

4. Ways of clarifying your long term goals.

It is well worth while spending a lot of time and effort on this stage. No one will tell you what to become (and be wary of anyone who does so!) - remember that YOU are the one who has to make the choice. Others can help by supplying information, by asking you questions about yourself and your interests, but ultimately YOU must make the decision.

If you have no idea whatsoever what you want to be then it is important to begin at the beginning and, either by choosing or by eliminating, get some broad idea of what you would enjoy becoming in 5 years time. There are several methods of doing this yourself, but it really is worth while to find some careers service and ask them to help. Your local Further Education College may well have such a service, but be careful that it is not really a recruiting agency for the College!

You may find the exercise in Section 4 useful in deciding broadly what sort of area you like - it is one which I have used with people - again don't rely on this as some sort of magic potion that will make everything clear - it is a tool to help you think clearly about yourself and your interests.

4.1 Colleges of Further Education

You should find good independent and personal advice at your local Further Education College, most of which have a Careers and Counselling Service. You could also contact your local University and ask if they can provide some career advice for you in the light of your present situation. It is possible that your local TEC will have some advice available, but be careful of this since their "advice" is often driven by a desire to place you onto one of their schemes in order to make money!

4.2 Libraries

Your local library will have information about careers, and that may be useful as a starting point, but it is often impersonal and the choice of books is probably left to you, which actually leaves you in the same state as before - not really knowing where to begin.

4.3 In general

Talking things over with family and friends can help. Certainly they should be included in your decision making, but again I must point out that this decision about where you want to be has to one that YOU make.

When you have made some progress with identifying your long term goal then I do urge you to find out what the career structure is within that career. At what sort of level do you seek entry?

Your local library and the College Careers and Counselling Service of your local College of Further Education will be able to help.

You should also try to make contacts with people who already work in the type of job you would like. Find someone who is doing the work or following the career/interest which attracts you and ask how they obtained their position.

There may be professional associations which you can contact.

Seek out the advice of those at the receiving Higher Education institutions and ask what people do when they leave with the qualification you intend to get.

**BE CLEAR ABOUT THE ROUTES YOU NEED TO FOLLOW
IN ORDER TO GET TO WHERE YOU WANT TO GET!**

SECTION 4
WHAT CAREER SHOULD YOU HAVE?

In this Section I try to start you off on thinking about what career is going to suit you best. I am trying to do no more than start you thinking. I do not want you to think that I can answer the question for you. There is only YOU who can do that. I suggest that you start with the series of questions overleaf[1] which may help you to decide the broad general area in which you have an interest and which you like doing.

After you have completed that series of questions and after you have talked the results over with other people including professional careers advisers, you might like to go on to the next series of questions which I hope will help you to narrow down your broader interests to more specific careers. Again I must urge you to go to careers advisers with your findings after you have thought through your reactions to your findings.

IMPORTANT NOTE

I must emphasise that whilst Part One can help you to clarify your thoughts about your future, you MUST get face to face advice from those trained to help in careers and educational guidance. The main providers of careers advice used to be the Careers Service which was run by Local Education Authorities. Look them up in your yellow pages, contact them and find out if they still offer a service to adults: the majority seem now to offer their advice only to young people in schools.

Your local Further Education College is another possibility. This is not quite as straight-forward as it may seem. Since Education has been forced into the "market place" you have to be wary of advisers who are actually sales-people! Each of the Colleges of Further Education is now a "corporate body" and it is their purpose to make money: thus you must be wary that they do not advise you to go on a course in their institution which may not be the perfect course for you, but which will generate income for them! However, the individual advisers within the Colleges will, I am sure, do their best for you. I would always be interested to hear from you about the effectiveness and objectivity of the advice you receive from the Colleges.

Training and Enterprise Councils (TEC's) can sometimes help, but they have information biased mainly towards training for jobs rather than educating for careers. It might be worth while trying them.

Another source of information about suitable courses for you is a computer database called ECCTIS. This may be available at your local school, College of Further Education, careers office or TAP (Training Access Point).

---

[1]. An IBM compatible computer programme version of the all the questions and interpretation in this section is available on from the publishers.

GROUP ONE

You like:*(1 =strongly disagree 2 =disagree 3 =not sure 4 =agree 5 =strongly agree)*

TO KEEP YOURSELF HEALTHY	① ② ③ ④ ⑤
FIXING THINGS THAT DON'T WORK PROPERLY	① ② ③ ④ ⑤
WORKING OUTSIDE	① ② ③ ④ ⑤
PRACTICAL TASKS	① ② ③ ④ ⑤
WORKING WITH YOUR HANDS	① ② ③ ④ ⑤
USING PRACTICAL TOOLS	① ② ③ ④ ⑤
WORKING WITH THINGS	① ② ③ ④ ⑤
FIXING THINGS THAT HAVE BROKEN⑤	① ② ③ ④ ⑤
WORKING WITH MACHINES	① ② ③ ④ ⑤
FIXING THINGS ABOUT THE HOUSE	① ② ③ ④ ⑤
WORKING IN THE GARDEN	① ② ③ ④ ⑤

Add up the totals in each column

GRAND TOTAL FOR GROUP 1

GROUP TWO

You like:*(1 =strongly disagree 2 =disagree 3 =not sure 4 =agree 5 =strongly agree)*

TO UNDERSTAND THINGS THOROUGHLY	① ② ③ ④ ⑤
EXPLORING NEW IDEAS	① ② ③ ④ ⑤
WORKING ON PROBLEMS	① ② ③ ④ ⑤
ASKING QUESTIONS	① ② ③ ④ ⑤
LEARNING ABOUT NEW THINGS	① ② ③ ④ ⑤
WORKING OUT OWN ANSWERS TO PROBLEMS	① ② ③ ④ ⑤
RESEARCHING A JOB WELL	① ② ③ ④ ⑤
SITTING & WORKING THINGS OUT THOROUGHLY	① ② ③ ④
⑤	
FINDING OUT FACTS FROM BOOKS	① ② ③ ④ ⑤
WORKING THINGS OUT IN YOUR HEAD	① ② ③ ④ ⑤
USING DIRECTORIES OR TIMETABLES	① ② ③ ④ ⑤

Add up the totals in each column

GRAND TOTAL FOR GROUP 2

GROUP THREE

You like:*(1 =strongly disagree 2 =disagree 3 =not sure 4 =agree 5 =strongly agree)*

GOING TO THE THEATRE	①	②	③	④	⑤
TO BE DIFFERENT	①	②	③	④	⑤
TO BE CREATIVE	①	②	③	④	⑤
TO HAVE BEAUTIFUL THINGS AROUND YOU	①	②	③	④	⑤
TO USE YOUR IMAGINATION	①	②	③	④	⑤
EXPRESSING YOURSELF ON PAPER	①	②	③	④	⑤
GOING TO THE CINEMA	①	②	③	④	⑤
TO HAVE UNUSUAL THINGS AROUND YOU	①	②	③	④	⑤
GOING TO ART GALLERIES	①	②	③	④	⑤
WRITING POEMS	①	②	③	④	⑤
EXPRESSING YOURSELF THROUGH PAINTING	①	②	③	④	⑤

Add up the totals in each column

GRAND TOTAL FOR GROUP 3

GROUP FOUR

You like:*(1 =strongly disagree 2 =disagree 3 =not sure 4 =agree 5 =strongly agree)*

BEING WITH PEOPLE & NOT WORKING ALONE	①	②	③	④	⑤
TALKING THINGS THROUGH WITH PEOPLE	①	②	③	④	⑤
TO PAY ATTENTION TO WHAT PEOPLE WANT	①	②	③	④	⑤
HELPING PEOPLE	①	②	③	④	⑤
HELPING PEOPLE DISCOVER & LEARN THINGS	①	②	③	④	⑤
LISTENING TO PEOPLE	①	②	③	④	⑤
GOING ERRANDS FOR OTHER PEOPLE	①	②	③	④	⑤
HELPING CRIMINALS FIT BACK INTO SOCIETY	①	②	③	④	⑤
TO WORK WITH MENTALLY HANDICAPPED	①	②	③	④	⑤
TO WORK WITH PHYSICALLY HANDICAPPED	①	②	③	④	⑤
WHO YOU'RE WITH IS MORE IMPORTANT THAN WHERE YOU ARE	①	②	③	④	⑤

Add up the totals in each column

GRAND TOTAL FOR GROUP 4

GROUP FIVE

You like:*(1 =strongly disagree 2 =disagree 3 =not sure 4 =agree 5 =strongly agree)*

TRYING TO PERSUADE OR INFLUENCE PEOPLE	①	②	③	④	⑤
USING A GREAT DEAL OF ENERGY AND EFFORT	①	②	③	④	⑤
PEOPLE TO DO WHAT YOU ASK OF THEM	①	②	③	④	⑤
TAKING RISKS	①	②	③	④	⑤
MAKING DECISIONS	①	②	③	④	⑤
GETTING PEOPLE ORGANISED					
& EXCITED ON A TASK	①	②	③	④	⑤
TO INFLUENCE PEOPLE	①	②	③	④	⑤
CARRYING FULL RESPONSIBILITY FOR A TASK	①	②	③	④	⑤
GIVING ORDERS	①	②	③	④	⑤
ORGANISING PEOPLE	①	②	③	④	⑤
DEALING WITH PEOPLE WHO DON'T AGREE	①	②	③	④	⑤

Add up the totals in each column

GRAND TOTAL FOR GROUP 5

GROUP SIX

You like:*(1 =strongly disagree 2 =disagree 3 =not sure 4 =agree 5 =strongly agree)*

TO GIVE CLEAR DIRECTIONS	①	②	③	④	⑤
GETTING THE DETAILS OF YOUR WORK RIGHT	①	②	③	④	⑤
A CLEAR STRUCTURE	①	②	③	④	⑤
BEING RELIED ON	①	②	③	④	⑤
WORKING WITH FIGURES	①	②	③	④	⑤
ORGANISING DOWN TO THE LAST DETAIL	①	②	③	④	⑤
A REGULAR ROUTINE	①	②	③	④	⑤
FILLING IN FORMS	①	②	③	④	⑤
WORKING WITH LISTS	①	②	③	④	⑤
FILING THINGS IN ORDER	①	②	③	④	⑤
MAKING SURE ALL IS DONE					
EXACTLY TO YOUR INSTRUCTIONS	①	②	③	④	⑤

Add up the totals in each column

GRAND TOTAL FOR GROUP 6

Interpreting your answers

SCORE FOR GROUP 1=[   ] SCORE FOR GROUP 4=[   ]
SCORE FOR GROUP 2=[   ] SCORE FOR GROUP 5=[   ]
SCORE FOR GROUP 3=[   ] SCORE FOR GROUP 6=[   ]

The scores relate to the groups below and, whilst there is no guarantee of accuracy in the interpretations, you may identify some aspects of your general interests.

GROUP	TITLE	WORK WITH	SCORE
1	PRACTICAL	THINGS	
2	INVESTIGATIVE	IDEAS	
3	ARTISTIC	IDEAS/PEOPLE	
4	SOCIAL	PEOPLE	
5	ENTERPRISING	PEOPLE/DATA	
6	ORGANISATIONAL/ADMINISTRATIVE	DATA/THINKING	

You should read the group where you have scored highest. The highest you can score in any group is 55. If you are scoring over 50 in any group then you are very strongly inclined towards that group. Scores of below 15 indicate very little interest in that group.

Group 1 = PRACTICAL - Working with things

If you have scored highly in this group then you might like to work with tools, objects, machines or animals. You seem to prefer to develop manual, mechanical, agricultural or electronic skills. You seem to prefer a job which could involve building or repairing things. You seem to like using your hands, using your body skilfully rather than words or thoughts or feelings. You admire physical co-ordination, strength agility and logic. You like being out of doors, dealing with concrete problems. You tend to be down to earth and matter of fact. You solve problems by DOING. You might look for jobs in skilled trades, technical & service, which involve physical co-ordination or strength, using, repairing and understanding machinery.

Group 2 = INVESTIGATIVE - Working with ideas

If you have scored highly in this group then you might like to work with mechanical principles or exploiting natural resources. You seem to enjoy using your mind. You tend to be curious, studious, independent, intellectual, sometimes unconventional and introspective. You like to develop skills in biology or the physical sciences. You like thinking through problems, trusting your own mind rather than other people and things. You admire logic, use insight and enjoy intellectual challenges. You appear to solve problems by THINKING. You might seek work in scientific or technical areas, which involve an interest in how and why things work or happen and interest in discovering the facts of a situation, analysing and solving problems.

Group 3 = ARTISTIC - Working with ideas and people

If you have scored highly in this group then you seem to prefer work which is free from routine. You might like to develop skills in language, art, music, drama or writing. You seem to trust your mind, body and feelings and are suspicious of things. You enjoy beauty, unstructured activity, interesting and unusual sounds, sights, textures and people. You perhaps see yourself as creative, talented and free-wheeling, often non-conformist, sensitive, independent, introspective and expressive. You would seem to like a job where you can express your creative skills. You appear to solve problems by being CREATIVE. You might seek work in visual and performing arts, design or literary areas.

Group 4 = SOCIAL - Working with people

If you have scored highly in this group then you might like work which is dealing with people. You seem to like/dislike through your feelings. You appear to rely on gut reactions. You perhaps would like activities that involve informing, training, educating, understanding and helping others. You seem to like the idea of working with people. You appear to be helpful, friendly, concerned, sensitive, supportive, responsible, perceptive, genuine, tactful and empathetic. You may enjoy being close to people, sharing problems, being in charge and unstructured activities. You might like a job in teaching, nursing or counselling. You appear to solve your problems by USING YOUR FEELINGS. You might seek work in educational or social welfare, or an occupation which involves advising, understanding and or helping people with their problems.

Group 5 = ENTERPRISING - working with people and data

If you have scored highly in this group then you might like work which is concerned with organising people to do things. You seem to love projects and leading and influencing people. You appear ambitious, outgoing, energetic, self-confident, independent, enthusiastic, sensitive and logical. You seem to like developing skills to lead, motivate and persuade people. You might enjoy managing/organising in a job which gives variety, status, power and money. You appear to solve problems by RISKING YOURSELF and even others. You might seek work in managerial, sales, financial and service occupations, which involve an interest in managing, leading or negotiating with others or promoting projects. You might enjoy setting up and running your own business.

Group 6 = ORGANISATIONAL/ADMINISTRATIVE - working with data and thinking

If you have scored highly in this group then you might like to work in a job where there is order and routine. You seem to enjoy activities that encourage organising information in a clear logical way. You appear to be responsible, dependable, careful, logical and accurate, having an eye for detail. You appear to enjoy order, security and certainty and identify with power and status. You would perhaps enjoy work which involves systems, operating computers and word processors. You might be happy developing office and arithmetical skills. You might enjoy work which involves systems, operating computers and word processors. You would probably enjoy working in large organisations. You appear to solve your problems by following routines. You might seek work in office/clerical occupations, public administration or security, and any job which involves directing or organising procedures by means of paper work.

Further interpretation

You should have a look at the group where you have scored the lowest and remember that that is an area you should avoid!

If you are interested you can gain further insight into your interests by listing **all** the points above where you have marked a ⑤ and then **all** those you have marked a ④ and so on. This will supply you with a list of interests in order of intensity, from highest to lowest.

Taking it further

You may wish to look more closely at some specific career interests and below you will find a similar set of questions which will indicate some more specific career interests you may have. The following questions are based on an excellent system used by CASCAID who publish an excellent book each year called "The Careers Guide". It contains information about 400 jobs, describing work content and training routes and listing sources of further information. This really is one of the best books for those who want to find out what a particular job/career entails and what qualifications you need to get into it. Check in your local library and if you want your own copy then they can be ordered from:
CASCAID
West Annex
County Hall
Glenfield
Leicester
LE3 8YZ

AREA ONE

You like:*(1 =strongly disagree 2 =disagree 3 =not sure 4 =agree 5 =strongly agree)*

WORKING WITH CHILDREN	① ② ③ ④ ⑤
PLANNING THINGS VERY CAREFULLY	① ② ③ ④ ⑤
DEALING WITH CRISES	① ② ③ ④ ⑤
TAKING HEAVY RESPONSIBILITY	① ② ③ ④ ⑤
WORKING IN A TEAM	① ② ③ ④ ⑤
WORKING ON YOUR OWN	① ② ③ ④ ⑤
TAKING THINGS CAREFULLY AND SLOWLY	① ② ③ ④ ⑤
DEALING WITH DIFFICULT SITUATIONS	① ② ③ ④ ⑤
COPING WITH DIFFICULT CHILDREN	① ② ③ ④ ⑤
ORGANISING YOURSELF	① ② ③ ④ ⑤
CONTROLLING YOUR SELF	① ② ③ ④ ⑤

Add up the totals in each column

GRAND TOTAL FOR AREA 1

AREA TWO

You like:*(1 =strongly disagree 2 =disagree 3 =not sure 4 =agree 5 =strongly agree)*

EXAMINING FINANCIAL MATTERS	① ② ③ ④ ⑤
ANALYSING/INTERPRETING FIGURES	① ② ③ ④ ⑤
WORKING WITH NUMBERS	① ② ③ ④ ⑤
USING A COMPUTER	① ② ③ ④ ⑤
COMMUNICATING IN WRITING	① ② ③ ④ ⑤
COMMUNICATING VERBALLY	① ② ③ ④ ⑤
WORKING OUT TAX FORMS	① ② ③ ④ ⑤
ANALYSING ORGANISATIONS	① ② ③ ④ ⑤
WORKING WITH OTHERS	① ② ③ ④ ⑤
UNDERSTANDING LEGAL DOCUMENTS	① ② ③ ④ ⑤
TAKING EXAMINATIONS	① ② ③ ④ ⑤

Add up the totals in each column

GRAND TOTAL FOR AREA 2

AREA THREE

You like:*(1 =strongly disagree 2 =disagree 3 =not sure 4 =agree 5 =strongly agree)*

BEING RESPONSIBLE FOR THE ORGANISATION	①	②	③	④	⑤
UNDERTAKING FINANCIAL DUTIES	①	②	③	④	⑤
PRODUCING REPORTS	①	②	③	④	⑤
ARRANGING MEETINGS	①	②	③	④	⑤
UNDERSTANDING THE LAW	①	②	③	④	⑤
INTERPRETING ACCOUNTS	①	②	③	④	⑤
HANDLING CORRESPONDENCE	①	②	③	④	⑤
PREPARING BRIEFS FOR OTHERS	①	②	③	④	⑤
SUPERVISING OTHERS	①	②	③	④	⑤
FINANCIAL PLANNING	①	②	③	④	⑤
TAKING RESPONSIBILITY	①	②	③	④	⑤

Add up the totals in each column

GRAND TOTAL FOR AREA 3

AREA FOUR

You like:*(1 =strongly disagree 2 =disagree 3 =not sure 4 =agree 5 =strongly agree)*

WRITING ORIGINAL WORK TO A PRESCRIPTION	①	②	③	④	⑤
UNDERSTANDING WHAT MOTIVATES PEOPLE	①	②	③	④	⑤
WORKING CLOSELY WITH OTHERS	①	②	③	④	⑤
WORKING TO TIGHT DEADLINES	①	②	③	④	⑤
TAKING CRITICISM	①	②	③	④	⑤
FOLLOWING OTHER PEOPLE'S INSTRUCTIONS	①	②	③	④	⑤
DEVELOP OTHER PEOPLE'S IDEAS	①	②	③	④	⑤
WORKING IRREGULAR HOURS	①	②	③	④	⑤
WORKING UNDER PRESSURE	①	②	③	④	⑤
HAVING YOUR WORK ALTERED BY OTHERS	①	②	③	④	⑤
WORKING WITH VISUAL MATERIAL	①	②	③	④	⑤

Add up the totals in each column

GRAND TOTAL FOR AREA 4

AREA FIVE

You like:*(1 =strongly disagree 2 =disagree 3 =not sure 4 =agree 5 =strongly agree)*

UNDERSTANDING AGRICULTURAL MATTERS	①	②	③	④	⑤
UNDERSTANDING SOIL	①	②	③	④	⑤
UNDERSTANDING ANIMALS	①	②	③	④	⑤
CHEMICAL SCIENCE	①	②	③	④	⑤
BIOLOGICAL SCIENCE	①	②	③	④	⑤
DOING RESEARCH	①	②	③	④	⑤
INVESTIGATING COMPLEX PROBLEMS	①	②	③	④	⑤
BEING PAINSTAKING IN DETAIL	①	②	③	④	⑤
COMMUNICATING COMPLEX MATERIAL	①	②	③	④	⑤
WORKING WITH OTHERS IN A TEAM	①	②	③	④	⑤
UNDERSTANDING PLANTS & GROWTH	①	②	③	④	⑤

Add up the totals in each column

GRAND TOTAL FOR AREA 5

AREA SIX

You like:*(1 =strongly disagree 2 =disagree 3 =not sure 4 =agree 5 =strongly agree)*

STUDYING HISTORY	①	②	③	④	⑤
BEING PAINSTAKING WITH DETAIL	①	②	③	④	⑤
RELATING DETAIL TO A LARGER PERSPECTIVE	①	②	③	④	⑤
WORKING WITH MAPS	①	②	③	④	⑤
KEEPING METICULOUS NOTES	①	②	③	④	⑤
PRODUCING WRITTEN REPORTS	①	②	③	④	⑤
WORKING IN A TEAM	①	②	③	④	⑤
WORKING UNDER PRESSURE	①	②	③	④	⑤
SURVEYING	①	②	③	④	⑤
WORKING SCIENTIFICALLY	①	②	③	④	⑤
CLASSIFYING THINGS	①	②	③	④	⑤

Add up the totals in each column

GRAND TOTAL FOR AREA 6

AREA SEVEN
You like:*(1 =strongly disagree 2 =disagree 3 =not sure 4 =agree 5 =strongly agree)*

BEING VISUALLY CREATIVE	①	②	③	④	⑤
WORKING WITH MATHEMATICS	①	②	③	④	⑤
DESIGNING THINGS	①	②	③	④	⑤
UNDERSTANDING STRUCTURE OF OBJECTS	①	②	③	④	⑤
WORKING WITH BUILDINGS	①	②	③	④	⑤
DOING METICULOUS RESEARCH	①	②	③	④	⑤
ENGINEERING PROBLEMS	①	②	③	④	⑤
WORKING AS A MEMBER OF A TEAM	①	②	③	④	⑤
NEGOTIATING WITH OTHERS	①	②	③	④	⑤
SUPERVISING OTHERS	①	②	③	④	⑤
DRAWING ACCURATELY	①	②	③	④	⑤

Add up the totals in each column

GRAND TOTAL FOR AREA 7

AREA EIGHT
You like:*(1 =strongly disagree 2 =disagree 3 =not sure 4 =agree 5 =strongly agree)*

DEALING WITH COMPLEX ARGUMENTS	①	②	③	④	⑤
PRESENTING IDEAS TO OTHERS	①	②	③	④	⑤
WORKING UNDER PRESSURE	①	②	③	④	⑤
UNDERSTANDING COMPLEX IDEAS	①	②	③	④	⑤
WORKING WITH DIFFICULT PEOPLE	①	②	③	④	⑤
PREPARING DETAILED ARGUMENTS	①	②	③	④	⑤
BEING UNDER PUBLIC SCRUTINY	①	②	③	④	⑤
BEING CRITICISED	①	②	③	④	⑤
THINKING ON YOUR FEET	①	②	③	④	⑤
WORKING UNSOCIAL HOURS	①	②	③	④	⑤
SUMMARISING COMPLEX ISSUES	①	②	③	④	⑤

Add up the totals in each column

GRAND TOTAL FOR AREA 8

AREA NINE

You like:*(1 =strongly disagree 2 =disagree 3 =not sure 4 =agree 5 =strongly agree)*

UNDERSTANDING MECHANISMS OF TISSUE	①	②	③	④	⑤
UNDERSTANDING THE GROWTH OF PLANTS	①	②	③	④	⑤
BEING CLEAR AND EXTREMELY LOGICAL	①	②	③	④	⑤
CREATING, IMPLEMENTING EXPERIMENTS	①	②	③	④	⑤
BEING VERY PATIENT	①	②	③	④	⑤
BEING TENACIOUS	①	②	③	④	⑤
DOING METICULOUS/PAINSTAKING RESEARCH	①	②	③	④	⑤
GENETICS	①	②	③	④	⑤
WORKING IN A TEAM	①	②	③	④	⑤
COMMUNICATING SCIENTIFIC DATA	①	②	③	④	⑤
SEEING THINGS THROUGH TO THEIR END	①	②	③	④	⑤

Add up the totals in each column

GRAND TOTAL FOR AREA 9

AREA TEN

You like:*(1 =strongly disagree 2 =disagree 3 =not sure 4 =agree 5 =strongly agree)*

BEING VERY WELL ORGANISED	①	②	③	④	⑤
PLANNING AND BUDGETING VERY CAREFULLY	①	②	③	④	⑤
TAKING RESPONSIBILITY	①	②	③	④	⑤
GIVING ORDERS TO OTHERS	①	②	③	④	⑤
DEALING WITH A WIDE RANGE OF PEOPLE	①	②	③	④	⑤
TO COMMUNICATE CLEARLY VERBALLY	①	②	③	④	⑤
COMMUNICATE CLEARLY IN WRITING	①	②	③	④	⑤
BEING AN ENTREPRENEUR	①	②	③	④	⑤
WORKING UNDER PRESSURE	①	②	③	④	⑤
WORKING WITH MONEY AND NUMBERS	①	②	③	④	⑤
ANALYSING SITUATIONS	①	②	③	④	⑤

Add up the totals in each column

GRAND TOTAL FOR AREA 10

AREA ELEVEN

You like:*(1 =strongly disagree 2 =disagree 3 =not sure 4 =agree 5 =strongly agree)*

HELPING PEOPLE IDENTIFY THEIR AMBITIONS	① ② ③ ④ ⑤
WORKING WITH PEOPLE	① ② ③ ④ ⑤
LISTENING/ENCOURAGING PEOPLE TO TALK	① ② ③ ④ ⑤
SUMMARISING WHAT PEOPLE SAY TO YOU	① ② ③ ④ ⑤
BEING SENSITIVE TO OTHER'S FEELINGS	① ② ③ ④ ⑤
EXPLAINING THINGS CLEARLY AND SIMPLY	① ② ③ ④ ⑤
WORKING ON YOUR OWN	① ② ③ ④ ⑤
PERSUADING OTHER PEOPLE	① ② ③ ④ ⑤
DEALING WITH DIFFICULT PEOPLE	① ② ③ ④ ⑤
RESEARCHING CAREERS METICULOUSLY	① ② ③ ④ ⑤
WRITING REPORTS	① ② ③ ④ ⑤

Add up the totals in each column

GRAND TOTAL FOR AREA 11

AREA TWELVE

You like:*(1 =strongly disagree 2 =disagree 3 =not sure 4 =agree 5 =strongly agree)*

EXAMINING EXACT CHEMICAL COMPOSITIONS	① ② ③ ④ ⑤
BEING CLEAR AND EXTREMELY LOGICAL	① ② ③ ④ ⑤
CREATING/IMPLEMENTING EXPERIMENTS	① ② ③ ④ ⑤
BEING VERY PATIENT	① ② ③ ④ ⑤
DOING METICULOUS PAINSTAKING RESEARCH	① ② ③ ④ ⑤
EXAMINING MINUTE DETAILS	① ② ③ ④ ⑤
WORKING IN A TEAM	① ② ③ ④ ⑤
COMMUNICATING SCIENTIFIC DATA	① ② ③ ④ ⑤
SEEING THINGS THROUGH TO THEIR END	① ② ③ ④ ⑤
HAVING AN ENQUIRING MIND	① ② ③ ④ ⑤
HAVING AN INTEREST IN SCIENCE IN GENERAL	① ② ③ ④ ⑤

Add up the totals in each column

GRAND TOTAL FOR AREA 12

AREA THIRTEEN

You like:*(1 =strongly disagree 2=disagree 3=not sure 4=agree 5=strongly agree)*

WORKING WITH PEOPLE	①	②	③	④	⑤
UNSOCIAL HOURS	①	②	③	④	⑤
DEALING WITH VERY DIFFICULT SITUATIONS	①	②	③	④	⑤
UNDERSTANDING DISEASES AND THEIR CURE	①	②	③	④	⑤
SPENDING EXTRA TIME READING	①	②	③	④	⑤
BEING PATIENT	①	②	③	④	⑤
BEING TACTFUL	①	②	③	④	⑤
WORKING UNDER PRESSURE	①	②	③	④	⑤
SPENDING AT LEAST 6 YEARS IN TRAINING	①	②	③	④	⑤
UNDERSTANDING ANATOMY AND BIOLOGY	①	②	③	④	⑤
TAKING A GREAT DEAL OF RESPONSIBILITY	①	②	③	④	⑤

Add up the totals in each column

GRAND TOTAL FOR AREA 13

AREA FOURTEEN

You like:*(1 =strongly disagree 2=disagree 3=not sure 4=agree 5=strongly agree)*

ORGANISING THE WORK OF OTHER PEOPLE	①	②	③	④	⑤
SUPERVISING THE WORK OF OTHERS	①	②	③	④	⑤
IMPLEMENTING SUPERIOR'S INSTRUCTIONS	①	②	③	④	⑤
ARRANGING MEETINGS	①	②	③	④	⑤
WRITING REPORTS	①	②	③	④	⑤
COLLECTING INFORMATION	①	②	③	④	⑤
EXPLAINING THINGS CLEARLY IN WRITING	①	②	③	④	⑤
DEALING WITH PERSONAL PROBLEMS	①	②	③	④	⑤
OVERSEEING RECORDS	①	②	③	④	⑤
WORKING WITH OTHERS	①	②	③	④	⑤
APPRAISING OTHERS AND BEING APPRAISED	①	②	③	④	⑤

Add up the totals in each column

GRAND TOTAL FOR AREA 14

AREA FIFTEEN

You like:*(1 =strongly disagree 2 =disagree 3 =not sure 4 =agree 5 =strongly agree)*

WORKING WITH A WIDE SECTION OF SOCIETY	① ② ③ ④ ⑤
DEALING DIFFICULT PEOPLE	① ② ③ ④ ⑤
DEALING WITH DIFFICULT SITUATIONS	① ② ③ ④ ⑤
WRITING REPORTS	① ② ③ ④ ⑤
WORKING IN DIFFICULT CONDITIONS	① ② ③ ④ ⑤
WORKING WIDELY DIFFERING CULTURES	① ② ③ ④ ⑤
WORKING UNSOCIAL HOURS	① ② ③ ④ ⑤
TAKING CRITICISM	① ② ③ ④ ⑤
HELPING OTHERS TO WORK TOGETHER	① ② ③ ④ ⑤
LISTENING CAREFULLY TO OTHERS	① ② ③ ④ ⑤
DEALING WITH PERSONAL PROBLEMS	① ② ③ ④ ⑤

Add up the totals in each column

GRAND TOTAL FOR AREA 15

AREA SIXTEEN

You like:*(1 =strongly disagree 2 =disagree 3 =not sure 4 =agree 5 =strongly agree)*

WORKING WITH COMPUTERS	① ② ③ ④ ⑤
WORKING WITH METICULOUS ACCURACY	① ② ③ ④ ⑤
WORKING MAINLY IN OFFICES	① ② ③ ④ ⑤
ANALYSING PROBLEMS ACCURATELY	① ② ③ ④ ⑤
SOLVING PROBLEMS LOGICALLY	① ② ③ ④ ⑤
CONCENTRATING FOR LONG PERIODS OF TIME	① ② ③ ④ ⑤
WRITING REPORTS	① ② ③ ④ ⑤
COMMUNICATING DIFFICULT PROBLEMS	① ② ③ ④ ⑤
MATHEMATICS	① ② ③ ④ ⑤
WORKING ON YOUR OWN FOR LONG PERIODS	① ② ③ ④ ⑤
ELECTRONICS	① ② ③ ④ ⑤

Add up the totals in each column

GRAND TOTAL FOR AREA 16

AREA SEVENTEEN

You like:*(1 =strongly disagree 2 =disagree 3 =not sure 4 =agree 5 =strongly agree)*

BEING CREATIVE	① ② ③ ④ ⑤
WORKING CLOSELY WITH OTHER PEOPLE	① ② ③ ④ ⑤
DRAWING FREEHAND	① ② ③ ④ ⑤
TWO AND THREE DIMENSIONAL ART	① ② ③ ④ ⑤
WORKING IN A WIDE VARIETY OF MEDIA	① ② ③ ④ ⑤
BEING RESPONSIVE TO OTHER'S DESIGN NEEDS	① ② ③ ④ ⑤
TAKING CRITICISM	① ② ③ ④ ⑤
BEING PRACTICAL IN MATERIAL/ECONOMY	① ② ③ ④ ⑤
BEING HIGHLY SELF-MOTIVATED	① ② ③ ④ ⑤
UNDERSTANDING MACHINES AND PROCESSES	① ② ③ ④ ⑤
COMMUNICATING WITH OTHERS	① ② ③ ④ ⑤

Add up the totals in each column

GRAND TOTAL FOR AREA 17

AREA EIGHTEEN

You like:*(1 =strongly disagree 2 =disagree 3 =not sure 4 =agree 5 =strongly agree)*

STUDYING PLANTS/ANIMALS/ENVIRONMENT	① ② ③ ④ ⑤
EXAMINING HUMAN ENVIRONMENTAL EFFECT	① ② ③ ④ ⑤
STUDYING BIOLOGY	① ② ③ ④ ⑤
DOING FIELD STUDIES	① ② ③ ④ ⑤
RECORDING DATA METICULOUSLY	① ② ③ ④ ⑤
COMMUNICATING COMPLEX IDEAS	① ② ③ ④ ⑤
WRITING REPORTS	① ② ③ ④ ⑤
WORKING WITH MATHEMATICS	① ② ③ ④ ⑤
DOING EXPERIMENTS	① ② ③ ④ ⑤
BEING PATIENT	① ② ③ ④ ⑤
USING COMPUTERS	① ② ③ ④ ⑤

Add up the totals in each column

GRAND TOTAL FOR AREA 18

AREA NINETEEN

You like:*(1 =strongly disagree 2 =disagree 3 =not sure 4 =agree 5 =strongly agree)*

EXAMINING USE/DISTRIBUTION OF RESOURCES	①	②	③	④	⑤
ANALYSING ECONOMIC SITUATIONS	①	②	③	④	⑤
HANDLING FINANCIAL DATA	①	②	③	④	⑤
USING A COMPUTER	①	②	③	④	⑤
COMMUNICATING COMPLEX ECONOMICS	①	②	③	④	⑤
MATHEMATICS	①	②	③	④	⑤
SPENDING A LOT OF TIME READING	①	②	③	④	⑤
WRITING REPORTS	①	②	③	④	⑤
BEING CRITICISED	①	②	③	④	⑤
RELATING FROM BROAD TO SPECIFIC TERMS	①	②	③	④	⑤
TAKING RESPONSIBILITY FOR OWN DECISIONS	①	②	③	④	⑤

Add up the totals in each column

GRAND TOTAL FOR AREA 19

AREA TWENTY

You like:*(1 =strongly disagree 2 =disagree 3 =not sure 4 =agree 5 =strongly agree)*

APPLYING MATHS/SCIENCE TO PROBLEMS	①	②	③	④	⑤
APPLYING THEORY TO PRACTICE	①	②	③	④	⑤
STUDYING SCIENCE	①	②	③	④	⑤
STUDYING MATHEMATICS	①	②	③	④	⑤
ANALYSING PRACTICAL DESIGN PROBLEMS	①	②	③	④	⑤
CONSTRUCTING SCIENTIFIC SOLUTIONS	①	②	③	④	⑤
COMMUNICATING COMPLEX ENGINEERING	①	②	③	④	⑤
WORKING ON YOUR OWN	①	②	③	④	⑤
WORKING WITH A TEAM OF PEOPLE	①	②	③	④	⑤
FOLLOWING INSTRUCTIONS AND DESIGNS	①	②	③	④	⑤
SUPERVISING THE WORK OF OTHERS	①	②	③	④	⑤

Add up the totals in each column

GRAND TOTAL FOR AREA 20

AREA TWENTY ONE

You like:*(1 =strongly disagree 2 =disagree 3 =not sure 4 =agree 5 =strongly agree)*

UNDERSTANDING COMPOSITION OF FOOD	① ② ③ ④ ⑤
INVESTIGATING CHANGES IN COOKING	① ② ③ ④ ⑤
OBSERVING FREEZING/PRESERVING PROCESS	① ② ③ ④ ⑤
BIOCHEMISTRY	① ② ③ ④ ⑤
MICROBIOLOGY	① ② ③ ④ ⑤
PHYSICAL CHEMISTRY	① ② ③ ④ ⑤
NUTRITION	① ② ③ ④ ⑤
CHEMICAL ENGINEERING	① ② ③ ④ ⑤
AGRICULTURE	① ② ③ ④ ⑤
BEING EXTREMELY METICULOUS	① ② ③ ④ ⑤
WRITING ACCURATE REPORTS	① ② ③ ④ ⑤

Add up the totals in each column

GRAND TOTAL FOR AREA 21

AREA TWENTY TWO

You like:*(1 =strongly disagree 2 =disagree 3 =not sure 4 =agree 5 =strongly agree)*

UNDERSTANDING EARTH'S STRUCTURE	① ② ③ ④ ⑤
STUDYING ROCKS, FOSSILS AND MINERALS	① ② ③ ④ ⑤
WORKING WITH AND MAKING MAPS	① ② ③ ④ ⑤
BEING PHYSICALLY FIT	① ② ③ ④ ⑤
PHYSICS	① ② ③ ④ ⑤
MATHEMATICS	① ② ③ ④ ⑤
CHEMISTRY	① ② ③ ④ ⑤
BIOLOGY	① ② ③ ④ ⑤
ENGINEERING	① ② ③ ④ ⑤
WORKING OUT OF DOORS	① ② ③ ④ ⑤
BEING EXTREMELY PRECISE	① ② ③ ④ ⑤

Add up the totals in each column

GRAND TOTAL FOR AREA 22

AREA TWENTY THREE
You like:*(1 =strongly disagree 2 =disagree 3 =not sure 4 =agree 5 =strongly agree)*

ADVISING/EDUCATING OTHER PEOPLE	①	②	③	④	⑤
DEALING WITH A WIDE VARIETY OF PEOPLE	①	②	③	④	⑤
DEALING WITH DIFFICULT AND ILL PEOPLE	①	②	③	④	⑤
HELPING OLD PEOPLE	①	②	③	④	⑤
HELPING YOUNG PEOPLE	①	②	③	④	⑤
HELPING WITH PREGNANCY	①	②	③	④	⑤
HELPING DISABLED PEOPLE	①	②	③	④	⑤
BEING TACTFUL	①	②	③	④	⑤
BEING OBJECTIVE WITH PEOPLE	①	②	③	④	⑤
KEEPING UP TO DATE BY READING A LOT	①	②	③	④	⑤
KEEPING ACCURATE RECORDS	①	②	③	④	⑤

Add up the totals in each column

GRAND TOTAL FOR AREA 23

AREA TWENTY FOUR
You like:*(1 =strongly disagree 2 =disagree 3 =not sure 4 =agree 5 =strongly agree)*

SPEAKING A FOREIGN LANGUAGE FLUENTLY	①	②	③	④	⑤
EXAMINING YOUR OWN LANGUAGE	①	②	③	④	⑤
UNDERSTANDING FINE MEANING NUANCES	①	②	③	④	⑤
LISTENING TO OTHER PEOPLE	①	②	③	④	⑤
TAKING A BACK SEAT IN CONVERSATION	①	②	③	④	⑤
PERCEIVING MOOD/TONE OF OTHER PEOPLE	①	②	③	④	⑤
CONCENTRATING DEEPLY FOR LONG PERIODS	①	②	③	④	⑤
RESEARCHING SPECIALIST TERMS	①	②	③	④	⑤
WORKING WITH PEOPLE	①	②	③	④	⑤
TAKING RESPONSIBILITY	①	②	③	④	⑤
BEING VERY PRECISE AND ACCURATE	①	②	③	④	⑤

Add up the totals in each column

GRAND TOTAL FOR AREA 24

AREA TWENTY FIVE
You like:*(1 =strongly disagree 2 =disagree 3 =not sure 4 =agree 5 =strongly agree)*

BEING UP TO DATE WITH NATIONAL EVENTS	① ② ③ ④ ⑤
KNOWING WHAT IS GOING ON LOCALLY	① ② ③ ④ ⑤
USING LANGUAGE EFFECTIVELY	① ② ③ ④ ⑤
COPING WITH DANGEROUS SITUATIONS	① ② ③ ④ ⑤
WRITING	① ② ③ ④ ⑤
WORKING TO TIGHT DEADLINES	① ② ③ ④ ⑤
BEING PERSISTENT	① ② ③ ④ ⑤
BEING EXTROVERT	① ② ③ ④ ⑤
BEING INQUISITIVE	① ② ③ ④ ⑤
INTERVIEWING A WIDE RANGE OF PEOPLE	① ② ③ ④ ⑤
FOLLOWING INSTRUCTIONS	① ② ③ ④ ⑤

Add up the totals in each column

GRAND TOTAL FOR AREA 25

AREA TWENTY SIX
You like:*(1 =strongly disagree 2 =disagree 3 =not sure 4 =agree 5 =strongly agree)*

BOOKS	① ② ③ ④ ⑤
BEING METICULOUS IN CATALOGUING	① ② ③ ④ ⑤
DEALING WITH A WIDE VARIETY OF PEOPLE	① ② ③ ④ ⑤
USING COMPUTERS	① ② ③ ④ ⑤
BEING LOGICAL	① ② ③ ④ ⑤
BEING WELL ORGANISED	① ② ③ ④ ⑤
HAVING A RETENTIVE MEMORY	① ② ③ ④ ⑤
BEING PATIENT	① ② ③ ④ ⑤
ROUTINE REPETITIVE TASKS	① ② ③ ④ ⑤
BEING PHYSICALLY FIT	① ② ③ ④ ⑤
CONCENTRATING FOR LONG PERIODS OF TIME	① ② ③ ④ ⑤

Add up the totals in each column

GRAND TOTAL FOR AREA 26

AREA TWENTY SEVEN
You like:*(1=strongly disagree 2=disagree 3=not sure 4=agree 5=strongly agree)*

WORKING WITH NUMBERS	① ② ③ ④ ⑤
ANALYSING COMPLEX PROBLEMS	① ② ③ ④ ⑤
COMMUNICATING COMPLEX IDEAS	① ② ③ ④ ⑤
STATISTICS	① ② ③ ④ ⑤
GEOMETRY	① ② ③ ④ ⑤
ALGEBRA	① ② ③ ④ ⑤
FORMULATING MATHEMATICAL SOLUTIONS	① ② ③ ④ ⑤
WORKING WITH OTHERS	① ② ③ ④ ⑤
BEING PRECISE AND EXACT	① ② ③ ④ ⑤
USING COMPUTERS	① ② ③ ④ ⑤
APPLYING THEORY TO PRACTICE	① ② ③ ④ ⑤

Add up the totals in each column

GRAND TOTAL FOR AREA 27

AREA TWENTY EIGHT
You like:*(1=strongly disagree 2=disagree 3=not sure 4=agree 5=strongly agree)*

LEADING PEOPLE IN WORSHIP	① ② ③ ④ ⑤
WORKING WITH PEOPLE	① ② ③ ④ ⑤
VISITING THE SICK	① ② ③ ④ ⑤
DEALING WITH BEREAVEMENT	① ② ③ ④ ⑤
STUDYING TEXTS	① ② ③ ④ ⑤
BEING CRITICISED	① ② ③ ④ ⑤
TAKING ON RESPONSIBILITY	① ② ③ ④ ⑤
COUNSELLING PEOPLE	① ② ③ ④ ⑤
INTERPRETING BELIEF TO OTHERS	① ② ③ ④ ⑤
PREACHING	① ② ③ ④ ⑤
PRAYING	① ② ③ ④ ⑤

Add up the totals in each column

GRAND TOTAL FOR AREA 28

AREA TWENTY NINE

You like:*(1 =strongly disagree 2=disagree 3=not sure 4=agree 5=strongly agree)*

DOING RESEARCH	①	②	③	④	⑤
BEING METICULOUS IN CATALOGUING	①	②	③	④	⑤
HISTORY	①	②	③	④	⑤
ENTHUSING OTHER PEOPLE	①	②	③	④	⑤
CONSERVATION/RESTORATION OF OBJECTS	①	②	③	④	⑤
ADMINISTRATIVE WORK	①	②	③	④	⑤
DISPLAYING OBJECTS	①	②	③	④	⑤
SUPERVISING THE WORK OF OTHERS	①	②	③	④	⑤
LIAISING WITH OTHERS	①	②	③	④	⑤
PAYING GREAT ATTENTION TO DETAIL	①	②	③	④	⑤
WRITING REPORTS	①	②	③	④	⑤

Add up the totals in each column

GRAND TOTAL FOR AREA 29

AREA THIRTY

You like:*(1 =strongly disagree 2=disagree 3=not sure 4=agree 5=strongly agree)*

DEALING WITH PEOPLE IN GENERAL	①	②	③	④	⑤
WORKING IN HOSPITALS	①	②	③	④	⑤
DEALING WITH DIFFICULT AND ILL PEOPLE	①	②	③	④	⑤
INJECTIONS, CHANGING DRESSINGS ETC	①	②	③	④	⑤
KEEPING ACCURATE RECORDS	①	②	③	④	⑤
FOLLOWING INSTRUCTIONS	①	②	③	④	⑤
HAVING UNSOCIAL HOURS	①	②	③	④	⑤
STUDYING ANATOMY AND PHYSIOLOGY	①	②	③	④	⑤
WORKING WITH OTHERS	①	②	③	④	⑤
TAKING CRITICISM	①	②	③	④	⑤
TAKING RESPONSIBILITY	①	②	③	④	⑤

Add up the totals in each column

GRAND TOTAL FOR AREA 30

AREA THIRTY ONE

You like:*(1 =strongly disagree 2 =disagree 3 =not sure 4 =agree 5 =strongly agree)*

BEING OBSERVANT OF PEOPLE	①	②	③	④	⑤
PSYCHOLOGY/SOCIOLOGY	①	②	③	④	⑤
DEALING WITH PEOPLE WHO ARE NOT WELL	①	②	③	④	⑤
ENCOURAGING, INSPIRING PEOPLE	①	②	③	④	⑤
BEING SENSITIVE WITH NERVOUS PEOPLE	①	②	③	④	⑤
INTERPRETING REPORTS FROM OTHER PEOPLE	①	②	③	④	⑤
WORKING WITH GROUPS OR INDIVIDUALS	①	②	③	④	⑤
STUDYING MEDICAL/SURGICAL CONDITIONS	①	②	③	④	⑤
ACTIVITY ANALYSIS	①	②	③	④	⑤
PROBLEM SOLVING	①	②	③	④	⑤
ANATOMY/PHYSIOLOGY	①	②	③	④	⑤

Add up the totals in each column

GRAND TOTAL FOR AREA 31

AREA THIRTY TWO

You like:*(1 =strongly disagree 2 =disagree 3 =not sure 4 =agree 5 =strongly agree)*

STUDYING SEA PROCESSES	①	②	③	④	⑤
THE MARINE ENVIRONMENT	①	②	③	④	⑤
ECOLOGY	①	②	③	④	⑤
BEING METICULOUS	①	②	③	④	⑤
WORKING OUTDOORS	①	②	③	④	⑤
PHYSICS	①	②	③	④	⑤
MATHEMATICS	①	②	③	④	⑤
USING COMPUTERS	①	②	③	④	⑤
GEOLOGY	①	②	③	④	⑤
WRITING REPORTS FOR LAY PEOPLE	①	②	③	④	⑤
WORKING WITH OTHER PEOPLE	①	②	③	④	⑤

Add up the totals in each column

GRAND TOTAL FOR AREA 32

AREA THIRTY THREE

You like:*(1 =strongly disagree 2 =disagree 3 =not sure 4 =agree 5 =strongly agree)*

STUDYING THE PROPERTIES OF MATTER	①	②	③	④	⑤
WORKING IN LABORATORIES	①	②	③	④	⑤
MATHEMATICS	①	②	③	④	⑤
UNDERSTANDING COMPLEX THEORIES	①	②	③	④	⑤
BEING METICULOUS	①	②	③	④	⑤
COMMUNICATING COMPLEX IDEAS TO OTHERS	①	②	③	④	⑤
APPLYING THEORIES TO PRACTICE	①	②	③	④	⑤
WRITING REPORTS	①	②	③	④	⑤
WORKING WITH OTHERS	①	②	③	④	⑤
STUDYING THE PROPERTIES OF ENERGY	①	②	③	④	⑤
STUDYING BEHAVIOUR OF MATTER/ENERGY	①	②	③	④	⑤

Add up the totals in each column

GRAND TOTAL FOR AREA 33

AREA THIRTY FOUR

You like:*(1 =strongly disagree 2 =disagree 3 =not sure 4 =agree 5 =strongly agree)*

HELPING RESTRICTED MOVEMENT PEOPLE	①	②	③	④	⑤
WORKING WITH OLD PEOPLE	①	②	③	④	⑤
SEVERE CASES (E.G. AMPUTEES. STROKE VICTIMS)	①	②	③	④	⑤
BEING PATIENT	①	②	③	④	⑤
BEING SYMPATHETIC AND FIRM	①	②	③	④	⑤
ENCOURAGING, EVEN INSPIRING	①	②	③	④	⑤
LISTENING	①	②	③	④	⑤
REPORT WRITING	①	②	③	④	⑤
SCIENCE	①	②	③	④	⑤
PHYSICAL EDUCATION	①	②	③	④	⑤
BEING FIT	①	②	③	④	⑤

Add up the totals in each column

GRAND TOTAL FOR AREA 34

AREA THIRTY FIVE

You like:*(1 =strongly disagree 2 =disagree 3 =not sure 4 =agree 5 =strongly agree)*

REPRESENTING OTHER PEOPLE	① ② ③ ④ ⑤
BEING A MEMBER OF A COMMITTEE	① ② ③ ④ ⑤
PUBLIC SPEAKING	① ② ③ ④ ⑤
LISTENING TO OTHERS	① ② ③ ④ ⑤
PERSUADING PEOPLE	① ② ③ ④ ⑤
RESEARCHING METICULOUSLY	① ② ③ ④ ⑤
GETTING ON WITH PEOPLE	① ② ③ ④ ⑤
WORKING UNSOCIAL HOURS	① ② ③ ④ ⑤
BEING A MEMBER OF A POLITICAL PARTY	① ② ③ ④ ⑤
CURRENT AFFAIRS	① ② ③ ④ ⑤
RESPONDING TO THE NEEDS OF OTHERS	① ② ③ ④ ⑤

Add up the totals in each column

GRAND TOTAL FOR AREA 35

AREA THIRTY SIX

You like:*(1 =strongly disagree 2 =disagree 3 =not sure 4 =agree 5 =strongly agree)*

STUDYING HUMAN/ANIMAL BEHAVIOUR	① ② ③ ④ ⑤
INVESTIGATING THE WORKINGS OF THE MIND	① ② ③ ④ ⑤
TO SOLVE PROBLEMS OF BEHAVIOUR	① ② ③ ④ ⑤
WORKING WITH PEOPLE	① ② ③ ④ ⑤
BEING INTERESTED IN PEOPLE IN GENERAL	① ② ③ ④ ⑤
BEING PATIENT	① ② ③ ④ ⑤
BEING METHODICAL AND METICULOUS	① ② ③ ④ ⑤
WRITING REPORTS	① ② ③ ④ ⑤
INTERPRETING THE REPORTS OF OTHERS	① ② ③ ④ ⑤
KEEPING METICULOUS RECORDS	① ② ③ ④ ⑤
KEEPING UP TO DATE BY A LOT OF READING	① ② ③ ④ ⑤

Add up the totals in each column

GRAND TOTAL FOR AREA 36

AREA THIRTY SEVEN

You like:*(1 =strongly disagree 2 =disagree 3 =not sure 4 =agree 5 =strongly agree)*

HELPING PEOPLE WITH PERSONAL PROBLEMS	① ② ③ ④ ⑤
DIFFICULT(E.G.) PSYCHIATRIC PATIENTS)	① ② ③ ④ ⑤
DIFFICULT/DANGEROUS SITUATIONS	① ② ③ ④ ⑤
DEALING WITH A WIDE VARIETY OF PEOPLE	① ② ③ ④ ⑤
SOCIOLOGY	① ② ③ ④ ⑤
ESTABLISHING TRUSTFUL RELATIONSHIPS	① ② ③ ④ ⑤
GIVING ADVICE TACTFULLY	① ② ③ ④ ⑤
DEALING WITH FAMILIES	① ② ③ ④ ⑤
COPING WITH PERSONAL ABUSE	① ② ③ ④ ⑤
BEING PATIENT	① ② ③ ④ ⑤
KEEPING METICULOUS RECORDS	① ② ③ ④ ⑤

Add up the totals in each column

GRAND TOTAL FOR AREA 37

AREA THIRTY EIGHT

You like:*(1 =strongly disagree 2 =disagree 3 =not sure 4 =agree 5 =strongly agree)*

STUDYING THE MECHANICS OF SPORT	① ② ③ ④ ⑤
PHYSIOLOGY	① ② ③ ④ ⑤
ANATOMY	① ② ③ ④ ⑤
THE SOCIOLOGY OF SPORT	① ② ③ ④ ⑤
USING COMPUTERS	① ② ③ ④ ⑤
MEASURING INDIVIDUAL PERFORMANCE	① ② ③ ④ ⑤
BEING FIT	① ② ③ ④ ⑤
WRITING REPORTS	① ② ③ ④ ⑤
KEEPING RECORDS	① ② ③ ④ ⑤
ORGANISING OTHER PEOPLE	① ② ③ ④ ⑤
ENCOURAGING OTHERS	① ② ③ ④ ⑤

Add up the totals in each column

GRAND TOTAL FOR AREA 38

AREA THIRTY NINE

You like:*(1 =strongly disagree 2 =disagree 3 =not sure 4 =agree 5 =strongly agree)*

WORKING WITH ANIMALS	①	②	③	④	⑤
WORKING WITH PEOPLE	①	②	③	④	⑤
DIAGNOSING/TREATING INJURED/ILL ANIMALS	①	②	③	④	⑤
MEETING PEOPLE & SENSITIVE SITUATIONS	①	②	③	④	⑤
ANIMAL PHYSIOLOGY/ANATOMY	①	②	③	④	⑤
ASPECTS OF MEDICINE	①	②	③	④	⑤
WORKING IN UNCLEAN CONDITIONS	①	②	③	④	⑤
CHEMISTRY	①	②	③	④	⑤
PHYSICS	①	②	③	④	⑤
BIOLOGY	①	②	③	④	⑤
KEEPING METICULOUS RECORDS	①	②	③	④	⑤

Add up the totals in each column

GRAND TOTAL FOR AREA 39

What to do with the results

Over the page you will find a scoreboard into which you should enter the scores you have noted for each area. When you have entered them find the highest scores, say the top 5 and look at the description of that career area. I must emphasise again that you do need to seek professional careers advice. This exercise is just to give you a very broad idea of where your interests lie.

It is also useful for you to be aware of the areas where you have shown no interest and obviously to avoid these areas when looking for a career.

You could also make a list of the statements to which you gave 5 marks, since these aspects are the ones which you like a great deal. This may give you further areas you would like to explore.

Don't just rely on this book - seek professional careers advice.

SCORES FOR EACH AREA

AREA 1=[ ]	AREA 2=[ ]	AREA 3= [ ]
AREA 4=[ ]	AREA 5=[ ]	AREA 6= [ ]
AREA 7=[ ]	AREA 8=[ ]	AREA 9= [ ]
AREA 10=[ ]	AREA 11=[ ]	AREA 12= [ ]
AREA 13=[ ]	AREA 14=[ ]	AREA 15= [ ]
AREA 16=[ ]	AREA 17=[ ]	AREA 18= [ ]
AREA 19=[ ]	AREA 20=[ ]	AREA 21= [ ]
AREA 22=[ ]	AREA 23=[ ]	AREA 24= [ ]
AREA 25=[ ]	AREA 26=[ ]	AREA 27= [ ]
AREA 28=[ ]	AREA 29=[ ]	AREA 30= [ ]
AREA 31=[ ]	AREA 32=[ ]	AREA 33= [ ]
AREA 34=[ ]	AREA 35=[ ]	AREA 36= [ ]
AREA 37=[ ]	AREA 38=[ ]	AREA 39= [ ]

Interpreting your answers

1. TEACHING.
2. ACCOUNTANCY
3. ADMINISTRATION
4. ADVERTISING
5. AGRICULTURAL SCIENCE
6. ARCHAEOLOGY
7. ARCHITECTURE
8. THE LAW
9. BIOCHEMISTRY
10. BUSINESS MANAGEMENT
11. CAREERS ADVISING
12. CHEMISTRY
13. MEDICINE
14. CIVIL SERVICE
15. COMMUNITY WORK
16. COMPUTING
17. DESIGNING
18. ECOLOGY
19. ECONOMICS
20. ENGINEERING
21. FOOD SCIENTIST
22. GEOLOGY
23. HEALTH VISITING
24. INTERPRETING
25. JOURNALISM
26. LIBRARIANSHIP
27. MATHEMATICS
28. MINISTRY OF RELIGION
29. MUSEUM CURATING
30. NURSING
31. OCCUPATIONAL THERAPY
32. OCEANOGRAPHY
33. PHYSICS
34. PHYSIOTHERAPY
35. POLITICS
36. PSYCHOLOGY
37. SOCIAL WORK
38. SPORTS STUDIES
39. VETERINARIAN STUDIES

Further interpretation

You should have a look at the Sections where you have scored the lowest and remember that that is an area you should avoid! Look carefully where you have scored highly and see if you can establish any pattern.

If you are interested you can gain further insight into your interests by listing all the points above where you have marked a ⑤ and then those you have marked a ④ and so on. This will supply you with a list of interests in order of intensity, from highest to lowest.

Choosing a specific career

Obviously you will need to research the career(s) suggested much further with professional careers guidance help. But remember there is a lot you can do yourself:
- talk to people doing that work and see if you go and observe, or even work along side them. See if there is any work experience available there.
- Contact any unions, associations, professional bodies and ask for their help.
- Get relevant books from your library of careers advisers.

Whatever you do always remember that you are choosing a career that is going to take 2-4 years of education before you enter it.

Remember that you should use this to think about your future. There's only you who can make the decisions about the type of work to which you will commit yourself. Use this exercise as a starting point for further discussion and thinking about your future career. Call at your local Further Education College and visit careers advisers NOW.

Some books to read

The working in series	COIC	COIC
Careers A-Z (Latest Edition)	Daily Telegraph	Collins
Personal values and Work	Dauncey	CRAC/Hobson
Successful interviewing	Gratus	Penguin
Job Hunting	Hossack	Penguin
In Search of Work	Leadbeater/Lloyd	Penguin
Annual Careers Guide (latest Edition)	MSC	COIC Moorfoot
Second Chances (latest Edition)	Pates and Good	COIC Moorfoot
Unqualified Success		Penguin
The Careers Guide		CASCAID[1]

---

[1]. *See p.1 above for address.*

SECTION 5
WHAT SUBJECT SHOULD YOU STUDY?

Some people know already which subject they wish to study that will lead them to their to their long term career goal. Others are not sure, and that's fine if you really don't want to go on to something beyond the degree. My own opinion is that it is better to decide **before** you go on a course, since you really can waste a lot of time half way through it wondering if it really will get you to a worthwhile long term goal. This is especially true for older students who perhaps do not have time with which to experiment!

There are many subjects to study at the present time! New ones appear, old ones disappear! You can even get "pick and mix degrees" now, tailor made to suit specific needs.

The problem which potential students have is selecting from the enormous number of possibilities one which is going to be the best for them.

I don't think looking at long lists of subjects will help you to decide what to study. The answer lies rather in answering the question:

"What do you want to become and therefore what do you need to study in order to get to that career?"

If you haven't already done so, then you may find it useful to go through Section 4 which is designed to start you thinking about what long term career you should be aiming at.

One of the best books on suggesting courses which will lead to specific careers is the one already mentioned in the previous Section:

"The Careers Guide"

from:

CASCAID

West Annex

County Hall

Glenfield

Leicester

LE3 8YZ

If you cannot obtain a copy of it then check with your local library and/or College of Further Education.

Having decided on your long term goals be sure you know exactly what qualifications you need in order to get in to the course in the first place and then list the qualifications you need (if any) that you may need after gaining your HE qualification.

Make sure you know precisely what degree/diploma you need.

SECTION 6
WHAT COURSE SHOULD YOU TAKE?

1. Find out specifically what qualifications are required for the career you have identified

In some cases this is simple, for example teaching and social work. In others it is more complex because of the range of entry points, or because there is no set pattern of qualifications required. It should, however, be possible for you to make a list of the qualifications required for entry at the point you want.

Obviously it is worth while checking if you already have these qualifications! If you have, then you can close this section now and go and apply for the career at once!

Start with a list of what you already have in terms of qualifications...and don't panic if you haven't got any.

Consider what you have - and what you need.

2. Seek professional advice as to what course(s) you need to get the qualification(s) necessary

Your local Further Education College should be able to help you with information about the route you need to follow in order to get the main qualification you require. For example, to get into teaching at present you would need 5 GCSE (old O levels) passes, including Maths and English, at Grade C and quite soon Science, as well as 2 A levels, OR an Access Course certificate. You will need to get the Maths and the English at GCSE Grade C or equivalent BEFORE you enter teacher training.

It is very sensible to ring the college or University and ask the people running the course if you can join the course at the next entry (usually September/October). This is because many Universities and colleges allow mature students to enter without the usual formal qualifications. If an applicant shows enthusiasm and evidence of recent study then that may be sufficient for entry - but this is becoming less and less the case: many now suggest that the student first does an Access

As a result of your decision about your long term destination you need to be asking:

1. What qualifications/experience do I need?
2. And therefore, for which course at Higher Education should I be aiming?

These questions can be answered only by thorough research by yourself with College Careers Service and especially by tutors from the relevant courses at the Universities where the main qualification is taught. Question 1 will need you to be sure of the entry qualifications to the particular career you have chosen.

For example: if you want to go into Teaching, you will need in addition to an Access to Higher Education Course, 'GCSE' or 'O' Level (or equivalent) Maths and English BEFORE you can proceed to train as a teacher. Thus, if you don't have these qualifications then you will need to get them during or before your Access Course.

3. Check if specific experience is required in addition to the qualifications

Check if the receiving University wants you to have had particular experience.

For example: if you wish to gain a place to do the Dip. SW., or most Social Work courses, then you will need to show that you are at present doing some form of social work either on a voluntary basis, or in relevant paid employment.

It's no good arriving at your HE institution and realising that you should have got a Maths GCSE before getting there! It's no good arriving for a course in Social Work to find out they won't accept you because you haven't the necessary experience.

BEFORE GOING ANY FURTHER

- Make 100% certain that you know what you need to get in order to get to where you want to get to in terms of your long term career goals.

- Before making any step, make sure that it is taking you in the direction of your ultimate aim.

- So often I have encountered students who get side-tracked into taking extra bits and pieces which do not in fact further their progress towards that goal.

---

5. Information

For your own information you will need at this stage to begin to get an idea of all the possible courses offered that are going to be of use to you. Therefore if you haven't already done so, send off at once for the UCAS Handbook and see if you can get, from your local library or college, a copy of "University and Colleges Entrance: The Official Guide" and make sure it is for the current or the coming year of entry. It is expensive to buy, £12.00 in bookshops, + postage and packing of £3.00 (UK) from Sheed and Ward Ltd, 14 Coopers Row, London EC3 2BH.

You need to begin to accumulate information about which courses appeal to you and, realistically which places are available to you. Thus you need to start seeking out the prospectuses of those Universities whose courses appeal to you. They should be available at your college or school or library. You can get copies direct form the Universities and will find their addresses in the UCAS Handbook.

Another source of information about suitable courses for you is a computer database called ECCTIS. This may be available at your local school, college of Further Education, Careers Office or TAP (Training Access Point).

The advice given in the UCAS Handbook should be followed carefully.

If the information you get from this variety of sources does not fully answer your questions then call at or write to the University and ask for more detail.

6. Will you be able to enjoy the course?

- After getting the course prospectus and details read them carefully. Subjects tend to be very different from those at school. English, for example, will probably include a study of the history of the language and linguistics as well as Literature. Read the course details carefully and be aware of all aspects of the curriculum.

- Do not rush into making a decision. Compare the courses offered in different institutions.

SECTION 7
WHERE SHOULD YOU GO?

1. Narrowing down the choice

There are some 80 Universities, 50 Institutes of Higher Education and many other places running Higher Education Courses[1]. Choosing the right place is a difficult business. Many people tend to drift into a University rather than actively investigating which place is best going to suit them. You should set yourself a deadline for when you will make the final decision. Before you start you need to be clear about what course you wish to go on. You will need to select 6 courses to apply to[2]. They can be all in the same University or at different ones.

1.1 Where can you reach?

Many returning to education are limited as to where they can apply because of local commitments, thus they are restricted to their local Universities. Others can be much more mobile and can choose from all of England, Wales, Scotland and now many places in Europe.

1.2 Where is the course run?

- You should have found out which Universities run the course(s) that you wish to join.
- You should get the prospectuses from all of the Universities which are accessible to you and which are running the course you wish to take.

You may find that there are a limited number of Universities running the course which you wish to apply for, and this obviously makes choosing much simpler.

1.3 What is the status of the place?

There is quite a lot of snobbery connected with the reputation and status of Universities. Oxford and Cambridge are generally regarded as the most prestigious, followed by the older Universities such as Durham, then the "red-brick" Universities like Leeds and Sheffield, and then the "New Universities" such as Kent, and finally the Universities which were originally Polytechnics. (In fact, standards in the "Polyversities", as they are sometimes called, are very high, since the vast majority of their courses used to be externally examined as opposed to the Universities who could validate their own courses!) **I do not advise you to get into this sort of criteria for selecting the best place for you.** Having said that you should be aware that someone with a degree from the more prestigious Universities may well be given preference over someone who has a degree from a

---

[1]. *I use the term University to cover all these in this Section.*
[2]. *For more detail on this see Section 10 on how to apply.*

---

lower status place! Seek out someone who is knowledgeable about your choice of course and ask their advice.

1.4 Advice on course quality

As should be fairly obvious there will be good and bad and average departments in each of the Universities, whatever their pedigree! You really need someone who knows your subject area to advise you. Most Careers Sections of Colleges of Education have a lot of experience in this and should be consulted.

1.5 Make a short list

Bearing in mind the above, make a list of all the places which are accessible and which run an appropriate course. Delete any which your advisers have said are not good and then read very carefully the prospectuses which describe both the course and the University itself. There may be other criteria which you need to apply. Then, if you can, visit.

2. Visiting the Universities

Remember that you will be spending several years at the place to which you apply, so make sure that it does in fact appeal to you. If you are applying locally you should visit all the local Universities to compare the facilities, talk to students and "get a feel for the place". If you are considering places away from your area you really should go and have a look at the facilities and the prospects of accommodation available to you.

The purpose is to select the best place for you by:
- meeting staff
- meeting students
- looking at the learning environment
- looking at the living environment

2.1 Making contact

Ring up the University and ask for an informal chat with a Tutor from the course to which you wish to apply. If this is not possible, ask if there are any open days. If these are not possible then visit the University anyway, just to get the "flavour" of the place.

2.2 Open Days

Many Universities run Open Days for prospective students. It saves them time if all prospective students visit at the same time and the advantages to you are that you will gain access to the facilities in a way you probably wont if you just go and have a chat with a Tutor. The Open Days are an excellent way of getting the feel of the University. They are usually well structured and you often get the opportunity to meet students at present studying the course you wish to join.

2.3 Talking with the Tutor(s)

You should check up at this chat on the following:
- What will you need to do in order to ensure entry to the course? (e.g. will successful completion of the course(s) you are taking at present, or intend to take, be sufficient for entry onto the course?)
- Will you need to do any courses in addition to that course (e.g. Maths/English GCSE)?
- will you need to have any experience in any area before going on the course (e.g. voluntary social work)?
- which subject specialism would they recommend? (In some Science and Paramedical subjects sometimes there is a question of whether technology or Science or Health Studies would be most appropriate. Sometimes a customised "package" is recommended combining several subjects.)
- is there anything else you need to be doing in order to maximise your chances of acceptance (e.g. taking an additional GCSE)?
- is there any relevant reading which they recommend?

You may wish to ask about:
- the range of careers open to those successfully completing the HE course,
- the department's attitude to mature students,
- other students' experiences of the course,
- the facilities available to you (accommodation, sports, Union etc),
- the price and standard of accommodation available (if you need it)[3]

If not already answered in the prospectus:
- what precisely will you be studying?
- how will you be assessed?
- where will you live?

2.3 Talking with the students

ISLE COLLEGE
LIBRARY

If at all possible meet students following your course. Don't take the opinion of only one, try to talk to as many as you can and ask them about:
- the course and their re-actions to it,
- the University itself and its attitude to people like yourself,
- the place (what facilities are in the town/city/campus[4]),
- transport,
- accommodation,
- hints and tips about where best to eat.

and any other aspects which you need to know about.

---

[3]. *Many Universities now have contracts which they ask you to sign with regard to accommodation. Be careful that you read them carefully. Especially with regard to price. Do try to see the accommodation too, before agreeing to sign the contract.*
[4]. *"campus"=name given to the University site, its buildings and facilities in general.*

2.4 Looking round the place

The University's facilities

You may be given a guided tour of the place which might tend to show you what is attractive and leave out the dull bits. Make sure you see the library, the lecture rooms your course uses and any other resources **available to you**. Are there places available to you for private study in the library? How many books can you take out?

The Students' Union

How active is the Students' Union and what facilities are there? Can you get help from them about accommodation? Or any other aspects which concern you? Try to get some idea of the Clubs and Societies that are active and which may be of interest and use to you.

The "town"

Having seen the campus you should have a good look at the place in which it is set. There are several University campuses which are some distance from the nearest centre of population. Others are in the centre of cities, some have split sites, some are purpose built and others are commandeered accommodation in terraced houses and flats. You should think carefully about how you will get around from where you live, to where you have your lectures, tutorials etc, and back to where you live. Buy as many local papers as you can and fetch them home. These will give you useful information about prices for accommodation, eating places, theatres, cinemas and generally what goes on in the place.

2.5 Accommodation

This may be one of the deciding factors. If you are not living at home, then you will need to find out where you will be living. Some Universities have spacious accommodation for their students. Others, the majority, have not and you will have to find your own accommodation, sometimes with little or no assistance from the University. You should be able to find out about this from the prospectus, and if not then ask about it on your visit.

Many Universities have "Halls of Residence" which provide accommodation for students. Again the quality varies enormously and you MUST inspect what is offered before making up your mind.

YOU MUST get accommodation sorted out BEFORE you start the course.

3. Making up your mind

You will need to make a decision about where you want to go to, bearing in mind that you need to apply to 5 courses, well before the time you need to get your application in. The above approach should provide you with information on which to make a decision about which you prefer. Remember that you will be spending a long time on your course and that it isn't easy to change your mind once you have started.

SECTION 8
SHOULD YOU BE FULL TIME
OR PART TIME?

1. The choice

Many courses are offered as either full time or part time. Your choice will depend on several factors, but it is essentially a balance between the time you can afford and the money and the time you have available! Part Time courses are longer and cheaper by the year, but last longer that the full time versions. Full Time Courses are more expensive per year, take up almost all of your time, but do not last as long in years as the equivalent part time courses.

There is no way you can have the time to do a full time job and a full time Higher Education course.

2. Part time courses

Part Time students are entitled to claim benefit, providing the course takes up less than 18 hours per week, AND YOU MUST STILL BE AVAILABLE FOR AND ACTIVELY SEEKING WORK[1].

3. Full time courses

There are some financial advantages in being a Full Time student:
- You can apply for a grant from your Local Education Authority,[2] which will give you money for living expenses and will pay the fees of the course.

There are financial disadvantages: You lose all your benefits.

4. Access Courses

If you are going on a part time Access course, you may be able to make it into a full time course by taking extra hours for extra subjects which are appropriate for your HE subject. This can enhance your chances of acceptance at HE level because you will be acquiring more experience of learning and will be able to say so in your application and interview. You **MAY** also be eligible for a Discretionary Award from your Local Education Authority, BUT don't forget this will mean that you will lose any benefits that you are receiving.

> **Check with your Citizen's Advice Bureau to make sure you know what your financial position is in either case**

---

[1]. *See Section 9 for more detail.*
[2]. *Open University students are not eligible for a Mandatory Grant.*

SECTION 9
HOW WILL YOU PAY?

1. Education and those on benefit

1.1 It is important to point out that:

AT PRESENT (1995)

- If you are in receipt of unemployment benefit then you must be available for work and be actively seeking work whilst attending part time courses at College or University.

- you will lose benefit if following a course of more than 21 hours per week (in effect this is 18 hours per week since three hours is added for lunch times). This is under review and there is a strong possibility that it will be reduced further.

- if you are following a Part-time course and signing on as available for work and actively seeking work, then a claim for unemployment benefit (where you must have the correct amount of NI contributions) or for income support may succeed. You must agree to give up the course if suitable employment/training is offered.

Ring Freephone 0800 666 555 or your local social security benefits agency office to check what the latest position is. There is a leaflet from there too: FB23: Young people's guide to social security.

Some Local Authorities can award Housing Benefit and Council Tax Benefit to some students. Contact them and ask!

1.2 Full time students and benefits

- Full time students are not entitled to claim unemployment benefit. The new regulations prevent full time students from claiming housing benefit during both term time and holidays with very few exceptions.

- Full time students do not pay the Council Tax.

1.3 Those on invalidity Benefit

If you are claiming invalidity benefit or sickness benefit then you have been certified by a GP as unfit for any work. Thus ability to do a College course may be construed by DSS as work, and therefore benefit is at risk. A small amount of study would be allowed but there is no fixed rule about how much: it is entirely at DSS discretion.

The DSS advises students on sickness/invalidity benefit to contact them for advice on the number of hours of study but could subsequently withdraw benefit if they consider the claimant fit for work. There is a right of appeal against this decision but until heard the claimant would be without sickness or invalidity benefit.

A limited amount of study may be considered if the claimant's GP and the DSS agree that it would be therapeutic. This should be investigated BEFORE embarking on the course.

Disabled students may be entitled to special grants to help them with study. If you think you may be entitled to this then please let your Tutors know and they should help you to apply for these grants.

Ring Freephone 0800 666 555 or your local Social Security Benefits Agency Office to check what the latest position is. There is a "Disability Working Allowance Pack available free. Freephone 0800 100 123.

2. Part-time courses in Further Education

If you are 19 or over, **or**

studying part-time at any age,

you (or your employer) may be charged by the College the full fee for the course. There may be reductions - this depends upon the policy of the individual College.

Some part-time courses are free for those who are:

single, unemployed, and in receipt of unemployment benefit

or:

married, unemployed with a spouse who is unemployed and either one or both are in receipt of unemployment benefit,

or:

in receipt of income support or family credit.

or:

unemployed and over the age of 60.

3. Full time courses in Further Education

3.1 In general

If you are 16-18 and want to study full time you are entitled to a place in a school or a College. Full time students aged 16-18 who are ordinarily resident in the European Community are entitled to free tuition.

If you are 19 or over you (or your employer) may be charged by the College the full fee for the course. There may be reductions - this depends upon the policy of the individual College. Some Colleges make arrangements so that you can pay by instalments.

Fees for the full-time courses are high. You should enquire immediately about the cost of the course and the possibility of a grant. Some students following certain courses are eligible for grants. If you manage to get a grant then the fees are paid by the Education Authority. I advise you to contact your own LEA (in the area where you live permanently) and make sure that they have your name and address, so that they can send you an application form any Grants or Awards if they are available.

There may be help with transport costs too, again this depends on the College and/or the Local Education Authority.

3.2 NVQ/GNVQ Courses

If you are studying for an NVQ at levels 1-4 or a GNVQ and pay your own course fees then you are entitled to tax relief. This means you will pay only 75% of the course fees.

3.3 The Discretionary Grant for some Full Time Courses in Further Education

Note: Some LEA's have retained this for Access Courses

If it is available then you should apply direct to your Local Education Authority Grants Section. They will give you details of their regulations and of how much the grant would be for you in particular.

Getting such a grant in no way affects the provision of a Mandatory Grant if you decide later to progress to Higher Education.

It is essential that you apply for these grants as soon as you are committed to the course.

3.4 Criteria for eligibility for a Discretionary Grant

IMPORTANT:These criteria were used in the my area in 1993 - they have changed by now. You must check this with your own LEA

Those applying for a grant should be ordinarily resident within the County of Durham for at least 12 calendar months preceding the 30th June of the year that the course commences.

If the student is found to be primarily resident to receive full time education (and would normally be resident elsewhere), the student will not be regarded as having ordinary residence thus rendering themselves ineligible for an award.

The applicant must be aged between 18 and 50[1] years on 31st August prior to the commencement of the course.

The applicant must not be repeating a course for which the applicant has previously enrolled, or any course at the same level, irrespective of whether the applicant completed or had any previous financial assistance. Thus if you even started any course above 'O' Level standard then you will not be eligible for a grant.

The applicant must not be undertaking a course with a similar, or lower level of qualification to that already held, or studied by the applicant.

Applicants must not have been in full time education for 5 years prior to the course.

Applicants must not possess A level qualifications or equivalent (e.g. some BTec's, some City & Guilds courses).

All applications must be made before the end of the first term of the course.

The rates for **1991-1992** for the Durham area were £1730 for students living in the parental home and £2181 for those living elsewhere. Awards do not include the payment of Student Union fees.

---

[1] *I believe it is now 40.*

3.5 Access funds

In 1994 Full Time or sandwich students were eligible to apply for Access Fund money. The "Access Funds" are used to assist students who are not eligible for discretionary awards. They may also be used to supplement the income of students who will receive such grants /awards but who may still be in serious financial difficulties. Assistance may be provided for fees, travel and/or maintenance.

Any student on an Access Course could apply, but owing to limited resources there is no guarantee of assistance. Within each College a panel of staff is usually set up to consider applications for "Access Funds". You should check if these funds still exist. Some Colleges have "hardship funds" for students in difficulty.

3.6 Career Development Loans

If you do not qualify for a Discretionary Award and are 18 or over and study a vocationally relevant training course (full-time, part-time or distance learning course) then you may be eligible for a "career development loan".

The course has to be related to a job (even if it isn't your present job), last no longer than a year², isn't paid for by an employer, and you are not getting any award or grant for it anyway. If it does last longer than a year the loan can be to cover only 1 year of it.

These loans are designed to cover course fees, books, materials child-care, and, if the course is full-time, living expenses.

You can apply for such a loan of between £200 and £5000 to cover up to 80% of course fees plus other costs. You make no re-payments while training and for up to 3 months after that. Then you become responsible for the loan repayments and any further interest.

There is a Department of Employment booklet on Career Development Loans which you can order from Freephone 0800 585 505

---

²*If it costs more than £5000, or lasts longer than 12 months then contact the Training and Enterprise Council to ask them if they would be willing to sponsor your loan. If they do then you may be able to apply for up to 24 months and a loan up to £10,000.*

---

4. Full time courses at Higher education level

4.1 Grants

If you are accepted as a Full Time student at an Institute of Higher Education you will almost certainly be eligible for a Mandatory Grant from your Local Authority.

4.2 Loans

You will also be able to apply for a loan to "top up" the grant. It is sad to note that as of November 1994 half of all graduates who have taken out loans are too poor to make repayments or are failing to settle their debts. Statistics prepared for the Department for Education show that £751 million has been lent to students since the scheme began in 1990 and only £19 million has been repaid. Student borrowers are entitled to defer payments if they earn less than 85% of the national average wage, about £14,000 a year or about £1200 a month. About 111,000 (41%) of the 296,000 graduates eligible for repayments have been granted deferment which is up from 36% in 1993. A further 23,000 graduates have fallen behind in their repayments, 18,000 by 2 months or more. Only 47% of students eligible actually take out the loans despite widespread hardship. Many students take on part-time jobs and, in my opinion, spend time and energy doing that rather than in studying. The average loan is £736, costing about £13 a month to repay over 5 years. There is a booklet available from the Department for Education called "Student Grants and Loans - A brief guide for Higher Education students" which shows in detail how all the means testing of the grants is calculated. It covers grants, loans and access funds. (Scotland and Northern Ireland have their own guides "Student Grants in Scotland" and "Grants and Loans to Students". Contact either Student Loans Company Limited, 100 Bothwell Street, Glasgow, G2 7JD, 0345 300 900, or your school or College.)

4.3 Paramedical courses

There are awards for some paramedical courses (e.g.occupational therapy, radiography, orthoptics, dental hygiene and dental therapy). Details are available from those Colleges running such courses.

4.4 Nurse Education

There are bursaries for people entering the "Project 2000" nurse education and training programme. You should contact your Local Health Authority. In Scotland, Wales or Northern Ireland contact the National Board for Nursing, Midwifery and Health Visiting, or local College of Nursing and Midwifery.

4.5 Sponsorship

There are sponsorships for students, but they are few and far between! There is a useful publication which lists the articles and profiles of Hobsons' Students and Scholarships with the sponsorship listings from COIC's "Sponsorships". It costs about £5 from COIC. It should be in your local library.

5. Student Grants and Loans 1994/1995

	Grants	Loans Full year　Final year
Basic amount available	London　　　　£2560 Elsewhere　　£2040 Living in parental home £1615	£1375　£1005 £1150　£840 £915　£670
Who decides if you get it?	Your LEA	Your College
Is it means tested?	Yes	No
When can you apply?	Not earlier than January if course starts in Autumn and not more than 4 months from start of the course.	After your academic year has started if applying for first time. From around May of previous year if you've had one before. Agreements to be returned by 31 July
Where do you get application forms?	College/school or LEA	College or Student Loans Company.
Who pays you the money?	Your LEA	Student Loans Company.
How is it paid?	By cheque termly	Transfer to your Bank/ Building Society Account
Do apply each year?	No, but LEA send forms to review your situation	Yes
Do you have to pay money back at the end?	No	Yes, in monthly instalments. Loan is index linked to inflation from day loan paid to your account You can defer if your income is less than 85% national average

There are extra allowances to grants which seem to change quite frequently.
For 1994-1995 there were extra allowances for disabled people, and students over the age of 26 and for those with dependants.

You should note that even though the grant is means tested and you may not get a great deal of money if you or your spouse is earning, the LEA may pay the fees of the course, even though you may not be eligible for a large grant.

I think it is most important that you contact your Local Education Authority and find out what the regulations are that apply to your area. Having got the answer to the question HOW MUCH WILL I GET? you'll be in a better position to decide if you can afford it!

6. Taking on jobs to pay for the course

Almost all the students I know at present, including members of my own family, take on extra jobs (both part time during the term and full time during holidays[3]) to earn money to pay their way through the system. They ought not to have to do this, but it is very difficult to live on a student grant. I do hope that the extra effort put into the jobs will not take away the student from study.

You can to some extent prepare for this by perhaps saving money before you get there and asking relatives and friends to give you book tokens, but perhaps more important acquiring some skill so that you wont be limited to the jobs which almost all students seek (and there are therefore not many of them in University towns and cities!) of baby-sitting, pub-work and labouring. We are hoping that, rather than washing up for about £2 an hour, our son Tom will be able to earn his way through University by teaching the flute at about £10 an hour!

You should check very carefully with your local Citizen's Advice Bureau to make sure what your financial position will be if you choose go ahead with becoming a student in either Further or Higher Education.

It is also important that you consult carefully with those with whom you live, since you will be asking them to make changes as well as yourself.

---

[3]. _There are 2 useful publications: "Summer Jobs in Britain" and "Summer Jobs Abroad" for about £8 each by Vacation Work, 9 Park End Street, Oxford, OX1 1HJ. You'll probably find copies in your local library._

SECTION 10
HOW DO YOU APPLY FOR A PLACE
IN HIGHER EDUCATION?

1. The system

1.1 Getting into the Universities and Colleges Admissions Service (UCAS) system

If you wish to get into an Institute of Higher Education[1] then you MUST obtain the latest UCAS application form and Handbook. This is the only way that you will be able to get into a University. You should get these IMMEDIATELY, like NOW (!), even if you don't plan at present to go to a University! I say NOW, because it is a complex and crucial process which takes some time to complete properly.

If you are following a course at a school or college then you should get your UCAS form from there since it will have a special number to let the UCAS organisation know from where you are applying. It also helps UCAS to get your examination results from them. Make sure you get the Handbook as well.

If you are not at a school or college then get the form and the Handbook direct from UCAS:

Universities and Colleges Admissions Service
Fulton House
Jessop Avenue
Cheltenham
Gloucestershire
GL50 3SH

The telephone number of their main office is : 01242 222 444.
The telephone number for general enquiries is: 01242 227 788.
If you are a mature student (21 or over), then ask also for the leaflet "Stepping Up: A Mature Student's Guide to Higher Education".

The Handbook is very clear and well written and lists all the courses you can apply to in Higher Education. It supplies all the addresses you will need[2].

---

[1]. *"University" is used in this Section to apply to all Institutes of Higher Education.*
[2]. *Applications to the Universities of London and Wales should be addressed to the individual colleges and not to the University.*

1.2 UCAS regulations

NB. The regulations affecting application to Universities are changing each year[3]. Thus you must check very carefully what the regulations are for the year in which you are applying.

1.3 The procedures

- Applications for most places in Higher Education[4] must go through UCAS.
- You may apply for up to 6 courses.
- You fill in the official UCAS form. (Keep a copy of it.)
- You pass it on to someone whom you will use a referee. You also give the referee the UCAS fee and a card on which you put a stamp and your name and address.
- The referee writes a reference for you on the form and then, without necessarily showing what has been written about you, sends it, together with your fee and your card, to UCAS.
- The card is returned to you to acknowledge that UCAS have received your form, reference and fee[5].
- UCAS then photocopies your application form and sends copies to each of the University departments to which you have applied.
- Later you will receive a letter telling you that your application has been processed by UCAS. This could be up to six weeks after UCAS receives your application form. The letter will list the choices you have made and give you an application number. Obviously you should check that the choices UCAS list are the ones you have made. You will also get a leaflet of advice to applicants describing the stages through which your application will pass.

---

[3]. *There is already a committee, chaired by Tony Higgins, which is trying to make the whole process more smooth. It is hoped that by 1998, with the use of computing systems, that students will not have to apply to specific Universities. They will be able to apply generally by saying:" This is who I am. This is the sort of course I want, and these are the probable Universities I'll apply to." The application would be made well before the students sit their exams. This information is put into the computer. The computer distributes the information to all those Universities with such courses, who are looking for that type of person and the University then says to the student, "Come to an interview/open day, and if we like your personality, and, if you want to come to us then you can, providing you get the grades that we specify." When the results come out, those students who do not get the required grades will be able to use the computer again to sort them into the available places.*

[4]. *Social work applications go through SWAS at the same address as UCAS. See page 9 in this Section for more detail.*

[5]. *If you do not receive your card within a few days of it being submitted by your referee then check with the referee that the forms, the fee and the reference have been sent. If they have then get in touch with UCAS to find out what has happened.*

- You cannot change your application form once it has reached UCAS. If, after receiving your letter from UCAS there are problems that are not answered in the advice leaflet then contact UCAS giving your full name, your application number, the course(s) applied for, and your correspondence address as given on your application form.

- Each of the University departments to which you have applied receives via UCAS a photocopy of your application form and reference. The Admission Tutor in each University department examines these and then sends out a letter to you saying **one** of the following:

1. we accept you without an interview,
2. we accept you, conditional on you getting specific grades in specified exams, without an interview,
3. we reject you without interview,
4. we ask you to attend for interview.

- After an interview UCAS will write to you and tell you that the University department has done **one** of the following:

1. U=accepted you, unconditionally,
2. C=accepted you, conditional on gaining specific grades in specified exams,
3. R=rejected you.

2. How many courses to apply to

Because there is an increasing number of applicants for the places available in the Universities it is VITAL to apply to more than one. You can apply for up to 6 different courses under the present system. I strongly recommend that you apply to the maximum and that you consider applying to courses which may be regarded as a "safety net". For example, there are few places available on Physiotherapy courses and you may not be accepted because of large numbers applying for those few places. Thus you should also apply to related courses which have more places, such as Health Studies, and which are therefore more likely to be able to accept you.

I suggest this just in case you are not accepted for your first choice. It is important that you take advice about this[6] from your local College.

If you wish, you may apply for more than one type of course. For example, if you want to get into Social Work in general, then you could apply for the Dip.SW., Sociology, Social Policy, Community and Youth etc. If, on the other hand you want to do a degree in English Literature and nothing else appeals to you, then apply to 6 different English Literature courses. You will need to seek sound advice from your local College of Further Education on the choice of courses. These decisions really are crucial.

---

[6]. *Applicants for Medicine and Dentistry have slightly different application procedures in this respect which are clearly explained in the UCAS Handbook.*

> **Your applications should be realistic and well founded on advice from experts and lead to your previously identified 5 year goal.**

3. Writing the application

3.1 When to apply

> **DO NOT APPLY UNTIL YOU ARE SURE ABOUT THE ANSWERS TO THE QUESTIONS POSED IN THE PREVIOUS SECTIONS.**

> The closing date for applications via the UCAS form and other Higher Education Clearing Houses forms has been around December 15th and it is vital that applications get into the system as soon as possible AFTER 1st September. You should aim to get applications in no later than mid-November but preferably even sooner. Avoid applying late. Courses fill up. They are really filled on a first come first served basis[7].

Some courses have had early closing dates. It is important that you check on the closing dates for application to the specific courses you choose[8]. If you are applying to Oxford or Cambridge then note that they usually also have earlier closing dates as well as different forms[9].

3.2 General points
- Write the form very clearly, remembering that it will be photocopied smaller.
- Do not write extra sheets. UCAS do not allow extension sheets to be attached. All the information must be concentrated on the actual form itself.

3.3 Later applications
Applications are still accepted up until May 26th or thereabouts and you will go

---

[7]. *There are slightly different regulations for application to Fine Art Courses which need the submission of portfolios of work. These are detailed in the UCAS Handbook.*
[8]. *The information about deadlines is usually in the UCAS book. If in doubt then ring the University department concerned and check.*
[9]. *See page 8 of this Section.*

through the normal procedures. Between that time and about 26th July UCAS send your applications to the Universities. It is then up to the Universities to contact you direct or wait until the results are out. After that date you must wait until UCAS begins to clear all the applications which have not fulfilled their conditional offers. This process is called "clearing".

3.4 Preparatory work

Before filling in the form
Check very carefully that:
- the University does offer the course that you want to take and that the University is the right one for you,
- you actually do have (or hope to have) the necessary qualifications/experience necessary to fulfil the entry requirements[10],
- that the course is actually running[11],
- that you have used the correct UCAS reference numbers to identify the courses for which you have applied.

Your referee
You will notice that some one has to provide a reference for you. This reference is written by your referee directly on the UCAS form itself. This, together with the fee (usually in the form of a cheque or Postal Order), is sent off by the referee, so you may not actually read what the referee has written about you.

This does mean that you should be careful whom you choose! Try to get someone who can talk about your keenness to learn, your determination to succeed and your capacity to learn in a University environment.

The referee is usually your Tutor on the course you are doing before you go on to Higher Education. If you are not on a course at present then try to choose someone who will be able to give an authentic reference about your ability to study and/or your knowledge of the subject for which you are applying.

Choose someone reliable!

After they have received your application form and fee from you, do check up with them that they have in fact sent off the form, the reference and the fee to UCAS!

4. Filling in the form

4.1 The notes supplied

- **The comprehensive and lengthy notes supplied with the UCAS form are very**

---

[10]. *Details of such requirements are in "University and Colleges Entrance: The Official Guide".*

[11]. *Some are written up in the Handbook before approval is given, others are withdrawn sometimes because of lack of student interest. Most colleges and schools are given updates by UCAS about such courses. Always check these lists before filling in your form.*

---

thorough and you should follow them carefully. Read them slowly and check off each paragraph as you complete reading and understanding it. I do not wish to complicate matters by re-iterating the points made in the notes.

Some hints

- Get a photocopy of the blank form and fill that in first in pencil. Then check, perhaps together with a friend, that you have followed the accompanying notes accurately.

- Use black ink for the final version and do not write too small since the form will be reduced by about 2/3rds on a photocopier by UCAS who then send on the photocopies to the relevant Universities.

4.2 Suggested starting point

This is a crucial document. Your acceptance for an interview really does depend on you filling in the form accurately and thoughtfully.

Do not rush filling in the form. Take your time and do some careful thinking and writing down of preliminary ideas before committing yourself to the actual form.

There are various factual pieces of information required. Make sure these are accurate. Then look at the areas where you have to give a picture of your personality and your reasons for wanting to go into Higher Education.

Do this BEFORE you attempt to fill in your UCAS form, and then fill in the copy first and, if you are at school or College, ask a Tutor to check it over before you fill in the actual form itself.

You may find it useful to jot down here your initial thoughts on what you would put under the following headings, then talk with others and think carefully about how you can present the best elements of yourself. Do this before attempting the UCAS form.

FACTUAL INFORMATION.

Name. Age. Date of Birth. Male/Female.

Schools etc attended (with places and dates).

Details of qualifications already gained (in detail, when and where and what grades).

Details of any course(s) you are at present following (where it is, what qualification it leads to, when it will be finished).

Present family background.(e.g. married with girl(4), boy(9)).

Main subject area.

University(s), college(s) and course(s) to which you are applying.

Your previous jobs and/or experience.

Any health problems you have.

Any posts of responsibility, or experience of supervisory/organisational or other relevant activities (give details).

INFORMATION ABOUT YOUR PERSONALITY ETC
Your range of interests (cultural, athletic, social etc).
Reading you do relevant to your intended course.
Other reading.
Your career aspirations.
Aspects of your character and personality. Include in what way(s) you will get something from HE and also give something.
Why you want to come on this course and how committed you are to HE.
Why you want to become a teacher/social worker...whatever.
Anything else you feel should be mentioned in support of your application for Higher Education.

4.3 False statements and omissions

If you make false statements or omit significant information about your circumstances the University has the right to withdraw at any time any offers made.

5. Applications to Oxford and Cambridge

- You cannot apply to both Oxford and Cambridge in the same year.
- You must apply via UCAS and:

if to Oxford then submit a completed Oxford Application Card to the Oxford Colleges Admissions Office by October 15th (this date varies each year),

if to Cambridge, then submit a completed Preliminary Application Form to the Admissions Tutor of the Cambridge College listed as your first choice, or in the case of an open application to the Cambridge Inter-collegiate Applications Office by October 15th (this date varies each year).

You should also submit your completed UCAS form as soon as possible.

6. Initial Teacher Training Courses (ITT)

- If you wish to become a teacher in publicly maintained schools in England and Wales you must obtain Qualified Teacher Status (QTS). This is obtained by successfully completing an approved course of ITT. There are 2 main routes:

Bachelor of Education (B.Ed.) degree (some Universities offer Bachelor of Arts (B.A.) or Bachelor of Science (B.Sc.) with QTS). These degrees take 4 years, although there are some institutions which have 3 year B.Ed. courses.

A relevant subject degree (3 years) followed by a (1 year) Post Graduate Certificate in Education (4 years in all). Note that degrees in Modern Languages, classics, business studies, social science and sociology are acceptable for entry to secondary school teacher training courses but are not generally considered suitable for entry to primary school teacher training courses.

There are arguments for and against which is the better route. The specialised teacher training degree really closes routes other than teaching but probably gives a longer period of time to learn the skills of teaching. It also forces you to make a decision about what age range you will teach. The degree +PGCE leaves more options open in terms of jobs. It also leaves the question of age range until the fourth year. - Each ITT University is responsible for its own recruitment and admissions policy. It is therefore important that applicants check entry requirements with the Universities of their choice.
- All applicants to courses that lead to QTS must have achieved at least Grade C level in GCSE English Language and Mathematics BEFORE commencing their training as a teacher.
- All applicants to courses that lead to QTS should be aware that the Universities usually require that they have studied their main curriculum subject to a level higher than GCSE. Applicants who have not studied A level or BTEC level or the equivalent may find it difficult to be accepted at an ITT University.
- All applicants to courses that lead to QTS must undergo a medical examination before starting the course. The University will let you know the details and procedures.

7. Social Work Courses

Application procedures vary. Most undergraduates recruit through UCAS. You should write to the CCETSW (The Central Council for Education and Training in Social Work), which has the same address as UCAS[12]. They will send you the appropriate application forms and explanatory material.

The main qualification is the Dip.SW, the Diploma in Social Work.

The Dip.SW has been designed to be the professional qualification for all social workers in the UK.

The programmes (courses) for Dip.SW:
- are at least 2 years of study and supervised practice,
- emphasise knowledge, skills, values and competence,
- assess students to a national minimum standard,
- are planned and run by educational Institutions and social work agencies working together,
- are designed flexibly to meet the needs of a wide variety of students,
- provide students with the opportunity for an extended placement and associated study to allow them to practice their skills in one particular practice setting.

Some programmes are employment based. Others are college based. Some offer both. There are some part time courses.

---

[12]. *See page 1 of this Section.*

Students are expected to confront racism and demonstrate they can work in a multi-cultural setting.

Successful students receive their Dip.SW together with a description of their work on practice.

All applicants must, in the opinion of the people selecting, be:
- likely to be able to succeed in completing the course,
- likely to succeed in meeting the assessment requirements,
- suitable to become a social worker, and not rendered unsuitable by a criminal conviction.

The main entry qualifications required are two passes at Advanced Level with grade A,B,C,D, E and passes in 3 other GCSE subjects with grade A,B or C, or any other qualification that is deemed to be equivalent. This includes most Access Courses. Many of the providers ask for experience of social work either paid or voluntary.

The application material sent to you by CCETSW is self explanatory, but you should study it carefully and get someone to go through it with you.

8. Working with children

Local police forces may be asked to disclose details to prospective employers of any criminal conviction of those who have applied to work with children. This also applies to students who, as part of their course are required to work with children. Each local authority has its own procedures. You will be contacted before enquiries are made.

9. Making the final decision

- UCAS will ask you AFTER the examinations are taken, BUT BEFORE the examination results are known, for which TWO University places you wish to be considered.

These two are the only two which can be offered to you when the results are known.

At this stage, remember, you do not know what your results will be since you have not yet even sat the examinations!!

So what will you chose?

This can be a very difficult decision!

For example:
You are offered a place at University 1 if you get 2 A's and a B at A level.
You are offered a place at University 2 if you get 2 A's and a C at A level.
You are offered a place at University 3 if you get 1 A, a B and a C at A level.
You are offered a place at University 4 if you get 2 B's and a C at A level.
You are offered a place at University 5 if you get 3 C's at A level.[13]

- There is a large element of gambling in the system at present. If you think you are going to do well then you put down the two highest offers. If you think you have done badly then you might be tempted to put down the two lowest, but...what happens if you DO get the high scores?

- The best advice I can give is to put down the two top offers. I say that for this reason: you are allowed to go through the clearing system if you do not achieve the levels required for your two chosen University places. This does involve a lot of rushing about once the results are out! But you will get a place offered to you and it does mean that the two courses you really want to get on to are safe if you do get the results asked for.

Read the above paragraphs carefully again, because it is important that you are completely clear about this part of the system. It is not perfect and places a great deal of stress on people, but it is the only one we have at present.

10. The results

10. 1 Results affected by illness etc

- If you have any adverse circumstances which may have affected your examination results then contact your University as soon as possible after the examination and let them know about it. If it is a medical condition then you must additionally get a doctor to write on your behalf.

10.2 The time between the examination and the results

This is probably one of the most difficult times for anyone. It is like a limbo. You might be going to your first choice. You might be going to your second. You may not be going to either. You may fail to get anywhere! Your whole personality and future development can go in so many different directions. It can be most unsettling.

---

[13]. *Some Universities offer the places based on a points system where an in A level A is 10 points, a B is 8 points, a C is 6 points, a D is 4 points and an E is 2 points. In AS level A is 5 points, a B is 4 points, a C is 3 points, a D is 2 points and an E is 1 point. In Scottish Highers: A is 6 points, a B is 4 points, a C is 2 points.*

In many European countries this period of time is about 3 weeks. In the UK it stretches from your last examination, which can be as early as mid-May until the third week of August.

You could get a job (if only to offset the comparative poverty into which you will go when you get to your University!).

You could go abroad and become self-indulgent with all the opiates you can afford (but be back clear-headed by the time the results come out)!

I cannot honestly say that there is a solution to controlling your feelings about this period of time! It is probably the most uncertain time you will experience in your life!

10.2 Getting the results

- DO NOT BE AWAY ON HOLIDAY WHEN THE RESULTS OF YOUR EXAMINATIONS ARE PUBLISHED.

This is because if you have not got the results required by the two choices you have made you will need to go into the clearing system.

UCAS warns that:

> "You will need to be available personally, particularly if you wish or need to enter Clearing. You should understand that it is very unlikely that you will be able to obtain a place in Clearing while on holiday abroad."

- Clearing operates from late August and September for:
  - those who did not receive any offers earlier in the year,
  - those who did not get the required grades for their conditional offers,
  - late applicants.

11. Taking out a year (deferring)

- There are other possibilities to consider too. **If you have time to spare** then rather than going on to University in your next year, there is always the possibility of getting an acceptance to go, but not immediately. It is possible that you could benefit more in the long run by taking a year off before going on to University. I do NOT advise taking a year off and then applying. I mean that you should get your acceptance and THEN ask for deferment for a year.

- Most Universities are prepared to consider you during the present year of application for deferred entry in the following year. You should have a clear and specific reason for doing so. Do NOT be vague and say what your HOPES are: your plans must be specific and firm, and you should give clear detail as to WHY this deferment is preferable to entering this year, and precisely how the year off will be relevant to your studies and future career. You MUST check with the University before filling in the UCAS form. You will need to present a good reason for asking for deferment. See the UCAS Handbook on these points.

- Some people feel that it is less stressful to apply AFTER the results are known, but it is unlikely that you will have the choice of places by going through Clearing. Some students, however, prefer to wait a full year and then apply, knowing what their results are.

- Let me make it clear too that I don't mean have a year off to do nothing but lounge around and get bored and self-indulgent! I mean take off a year to do something with a specific purpose. Whatever you choose make sure that it has relevance to your future - wandering over Europe without any attempt to learn a language, or get some form of income is pointless and you will regress rather than develop!

12. Summary of procedures

1. Obtain the latest UCAS application form and Handbook IMMEDIATELY.
2. Fill in the official UCAS form. (Keep a copy of it.)
3. Pass it, with the UCAS fee and stamped self-addressed card, to your referee
4. The referee sends his reference with your form, fee and card, to UCAS.
5. The card is returned to you to acknowledge receipt.
6. UCAS sends photocopies of your application form and reference to courses to which you've applied.
7. You will receive a letter telling you that your application has been processed.
8. You cannot change your application form once it has reached UCAS.
9. Each department will do **one** of the following:
    1. accept you without an interview,
    2. accept you, conditional on you getting specific grades in specified exams, without an interview,
    3. reject you without interview,
    4. ask you to attend for interview.
10. After an interview UCAS will write to you and tell you that you've been:
    1. U=accepted unconditionally,
    2. C=accepted conditionally,
    3. R=rejected.
11. UCAS will ask you AFTER the examinations are taken, BUT BEFORE the examination results are known, for which TWO University places you wish to be considered. These two are the only two which can be offered to you when the results are known.
12. Do not be away on holiday when the results are published.

YOU MUST APPLY AS SOON AS POSSIBLE AFTER 1ST SEPTEMBER AND NO LATER THAN MID-NOVEMBER BUT PREFERABLY EVEN SOONER.

SECTION 11: INTERVIEWS
Introduction

Mature students[1] without the traditional entry requirements usually have to be interviewed because, unlike school leavers, their academic reference is not usually based on a 6 year acquaintance. Also the Admissions personnel have no 'A' level grades on which to base their decisions. The interview is not an obstacle but rather an opportunity to impress them with your strengths and qualities. Hopefully by the time you have worked through this Section you will be more aware of those qualities. Remember an interview is a two-way transaction. Ask questions! This is an opportunity to find out so much. You don't want to commit yourself to three or four years of an inappropriate, unsatisfactory or irrelevant course.

There are six "P"s to remember when preparing for an interview. The first three are:

PLANNING

You need to plan a strategy based upon what you have to offer, your special qualities, coupled with an image of the "perfect" mature student

PREPARATION

You need to prepare thoroughly by working through this hand-out in your own time

PRACTICE

Do a dummy run with a willing friend. Role play the interview taking turns to be both the interviewer and the interviewee.

1. PLANNING

The next page itemises some of the qualities of the perfect mature student. You can probably come up with others which are not included. The following pages provide guidelines which encourage you to analyse your own strengths in these areas.

Work through these guidelines with a "hi-lite" pen, emphasising your own strong points, and looking at the ways in which you measure up to the image. REMEMBER NO-ONE EXPECTS YOU TO SHINE IN ALL AREAS. DON'T SET YOUR PERSONAL STANDARDS TOO HIGH.

When you've done this, hi-lite, in a different colour, the strengths/qualities you feel are the most important ones for you. Keep this to 4 or 5 main points. You don't want to overwhelm the interviewer. Working systematically through this section will help you to have a clear idea of the essential points that you have to communicate. In your preparation and practice, consider ways in which you can "engineer" these points into your answers. It means that you won't come away saying, "Oh, why didn't I say that!" or "I wish I'd remembered to tell him this!"

[1]. *Some students in 6th forms may have to attend interviews too. There seems no pattern as to who is interviewed and who isn't! You'll be interviewed almost certainly if you apply to a course which is very popular, or if you apply to Oxford or Cambridge.*

WHAT IS THE PERFECT STUDENT?
POSSIBLE QUALITIES
studious

academic

hard working

knows all the study skills

ability to see more than one side of an issue

honest

dedicated

well organised

sociable

supportive

keen/enthusiastic

open minded/flexible

enquiring mind

fit

healthy

cultured

politically aware

good communicator

able both to give and gain from HE.

able to cope under stressful conditions

someone with a clear idea of their direction in life

STUDIOUS

- Evidence of this quality could be seen perhaps in a portfolio of work done recently on the course you are on (including marking sheets), or work done previously.
- You could tell the interviewer about your work schedule and projects you have undertaken on this course.
- If your school record in this area was good this also could be evidence of your strength in this area.

EVIDENCE THAT YOU HAVE THIS QUALITY - your answer

_____

_____

_____

_____

_____

_____

ACADEMIC

- Take along a good, well-structured, well-substantiated academic essay for the interviewer to look at.
- Again produce a portfolio with marking sheets if they provide such evidence.
If your school record (perhaps "O" and"A" level grades if you have them) was good on this score that's good evidence.
- Perhaps you've read some relevant academic literature that you feel confident about holding an intelligent conversation or discussion about.

EVIDENCE THAT YOU HAVE THIS QUALITY - your answer

_____

_____

_____

_____

HARD WORKING

- A well-organised portfolio of work completed since your course began could demonstrate your capacity in this area.
- If you're one of these superwomen/men who raise 7 children, stack shelves at Sainsbury's, do part time child-minding, midwifery, skiing courierring, make your own bread and sew your own sequins on by hand point this out to the interviewer.
- Draw on past experience where perhaps in a previous employment you have proven yourself to have been hard working. Point out your achievements in this area.
- Draw the interviewer's attention to past achievements which were accomplished through application and hard work.

EVIDENCE THAT YOU HAVE THIS QUALITY - your answer

_____

_____

_____

_____

_____

_____

KNOWS ALL THE STUDY SKILLS

- Show her/him an essay that you have written.
- Talk about any research skills you have used.
- Tell him/her about any proposed special study and how you would intend to approach it, what research you hope to be able to do[2].
- Tell them where you feel you have grown in the area of study skills since the course began.

EVIDENCE THAT YOU HAVE THIS QUALITY - your answer

_____

_____

_____

[2]. See Sections 19 and 20.

ABILITY TO SEE MORE THAN ONE SIDE OF AN ISSUE
- This can be demonstrated by way of a discussion of some topical issue, or something relevant to the area you hope to study at HE level.
- Perhaps you have an essay which demonstrates this ability, "...according to Piaget...this! Whereas Luria asserts...that! On close examination it would appear that Piaget's theory is correct if applied to... and Luria's viewpoint can be justified when taken in the context of...."
EVIDENCE THAT YOU HAVE THIS QUALITY - your answer

_____

_____

_____

_____

_____

_____

_____

HONEST
- Don't say you've read Proust if you haven't: you might get caught out!
- Give genuine reasons for your decision to enter HE and your chosen career course.
- Be yourself. They like mature students!
EVIDENCE THAT YOU HAVE THIS QUALITY - your answer

_____

_____

_____

_____

_____

_____

DEDICATED
- "I gave up my job."
- Your family and you have made financial sacrifices to pursue this course.
- Your attendance record and your work record testify to this dedication.
- In your previous employment as a .... dedication was a crucial requirement.

EVIDENCE THAT YOU HAVE THIS QUALITY - your answer

_____

_____

_____

_____

_____

WELL ORGANISED
- Perhaps you could describe to your interviewer "a day in the life" to demonstrate the number of "hats" you wear and how you successfully accomplish all the roles in which you find yourself as a homemaker, parent, volunteer social worker, shelf stacker, pig breeder etc.
- Show her/him your time-planner, organiser, filofax if it demonstrates the systematic way in which you schedule your work for College and your other commitments.
- Is there evidence from previous employment/voluntary work that you are a systematic, thorough, organised person?
- Have you done office work?
- Were you a secretary?
- Have you been involved in the organisation of charity work?
- Have you been involved with committee work?

EVIDENCE THAT YOU HAVE THIS QUALITY - your answer

_____

_____

_____

_____

_____

SOCIABLE

- Do you belong to any clubs, societies, etc?
- Are you a cinema/theatre goer?
- Do you play in a band?
- Do you play football?
- "Do you row?"[2]

EVIDENCE THAT YOU HAVE THIS QUALITY - your answer

_____

_____

_____

_____

_____

_____

_____

SUPPORTIVE

- Do you support your fellow students?
- Do you engage in self help groups either to tackle academic work or to give social/emotional support?
- Do you support your tutor?
- Do you smile and nod and say "Hear,hear!"?
- Do you hand in your work on time?

EVIDENCE THAT YOU HAVE THIS QUALITY - your answer

_____

_____

_____

[2]. *This is a reference to one of our students who was interviewed at Durham University for a teaching course. The particular student was female and approaching a stage of development where voluntary hard physical activity was not really one of her priorities. Towards the end of a rather academic interview the interviewer suddenly asked "Do you row?". Remember that you can easily be asked questions which are unexpected and apparently irrelevant! Be prepared!!!*

KEEN/ENTHUSIASTIC

- Do you engage in self help groups either to tackle academic work or to give social/emotional support?
- Do you support your tutor?
- Do you smile and nod and say "Hear, hear!"?
- Do you hand in your work on time?
- Do you contribute to group discussions?
- Do you come up with useful suggestions for improving the course?
- Do you come up with useful suggestions for solving problems encountered by the group?
- Do you enjoy the course?
- Do you enjoy the work?
- Have you made long term academic plans e.g. planned your special study, planned your dissertation or preferred area of interest at HE level?
- Have you taken on additional academic work over and above the course requirements? (e.g. those of you taking additional GCSE's and "A" levels).

EVIDENCE THAT YOU HAVE THIS QUALITY - **your answer**

OPEN MINDED/FLEXIBLE

- How in the past have you have demonstrated this quality?
- As most of you have had to make huge life-changes this would indicate a certain flexibility and openness to change.
- Again, this can be demonstrated by way of a discussion of some topical issue, or something relevant to the area you hope to study at HE level.
- Perhaps you have an essay which demonstrates this ability, "...according to Piaget...this! Whereas Luria asserts...that! On close examination it would appear that Piaget's theory is correct if applied to... and Luria's viewpoint can be justified when taken in the context of...."

EVIDENCE THAT YOU HAVE THIS QUALITY - **your answer**

ENQUIRING MIND

- What are the things that interest you academically, hobbies, in current affairs etc?
- Have you done any courses in the past? e.g. at night school.
- Have you made long term academic plans e.g. planned your special study, planned your dissertation or preferred area of interest at HE level?
- Have you taken on additional academic work over and above the course requirements? (e.g. those of you taking additional GCSE's and "A" levels).

EVIDENCE THAT YOU HAVE THIS QUALITY - your answer

_____

_____

_____

_____

_____

_____

_____

FIT/HEALTHY

- Are you fit?
- How do you keep yourself fit?

EVIDENCE THAT YOU HAVE THIS QUALITY - your answer

_____

_____

_____

_____

_____

_____

CULTURED

What types of music do you listen to?
- What books do you read?
- Do you go to the cinema?
- What types of film do you like?
- Do you go to the theatre?
- What types of plays do you like?
- Have you ever been to the Opera or the Ballet?
- Do you play in a brass band?

EVIDENCE THAT YOU HAVE THIS QUALITY - your answer

_____

_____

_____

_____

POLITICALLY AWARE

- Can you hold your own in a discussion about current affairs?
- What newspapers do you prefer to read?
- Do you watch "Question Time", listen to "Any Questions" etc.?
- Are you actively involved in local politics?

EVIDENCE THAT YOU HAVE THIS QUALITY - your answer

_____

_____

_____

_____

_____

_____

GOOD COMMUNICATOR
- If yes, how can you prove this? Especially if you are not at your best in interview conditions?
- Did your previous employment require communication skills?
- Are you involved in any clubs, groups, societies etc.?
- Have you ever communicated through art, music, drama, etc.?
- Have you ever done charity work or voluntary work which involved communicating with / helping others?
- Do you communicate well on paper? Show interviewer an essay.

EVIDENCE THAT YOU HAVE THIS QUALITY - your answer

_____

_____

_____

_____

_____

ABLE TO GIVE AND GAIN FROM HE
- Tell them what you will be able to achieve in career terms.
- Tell them what you will gain in academic terms, e.g. stimulation, your "greed for knowledge".
- Mention your commitment, your desire to contribute positively to the course and the students.
- Tell them how much you have gained and given on your present course e.g. sense of achievement, confidence, support and friendship etc..

EVIDENCE THAT YOU HAVE THIS QUALITY - your answer

_____

_____

_____

_____

_____

_____

ABLE TO COPE UNDER STRESSFUL CONDITIONS

- Most mature students, because of their life experience, have experienced stressful events. You may have had a highly pressured job. You may have had children!
- Cite examples of past experiences where you have experienced / coped with / thrived on stress.

EVIDENCE THAT YOU HAVE THIS QUALITY - your answer

SOMEONE WITH A CLEAR IDEA OF THEIR DIRECTION IN LIFE

- You will probably be asked, "Why do you want to be a social worker/teacher etc?"
- You need to provide genuine and worthy reasons.
- "I believe that everyone should be allowed the chance to become the very best that they can become, that everyone should be given the opportunity to develop her/his potential. As a teacher, I believe I can be instrumental in helping children on their way to achieving their personal goals."
sounds better than
"..Well the holidays are good... fits in nicely with the kids' school holidays."
- If you have done voluntary work in this or another related field, point this out. It is a great selling point. It proves that this is an informed, considered decision based on real knowledge and experience and not just a whim.
- If you have been through some major personal transition which has influenced your calling to this career, tell them. You are probably far more committed to this calling than a school leaver who just drifted into this career without much thought or consideration.
- If you are following this degree primarily for the pursuit of knowledge, that's good. Don't feel ashamed of that noble quest. Convince them of your genuine desire to stretch your mind. Not everyone takes a degree with a career goal in mind.

EVIDENCE THAT YOU HAVE THIS QUALITY - your answer

_____

_____

_____

_____

_____

_____

_____

_____

2. PREPARATION

- There are a number of considerations as far as preparation goes
- How can you prepare your answers when you don't know the questions?
- How can you keep calm?
- How do you get there?
- What should you wear?
- What should you take with you?

How can you prepare your answers when you don't know the questions?

Accept that there will always be the unexpected question that you couldn't have planned for, but remember there are many predictable questions for which you can prepare and if you impress them with your considered answers to these questions, they're not going to be too bothered if you find it difficult to think on your feet for the unexpected one! Below you will find a collection of typically asked questions, along with guidelines to help you answer them.

2.1 "Why do you want to do this course?"

- It's probably the passport to your chosen career, so say why you want to pursue that career, and why this particular course appeals.
- Give genuine reasons which are evidence of your interest in this area.
- How did that interest develop?
- What do you like about the course content at this institution in preference to the same subject on offer elsewhere?

YOUR ANSWER

_____

_____

_____

_____

_____

_____

_____

_____

2.2 "Why have you chosen this University?"

You can point out its reputation.

You like the content of the course from what you've heard about it.

You will be able to continue living at home (a huge advantage when applying locally as all the HE institutions are short of accommodation).

Maybe there are other advantages to this particular institution: sports facilities, clubs and societies etc.

YOUR ANSWER

_____

_____

_____

2.3 "How do you think you will cope with the demands of this course considering all your outside commitments?"

If you are already studying then:

- Point out that you are coping well with the considerable demands of an intensive course.

- Explain that the family and friends are very supportive (if this is the case) and that from necessity you have developed organisational and time-management skills in order to survive on your present course.

If you are not on a course then point out that you are aware of these demands and that you have already made careful plans to take into account all the different aspects of your life. Give specific examples, e.g. show completed filofax, year planner etc.

YOUR ANSWER

_____

_____

_____

2.4 "What are your interests and hobbies?"

- Point out your genuine interests and hobbies and make them interesting. Be enthusiastic about them. Be specific about them. If you like reading then which authors? If you play in a band then which band? Tell them how you keep fit.

YOUR ANSWER

_____

_____

_____

_____

_____

_____

2.5 "What reading have you done that is relevant to the course?"

- Be prepared for this question and talk about readings with which you are thoroughly familiar.
- Make sure you know the books on the specialism you have chosen.

YOUR ANSWER

_____

_____

_____

_____

_____

_____

_____

_____

2.6 "I am not familiar with Access/mature/students/Courses.[4] "Can you tell me more about the Access Course?"

OR

"I see you don't have any "O" levels or "A" levels!"

- It's essential that you respond very positively to a question like this. You must allay any doubts the interviewer may have about your ability to to perform well at HE level.
- The Access Certificate IS matriculation.
- Tell them by whom the course is validated.
- If it is an Access or equivalent course then point out that it is the accepted alternative route to HE for mature people who do not have the traditional entry requirements.
- Be prepared to indicate the main areas of study which your course involves.
- If you do any study skills then list them.

---

[4]. *This obviously assumes you are on an Access Course: you should adapt this to meet the particular course you are at present following.*

Tell them how you have studied this book which aims to help you:
to experience all the learning methods you will encounter at HE level,
to develop research skills, essay writing skills, presentation skills,
  to be practised in the areas of academic rigour, substantiation, data selection,
enquiry, analysis, synthesis, structuring and presentation.
- Say it also helps with personal development, confidence building, assertion
training, interpersonal skills, time management and stress reducing strategies.
- Say how it helps you with developing library and computing skills.
- Be prepared to explain the nature of your particular specialism. Be aware of its
aims, objectives, its basic concepts and underpinning theories.
YOUR ANSWER

_____

_____

_____

_____

_____

_____

_____

_____

_____

_____

_____

_____

_____

_____

_____

_____

2.7. "Why have you left your return to study until so late in life?"

- "I felt I had to put my family first but now they're less dependant it's time for me to have my chance to progress."
- "It wasn't until recently I realised that, what seemed an unreachable goal, could actually be within my reach."
- "No one in our family had ever been to University so I never considered it until recently. I feel optimistic. I appear to be on line for an overall credit."
- "I never considered HE but when I was made redundant I felt I had nothing "and when you got nothing, you got nothing to lose"!" (Dylan,196?). So I thought, "Why not!"

YOUR ANSWER

_____

_____

_____

_____

_____

_____

2.8 "How do you feel you'll relate to younger students?"

- "I look forward to working with them, hearing their fresh ideas and new approaches, learning from them and in turn being able to offer them support and worldly wisdom when they have their inevitable crises."

YOUR ANSWER

_____

_____

_____

_____

2.9 "Do you think you'll be able to manage on a student grant?"

- This is something that by now I'm sure you have looked into. If it's going to be difficult admit this but reassure them that your determination "will out", even if it means shelf stacking etc.

YOUR ANSWER

_____

_____

_____

_____

_____

_____

_____

_____

2.10. "What do you think of the course you are doing now?"

- Give an honest answer: "The tutors are wonderful" "It's the best thing that ever happened to me!"
- Seriously be positive. Explain the areas where you have grown, academically, personally etc. Tell her/him what you particularly like about the course.
- Use this as an opportunity to sell the course's strengths. See question 2.6.
- Your enthusiasm will pay dividends for yourself and other students from the same course who apply there.

YOUR ANSWER

_____

_____

_____

_____

2.11. "What do you know about this course?"

- It is an advantage if you have been able to find out, prior to the interview, a more detailed knowledge of this particular degree course. This question gives you an opportunity to demonstrate that knowledge, to ask any relevant questions and to say why you think this course will suit you.

- Take along a photocopy of their course information publicity on which you have scribbled notes, and been through with a "hi-liter" pen. It shows you have done your research and thought seriously about the course.

- If you don't know much about the course ASK!

YOUR ANSWER

_____

_____

_____

_____

2.12. "What are your long term goals?"

- You should be aware of these by the time you come to the interview and it's just a matter of stating them very clearly, precisely and positively to show that you know where you're going.

- If you are in the minority whose main ambition is the pursuit of knowledge make this a "plus", be proud of your quest!

- "My main concern is to pursue knowledge, to develop intellectually, to realise my academic potential...." etc.

YOUR ANSWER

_____

_____

_____

_____

_____

_____

2.13. "What books do you read?"

- Be specific and enthusiastic about the books you like, and be able to justify your choice.

YOUR ANSWER

_____

_____

_____

_____

2.14. What newspapers do you read?"

See previous answer.

YOUR ANSWER

_____

_____

_____

2.15. "What do you consider to be the most significant world event over the past twelve months?"

- Prepare in advance items of world, national and local news, in areas in which you are interested, and fairly knowledgeable.

YOUR ANSWER

_____

_____

_____

_____

2.16. "What have you enjoyed most about your return to study"

YOUR ANSWER

Be honest and be positive. Pick out the things that show how you enjoy the academic aspects of the study, perhaps too how well those around you have responded and how you feel you are progressing and moving forward.

_____

_____

_____

_____

_____

_____

_____

2.17. "What do you hope to get out of this course?"

- Consider the wider advantages of doing a course, not just the degree but the personal, social, and intellectual development involved.
- THEY WILL ALSO PROBABLY PICK UP ON INFORMATION FROM YOUR APPLICATION FORM PREVIOUS WORK, FAMILY BACKGROUND etc.
BE PREPARED TO EXPAND ON ANYTHING YOU HAVE MENTIONED IN YOUR APPLICATION. CHECK WITH YOUR REFEREE IF S/HE HAS PUT IN ANYTHING THAT MAY BE QUESTIONED.

YOUR ANSWER

_____

_____

_____

ADDITIONAL PREPARATION

How can you keep calm?
- Deep breathing and relaxation techniques[5].

- Stress reducing strategies which have worked for you in the past.

- "Psyching yourself up" by reminding yourself of all your qualities and strengths. If you have worked through this Section you will be well aware of them.

- Remind yourself that they like mature students (if you are one!).

- Arrive at least 10 minutes before to give yourself time to focus your mind to the task in hand.

- Make sure you are well rested have an early night the night before.

- "Sparkle!"

How do you get there?
- Do a dummy run in advance.

- Allow time for bus cancellations.

- Find out where in the building you need to be.

What should you wear?
- Something presentable and above all comfortable (especially your shoes)!

What should you take with you?
- Portfolio of work you have done or at least some essays.
- Any of your work which you feel may be relevant even if it was done some time ago. e.g. Art work, if your going for an art degree, samples of creative writing if you're going for a creative writing course.
- Information about the course you are now on.
- Your Tutor's phone number and work address in case you need to put the interviewer in touch with him/her.
- Any previously gained certificates.

---

[5]. *See Section 16 p.28ff.*

---

3. PRACTICE

- Do a role play interview in advance, preferably with a friend on the course who has read this hand out. Role play the interviewer and the interviewee.

GENERAL HINTS AND TIPS

Be positive
- They like mature students. Mature students are dedicated, committed and hard working.

Be yourself
- Don't feel you have to impress by using "big" words or claiming to have read books which you think will impress. Chances are they won't.

Be comfortable
- Wear clothes which are presentable and comfortable.

Be there
- Make sure you know how to get there, and how long it takes. Leave yourself enough time.

Be prepared
- Work through this section a few days before. As you work through it, hi-lite your strong points and consider how they can be included in your answers to the "typically asked questions".

Be proud
- Be proud of your maturity. It is a very strong point in your favour.

Be precise
- If you don't understand the question, say so. Don't waffle, in the hope that you've understood. Have a list of questions about the course, the University, etc. prepared.

- Take with you examples of your academic work and information about your course (in case the interviewer is unfamiliar with the course you are on)..

Be relaxed
- Be in the habit of practising relaxation techniques which work for you.

Be fresh
- Have an early night the night before.

SUMMARY

The first 3 "P"s of interview skills are

PLANNING

PREPARATION

PRACTICE

The final 3 "P"s are

be POSITIVE

be PRECISE and...

be PROUD of yourself!

GOOD LUCK!!!

SECTION 12:
HOW SHOULD YOU PREPARE?

1. Get your home sorted out to help you study

You will need three things from home:

- time of your own, which is uninterrupted and guilt free! This is time which you devote to study,
- space of your own, which is uninterrupted and guilt free! This is where you can spread out your books and writing papers without fear of them being tidied away etc,
- support, understanding and encouragement! You should consult carefully with those with whom you live and gain their support and understanding for what may well be a difficult set of changes for them as well as yourself if you decide to go ahead with the taking on a course. It is not an easy position for those around you to be in, seeing you with all the pressures of your new way of life and they may well feel threatened by it. Be very aware of their needs as well as your own. They too will need your support, understanding and encouragement!

1.1 Time and money

The time factor

You must consider the time factor: it will be AT LEAST 2 years after the Access Course before you can be qualified, and in some cases it can be 4 years.

The money factor

You must find out about money and how you will be able to support yourself for the time you spend in education. Grants for courses at Higher Education level are not high and there is a strong possibility you may need to take out a loan For more detailed information about this see Part One Section 9. Get in touch with Citizens' Advice Bureau/County Hall/Benefit Office re finance to make sure that you are in the best financial position possible.

1.2 Feel organised and in control

You need to be organised and clear in your own mind about priorities and timetables and plans. This is a high priority. I recommend that you begin by setting out all the important deadlines in your life for the coming year(s), including the course you join, family birthdays, holidays, appointments etc etc, in a way where you can see them all. Something like a year planner. There is more about this in Section 16. If you are organised and you know how you are distributing your time, then you will feel in control of your life.

2. Get to know the place you are going to

2.1 The place

Once you know to which University you will be going I do suggest that you visit it if you possibly can so as to become familiar with it.

If you need accommodation then try to get it sorted out before the term starts.

2.2 The staff

You should try to contact the staff of the course onto which you intend to go and ask for information about the structure of the course and a reading list and answers to any general questions you may have.

Tutors in most Institutions are becoming more and more experienced with and used to mature students and their problems. Do not hesitate to talk over any problems, either personal, or financial or academic with your Tutor. They ought to be there to help.

You MUST use them fully.

They have a responsibility to you to keep you informed about your progress and to give you all the help and encouragement they can.

Your Tutor should be your friend. Your Tutor should be on your side. Your Tutor is PAID to help you. They do NOT see themselves as people putting obstacles in your way, but as friends helping you to get over the obstacles which are there. Always share with your Tutor your worries and concerns.

2.3 Clarify your responsibilities on the course

Responsibility to attend

You must attend the course regularly, making sure that you go to all the elements of the course and not just the bits that seem attractive. Make a habit, a ritual of it.

Responsibility to complete work

You must complete all the assignments you are given by the deadlines that you are given, so make sure you don't leave essays etc till the last minute. Get the deadlines written into that diary!

Responsibility to be honest

If you are found to have cheated or attempted to gain an unfair advantage, the examiners have the authority to deem you to have failed part or all of the assessment, and the authority to determine whether or not you shall be re-assessed.

Responsibility to your Tutor

You have a responsibility to your Tutor know what is going on! If you decide not to attend for whatever reason then you MUST let your Tutor know, preferably before the absence.

3. Broaden your knowledge in general

When you go to a University or College you will find that the study of your subject will be enhanced if you have a broad general knowledge beyond that of your subject. It is important that you should be aware of the society in which we live:
- what is going on in that society,
- how our society has evolved
- the people who have been considered as important contributors to our society.

There is much more about this in Section 24, but for the time being it is important that you should get into the habit of broadening the base of your knowledge and thinking carefully about events and experiences which are part of our present culture.

You should become more aware of:
- current events, listening to programmes like

    "PM" (BBC Radio 4 at 5.00 p.m.-6.00 p.m.)

    "The World at One" (BBC Radio 4 at 1.00 p.m.-1.40 p.m.)

    "Today" (BBC Radio 4 at 6.30 a.m.- 8.40 a.m.)

    Channel 4 News (TV Channel 4 at 7.00 p.m.- 7.50 p.m.) This news bulletin is presented by journalists who do their own interviewing with people in the news and much background is given as opposed to the BBC and ITV news bulletins which are shorter and do not seem to have the time for as much depth.

- the background to current affairs, listening to the documentaries like

    "File on Four", "Analysis" and "Special Assignment" (all on Radio 4 at various times throughout the week)

- newspapers you don't normally read, to see the different ways in which news is presented.

- current events in the arts, listening to radio programmes like

    "Kaleidoscope" (BBC Radio 4 at 4.05 p.m.- 4.45 p.m.)

- music you do not usually listen to,

    Classic FM, Radio 3 for classical music

I suggest many radio programmes since you can be doing other things whilst listening to them. For example, I usually listen to Kaleidoscope whilst I am getting the tea ready for the family's return. I time my lunch to coincide with the "World at One" and the ironing gets done Saturday morning whilst I listen to the top 20 classical releases on Classic FM. Journeys in the car I tend to be tuned to radio 4. As a result of this I feel I am in contact with what is happening in the society in which I live and I can relate much of what I do to that information and vice versa.

4. What you know already

4.1 Current affairs

I hope that when you first go through the following section that you do not get many right! That will mean that you can identify what you do need to get to know about! Try answering the following questions. If you get less than half right (and you will have to a bit of research to check up the answers, since what is correct as I write this part won't be correct by the time you read it!) then you need to do a bit of listening to what's going on in the world of politics.

I am not asking you to agree with any of the political parties, nor am I saying that you have to become political. All I am suggesting is that if you wish to be considered an educated person then you should know who it is that is making decisions about many aspects of our lives.

Name the	[Your answer]	[Correct answer]	[✓✗]
Leader of the Conservative Party	[_____	][_____	][ ]
Leader of the Labour Party	[_____	][_____	][ ]
Leader of the SLD	[_____	][_____	][ ]
The Speaker	[_____	][_____	][ ]
Chancellor of the Exchequer:	[_____	][_____	][ ]
Home Secretary:	[_____	][_____	][ ]
Secretary of State for:	[_____	][_____	][ ]
Transport:	[_____	][_____	][ ]
Foreign/Commonwealth Affairs:	[_____	][_____	][ ]
Defence:	[_____	][_____	][ ]
Employment:	[_____	][_____	][ ]
Education and Science:	[_____	][_____	][ ]
Trade and Industry	[_____	][_____	][ ]
the Environment:	[_____	][_____	][ ]
Social Services:	[_____	][_____	][ ]
Lord Chancellor:	[_____	][_____	][ ]
First Lord of the Treasury and Minister for the Civil Service:	[_____	][_____	][ ]

Name the	[Your answer][Correct answer][..]
Minister of	[_____][_____][ ]
Agriculture and Fisheries:	[_____][_____][ ]
President of the NUM:	[_____][_____][ ]
General Secretary of the TUC:	[_____][_____][ ]
Director-General of the CBI:	[_____][_____][ ]
President of the Commission of the	
European Communities:	[_____][_____][ ]
Secretary General of	
the United Nations:	[_____][_____][ ]
Chairman of the	
Conservative Party:	[_____][_____][ ]
Deputy leader of	
the Labour Party:	[_____][_____][ ]
Deputy leader of the SLD:	[_____][_____][ ]
Leader of the House of Commons:	[_____][_____][ ]
Shadow Chancellor	
of the Exchequer:	[_____][_____][ ]
Shadow Home Secretary:	[_____][_____][ ]
Main Opposition Party spokespeople for:	
Transport:	[_____][_____][ ]
Foreign/Commonwealth Affairs:	[_____][_____][ ]
Defence:	[_____][_____][ ]
Employment:	[_____][_____][ ]
Education and Science:	[_____][_____][ ]
Trade and Industry	[_____][_____][ ]
the Environment:	[_____][_____][ ]
Social Services:	[_____][_____][ ]

You should be able to state very simply what the major policy differences are between the three main political parties in Great Britain.

4.2 Literature

Compile a list of books/authors which you already <u>have</u> read under the following headings:

Novels
Poems
Plays
Short Stories
Essays
Auto-biographies

4.3 Newspapers etc

Magazines (which do you take regularly?)

Because you will be short of time when you become a student you will need to decide if there are any regularly published magazines/periodicals which will help you with the subject you are studying and, if money has to be prioritised then you should perhaps cancel any of those which are not relevant to your study?

Newspapers (which do you take regularly?)

Without wanting to appear snooty about it I have to suggest that you should avoid reading the "tabloid" format newspapers as your main source of information about what is going on in the world. "The Times", "The Guardian", "The Independent" actually do gave you more value for money in terms of numbers of words! They do attempt to provide not only the news but comment and background information.

Read a copy of each of the newspapers you can find and see how each deals with the major political story of the day, the major "news" item of the day, and the major sporting item of the day. Try to get at least 4 of the following: "The Guardian", "The Times", "The Telegraph", "The Independent", "The Sun", "The Mirror", "The Daily Mail", "The Express". Make notes below about the differences.

4.4 Reference books

(Which do you have at home?)

Are there any which you will need for your life as a student?
Absolutely Essential:
You need to purchase one good small modern dictionary such as:
> *"Chambers New Compact Dictionary"*
> *"Collins Pocket Dictionary of the English Language"*
> *"The Pocket Oxford Dictionary"*

The rest of these books you do not need to purchase - but they are useful:
> *"Chamber 20th Century Dictionary"*
> *"Collins' Concise Dictionary of the English Language"*
> *"The Concise Oxford Dictionary"*
> *"Longman Modern English Dictionary"*

You should have a:
> Thesaurus - various publishers including Penguin and Longmans

Useful to have:
You need access to recent editions of:
> * *"Whitaker's Almanac"*
> * *"Pears Cyclopaedia"*
> * *"MacMillan Encyclopaedia"*

Make a list below of any reference books you will need in general and which ones you think may be useful for your main subject:

5. Broadening your base

Make a list of 5 names that are considered to be "significant" under the following headings and find out what those people have written - and at least sample it - try to find out what it is about these people's contribution that makes them acknowledged as "significant".

Novelists:	1:
	2:
	3:
	4:
	5:
Playwrights	1:
	2:
	3:
	4:
	5:
Poets	1:
	2:
	3:
	4:
	5:
Politicians	1:
	2:
	3:
	4:
	5:
Psychologists	1:
	2:
	3:
	4:
	5:
Philosophers	1:
	2:
	3:
	4:
	5:

Painters	1:
	2:
	3:
	4:
	5:
Sociologists	1:
	2:
	3:
	4:
	5:
Sculptors	1:
	2:
	3:
	4:
	5:
Scientists	1:
	2:
	3:
	4:
	5:
Visual artists	1:
	2:
	3:
	4:
	5:
Composers	1:
	2:
	3:
	4:
	5:
The 8 "significant" people in your specialism?	
	1:
	2:
	3:
	4:
	5:
	6:
	7:
	8:

Why is it that some people's contribution to our culture is of more significance than that
of others?

Compile a list of 5 scientific ideas with which an educated person should be familiar.

    1:
    2:
    3:
    4:
    5:

Join a library and ask to be shown around it so that you understand the classification system and the reference system.

6. Information technology and computers

You do need at least to become aware of the impact which the development of computers is having and will have on our society. See what you can find out about the following:

The use of computers in education.
The use of the "Internet" in increasing access to information.
The usefulness of word-processors for students.
The usefulness of other tools computers provide, such as spreadsheets and databases.

SECTION 13
WHERE ARE YOU NOW?

Introduction

By the time you reach this point in the book you should have been able to come to some decisions about the way that you see your life changing and developing. I think that before going further it is necessary for you to consolidate this new approach to your life and take stock of this pivotal point in your life, so that:

- you know where you are now,

- how you got to this point,

- where you going to be in a few years time,

- and how you are going to get there!

I'd like you to reflect upon your life and to use it as a resource both in terms of planning future action and in terms of becoming aware of the learning which has already been done, not only from school, but things like management skills in house-keeping, decision making skills in the factory: hence the title.

"Who I am - where I am now - how I got here - where I am going and how I'm going to get there!"

There is another good reason for putting pen to paper at this point and that is to give you a chance to write an essay with a given structure.

The structure

Any essay you write should have a structure.

It should have an introduction, some separate parts dealing with aspects of the main topic, and a conclusion.

Sometimes, as in this essay you will be given the structure, but usually you will be expected to work out your own structure to the essay.

The structure which I would like you to follow for this essay is set below. It is not absolutely essential to follow it in every detail, and if you find there are some aspects of your life upon which you wish to place more emphasis than others then certainly you should do that. However, do try not to be far short of the 3000 words, nor to exceed that number by too many.

The essay

Title:"Who I am - where I am now - how I got here - where I am going and how I'm going to get there!"

Introduction
This should state explicitly and clearly what you are going to do in the essay and in what order.

Part 1: Statement in <u>factual</u> terms of who you are now
- age, height, weight, colouring, etc., etc.(perhaps illustrate with photograph(s)),
- where you live and have lived (a geographic perspective),
- when you live (an historical perspective),
[You might try to identify the main outline of your life to date. Perhaps write down the year you were born and then for each year after that on the left hand side of the page write down what happened to you, on the right hand side what were the major events in the "world" outside.]
- a list of the skills and achievements, which you think you have acquired/developed over the years.
[You might try looking at the skills you have used as a housewife/husband, the skills you have developed in hobbies etc - don't think of them just as job skills. You can identify the learning which you have done from non-traditional sources. (e.g. management skills in house-keeping, decision making skills in the factory)

Part 2: Outline of the major "influences" on you
- the family you were born into - (family tree(?)), something of their background - and how their attitudes, values and beliefs have affected you,
- your education and its effect on you,
- other personal major events, people, jobs, experiences in your life and the effect they have had upon you,
- perhaps some thoughts about how broader issues like political/economic/social events you mention in Part 1 have affected your life.

Part 3: A summary of where you are now

This should be in terms of your beliefs, opinions, prejudices, qualifications, skills acquired, relationships, and anything else you feel is of relevance to a clear picture of your self.

Part 4: A statement of where you are hoping to get to

In the areas which you feel are important, particularly in terms of what you expect/hope to be doing in say 5 years time, and what you will need to do over the next 3-4 years in order to achieve that ambition.

Conclusion

This should attempt to draw together the main points made in the essay.

Rubric

The essay should be no longer than 3000 words - but you may wish to use appendices of supportive, illustrative material (such as diaries, photographs, newspaper extracts, diagrams, family tree...) which do not count in the 3000, but to which you can refer in the main text.

Marking

The marking of this piece of work will be based on the following scheme:

SPELLING	[15]-	accuracy.
PUNCTUATION	[15]-	correct usage.
GRAMMAR	[15]-	correct and appropriate usage.
PRESENTATION	[15]-	neatness and legibility.
STRUCTURE	[25]-	a clear and appropriate statement of intent which is then implemented.
CLARITY	[15]-	simple, straight-forward vocabulary and sentence structure.

TOTAL MARKS =   100

In this essay marks are not given for the actual CONTENT matter. The essay is a very personal one and I do not think it is appropriate to mark it for anything other than the above.

Some suggestions

- Start by writing down the headings of the different parts on separate sheets of paper (or if you are using a word-processor on separate pages of a document) and then spend time jotting down your ideas under the headings and begin to build the essay up in different parts. Don't try to do the introduction first.

- When you have got these notes so that they cover most of the points you wish to make, begin to write out a neat first draft. When you have got to this stage you could begin to think of introduction and conclusion.

- You may have to do this process several times, perhaps literally cutting bits out and moving them into different positions, adding bits and cutting other bits out, before you are satisfied.

- You should have a look at Section 25 on setting out of work.

- Then you should check carefully the following points for the final draft:
    - accurate spelling
    - accurate punctuation
    - correct and appropriate grammar
    - neat and legible presentation
    - clear and appropriate structure to the essay
    - simple and straight-forward vocabulary and sentence structure.

These qualities are the ones, along with several others, that you will need to develop in order to write competent essays for your more academic work.

You will need someone to diagnose and prescribe
        by pointing to areas where you need to improve,
        by suggesting action to be taken, and
        by identifying areas where you are strong.
You can do the evaluation yourself, indeed it is a very good exercise to do this anyway, but you will probably find it more realistic and satisfying if you get someone else to mark it for you. If you cannot think of anyone to do this, then send it, together with a fee of £5 for every 1000 words of the essay and a stamped self-addressed label for returning the package, to me via the address at the front of the book and I will return it to you marked and with comments as soon as I possibly can.
CONFIDENTIALITY: The essay is confidential between you and myself. No part of it will be read out or published or discussed with anyone other than yourself.

SECTION 14: CHECKLIST

Before you go on I would like you to fill in the following checklist so that you are sure that you have got to the stage where you can concentrate on your studying, knowing that you have tackled your long term plans and that you have a clear route ahead of you.

NOTE: Talk all these things over with those with whom you live. [ ]

1. Get your long term career goals sorted out with the help of professional careers advisers, if possible at the Careers Office, or at your local College of Further Education. [ ]

2. Make decisions about which HE Courses you would like to apply for in the light of the career you would like. [ ]

3. Write to the relevant and realistically accessible Universities and ask for their prospectuses. [ ]

4. Get in touch with the Departments within the Universities and see if you can go through for a chat with staff & students, and see the place. [ ]

5. In order to be realistic about your long term goals make sure you talk to those already working in that area, those who teach on or study those courses leading to that particular goal. [ ]

6. If you need to get qualifications before going on to Higher Education then consult carefully with College of FE as to what the best route is: Access courses usually provide the fastest route for older students, but be sure that the University is prepared to accept it as matriculation.[1] [ ]

7. Make sure you are clear about what experience(s) you need in order to fulfil entry qualifications to your University. This may mean again deferring entry until you have acquired that experience. [ ]

8. Get the UCAS application form and Handbook.

9. When you are clear about which courses will help you best achieve your goals, and which University(s) are the most appropriate for you, send off the application form.

---

[1]. *If you do go to Further education first then you will find Part 2 of this book, Sections 16-31 useful.*

---

10. If are going into Higher Eduction then make a decision about if you will be taking a full time or a part time course.   [ ]
11. Make sure you know how you are going to pay for the course. Get in touch with Citizens' Advice Bureau/County Hall/Benefit Office re finance to make sure that you are in the best financial position possible.   [ ]

12. Check that you know where you will be living! If not at home then can the college sort out a place for you? If not then what?

13. Check with Tutors to see if you need to do any pre-course work.   [ ]
14. Get some passport photographs taken. You will probably need to send some to your college before September.   [ ]

15. Get some sort of diary, planner and enter up all your known deadlines/commitments from now until (at least) July of next year[2].   [ ]
16. From the course get a list of books that you will need and get them. [ ]
17. Get your basic reference books collected.   [ ]
18. Broaden your knowledge of current affairs.   [ ]
19. Broaden your knowledge/experience of science/literature/music/art [ ]
20. Keep talking things over with those with whom you live.   [ ]

---

[2]*See Section 16 for more detail.*

SECTION 15: WILL YOU SUCCEED?

Introduction

I have discovered that people returning to the learning situation have three worries which hold them back:
- lack of knowledge of how you get into Higher Education,
- lack of confidence in skills which you need in writing essays and studying in general,
- lack of confidence in yourself complicates the issue further.

1. Lack of knowledge of how to get into HE

Hopefully this book will help you gain the knowledge! If you go systematically through Part One then you should be able to know how you can get in to Higher Education. This should clear away many of the fears of the unknown, and set your mind at rest that people like you really do get into it and benefit from it.

2. Lack of confidence in study skills

2.1 Using this book

Again this book will help you to develop these skills and enable you to apply what you learn to the course which you are following (or will shortly be following). Remember that you are not supposed to read this book all at once, cover to cover. It is designed so that you use a particular Section as you reach an appropriate stage in your development as a student. You already have the skills required, it is just a matter of practice and building your confidence through doing work for your course, having positive feedback from your Tutor(s) and realising that you are doing the work successfully. If you have problems then remember that the Tutor is there to help and advise.

Building confidence isn't something which I can do for you just by telling you what to feel! It will require you:
- to identify precisely where you feel a lack of confidence and then
- to take some positive and practical steps towards improving the skills in that area.

On the next pages are some guidelines to help you to identify those areas where you feel a lack of confidence and then plan to do practical things to build your confidence in your abilities. The good thing about these areas is that you can actually DO something PRACTICAL to improve your confidence! You will find more help with identifying lack of knowledge about study skills in the Introduction to Part Two of the book.

2.2 The ideal student!!!

(At the risk of petrifying you even more!!!) here is a list of qualities looked for in a student in Higher Education. Write down you what think each one does.

A person who is **studious**
(e.g. studies systematically)
A person who is **academic**

A person who is **hard working**

A person who **knows all the study skills**

A person has the **ability to see more than one side of an issue**

A person who is **dedicated**

A person who is **well organised**

A person who is **sociable**

A person who is **supportive**

A person who is **keen/enthusiastic**

A person who is **open minded/flexible**

A person who has an **enquiring mind**

A person who is **fit/healthy**

A person who is **cultured/politically aware**

A person who is **a good communicator**

A person who is **able both to give and gain from HE**

A person who is **able to cope under stressful conditions**

A person who is **someone with a clear idea of their direction in life**

2.3 Identifying where you lack confidence

Indicate how much you think that you have the qualities listed below.

(1 =strongly disagree 2 =disagree 3 =not sure 4 =agree 5 =strongly agree)					
You are...					
studious	①	②	③	④	⑤
academic	①	②	③	④	⑤
hard working	①	②	③	④	⑤
knowledgable about study skills	①	②	③	④	⑤
able to see more than one side of an issue	①	②	③	④	⑤
dedicated	①	②	③	④	⑤
well organised	①	②	③	④	⑤
sociable	①	②	③	④	⑤
supportive	①	②	③	④	⑤
keen/enthusiastic	①	②	③	④	⑤
open minded/flexible	①	②	③	④	⑤
enquiring and enjoy research	①	②	③	④	⑤
fit	①	②	③	④	⑤
healthy	①	②	③	④	⑤
cultured	①	②	③	④	⑤
politically aware	①	②	③	④	⑤
a good communicator	①	②	③	④	⑤
able both to give and gain from HE.	①	②	③	④	⑤
able to cope under stressful conditions	①	②	③	④	⑤
someone with a clear idea of their direction in life	①	②	③	④	⑤

Add up the totals in each column

GRAND TOTAL

Identify those which are your lowest scores.
List them on the next page.

2.4 Doing something about it

Make a list of some PRACTICAL things that you can DO to improve your skills in the areas on which you scored lowest.

To improve me being studious, *I should:*
(e.g. become more systematic about deadlines for work and organise myself with a filofax. I'll read Section 16 of this book!)

To improve me being academic, *I should:*

To improve me being hard working, *I should:*

To improve my knowledge of study skills, *I should:*

To improve my ability to see more than one side of an issue, *I should:*

To improve me being honest, *I should:*

To improve me being dedicated, *I should:*

To improve me being well organised, *I should:*

To improve me being sociable, *I should:*

To improve me being supportive, *I should:*
To improve me being keen/enthusiastic, *I should:*
To improve me being open minded/flexible, *I should:*
To improve me having an enquiring mind, *I should:*
To improve me being fit , *I should:*
To improve me being healthy, *I should:*
To improve me being cultured, *I should:*
To improve me being politically aware, *I should:*
To improve me being a good communicator, *I should:*
To improve me being able both to give and gain from HE., *I should:*
To improve me being able to cope under stressful conditions, *I should:*
To improve me being someone with a clear idea of their direction in life, *I should:*

You could use this technique to help in other facets of your life, identifying areas where you feel unconfident, and then making positive and practical plans to improve those areas.

3. Lack of confidence in being a student

3.1 What the problems are

There are two main problem areas which I found concerned our students who returned to education after a gap:

- a feeling that you are too old, not clever enough, or somehow different to those in education.
- logistic problems of how to organise your life to fit in studying.

3.2 Feeling that you are too old, not clever enough, or somehow different to those in education

Most people's image of students and studying is of young, very bright, 18 year olds with scarves!

Some facts about those who have returned to education

There is a massive increase in the numbers of older people returning to learning. As I have pointed out before the average age of those on Access Course was 35, the spread of ages was 19-71!

The vast majority of those who have returned to education have been able to cope. None of them have ever said that it is easy! But many of them have said how much they have enjoyed it, even though it is hard.

Look through Appendix 1 for comments by people who have followed the advice and guidance outlined in this book.

3.3 The shocking truth about Universities!

You do not have to be clever to get a degree! The most important single idea to remember is that you do NOT have to be CLEVER to be successful in Higher Education:

- you have to be keen to learn!
- you have to learn to be systematic and well organised![1]

These two qualities are ones which I am sure you have in abundance. I can say that confidently because I have met so many adults who have wanted to get back into education and who have, once they have realised that it is perfectly possible to become systematic and organised, been able to develop the necessary skills to cope with the business of being a student.

Most people think they are not as clever as other students. There is a sort of false modesty in the English character which almost teaches us that it's rude to boast, even if one is good at something, and that seems to have blunted our confidence to tackle things with which we are not familiar or which make us feel alien.

---

[1]. *See especially Section 16: Getting organised for learning.*

3.4 It's different to being at school

I have taught in schools and I have taught in Colleges. In schools the students are there because they have to be there. The teacher's job very often is to interest them and make them want to learn. In a College, or 6th form or University, the student is there because the student has chosen to be there. Thus the Tutor's job is made much, much easier because the student is highly motivated.

If you have the desire to succeed and the ability to stand back from your situation and coolly organise yourself then you will succeed.

Remember too that Tutors are on your side. A good Tutor is not there to pull you to pieces and put you down. A good Tutor is there to help you to identify the obstacles in your way of succeeding and to help you over them.

4. Lack of confidence in general

4.1 Identify your strengths

I have found that when people first return to education they have real difficulties in believing that they can succeed and they tend to get into a habit of almost putting themselves down: "Oh, I couldn't do that, I'm only a housewife, labourer, uneducated sort of person....and so on."

The only way we could get people to realise and articulate their worth was to encourage them to do a bit of more objective analysis of the skills they already possessed.

It is not easy to tell yourself what your strengths in skills are. You will have developed many skills throughout your life, and hardly be aware that you have got them. It is useful to be able to identify some of them and acknowledge that you are quite good at doing some things, otherwise you would not be reading this book at present.

We found it useful to encourage students to identify several things they had achieved in their life. These were things of which they were justifiably satisfied. They came from all aspects of their lives. They were often things which seemed trivial, but which on closer thought had involved all sorts of skills which had been developed.

Firstly, make a list of the 6 most important achievements you have had in your life, or the things that have given you most satisfaction. It might be bringing up a family, taking part in a marathon, gaining an exam success, organising a wedding, a job that you have had...the key thing is you should feel some satisfaction about it.

ACHIEVEMENTS
1=
2=
3=
4=
5=
6=

Now take achievement number 1 and look at each of the skills in the list below, asking: "How much of this skill was involved in me being able to achieve this?"

If it involved none of that skill   then put a 0 in the column.
If it involved a bit of that skill   then put a 1 in the column.
If it involved some of that skill   then put a 2 in the column.
If it involved quite a lot of that skill   then put a 3 in the column.
If it involved a great deal of that skill   then put a 4 in the column.

SKILLS	ACHIEVEMENTS						
	1	2	3	4	5	6	TOTALS
dealing with animals							
analysis							
dealing with plants							
basic calculation							
measurement							
drawing							
coping with weather							
artistic qualities							
caring/helping							
physical dexterity							
dealing with people							
being creative							
working hard physically							
designing							
being tactful/diplomatic							
being efficient							
having an eye for detail							
working with figures							
handling food							
healing							
thinking very carefully							
using your imagination							
showing your initiative							
being inventive							
leading other people							
making decisions							
solving problems							
managing money							
managing people							
having a good memory							

continues on next page....

SKILLS	ACHIEVEMENTS						
	1	2	3	4	5	6	TOTALS
organising carefully							
coping outdoors							
having patience							
being persistent							
planning							
being trustworthy							
repairing							
researching							
using science							
being self-disciplined							
selling/salesmanship							
having stamina							
talking to people							
listening to others							
working with a team							
working on your own							
being meticulous							
knowing machinery							
working with hands							
writing							
explaining to others							

Now add up the "scores" of each skill and list the top ten below. These skills are ones which you can consider to be your special skills, those which have helped you achieve the things from which you have gained satisfaction.

YOUR SPECIAL SKILLS
1=
2=
3=
4=
5=
6=
7=
8=
9=
10=

5. Doing something about it!

5.1 Your own support network

Don't try and cope with everything on your own. Build up a support network of people you know, or get to know, who will help. You may be in a position to offer help to others too.

You will find it useful to make a list of the people who can help you in the following situations and share with them the notion that you may well be going to ask for their advice, help and support.

To whom would you go for help with:

> medical problems?
>
> experiencing difficulties with writing an essay?
>
> a feeling of not being able to cope with the work load?
>
> difficulties with the family/friends?
>
> financial difficulties?
>
> accommodation problems?
>
> missing a lecture?
>
> not being able to find a particular book?
>
> finding discussion groups difficult?
>
> not knowing where a Tutorial is to be held?

Actually make a list of sources of help, from the immediate "good friend" to the more professional source of counselling. Your College/University will certainly have a form of counselling available to you. Your Students' Union should be able to give advice on a wide variety of matters.

REMEMBER

You do not have to be clever to get a degree! The most important single idea to remember is that you do NOT have to be CLEVER to be successful in Higher Education:

> - you have to be keen to learn!
> - you have to learn to be systematic and well organised![2]

These two qualities are ones which I am sure you have in abundance. I can say that confidently because I have met so many adults who have wanted to get back into education and who have, once they have realised that it is perfectly possible to become systematic and organised, been able to develop the necessary skills to cope with business of being a student.

---

[2]. *See especially Section 16: Getting organised for learning.*

Studying Successfully

PART TWO

Study Skills

You do NOT need to read every section in Part Two.
You can:
just dip into a section which looks interesting to you
(or which you think you need to read),
or you can do the diagnostic tests in the Introduction
(and then do the sections where you find you are weak).
Those of you using the book on your own note that:
you do not have to rush:
take things steadily and
work at your own pace.

INTRODUCTION TO PART TWO

Part Two is concerned with the skills of **academic rigour**. The following Sections, 16-31, deal with some of the major tools of study which most students need in their 6th Form "A" levels, in Access Courses in Colleges of Further Education, in undergraduate and graduate courses in Universities.

You need to learn how to collect relevant evidence about your subject, collate that evidence, weigh it carefully, come to tentative conclusions and then present it in an acceptable format. This process enables you to become familiar with and knowledgeable about the subject. Implicit in this approach is the notion that you must continually be reviewing the evidence in case anything new is revealed which affects the tentative conclusions to which you have come.

This part of the book is divided into the following Sections.

16. Getting organised	17. Reading	18. Writing essays
19. Special studies	20. Questionnaires	21. Statistics
22. Class	23. Culture	24. Setting out work
25. Taking exams	26. Interviews	27. Punctuation etc
28. Computers	29. Philosophy	30. Using the library
31. Lectures.		

YOU ARE NOT SUPPOSED TO KNOW ALL ABOUT THESE NOW! IF YOU DID THEN THERE WOULDN'T BE MUCH POINT IN READING THIS BOOK!

Self assessment and diagnosis in Study Skills

To start you should complete the following pages where I ask 20 questions about the areas with which each of the above Sections deals. This will enable you to identify the areas where you have weakness and work on those first. It depends upon you being honest! You should be able to interpret the results yourself, but you may prefer someone else to go through it with you.

Instructions
1. Indicate to what extent you know about the skills/knowledge listed in the Sections, on a scale of 1 = "Not at all." 5 = "Fully."
2. Add up the numbers you have chosen in each column.
3. Add up the total for that Section.
4. When you have answered all the questions look back and identify those Sections with the lowest scores: it is these Sections that I would advise you to tackle first. You can also identify the individual questions where you score low and then give more time to these areas within the Sections.

The purposes of this process are to:
- set out clearly what you will be able to do when you've finished the book!
- assess what you already know.
- identify what you need to find out about
- help you to prioritise your learning

Don't regard this exercise as a threat. Look at it as going to a doctor and getting a diagnosis before prescription!

I recommend that you use this as a means of monitoring your progress by going through the questions again as you progress through the book and re-marking yourself[1]. It's a bit like checking up with the doctor that you are actually getting better!

One of the most important developments you can make is being able to evaluate the adequacy and sufficiency of your own learning and begin to identify the next stage of your own personal development, so that in the long run you take on a major responsibility for your own learning.

You should start with seeing if you really are getting yourself organised in order to do that learning!

PLEASE REMEMBER:
YOU DO NOT HAVE TO READ EVERY SECTION
USE ONLY THOSE SECTIONS
WHICH ARE RELEVANT
TO YOUR PARTICULAR STAGE AT PRESENT
DO NOT TRY AND DO IT ALL AT ONCE!

---

[1]. *See page 19 of this section.*

16:GETTING ORGANISED FOR LEARNING

(1 = "Not at all." 5 = "Fully.")

To what extent have you identified clearly and precisely

your learning objectives	①	②	③	④	⑤
what and how you learn	①	②	③	④	⑤
how best to learn from learning experiences	①	②	③	④	⑤
relevant learning theory	①	②	③	④	⑤

To what extent have you been systematic and organised a timetable for

your academic work	①	②	③	④	⑤
your personal life	①	②	③	④	⑤

To what extent have you planned your activities

for the year/month/week/day	①	②	③	④	⑤

To what extent have you organised information on:

Addresses etc	①	②	③	④	⑤
Notes etc	①	②	③	④	⑤

To what extent have you consciously and systematically organised:

time of your own	①	②	③	④	⑤
space of your own	①	②	③	④	⑤
understanding, support and encouragement	①	②	③	④	⑤

To what extent have you dealt with

Distractions	①	②	③	④	⑤
Concentration span	①	②	③	④	⑤

To what extent have you dealt with your

physical health	①	②	③	④	⑤
mental health	①	②	③	④	⑤

To what extent would you be able to identify

stress in yourself	①	②	③	④	⑤
causes of stress	①	②	③	④	⑤

How much do you know about

relaxing	①	②	③	④	⑤
dealing with stress caused by study	①	②	③	④	⑤

Add up the totals in each column

GRAND TOTAL FOR SECTION 16
GETTING ORGANISED

17:READING

	(1 = "Not at all." 5 = "Fully.")				

To what extent are you aware of:

	1	2	3	4	5
the range of what is to be read on your course	①	②	③	④	⑤
where to obtain the books etc	①	②	③	④	⑤
how to avoid unnecessary reading	①	②	③	④	⑤
the various purposes of reading	①	②	③	④	⑤

To what extent are you aware of such strategies for reading as:

	1	2	3	4	5
Skimming	①	②	③	④	⑤
Scanning	①	②	③	④	⑤
Detailed reading	①	②	③	④	⑤
Speed of reading	①	②	③	④	⑤
Reading actively	①	②	③	④	⑤

To what extent are you aware of the stages in reading such as:

	1	2	3	4	5
Settling down to skim/scan	①	②	③	④	⑤
Establishing rituals	①	②	③	④	⑤
Wrapping your mind around a book	①	②	③	④	⑤
Skimming/scanning	①	②	③	④	⑤
Questioning the material	①	②	③	④	⑤
Reading the material	①	②	③	④	⑤
Recalling the material	①	②	③	④	⑤
Making notes about the material	①	②	③	④	⑤
Reviewing the material.	①	②	③	④	⑤

To what extent have you:

	1	2	3	4	5
evolved a system for recording what you've read	①	②	③	④	⑤
a good knowledge of associated abbreviations	①	②	③	④	⑤

Add up the totals in each column

GRAND TOTAL FOR SECTION 17
READING

18:PRESENTATION/SEMINAR

(1 = "Not at all." 5 = "Fully.")

To what extent do you know about

planning a presentation/seminar ① ② ③ ④ ⑤

choosing appropriate methods ① ② ③ ④ ⑤

being original/imaginative ① ② ③ ④ ⑤

To what extent do you know how to use your verbal skills i.e.

clarity ① ② ③ ④ ⑤

pacing ① ② ③ ④ ⑤

variety of tone, pitch, volume ① ② ③ ④ ⑤

"Liveliness" ① ② ③ ④ ⑤

To what extent do you know about ① ② ③ ④ ⑤

production of handout(s) ① ② ③ ④ ⑤

OHP's ① ② ③ ④ ⑤

blackboards ① ② ③ ④ ⑤

flip-charts ① ② ③ ④ ⑤

slides ① ② ③ ④ ⑤

wall displays ① ② ③ ④ ⑤

working with others in a group ① ② ③ ④ ⑤

controlling natural nervousness in front of a group ① ② ③ ④ ⑤

To what extent do you know how to

construct, administer, collate and interpret a questionnaire ① ② ③ ④ ⑤

plan and administer interviews ① ② ③ ④ ⑤

plan and execute visits ① ② ③ ④ ⑤

write appropriate letters ① ② ③ ④ ⑤

Add up the totals in each column

GRAND TOTAL FOR SECTION 18
PRESENTATIONS/SEMINARS

19:WRITING ESSAYS

(1 = "Not at all." 5 = "Fully.")

To what extent have you considered the problems of:

selecting essay titles	① ② ③ ④ ⑤
interpreting key words in essay titles	① ② ③ ④ ⑤

To what extent have you used

brainstorming ideas with essays	① ② ③ ④ ⑤
doing a preliminary plan	① ② ③ ④ ⑤

To what extent do you know how to

gather data for an essay	① ② ③ ④ ⑤
set out quotations	① ② ③ ④ ⑤
set out references	① ② ③ ④ ⑤
set out notes	① ② ③ ④ ⑤
structure the introduction to an essay	① ② ③ ④ ⑤
structure the main body of an essay	① ② ③ ④ ⑤
structure the conclusion to an essay	① ② ③ ④ ⑤

To what extent do you know how to

give shape to an essay	① ② ③ ④ ⑤
use an appropriate style in an essay	① ② ③ ④ ⑤
maintain clarity of expression	① ② ③ ④ ⑤

To what extent do you know how to set out ① ② ③ ④ ⑤

the Bibliography.	① ② ③ ④ ⑤
margins, paragraphs etc.	① ② ③ ④ ⑤
headers and footers.	① ② ③ ④ ⑤
titles for sections etc	① ② ③ ④ ⑤
numbering of paragraphs, pages etc.	① ② ③ ④ ⑤

Add up the totals in each column

GRAND TOTAL FOR SECTION 19
WRITING ESSAYS

20:SPECIAL STUDIES

(1 = "Not at all." 5 = "Fully.")

To what extent do you know how to

choose and make explicit the topic	① ② ③ ④ ⑤
plan the whole project	① ② ③ ④ ⑤
collect, organise & interpret data/evidence/substantiation	① ② ③ ④ ⑤
present the material	① ② ③ ④ ⑤
identify the broad area of the topic.	① ② ③ ④ ⑤
refine the broad area to a manageable size	① ② ③ ④ ⑤
refine the title, so it is clear	① ② ③ ④ ⑤

substantiate any claims you make
　　　　　　by primary research

questionnaires	① ② ③ ④ ⑤
interviews	① ② ③ ④ ⑤
letters	① ② ③ ④ ⑤
visits	① ② ③ ④ ⑤
archive material	① ② ③ ④ ⑤
by secondary research	① ② ③ ④ ⑤
structure the introduction to a study	① ② ③ ④ ⑤
structure the main body of a study	① ② ③ ④ ⑤
structure the conclusion to a study	① ② ③ ④ ⑤

To what extent do you know how to deal with

the style of a study	① ② ③ ④ ⑤
the shape of a study	① ② ③ ④ ⑤
the "voice" of a study	① ② ③ ④ ⑤
setting out title page, illustrative material etc, etc	① ② ③ ④ ⑤

Add up the totals in each column

GRAND TOTAL FOR SECTION 20
SPECIAL STUDIES

21:QUESTIONNAIRES

(1 = "Not at all." 5 = "Fully.")

To what extent do you know how to select appropriate questions in order to:

get appropriate factual details of the person questioned   ① ② ③ ④ ⑤

To what extent do you know how to

identify clearly what it is you are trying to find out   ① ② ③ ④ ⑤

use factual, attitudinal, behavioural questions   ① ② ③ ④ ⑤

use direct/indirect/multiple choice/hypothetical questions   ① ② ③ ④ ⑤

word questions re "when?", and "how often?"   ① ② ③ ④ ⑤

select samples that are appropriate, representative   ① ② ③ ④ ⑤

select samples large enough/reply in sufficient numbers   ① ② ③ ④ ⑤

random, captive   ① ② ③ ④ ⑤

word questions to ensure confidentiality   ① ② ③ ④ ⑤

word questions to avoid bias and offence   ① ② ③ ④ ⑤

use open ended/closed questions   ① ② ③ ④ ⑤

use questions with options/multiple choice   ① ② ③ ④ ⑤

select long/short questions   ① ② ③ ④ ⑤

decide the order?   ① ② ③ ④ ⑤

To what extent do you know about:

using techniques to measure intensity where appropriate   ① ② ③ ④ ⑤

the order of the questions   ① ② ③ ④ ⑤

trying out the questionnaire   ① ② ③ ④ ⑤

using tick boxes etc that produce countable answers   ① ② ③ ④ ⑤

using secondary research to set your work in perspective   ① ② ③ ④ ⑤

To what extent do you know how to present the results:

by using different types of graphs and charts   ① ② ③ ④ ⑤

Add up the totals in each column

GRAND TOTAL FOR SECTION 21
QUESTIONNAIRES

22:STATISTICS

(1 = "Not at all." 5 = "Fully.")

To what extent do you know about how to

present data gathered from your questionnaires	① ② ③ ④ ⑤
understand statistics presented in other people's work	① ② ③ ④ ⑤

To what extent do you know about

the mean	① ② ③ ④ ⑤
the mode	① ② ③ ④ ⑤
the median	① ② ③ ④ ⑤
the midrange	① ② ③ ④ ⑤
To what extent do you know about which to use	① ② ③ ④ ⑤

To what extent do you know about

variance	① ② ③ ④ ⑤
the range	① ② ③ ④ ⑤
variance and standard deviation	① ② ③ ④ ⑤

Add up the totals in each column

AND DOUBLE THEM(since there are only 10 questions for this section)

GRAND TOTAL FOR SECTION 22
STATISTICS

23:CLASS

	(*1* = *"Not at all."* 5 = *"Fully."*)
To what extent do you know about	
how to define social class	① ② ③ ④ ⑤
the main factors generally used to define it	① ② ③ ④ ⑤
what is used in Britain for official statistics	① ② ③ ④ ⑤
what is used in America for official statistics	① ② ③ ④ ⑤
definition of social class by Karl Marx	① ② ③ ④ ⑤
definition of social class by Max Weber	① ② ③ ④ ⑤
the distribution of social class in Britain	① ② ③ ④ ⑤
the Registrar General's classification system	① ② ③ ④ ⑤
To what extent can you	
allocate social class to specific occupations	① ② ③ ④ ⑤
give examples of occupations from specific social classes	① ② ③ ④ ⑤
describe in general terms each social class	① ② ③ ④ ⑤
give the specific characteristics of each social class	① ② ③ ④ ⑤
To what extent do you know about	
'A' UPPER MIDDLE CLASS	① ② ③ ④ ⑤
'B' MIDDLE CLASS	① ② ③ ④ ⑤
'C1' LOWER MIDDLE CLASS	① ② ③ ④ ⑤
'C2' SKILLED WORKING CLASS	① ② ③ ④ ⑤
'D' UNSKILLED WORKING CLASS	① ② ③ ④ ⑤
'E' LOWEST LEVELS OF SUBSISTENCE	① ② ③ ④ ⑤
social grade of occupations	① ② ③ ④ ⑤
classifications used by market research companies	① ② ③ ④ ⑤

Add up the totals in each column

GRAND TOTAL FOR SECTION 23
CLASS

24:CULTURE

(1 = "Not at all." 5 = "Fully.")

To what extent do you know about

    today's significant people and events   ① ② ③ ④ ⑤

    the cultural heritage of our civilisation   ① ② ③ ④ ⑤

To what extent have you evaluated the "significance" of WRITERS

    historians   ① ② ③ ④ ⑤

    novelists   ① ② ③ ④ ⑤

    dramatists   ① ② ③ ④ ⑤

    poets   ① ② ③ ④ ⑤

    journalists   ① ② ③ ④ ⑤

To what extent have you evaluated the "significance" of VISUAL ARTISTS

    painters   ① ② ③ ④ ⑤

    sculptors   ① ② ③ ④ ⑤

    film makers   ① ② ③ ④ ⑤

    photographers   ① ② ③ ④ ⑤

To what extent have you evaluated the "significance" of COMPOSERS

    classical   ① ② ③ ④ ⑤

    pop   ① ② ③ ④ ⑤

To what extent have you evaluated the "significance" of SCIENTISTS

    biologists   ① ② ③ ④ ⑤

    chemists   ① ② ③ ④ ⑤

    physicists   ① ② ③ ④ ⑤

To what extent have you evaluated the "significance" of PHILOSOPHERS

                ① ② ③ ④ ⑤

To what extent have you evaluated the "significance" of POLITICIANS

    of left   ① ② ③ ④ ⑤

    of right   ① ② ③ ④ ⑤

    of green   ① ② ③ ④ ⑤

Add up the totals in each column

GRAND TOTAL FOR SECTION 24
CULTURE

25:SETTING OUT

(1 = "Not at all." 5 = "Fully.")

To what extent do you know about

presentation of academic work in general	①	②	③	④	⑤

To what extent do you know about the setting out of

margins	①	②	③	④	⑤
paragraphs	①	②	③	④	⑤
spaces	①	②	③	④	⑤
white space	①	②	③	④	⑤
headers and footers	①	②	③	④	⑤
title pages etc	①	②	③	④	⑤
a preface	①	②	③	④	⑤
photographs	①	②	③	④	⑤
diagrams and tables	①	②	③	④	⑤
maps	①	②	③	④	⑤
video and audio tapes	①	②	③	④	⑤

To what extent do you know about the setting out of

quotations	①	②	③	④	⑤
incomplete quotations	①	②	③	④	⑤
references	①	②	③	④	⑤
notes	①	②	③	④	⑤

To what extent do you know about

numbering sections, paragraphs pages etc	①	②	③	④	⑤
setting out bibliographies	①	②	③	④	⑤
setting out glossary of terms used	①	②	③	④	⑤
setting out appendices	①	②	③	④	⑤

Add up the totals in each column

GRAND TOTAL FOR SECTION 25
SETTING OUT

26:EXAMINATIONS

(1 = "Not at all." 5 = "Fully.")

To what extent do you know about checking up in advance re:

course assessment procedures, format and dates of exams	①	②	③	④	⑤

To what extent do you know about

making a revision plan	①	②	③	④	⑤
practising the exam	①	②	③	④	⑤
essay type answers	①	②	③	④	⑤
short answer questions	①	②	③	④	⑤
objective tests	①	②	③	④	⑤
practical	①	②	③	④	⑤
multiple choice questions	①	②	③	④	⑤
oral questions	①	②	③	④	⑤
seen questions	①	②	③	④	⑤
unseen questions	①	②	③	④	⑤
"ongoing revision"	①	②	③	④	⑤
specific revision	①	②	③	④	⑤
optimization of your best time	①	②	③	④	⑤

To what extent do you know about preparing mentally for the examination by

identifying your fears	①	②	③	④	⑤
using relaxation techniques	①	②	③	④	⑤
focusing	①	②	③	④	⑤

To what extent do you know about examination techniques

before the exam	①	②	③	④	⑤
during the exam	①	②	③	④	⑤
reflecting on your performance	①	②	③	④	⑤

Add up the totals in each column

GRAND TOTAL FOR SECTION 26
EXAMINATIONS

27:GRAMMAR AND PUNCTUATION

(1 = "Not at all." 5 = "Fully.")

To what extent do you know about the use of

the full stop, comma, colon, semicolon	①	②	③	④	⑤
apostrophe, quotation, question & exclamation marks	①	②	③	④	⑤
parentheses, square brackets	①	②	③	④	⑤
capital/small letters	①	②	③	④	⑤

To what extent do you know about spelling

adjectives and adverbs adding -ly	①	②	③	④	⑤
words that are often spelt incorrectly	①	②	③	④	⑤

To what extent do you know about the split infinitive   ① ② ③ ④ ⑤

To what extent do you know about

adjectives	①	②	③	④	⑤
adverbs	①	②	③	④	⑤
the articles	①	②	③	④	⑤
conjunctions	①	②	③	④	⑤
nouns/pronouns	①	②	③	④	⑤
prepositions	①	②	③	④	⑤
singular and plural	①	②	③	④	⑤
verbs	①	②	③	④	⑤
clauses and phrases	①	②	③	④	⑤
figures of speech	①	②	③	④	⑤
antonyms/synonyms/homonyms/acronyms	①	②	③	④	⑤
consonants and vowels	①	②	③	④	⑤
the direct object, indirect object, subject, main verb	①	②	③	④	⑤

Add up the totals in each column

GRAND TOTAL FOR SECTION 27
GRAMMAR AND PUNCTUATION

28: COMPUTERS

(1 = "Not at all." 5 = "Fully.")

To what extent are you

familiar with computers	①	②	③	④	⑤
aware of their use as a tool for writing essays	①	②	③	④	⑤
aware of their use as a tool for storing information	①	②	③	④	⑤

To what extent do you know about

PC's	①	②	③	④	⑤
PCW's	①	②	③	④	⑤
Apple-Macs	①	②	③	④	⑤
Acorns	①	②	③	④	⑤
Processors	①	②	③	④	⑤
Memory	①	②	③	④	⑤
Random Access Memory or RAM	①	②	③	④	⑤
Hard disc	①	②	③	④	⑤
Floppy discs	①	②	③	④	⑤
Operating systems	①	②	③	④	⑤
Windows	①	②	③	④	⑤
VGA	①	②	③	④	⑤
SVGA	①	②	③	④	⑤
Dot matrix	①	②	③	④	⑤
Daisywheel	①	②	③	④	⑤
Bubblejet	①	②	③	④	⑤
Laser	①	②	③	④	⑤

Add up the totals in each column

GRAND TOTAL FOR SECTION 28
COMPUTERS

29:PHILOSOPHY

(1 = "Not at all." 5 = "Fully.")

To what extent do you know about

philosophy in general	① ② ③ ④ ⑤
definitions of philosophy	① ② ③ ④ ⑤
philosophy as a "second order discipline"	① ② ③ ④ ⑤
metaphysics	① ② ③ ④ ⑤
epistemology	① ② ③ ④ ⑤
logic	① ② ③ ④ ⑤
ethics	① ② ③ ④ ⑤
aesthetics	① ② ③ ④ ⑤
philosophy of mind	① ② ③ ④ ⑤
political philosophy	① ② ③ ④ ⑤
social philosophy	① ② ③ ④ ⑤
the tools which philosophy provides	① ② ③ ④ ⑤
linguistic analysis	① ② ③ ④ ⑤
identifying the type of statement being dealt with	① ② ③ ④ ⑤
different types of statement	① ② ③ ④ ⑤
imperative attitude statements	① ② ③ ④ ⑤
empirical statements	① ② ③ ④ ⑤
analytic statements	① ② ③ ④ ⑤
value statements	① ② ③ ④ ⑤
metaphysical statements	① ② ③ ④ ⑤

Add up the totals in each column

*GRAND TOTAL FOR SECTION 29
PHILOSOPHY*

30: LIBRARIES

(1 = "Not at all." 5 = "Fully.")

To what extent do you know about

finding them ① ② ③ ④ ⑤

getting to know their "house rules" ① ② ③ ④ ⑤

working in a library ① ② ③ ④ ⑤

using the staff ① ② ③ ④ ⑤

classification systems in general ① ② ③ ④ ⑤

microfiche systems ① ② ③ ④ ⑤

computer based systems ① ② ③ ④ ⑤

Dewey Decimal Classification system ① ② ③ ④ ⑤

To what extent do you know about the use of

magazines, journals, periodicals and newspapers ① ② ③ ④ ⑤

To what extent do you know about choosing the right book(s) from lists of

readings etc ① ② ③ ④ ⑤

Add up the totals in each column

AND DOUBLE THEM(since there are only 10 questions for this section)

GRAND TOTAL FOR SECTION 30
LIBRARIES

31: LECTURES

(1 = "Not at all." 5 = "Fully.")

To what extent do you know about

techniques for dealing with lectures	① ② ③ ④ ⑤
becoming actively involved	① ② ③ ④ ⑤
taking notes	① ② ③ ④ ⑤
establishing a ritual	① ② ③ ④ ⑤
recording lectures	① ② ③ ④ ⑤
reviewing the lecture	① ② ③ ④ ⑤
keeping a formal record of your notes	① ② ③ ④ ⑤
integrating your lecture notes with other notes	① ② ③ ④ ⑤
the value of lectures	① ② ③ ④ ⑤
how to approach lecturers to ask questions	① ② ③ ④ ⑤

Add up the totals in each column

AND DOUBLE THEM(since there are only 10 questions for this section)

GRAND TOTAL FOR SECTION 31
LECTURES

SUMMARY OF YOUR PROGRESS

	Test 1	Test 2	Test 3	Test 4	Test 5	Test 6	Test 7
Date of test →							
16.Getting Organised							
17.Reading							
18.Presentations/Seminars							
19.Writing Essays							
20.Special Studies							
21.Questionnaires							
22.Statistics							
23.Class							
24.Culture							
25.Setting out							
26.Examinations							
27.Punctuation etc							
28.Computers							
29.Philosophy							
30.Using the library							
31.Lectures							

Use the above to keep a record of your progress whilst studying. Enter in the first column the results from the test before you read the various sections. After a suitable interval of studying, say a month, return to the tests and re-do them. I have put seven possible tests - you may not need as many as that. When you have finished your course do the test again and see in what areas you have improved.

SECTION 16
GETTING ORGANISED FOR LEARNING

Introduction

In this section I try to help you decide how best to set about the business of learning. Whether you have been away from learning for a long time, or if you are someone who has been at school or College since you were 5, I suggest that you will need to have a careful examination of the way in which you organise your life in order to learn. The onus is very much upon YOU to organise your learning. DO NOT rely on someone telling you how to do it.

What and how you learn

On any course you will be expected to study in order to learn knowledge and skills and to acquire concepts and to develop attitudes and values about the subject(s) you are studying.

Where you learn

You learn all these from a variety of experiences constructed by the course Tutor(s). There are also periods of time which you have on your own, or with colleagues, during which you are expected to study by writing essays etc, preparing presentations/seminars, reading books etc, and revising for exams.

How best to learn from these experiences

There are specific things you can do in order to maximise the learning you do from each of these learning experiences. Essentially you should prepare for the experience, participate actively in it, reflect on the experience and then record the essential points from it.

How to record and organise your learning experiences

You need to centralise your notes and other records of experience in a filed, cross-referenced system.

How best to learn from working on your own

Some theoretical considerations

It is important to examine the research done on learning so as to ensure that the effort you put into learning is maximised.

How to get rid of the clutter in your head

You should get rid of the tedious need to remember all the every-day commitments and contacts by centralising them into some sort of day by day diary.

How to get organised

Getting yourself organised to fit in the new academic commitments, with all the already existing personal and job commitments, as well as possible financial and health problems, is sometimes difficult.

1. WHAT and HOW you learn

It seems to me that there are 5 main types of learning. Look at these examples:

ATTITUDES	FACTS	CONCEPTS	SKILLS	VALUES
learning to be...	learning that...	learning to understand..	learning how to...	learning to believe in...
polite	a fork goes on the left	courtesy	curtsey	politeness
patient in traffic queues	Honda is a Japanese car company	Transport	drive a car	green issues
interested in cricket	Bradman had a score of 452	Tactics	spin the ball	playing to win
self-disciplined	a noun is a naming word	essay structure	write an essay	power of pen over sword
interested in poetry	these are the words of "Cargoes"	poetry	write a poem	the worth of poetry
interested in science	H2O=Water	science	dissect a frog	scientific method
LEARNED BY HABITUATION over a period of time, by becoming habituated. You don't fully control them. They change sometimes for no clear reason.	LEARNED BY MEMORISATION by rote, by repetition, self-testing	LEARNED BY HABITUATION over a period of time by accommod-ation of facts+skills into schemata, by question-ing,discussion testing,linking & relating.	LEARNED BY DOING by watching, by doing, trial+error. others.	LEARNED BY HABITUATION over a period of time, by thinking, comparing & talking to others.

2. WHERE you learn

As a student on a course you will be placed in various situations during the course from which you will be expected to learn. These experiences, which I have divided broadly into three categories[1], include the following:

Academic learning situations

A. Work organised/presented by the course tutor(s)
You can choose to be actively involved or not
attending a lecture*
taking dictated notes*
watching a demonstration*
watching a TV broadcast/video recording*
attending a residential course*
interacting with a computer programme†
listening to an audio cassette/radio programme*
going on a visit*

B. Work in groups
You can opt in or out of participation
taking part in a discussion†
attending a seminar/tutorial†
brain storming with others†
taking part in a role play, simulation or games†
taking part in problem solving exercises†

C. Work over which you have direct control
informal chats with Tutor(s)†
writing an essay/special study/case study
interviewing an "expert"*
conducting a questionnaire
preparing an individual presentation/seminar/tutorial
reading set texts*
reading relevant articles*
reading programmed learning text†
reading handouts from lectures/other people's notes etc*
reading your own broader reading*
reviewing your notes*
revising for examinations etc*
thinking about things on your own and coming to conclusions†

---

[1]. *Some could be in both of the first two groups, and you could be asked to do some of the activities in the third group with others, e.g. the presentations/seminars.*

---

3. How best to learn

3.1 Learning from Groups A and B

You can take full advantage of all these situations if you follow this pattern:

> ### HOW BEST TO LEARN FROM THESE EXPERIENCES
> #### PREPARE FOR THE EXPERIENCE
> #### BE ACTIVELY INVOLVED IN THE EXPERIENCE
> #### REFLECT ON THE EXPERIENCE

3.2 Preparing for the experience

Beforehand with ALL of the experiences above ALWAYS check the following:
- can you anticipate what the experience will be about?
- can you prepare a few questions you hope it will answer?
- have there been any previous ones in the series?
- read any notes you have from previous sessions

3.3 Being actively involved

All of the situations marked with a star (*) DEMAND that you
- take notes AT THE TIME of the experience. You MUST take notes. It is not easy if you allow your concentration to slip.[2]

Others, marked with a dagger (†), require you to
- jot down notes at the time if you can, or immediately following the experience (if you are too directly occupied with the experience that you are prevented from doing so).
- participate as fully as you can. It is important that you do not sit on the sidelines (unless that is your specific job within the experience)[3].

3.4 Reflecting on the experience

If you rush from one learning experience to another without time to pause for thought about what has happened and its significance for you and your learning then you may as well have stopped at home!

Three to four minutes sometimes, between lectures, spent thinking, or talking over the content matter with a friend, will help consolidate the learning that has taken place. Don't get into the habit of thinking that once finished these learning experiences are of no value again.

UNLESS YOU REFLECT the short term learning (i.e. the electrical changes in your brain) will fade. You need to convert the short term learning into long-term chemical changes in your brain.

---

[2]. See Section 31 on lectures for more detail on note taking in lectures
[3]. See below on working in groups.

Thus you will ALSO need to reflect on the learning during the evening. All of these situations need you to keep some record of what is significant for you in terms of:
- the facts/knowledge with which you are presented,
and also, in some situations:
- the important points in the skills you have been practising,
- the conclusions to which you may have come.
You need a filing system which enables you to bring together all the relevant information from these different sources.

4. How to record and organise your learning experiences

It is essential to file all the notes, handouts, photocopied articles etc, from all the learning experiences which you have in connection with your course, in a meaningful and accessible format. When you start you'll probably find a ring binder sufficient, but you will accumulate a huge amount of paper and I know from experience that the ring binder becomes a lever arch folder, that becomes a box file and then 2 box files and then a small filing cabinet. I have reduced mine now to four drawers, a cupboard under the stairs and an attic! There are problems with just keeping notes in files because you will get information etc about many different aspects of your subject in each set of notes and you will need to be able to find these references without ploughing through the whole set of files each time you want to see what you've learnt about one single aspect. Thus before you put the handout or set of notes or photocopied article in to the filing system, go through it and identify each of the key aspects within it and enter those into a "Key Word Index Book". This is a simple loose leaf folder with alphabetic divisions. In this book you will enter all the useful references to topics within your subject together with the number of the file in which the article etc is stored, so you'll be able to find it easily.

4.1 The Key Word Index Book
Thus on the page for H you may have a list like this

Keyword	See File Number
Handedness	7
Height	8,6,5
Heredity	4,9,3

For a more sophisticated (and useful) system you could add a little summary of what is contained in a particular file in addition to recording only file number.

Keyword	See File Number
Handedness	7:article by J.McGuiness on effect of handedness on whiskey drinking in Spain. *(Leave space between key words for future additions)*
Height	8:notes from J.Tanner's lecture on growth at adolescence 6:my presentation re genetic/environmental aspects 5:notes from S.Cohen's book "Dwarfs in Redcar" 1:p 3 of my notes from intro lecture by B Trenbirth
Heredity	6:my presentation re genetic/environmental aspects of height 9:P.Johnson's lecture re genetic tendencies to sloth 3:notes from K.Gorman's book "Heredity and the growth of beards"

You might make more than one entry for one aspect. For example, with the notes from J.Tanner's lecture on growth at adolescence, you could put entries under "adolescence" and under "growth" as well as under "height".

Some people prefer to use a card index system to record the key words, with a card for each key word on which you enter the number of each file in which that key word is mentioned. This is probably a better system than the book, in that it is infinitely expandable. I have transfered all mine onto a computer database.

There are other ways of organising notes, but this way seems simple. It also forces you to re-read the notes etc in a systematic and purposeful way (i.e. looking for relevant key-words to note in the Index Book, or Card Index, or computer database) before you put them to the filing system. Retrieval is simpler than searching through un-indexed notes.

> **The very process of keeping such a comprehensive and systematic record of your learning experiences will increase your learning and the retention of that learning because YOU will be organising the material in a way that is meaningful to you and making connections between new material and what you have already learned.**

5. Learning from Group C

5.1 An example

Before going any further, have a go at learning this list of letters IN ORDER and be prepared later on to recall it by writing it down in the same order. Use whatever method you like to learn it, but do not spend more than 2 minutes from now.

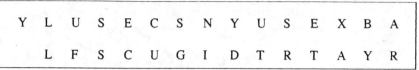

Y	L	U	S	E	C	S	N	Y	U	S	E	X	B	A
	L	F	S	C	U	G	I	D	T	R	T	A	Y	R

5.2 Some theoretical considerations

5.2.1 How much learning to learn something?

It is often assumed that the amount learned depends upon the amount of time put into learning. This is to some extent true, but research has shown that there are ways in which you can optimise the amount learnt and the time spent learning.

Experiments by Hermann Ebbinghaus almost 100 years ago show that the time spent on the first day learning a particular set of nonsense words means a reduction in the amount of time needed to learn the same words on the following day.

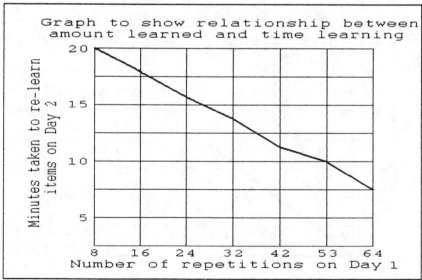

Graph to show relationship between amount learned and time learning

Minutes taken to re-learn items on Day 2 (vertical axis)
Number of repetitions on Day 1 (horizontal axis)

THE MORE TIME YOU SPEND LEARNING THE MORE YOU WILL LEARN.
But there are ways to optimise the amount learned in a given time.

5.2.2 Optimum use of time

If a group is divided into two in order to learn a skill (e.g. typing) and Group A learns the task for 1 hour per day and Group B learns it for 4 hours a day then in terms of TOTAL HOURS spent Group A takes only 55 hours, Group B takes 80 hours.

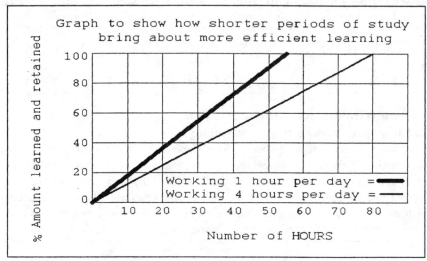

Graph to show how shorter periods of study bring about more efficient learning

BUT, in terms of DAYS, Group A takes 55 days and Group B takes only 20 days!

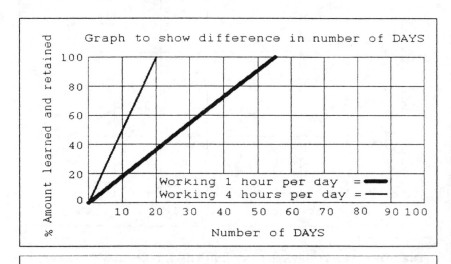

Graph to show difference in number of DAYS

LITTLE AND OFTEN IS BETTER THAN LARGE INFREQUENT CHUNKS!

5.2.3 When is the best time to learn

It is fairly clear from research that the evening is the preferred time for learning. We gave lists of words to some three groups of our students. Group A learned the material just before going to bed by reading through the list 10 times. Group B were asked to learn the same list in the same manner, but to do it just after breakfast. Group C were asked to do the same at noon. The three groups were then tested 24 hours later (i.e. Group A in the morning, Group B in the following morning, Group C at lunchtime). The results of the tests are shown below:

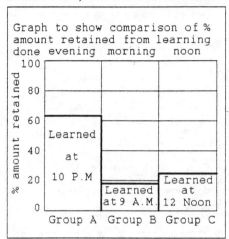

Group to show comparison of % amount retained from learning done evening morning noon

Group A recalled the material 24 hours later more successfully than those who learn it in the morning followed by a day's normal activity, and than those who learned it at noon, with the interference from the morning's activities and the thought and then the reality of the afternoon's activities. Group B did marginally better than Group C, possibly because they were further away from the night's sleep? Group A's much better performance may be able to be explained by the fact that there is little interference during the night's sleep, whereas the person learning in the morning has the full day of activity to place in competition with the learned material. **Having said all this, individuals do vary and some people are unable to function after a long day's work and prefer to get up at 6.00 a.m. and do their study then.** An evening's study could well be reviewed the following morning after sleep after an evening's study.

- During holidays you may find that different conditions apply and that your studying is best done when everyone is out of the house during the day time.
- It is also worth pointing out that a few minutes spent on buses, or between lectures or waiting for the kettle to boil, are not to be ignored in terms of either preparing for the next learning experience, reflecting on the previous one, or reviewing some material to be learned.

However, it is possible that the physiological conditions of sleep are more likely to help the electrical changes in the brain to become more permanent chemical ones. Little research at present has been done on this.

> THE QUALITY OF LEARNING DONE IN THE EVENING
> IS **PROBABLY** BETTER THAN THAT DONE AT OTHER TIMES

5.2.4 Concentration

You will know from your own experience that when you start a piece of studying concentration level is high, but that it falls off after a time and then picks up a little just after that. Each person has a different attention span, but it seems to average at about 20-25 minutes. The range is very wide and some people can manage as much as an hour at high concentration levels. You will be able to tell when your concentration wanes.

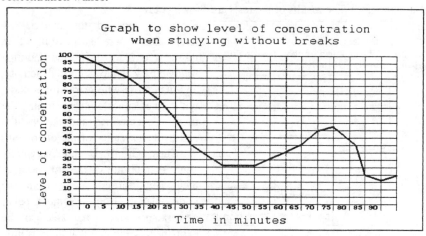

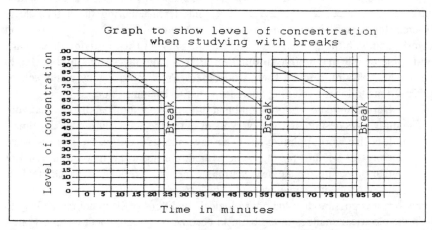

TAKE BREAKS WHEN CONCENTRATION WANES
AND YOU'LL CONCENTRATE MORE ON RETURN.
But do not concentrate on something different
or you may take time getting your mind back to where you were!

5.2.5 Memory

Research has shown that your ability to recall things has a similar pattern to that of concentration:

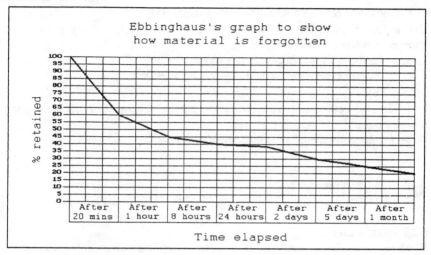

The interesting parallel continues: if you review the material regularly then the recall is improved:

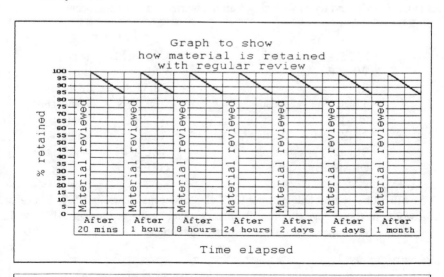

REVISE ALL MATERIAL AT REGULAR INTERVALS
MAKE A REVISION TIMETABLE IMMEDIATELY

5.2.6 The causes of forgetting/remembering

These are, perhaps surprisingly, not very clear. Some say that what we learn gradually fades away to nothing. Others say that we forget because other experiences interfere with what have previously learnt.

One aspect of forgetting is quite well researched and that is the physiological changes which occur within the brain.

memory has been shown to consist of two stages:

1. Electrical activity which links up a network of brain cells,

followed by:

2. Chemical changes in the brain cells which make a more permanent memory trace.

Stage 1 is not permanent and is thus subject to being lost quite quickly.

REVIEWING MATERIAL AFTER FIRST LEARNING MAKES
THE MORE PERMANENT CHEMICAL CHANGES MORE LIKELY TO OCCUR

5.2.7 Interference

It can be shown that it is more difficult to learn two lists of similar meanings than it is to learn two lists of widely different meanings. Read through LIST A twice, slowly, then try to write down all the words you remember. Now read through LIST B twice, slowly, and try to write down all the words you can remember.

LIST A		LIST B	
BLACK	quick	CARMINE	slow
WHITE	fast	GREY	angry
RED	rapid	SILVER	mobile
YELLOW	speedy	GOLDEN	clandestine
PURPLE	swift	AZURE	bald
PINK	fleet	ROSE	damp
BLUE	nimble	SALMON	obsequious
ORANGE	prompt	GREEN	shining

You will probably find that learning LIST B is easier than learning LIST A because the words in B are very different from each other, whereas those in LIST A are extremely close in meaning and difficult to differentiate.

DON'T REVISE THINGS THAT ARE SIMILAR TOO CLOSELY TOGETHER

5.2.8 The bad news: Retroactive interference

THE MORE YOU LEARN THE MORE YOU FORGET!

Try remembering the letters from the exercise I asked you to do on page 7 of this section! You have tried out so many different lists and read so many different pieces of information that, unless you have a remarkable memory, the interference from the new learning will have interfered with the learning of the first list that you tackled.

This has serious implications for the sort of learning which is required in many academic courses. This is especially bad news for those who are studying one undifferentiated subject where the learning of one aspect is closely similar to that in another since it has been shown that there is more likelihood of forgetting taking place in these cases.

5.2.9 Pro-active interference

Further problems can arise too from material you have learned in the past interfering with new material.

5.2.10 The good news

However, there is a piece of good news for you.

If you haven't already spotted it, that list of letters has a meaning, a meaning which if you **had** spotted, would have enabled you to write the list down with no difficulty whatsoever! Have another look at the list of page 7 and then have a look at my name and the title of this book and try to see the connection. First at it see don't you if backwards it try.

This is the good news and its implications are very important for the way you actually structure the material BEFORE you learn it.

NEVER LEARN WHAT YOU DON'T UNDERSTAND

YOU
MUST
STRUCTURE
THE MATERIAL YOU WISH
TO LEARN
---

6. Discussion and learning

6.1 Acquiring concepts

Don't worry too much about this! It tends to happen without you being aware of it! Not a great deal of meaningful experimental work has been done that can easily be transferred into the learning context. The broad general points that seem to emerge are that the acquisition of concepts can be done most speedily by learning examples from a narrow context. The ability to apply what is learned in a broader framework is more easily done by then having examples from the broader context. In a way a little like the teacher being trained to understand the theory of teaching and then being placed in a situation where s/he will encounter a narrow range of teaching problems on a teaching practice before being exposed to the full range when s/he starts teaching.

Much acquisition of concepts and formation of attitudes and values within your subject area comes from discussion. That is one of the reasons why studying alone, without contact with other students, is not recommended[4]. The discussions, both formally organised by the course Tutor(s) and the informal chats between lectures, and over lunch, or organised by self help groups, do much to encourage these developments. Self help groups are groups of students who organise themselves to meet regularly to discuss and to help each other to get through the course as easily and as painlessly as possible. They can be large or small, formal or informal. They are often the most effective way in which students learn the concepts, attitudes and values implicit within the course. We evaluated our course every year and one of the open ended questions was "What do you think was the source of most of your learning?" Each year over 76% of students replied: "Other Students" (Not very flattering to the lecturers)!!

6.2 Working in groups

Some students find being a member of a group quite difficult. I must point out the advantages of taking part in group activities, since they are situations where a great deal of learning takes place. Many of the other learning situations which we have listed under Group A (p.3 above) are essentially passive. The lecturer talks and if you wish you can sit there and let it flow in one ear and out of the other. You have to force yourself to become active and participate, simply by taking notes. There is little interaction and little challenge to which you can respond actively at the time.

---

[4]. *We were in a position to see this on our Access Course: we frequently had students who could not attend the discussion sessions following lectures and who left immediately after the formal lecture. They did all the work in terms of essays, questionnaires, special studies and so on, but had little contact with other students. Of the 17 students who were in this position, only 3 stayed the course which is only 17.64%, as opposed to a retention rate of over 90% for those who attended the full course.*

However, that doesn't help to cope with the exposure which is sometimes felt in such groups. I would hope that the Tutor(s) running the group would help all members to relax and feel at ease with other members. Most Tutors use "ice-breakers", or "getting to know each other sessions", which are very useful in breaking down barriers and relaxing the participants. If you do find problems (and that is not unusual) then don't hesitate to approach the Tutor(s) and express your concerns. Then the Tutor(s) will be able to respond to your difficulties. At the root of such problems is usually your lack of confidence in such situations and I can only say, keep trying with it. You cannot lose much in these situations and you can gain a huge amount of learning from them!

If you do find group work difficult, it may be useful for you to write down precisely what it is you find difficult. You could then share that the Tutor(s), or with a sympathetic member of the group. Remember that the Tutor is there to help, not to criticise or condemn.

Groups, **if you participate**, confront you with what you have learned and ask you to articulate it, use it, think about it actively and thus re-order it and thus review and re-structure it and make it your own and thus convert it from a purely electrical, short-term piece of learning into a chemical long term piece of learning. It may also help to develop concepts of the area since you begin to apply it to differentiated examples.

There are skills, which I am sure you have, but which you need the **confidence** to apply, in group work situations:

> **preparing for the group work**
> **participating in it by:**
> listening,
> encouraging others to express their ideas,
> questioning if you don't understand,
> thinking,
> sharing,
> responding by expressing your views,
> taking criticism of your ideas*(without seeing it as a criticism of you!)*.
> **reflecting after the experience**
> *(by making notes either during or as soon as possible after the session)*

> **Discussion**
> **forces you to USE and APPLY what you have learned,**
> **makes you think about it from different viewpoints,**
> **helps you convert the short term learning into long term by**
> **making you actively re-order the material in your mind.**

7. Learning and meaning

Read through LIST A twice, slowly, then try to write down all the words you remember. Now read through LIST B twice, slowly, and try to write down all the words you can remember. Finally read through LIST C twice, slowly, and try to write down all the words you can remember.

LIST A	LIST B	LIST C
abstract	scissors	that
epitome	pencil	Penny
inspiration	rubber	black
decrepitude	book	sequins
motivation	lamp	was
enthusiasm	chair	with
peace	computer	wearing
normality	notes	little
innocence	screen	dress
flexibility	paper	neat

I am sure that you found that LIST C is quicker to learn, by far. You can organise it into a list with meaning: *"Penny was wearing that neat little black dress with sequins"*. Look again at LIST B and consider if you could impose some meaning, or extract a meaning which is there, or create a situation where all these objects could be seen, that would make it easier to remember. It is a list of things I can see on my desk as I write this page. If you know that, it makes the list immediately more memorable, because you can, if stuck, guess what would be seen on the desk. LIST A is far more difficult. It does not make sense itself, as does LIST C, nor are there any inherent connections/meanings. Further the words themselves are randomly chosen abstract nouns, and difficult to visualise. You could attempt to make up a story which includes all the words, but it's not easy! *"The man made an abstract of the epitome of inspiration. His decrepitude lessened his enthusiasm and motivation but he gained peace from the normality of his own innocence and flexibility."* I find this **almost** as difficult to recall as the bare list. However, when I test myself, perhaps because I made up the story, I do find I score marginally better than when I just tried to recall the words. The two activities will have helped consolidate learning.

> Many people find it easier to recall things rather than abstract notions.

**LEARNING IS MADE EASIER IF WHAT IS TO BE LEARNED
HAS BEEN ORGANISED BY THE LEARNER
AND MAKES SENSE TO THE LEARNER.**

7.1 Retrieving information

You will have experienced the feeling that you know something, but just cannot get it into the conscious mind. If you do crosswords, you will know what I mean. You can stare at a clue and the blanks, think you do not know it, and then some time later as extra letters are added suddenly you realise that you have known it all the time, but just could not recall it. Another instance is trying to remember the name of an old acquaintance, which teases us and then again quite suddenly appears in our consciousness and we wonder why on earth it didn't appear there before.

The implication of this is that we do have a great deal stored in our memory, more than we seem able to bring into the conscious mind at will. Some psychologists have claimed that we store every bit of sense data and thoughts and feeling that we have ever experienced.

Whether we do or not is not really relevant. What matters is that we need to be able to retrieve for examination purposes and sometimes day to day living purposes specific bits of information we have learned, or to apply previously acquired concepts, or skills into situations as they arise.

Study the following list of 32 words by reading it through just three times:

gloves, red, window, hat, twig, green, rain, peach, roof, cherry, turnip, leaf, scarf, parsnip, trunk, orange, hail, potato, apple, carrot, blue, pear, mother, chimney, father, door, daughter, branch, snow, son, overcoat, sleet. Now, without reading further, close the book and try to write down as many of the words as you can.

Now that you have tried that, WITHOUT LOOKING AT THE LIST AGAIN, write down as many of the words as you can under the following 8 headings:

Outdoor clothing, colours, parts of a house, parts of a tree, precipitation, root vegetables, fruit, family members.

My informed guess is that you will be able to recall more, knowing the headings under which the words are grouped than when you attempted it first time without the classifications. Perhaps that is because you were searching the appropriate storage place in your memory?

**RETRIEVING IS MADE EASIER IF WHAT IS TO BE RETRIEVED
WAS ORGANISED BY THE LEARNER
AND MADE SENSE TO THE LEARNER WHEN LEARNT**

If it is organised well then there are fewer problems of recall. It is more difficult to find a particular book from a shelf of books in random order than one organised in alphabetic order.

Various experiments have been done to find out what element in the processing was most significant. Three possibilities were suggested:

Visual appearance, sound and meaning. As you have probably guessed meaning is by far the most significant.

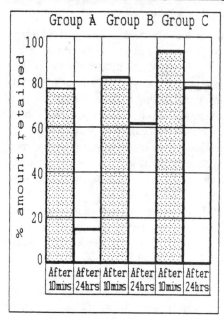

Further, the more actively involved you are at the learning stage, the higher the chance of retrieving the information at a later stage. Some of our students were divided into three groups and asked to learn the list of words above in 5 minutes. Group A were asked to learn it by silent repetition of each word. Group B were told about the categories and had the words listed under the categories before they learned it. Group C were told that the list was in categories, and were also told to categorise each word before learning the list. They were tested 10 minutes after learning the list and also without previous warning 24 hours later. Group C was by far the most successful.

THE MORE ACTIVELY INVOLVED YOU ARE AT THE LEARNING STAGE THE HIGHER THE CHANCE OF RETRIEVAL.

7.2 Motivation

If you have a good reason to learn the material then obviously you will try harder, BUT it is important to bear in mind that motivation to learn is useful only in so far as motivation enables you to spend more time learning. It is not a magic ingredient that improves anything other than your desire to learn. Motivation helps you concentrate more. Just wanting to learn will not in itself improve your skill in learning. You still need to organise and structure your learning carefully.

It is not sufficient for an athlete merely to want to win: the athlete must learn how to train systematically over a period of time before the race. Equally the athlete will find it easier to do that training if the motivation to win is there.

It is not sufficient for a student merely to want to learn: the student must learn how to learn systematically over a period of time before the exam. Equally the student will find it easier to do that learning if the motivation to learn is there.

---

8. Some aids to memory

Learning by rote

Learning lists etc

It has been shown that the learning of lists of formulae or vocabulary etc is much improved if the items are presented to the learner in such a way that a new item is tested after a short delay, then as that item is learned more securely, it is presented with a longer delay. The ideal delay is just short of the longest time that it can be remembered! You would have to rely here on a friend or a well constructed computer programme[5].

The computer asks for the list of items to be remembered in terms of a question and a correct answer. The programme then presents the question. The learner inputs the answer. If the answer is wrong the computer presents the student with the correct answer and asks that question again. It continues to do this until the student responds with the correct answer. It then asks the next question and does the same, following it with a re-test of the first question. If correct the computer presents the second question. If correct it moves to the third, after which it returns to the first and second and then third and so on. When each question has been correctly answered three times without an incorrect answer the computer leaves that question out and proceeds. The programme deals with 10 items in each session.

8.3 Chanting

Breaking down what is to be learned into small segments seems, to assist memory too. It is easier to learn a poem than a piece of prose for at least three reasons:

- 1. the rhymes suggest the following line
- 2. the lines are usually short
- 3. the rhythm allows you to break the material into natural chunks.

Examples: I before E except after C

> 30 days hath September, April June and November.
> All the rest have 31, except February alone,
> Which has 28 days clear
> And 29 in each Leap Year.

8.4 Read, write and recall

I find this one of the most potent ways of learning. I read what I am supposed to learn, in a manageable chunk and make a summary of it in my own words in writing. I then re-read the original and then read what I have written, make any adjustments and then put the book and my summary to one side and write out what I think I should re-call.

5. *A simple example of this is available from myself to work on IBM compatible PC's. It is on the disc which contains the diagnostic tests contained in this book. The disc costs £15.*

8.5 Other Mnemonics

I have never found these much use! But quite a few of our Access students have reported good results with several of them. They were frowned upon until recently when research has shown that some of the techniques do allow the brain to convert the short term electrical impulses acquired through them into the more permanent chemical changes. It is also possible that they help gain access quickly to the memory which is often "on the tip of the tongue". However, some people, myself included, find them irritating and actually get in the way of old fashioned chanting!!!

Acronyms

Making up a word, the initial letters of which represent the initial letters of what you want to recall:

QANGO: Quasi autonomous non-governmental organisation.

Mnemonic sentence

Making up a sentence, the first letters of each word being the initial letter of what you want to remember:

Richard of York Gained Battles In Vain, being the colours of the spectrum.

Every Good Boy Deserves Favour for EGBDF, notes on lines of treble clef.

Number rhyme

A rather complicated, but I am assured very effective, method of remembering lists where order is important:

Give each cardinal number a rhyming associated word:

1=gun, 2=shoe, 3=tea, 4=crow, 5=hive, 6=sticks, 7=heaven, 8=grate, 9=wine, 10=hen, 11=Devon, 12=shelf

Now you must imagine your list of items that you want to remember to be visually associated with each of the images above. If there are more than twelve then start again at one.

House walk

A rather similar one, but which enables you to pick out the items in non-sequential order, is to imagine a walk through your house where you leave each of the items in the list in given places and visualise them being there. The first might be the front door, then the living room, then the kitchen and so on.

9. Getting down to work!

9.1 Getting organised!

A thing to realise is that no one can do it for you! People going into Further and Higher Education very often wait for someone to tell them what to do. Don't wait for that to happen! The onus is on YOU to decide that you want to succeed and on YOU to find out what you need to do in order to succeed.

DO NOT WAIT FOR SOMEONE TO TELL YOU!! YOU must be the one in charge and making the decisions and making the plans and organising yourself.
At the beginning of this book I said that you don't have to be clever to get on in Higher Education: you need to be well organised. You need to manage your time.

NEVER WAIT FOR "THE MUSE" TO COME.
THE MUSE VISITS ONLY THOSE WHO ARE ALREADY WORKING!!

This rest of this section is concerned with getting you organised! You need to get the tools of the trade, so you are not "faffing about" borrowing pencils etc, and panicking because you don't know where the rubber is! And you need to get rid of the clutter of things to remember. Get them written down. Hopefully this will encourage you to become systematic and to set up regular rituals which make the task of learning and study so much easier.

9.2 Organise the "Tools of the Trade"!

The Tools of the Trade!
a decent pen, and/or a set of cheap but reliable ball point pens
pencils with rubbers on the end and good sharpener
(these are good for taking notes, provided you always re-write them in pen)
a set of coloured pencils, a calculator,
a transparent plastic ruler
(with inches in 10ths and 12ths and centimetres and millimetres)
paperclips, small stapler, hole punch, Tippex
a small pair of scissors
pads of A4 wide lined paper
(I prefer with margins on left and right)
ring binder(s), note-book(s)
any relevant books
a diary/filofax (see below)
a good briefcase that will take the above
(plastic bags do not protect delicate essays!)
You may also need specialised tools of your particular subject.
e.g. compasses, dividers etc for Maths.

Keep them in the briefcase. Always put them back when you've finished with them. Always know where the briefcase is. Make sure you have it with you and don't be spending time at the last minute asking to borrow a pen and a piece of paper at your lecture/tutorial! Don't let that become a cluttering worry. You wouldn't expect a plumber to ask you for a blowlamp!

9.3 Organise your information

There are so many things which you need not carry around in your head and which are better outside and visible and able to be seen at a glance and altered and updated and NOT left cluttering up your mind in an inefficient and haphazard muddle! Get the clutter out of your head! This takes another load out of your over filled memory! You no longer have to worry about remembering addresses, telephone numbers and names! You no longer have to worry about remembering to bring a set of notes!

Addresses etc

- Try to centralise all your addresses and contacts. At an appropriate place in your diary/filofax/computer database, put down all your important addresses and telephone numbers.

- These would include friends, relatives etc, but also contacts for your study, tutors, bookshops, libraries, experts to consult and so on. They are best put in alphabetic order by surname.

Notes etc

- Be systematic with your notes. Look at p.5 ff of this section for suggestions as to systematic note-taking.

GET THE CLUTTER OUT OF YOUR HEAD!
ORGANISE YOUR ADDRESSES AND YOUR NOTES

9.4 Organise your commitments

Get the clutter out of your head! Birthdays, shopping, write to a friend, walk the dog, see the Tutor, pay the papers, write the essay, make the supper, put a button on the shirt...each day has its list of things to be done.

GET IT OUT OF YOUR HEAD AND INTO AN ORGANISED LIST WHERE YOU CAN BEGIN TO TAKE CONTROL OF IT RATHER THAN YOU RE-ACTING TO THE FIRST THING YOU REMEMBER!

You need to get a year planner or an organiser and start filling in all the commitments of which you are aware[6]. My own preference is for a diary/filofax which has a page for each day so that each day can be broken down into hours, but also to have a year planner which gives an overview of the whole academic year. I prefer the loose leaf filofax which has pages inserted onto a 6 ring binder system because you can get rid of the pages you no longer need without ruining the binding

---

[6]. *If you have a computer then you will have access to many of the computer driven organiser diaries, which in the long run make life much simpler.*

---

as happens with a simple diary. A simpler and cheaper way is to use a small ring binder book[7].

Organise your time

The diary/filofax

Into the diary and the year planner you should enter:

Year by year
- Start and end of terms and holidays
- Birthdays of friends and family
- Any specific engagements you already have such as friends for a meal, sporting activities, walks etc.

Term by term(Some of these may belong in the year by year list)
- Dates by which important applications have to be completed and sent off
- Examination dates
- Lectures you must attend
- Tutorials seminars you must attend
- Deadlines for work to be handed in
- Revision timetable dates and content matter

This can be broken down later into deadlines for each piece of work, e.g.
- when letters must be sent off for a survey
- when a questionnaire is to be collated
- when particular revision must be repeated.

Look carefully at the balance and pattern of your time. Have you set aside time for your friends and family? Make sure if you have a family that you build in time to be with them wholeheartedly. One of the things I have found when teaching adults is that very often their enthusiasm for learning makes them forget their family! It is vital that the time you give to yourself is balanced by time you can devote entirely to others. If they know that you need to have time to yourself then make sure that when you do give time to them that it really is uncluttered by your preoccupations.

Week by week

Don't forget things like shopping and cleaning and eating have to be accounted for in your time allocation for each week! If you feel you are not using your time to best effect at present then keep a diary for a week noting carefully each day what you do in each hour from 12 midnight to 12 midnight. I am sure you will find that there are many hours which you can begin to "save". It is usually TV which takes

---

[7]. *I also find very useful a little electronic device, the size of a credit card, into which I can enter phone numbers and addresses and, most importantly, set alarms which sound a beeper and display a message telling me what I am about to be doing next!! There are even more sophisticated versions of these now on the market. But I think they are for the really absent minded/lazy person like me who can't be bothered to look in the filofax/diary!*

---

up a lot of time. Once you have become a student then you should perhaps re-consider the amount of time you devote to TV!

Day by Day "Rituals"

Plan each day carefully - trying to give yourself time at the beginning and end of the day for reflection on what is about to happen and what has happened.

Keep a section in your diary/filofax for jotting down anything which occurs to you that you want to do something about and look through it in the morning and evening sessions.

It is useful to have a THINGS TO DO section into which you can jot down things as they come to you under separate headings such as:

- - long term academic things to do
- - short term academic things to do
- - shopping
- - house work
- - odd things that came to you!

You then sort these things out when you next have a planning session either at the start or the end of the day[8].

THE START OF THE DAY.

- Spend time at the beginning of each day having a planning session:

- - checking your diary for the week ahead to make sure you haven't got some deadline in front of you, or a birthday, is time well spent!
- - checking your jotter pages.

- Plan your day carefully in the light of your deadlines, don't just rush into the day doing the first thing you happen to fancy doing!

- Write out a schedule for the day. There are things which you will need to do, but which are possibly unpleasant - you should fit these into your schedule for the day. Give yourself a treat too, at some point in the day, perhaps as a reward for doing a difficult or unpleasant task.

DURING THE DAY

- Jot down any things which occur to you that might be worth noting for you to take action on later in your jotter pages.

- Take notes as indicated above (pp 4 ff).

- Enter any new deadlines etc into the diary part.

---

[8]. *Postit notes also are useful, because you can put them in places where you will see them at the right time! "Phone Eleanor," said one of Tom's the other day stuck to the telephone! "Pay the milkman," said one of mine stuck to a milk bottle! Mary stuck one on the TV screen saying "Record film 8.55 BBC2". Because they are removable, they are also useful for sticking to papers for filing, indicating in which section of your system they are to be filed.*

THE EVENING - don't start until you've eaten!

- Spend time at the start of each evening session having a planning session:
    - checking your diary again for the week ahead to make sure you haven't got some deadline in front of you, or a birthday, is time well spent!
    - try to allocate time for each activity. This is hard at first when you may not be too sure of how long something takes, but with experience you'll get the feel for this.
    - enter any new deadlines onto your year planner
    - checking your jotter pages for anything that's cropped up during the day.
    - noting any things which are outstanding,
    - anything needed for tomorrow.
- Plan the evening's activities,
- Check if there are things coming up you need to start on this evening. Don't suddenly realise tomorrow morning that you needed to see someone, give in an essay or take the dog to the vet!
- Set aside some time during the evening to go over the day asking yourself the question what did I learn from today's learning experiences?
- Make sure you have coped with everything by at least allocating a time for it and then turn to the study for the evening with an uncluttered, unpreoccupied mind!!! (Well, that's the ideal situation to aim at!!!)

THE LAST THING AT NIGHT.

- **Write up your notes from lectures or reading and so on. Time spent reviewing these things on a regular basis pays enormous dividends.**
- Check again what is happening tomorrow.
    - e.g. - Is there a lecture or other learning experience?
        - What is it likely to be about, make a list of topics it should cover.
        - Check the previous one in the series and set the coming one in context.
- Set out all the things you will need for tomorrow.

9.5 Actually settling down to work

It's OK for me to say set aside this time for work and that time for housework and so on, but when you get to the hour you are supposed to be studying your mind is in a whirl, or you feel so drained, or the kids start up a racket...what should you do?!

Many of the distractions like cleaning the house, shopping can be allocated specific times.

Soon I'm sure you'll sort them so they don't interrupt your study time. Often you'll procrastinate by insisting on doing something mundane to put off returning to study.

Ask why can't you settle.

Why can't I settle?

1. Broad motivational reasons to do with the topic itself.
   you dislike the subject
   you've been told by the Tutor that it's useful but you aren't convinced
   you see no relevance to the aims of getting your qualification
   you know it's relevant, but it is deadly boring
2. Narrower motivational reasons to do with a particular aspect of the subject
   you are really keen and interested in this aspect
   you've missed a couple of lessons and are really at sea with this
3. Distractions that are nothing to do with either of the above
   you can't stand the Tutor...You are about to go to a party...You haven't eaten for 5 hours...You cannot find the right book!!! You've been studying for an hour and a half already...You also have 2 other essays for tomorrow morning...The TV is on...You have something you'd rather be doing.

You can do something about most of them, even if it is only to put things on the back burner! It does take time to get the system well organised, but it really is worth the effort in the long run. Get into the habit and it's all much easier.

ESTABLISH A DAY BY DAY RITUAL (p.18 above)
WHICH MAKES YOU TO DO AN HABITUAL/MECHANICAL TASK
AND WHICH ITSELF LEADS INTO
THE ACTUAL LEARNING TASKS THAT YOU HAVE.

---

10. Get home sorted out to help you study

You will need three things from home:

10.1 Time of your own

This is time which is uninterrupted and guilt free! This is time which you devote to study. This you should be able to arrange with agreement from others in your life, providing you give fully to them at other times.

10.2 Space of your own

This is space which is uninterrupted and guilt free! This is where you can spread out your books and writing papers without fear of them being tidied away etc. This is not easy to come by and should be done in consultation with those with whom you live. There is no point in commandeering a space which belongs to someone

---

else. The guilt will get you even if the other person doesn't! Together you need to be able to find a quiet space in the house which is going to be suitable for study.
Ask the following questions: have you got:
- easy access to main reference/text books (a bookshelf within arms length)?
- writing equipment - paper, ink, pens, pencils, rubbers, paper-clips, scissors, glue, Tippex etc? (i.e. all the things in your brief-case)
- good lighting?
- a comfortable chair and a good work space such as a desk/table?
- warmth?

10.3 Support, understanding and encouragement!

You should consult carefully with those with whom you live and gain their support and understanding for what may well be a difficult set of changes for them as well as yourself if you decide to go ahead with the taking on a course.

It is not an easy position for those around you to be in, seeing you with all the pressures of your new way of life and they may well feel threatened by that new way of life, a new set of friends, even a new way of thinking and new values and attitudes as time goes on. Be very aware of their needs as well as your own. They too will need your support, understanding and encouragement!

FROM HOME YOU NEED
TIME
SPACE AND SUPPORT
AND SO DO THOSE AROUND YOU!

---

11. You and your health

Be aware of your state of health. Always try to balance your days and your diet!
By balancing your days I mean ensure that you have varied activities and include some physical exercise, even if this is just going for a walk. Be aware too that stress can creep up on you unaware.

11.1 Physical health

Your brain

It is important for you to realise that the brain takes 25% of the oxygen you take in. The blood getting to the brain with the oxygen needs uncluttered veins through which to travel. Exercise of your body actually does help the body help the brain.

Check-up

Most General Practices run "well men" and "well women" clinics, where you are able to go and get a general check-up to make sure that you are normally fit and healthy.

If you haven't done this before then drop in to the surgery, or ring up and make an appointment. You will receive a check-up and advice on any aspect of your health which may be discovered to cause concern.

11.2 Mental health

No, I am not suggesting that you have gone crazy!

I am concerned that you should be aware of the fact that we live in an age of insecurity.

Abnormal loads of stress have been arriving on most people, be it from job insecurity, financial strain or relationships.

Joining a course of study, where you may well feel scrutinized by your fellow students and by your Tutors and examinations, will, unless you have the thickness of skin of an elephant, put some pressure on you. That and the change in patterns of what went in your home and other people within the family re-acting to you the student, can add to that pressure.

Very often just being aware that pressure is building up and then attempting to identify the causes can be enough for you to be able to bring it out into the open and talk it over with those concerned, well before any damage is done.

Identifying stress

Have you noticed any changes in?		
Sleep patterns	physical health	relationships
increase in dreams	eating	moods
decrease in dreams	blood pressure	level of anxiety

If there are significant changes in several of the above you could well be exhibiting signs of stress.

Stress and anxiety are in fact needed by human beings to cope with life! Anxiety is the body warning you that you need to do something to protect yourself from some perceived threat. Stress is a warning that you are reaching the limits of your body's resources. In bearable amounts they are normal and good healthy re-actions to human situations. If you have no stress/anxiety then you could well be so laid back that you will never succeed in actually doing anything! In excess, stress/anxiety can be very unpleasant. Stress and anxiety can be dealt with.

Try now taking a piece of paper and spend 7 minutes writing down any likely causes of the stress that you feel (if you have none then obviously don't make any up!). Don't try to control the writing. Let it flow by writing whatever comes to your mind in association with stress.

When your 7 minutes is up look at what you have written and try to identify what causes you have written about.

Causes of stress

- External causes

Some causes of stress are quite specific and are out there! They are things like next door's vicious Rottweiler, an examination that comes next week, a colleague who is constantly criticising.

- Internal causes

Others are more to do with our own inner fears and are less easily identified: a worry about how we appear to other people, fear of crossing a busy road, or driving in heavy traffic...sometimes just a vague fear of something...One of the worst aspects of stress is that it can come from within and the cause and root may be very difficult to identify.

Dealing with external causes of stress

Identify them! Become familiar with them. The unknown is always worse than the known! Remember the horror films: when the beast appears it is NEVER as bad as you imagined!

Dealing with external causes of stress

This is very much an attitude of mind. It is very little use anyone saying to you "Pull yourself together-things aren't as bad as you think they are!", if you are way down in a trough of depression. It is hard to get things into a clear perspective if you are suffering from anxiety and stress which is coming from within. Very often if you can identify the external causes of stress you will be better able to cope with them and that often reduces the internal stress.

If you find it impossible to identify causes of stress and yet you still have feelings of anxiety then I suggest that you consult with your GP.

Dealing with stress in general

Learning how to relax is a useful technique to help to cope with all kinds of feelings of anxiety, whatever their cause.

Lie down, or sit down in a position which is comfortable for you.

Become aware of your muscles.

Make them as tense and as tight as you can. Really pull on every one you can identify.

Then, starting with the neck muscles, say to yourself:

- "I will relax the muscles in my neck so that they are not tense and tight. They will be soft and relaxed and free."

Say this until the muscles in your neck really are soft and relaxed and free.

Then, go on to the muscles in your shoulders and say to yourself:

- "I will relax the muscles in my shoulders so that they are not tense and tight. They will be soft and relaxed and free."

Say this until the muscles in your shoulders really are soft and relaxed and free.

Then, go on to the muscles in your back and say to yourself:

- "I will relax the muscles in my back so that they are not tense and tight. They will be soft and relaxed and free."

Say this until the muscles in your back really are soft and relaxed and free.

Then go on and do the same with your stomach, your buttocks, your thighs, your ankles and finally your feet.

When you have finished that, concentrate on your breathing. Just be aware of it. Tell yourself you will be aware of the air going into your body, it resting there and then being expelled, slowly. Don't try deep breathing, just normal, light breathing. Just be aware of it and it's effect on your body. Listen to it carefully. Do this for about 3-5 minutes.

Still in the same position and still relaxed, take 6 very slow and deep breaths. again concentrating on being aware of the effect on your body. the extra oxygen travelling through your body will reach your tired muscles and exhausted brain and feed both of them. When you have completed the last of these, stay in that position and focus on the task in hand. Without moving and without tensing your muscles, focus on the plan you have for your work for the next hour or so. Make it clear in your mind. Don't try and start until you have then taken a further 4 slow deep and very aware breaths. Then you can move and start.

The whole process takes about 5 to 10 minutes and after it most people feel refreshed and calm. There are many other similar variations on this.

Relaxation and sleeping

People have problems sleeping when there is stress. If you do have problems then the relaxing exercise above can be done in bed. Instead of focusing on work you might like to focus on some repetitive and calming activity which you do. My own favourite is imagining me playing the perfect round of golf at my golf course. I have never actually got up to the 18th hole...I've always been able to drop off around the 11th or 12th holes and had the most calm and peaceful sleep!

Dealing with stress caused by courses of study

Get to know your course as ignorance of what is expected of you makes you believe you'll never succeeed, wheras the reality is never as bad as your imagined fears.

This may sound obvious but you need clear answers to the following questions:

What books do I need to read? What books do I need to purchase?

How will I be assessed?

What is the proportion of marks allocated to course work and what to examinations?

What are the deadlines for formally assessed work? What format do they take?

When are the examinations?

How long are they? What format do they take? Where do I find previous examination papers?

Are there any other forms of assessment (e.g. oral, practical)?

Where do I find previous examination papers?
Are there any other forms of assessment (e.g. oral, practical)?

BE SURE YOU ARE FIT AND TAKE REGULAR EXERCISE
BE AWARE OF STRESS AND PURPOSELY RELAX
REDUCE ACADEMIC STRESS BY IDENTIFYING
YOUR COMMITMENTS

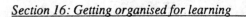

SECTION 17: READING

1.Introduction

Reading is studying and studying is reading! We may feel that the world is changing and that the future lies with interactive learning via computers and laser discs, but essentially the ability to learn from what we read, and the ability to search out and identify appropriate reading matter is at the heart of studying any topic. Certainly the job of finding appropriate references will be made easier by computers storing information and having the ability to find the particular bits we ask for, but essentially we will still have to read and interpret the relevant material and decide what weight to give it and so on.

Most of this section is about how best to read books, or large chunks of books articles etc., but much of what is said also applies to smaller extracts.

2. Deciding what to read

2.1 What is read

As a student of any subject you will be reading a huge amount of material from a wide variety of sources:

Basic text books
Recommended books
Government Reports
Research Reports
Specialist Journals
Newspaper articles
TV/Radio transcripts
Lecturer's handouts
Lecture notes from other people
Archive documents

ISLE COLLEGE
LIBRARY

2.2 Where to get books

Join as many libraries as you can! The pressure on books because of increases in student numbers is enormous and when readings are to be done for essays there is a stampede to obtain the relevant books. It is vital to make yourself known at the main library because librarians are useful allies in searching for relevant books. See Section 30, about using the library.

2.3 Some suggestions to save unnecessary reading

1. Make sure that what you read is actually relevant to your study,
2. Ask advice from Tutors about the recommended readings,
3. Ask advice from the Librarians,
4. Ask advice from other students (especially those who have successfully

completed the course) about which books and which parts are useful and in what way they are useful,

5. Try to follow up the authors mentioned by your Tutors,

6. Form self-help groups where you share out reading tasks and compare and exchange summaries.

Although I would urge you to be SELECTIVE in your reading I would also urge that: YOU **MUST** READ WHAT YOU ARE TOLD TO READ. IT IS POINTLESS GOING TO A TUTORIAL OR LECTURE WITHOUT HAVING DONE THE PRE-READING. Your Tutors will have carefully selected the books which they believe will illuminate your study, and you should never ignore their advice about relevant reading. It is impossible to criticise their choice of readings until you have read them!

3. Purposes of reading

3.1 Why identify the purpose?

It is crucial to identify the purpose of reading the material because the purpose should affect how you read the book. It's not always the same purpose as if you'd gone to the library, seen a book by an author you've enjoyed reading in the past and picked it up to read. Most people see reading as what they've always done with books. But there are different ways of reading, or STRATEGIES, depending on the PURPOSE of reading.

3.2 Some purposes

Why are you reading the book? Often it is because someone has told you to read it. Go beyond that and attempt to analyse the PURPOSE of being to told to read it.

1. to get a specific piece of information,
2. to find out if the material might be of some use,
3. to get a particular view of the author on a specific topic or topics,
4. to get some help with an assignment,
5. to understand the whole book,
6. to find out how to do something,
7. to memorise something,
8. to "criticise" the author's view(s), theory(s),
9. to "criticise" the author's style,
10. pleasure.

3.3 Scope of this section

This section is concerned essentially with how to read a book (or an extended piece of writing) in order to extract what you need from it. Thus it is referring mainly to numbers 1-7. That is not to say that reading books etc in this way for academic purposes is not pleasurable. It can become addictive!

4. Some strategies for different purposes

4.1 Skimming

This technique is useful when you don't know exactly what you are looking for! It is purposely reading about one sentence in 10, especially first and last of each paragraph.

4.2 Scanning

This technique is useful when you DO know what you are looking for! You should previously have identified several key words/phrases and/or some questions you want answering. Thus you can let your eye skip along looking for the key word or phrase in a section/chapter. You ignore all other material as much as possible and concentrate on finding the particular word/phrase for which you are searching. Just note where the relevant parts are and return to them later.

4.3 Detailed reading

This is reading almost every word from start to finish. It is not actually much use to the student until you've found out exactly what you want to read - even then it is very slow and cumbersome.

It is possible to speed up the reading process.

4.4 Speed of reading

The actual content matter of the material will affect the speed at which you are able to read: When the material is "easy", because we understand it and it is simply expressed, then we can read quite quickly. When it is less familiar, using difficult "jargon", or complex sentence structure, then we have to slow down. What is important is to realise that you can vary your reading speed. Unfortunately we tend to get into the habit of reading everything at the same pace.

4.5 Reading actively

As with all learning situations it is imperative to be involved with the reading. You cannot expect the book to teach you if all you do is look at the words!

You must be asking questions and seeking the answers while you read. For example: "Is there anything wrong with the views expressed?" "Has the author substantiated the points made?" "Is there a bias?"

5. A recommended approach

What follows is an approach which was worked out from a variety of sources by groups of students over the past 5 years on our Access course. It should be applied flexibly and taking into account the purpose of the reading and the nature of the content matter itself. It is a very useful strategy and can be applied to a wide variety of study situations, such as note taking in lectures, reading a whole book, or reading a short newspaper article.

5.1 The stages

1 = Settle
2 = Skim/Scan
3 = Question
4 = Read
5 = Recall
6 = Review

5.2 Settling down to skim/scan

Reading because you have to is not like reading for pleasure (although I have found that many students do get immense pleasure from reading for information and research once they have got over the initial fear of reading "experts").

Establish a ritual

Many students said they found it hard to start reading and that they could easily find excuses not to! One way which seems to help "get into" a book is to establish a pattern, a ritual, which you always follow to get you started.

- Get everything ready, obviously the book, but also yourself. Make the ritual a pleasurable one. It is worth being aware that you can choose the conditions in which you do your reading.

- Many students use both home and library for their reading. If you are using a library then make sure you know their house rules about which books can be taken home, and which must be read in the library itself. Many libraries provide excellent facilities for study, with individual carrells or desks for students. However, many do not and because of growing student numbers it is increasingly difficult to find places for study.

- Although sitting in a comfortable armchair may seem well suited to reading, you will find it more useful to sit at a table, since you will need to make notes. You will need your note-book, or your computer if you are using a computer to make notes. You may also want to have several other pieces of material open at relevant pages.

- Make sure you have adequate even lighting. Don't have too bright a light - use a low power bulb (less than 60 watts) in a desk lamp or diffused/reflected high powered lighting.

- Set out your favourite pen and your favourite note book at your favourite chair and desk.

- It isn't easy to read with TV on, people in the room, or other distractions. Some people find wearing headphones with "wall-paper" music to cut out other noise useful - others find that in itself distracting. Experiment and see what helps you to concentrate.

- If it is a book you have not read before then FEEL the book! Flip through the pages. Smell it. Get to its texture! And then begin to wrap your mind around it!

5.3 Skim/scan the book

Start to wrap your mind around the book

- Is there a "blurb" - the bit that is written by the publisher to entice people to read and buy the book? - Does this tell you anything about the book?
- Is there anything about the author? - Does this tell you anything about the book?
- Is there an introduction, or preface? - Does this tell you anything about the book?
- Have a look at the index and skim through the references there. - Does this tell you anything about the book?
- Are there any illustrations? - Does this tell you anything about the book?
- Are there any diagrams, tables, graphs? - Do these tell you anything about the book?

Look through it and get its structure

- What does the contents page tell you about the structure?
- Why is it organised in the way it is?
- What are the main chapter headings? (Or, with a short reading, just the main headings, or paragraphs.)

Make notes

- It's a good idea to keep notes about the books you read. It is also a useful part of the ritual. You won't be waiting for some way of starting. Over leaf is a suggested format that you may wish to use for keeping records of your reading.
- Just going through the book and jotting down the answers to the questions will get you into the book.
- I suggest this as part of the ritual. If you have a specific task to do with each book that you read then the business of getting into the book is made easier.
- Remember that reading a book does NOT mean starting at page one and forcing yourself to read every page.
- User the record card format on the next page to get you into the habit of starting each book in the same way, so that the ritual actually helps you to get into the frame of mind you need to be in in order to extract from the book what is useful to you.
- This approach also forces you to be actively involved in the process, rather than just sitting there staring as each paragraph slips by!

Possible format for record card

BOOK RECORD CARD NO:
Title:_____

Type: (e.g. Basic Text Book, Recommended book, Government Report, Research Report, Journal, article, TV, Radio Programme.)_____
Sub-Title:_____
Author(s)/Editor:_____
Nationality of author:_____
Qualifications of Author(s):_____
Publisher:_____
Address of Publisher:_____
Year of this edition:_____
Other editions:_____
Catalogue information:_____
Dewey number:_____ISBN:_____
Where it is to be found:_____
Is there a Contents?:_____
How is it divided?
(Parts/Chapters/sections?)?:_____
Are there Conclusions/Recommendations?:   [ ]
Are there any summaries?:   [ ]
Are there any appendices?:   [ ]
Is there a list of references?:   [ ]
Is there a bibliography?:   [ ]
What type of index or indices?:_____
Is there a Preface?[ ] What does this say the material's about?:

_____

Is there an Introduction? [ ]What does this say the material's about?:

_____

Is there a"blurb"? [ ]What does this say the material's about?:

_____

_____

Does it look as though it will be of use or not?:
USEFUL [ ]   NOT USEFUL [ ]   NOT SURE [ ]

5.4 Question the material

- Be clear about what you are wanting from the material. (Sometimes specific
  · sometimes just what is the author saying?)
- What specific questions are to be answered?
- Are there any key words/phrases to find?

MAKE A SPECIFIC LIST

Choose two (or more) key words (or synonyms of the key words):

Key Word 1:_____

Key Word 2:_____

Other Key words:_____

_____

_____

Main questions to be answered:

_____

_____

_____

---

and then look for these in the:

    Contents
    Index
    summaries
    headings
    first and last paragraphs of each chapter

and note which bits are relevant

Use the "skimming" technique to get an overview - don't try to read it all with detailed reading.

5.5 Read the material

- Read only those parts which are of use.
- Check off the questions/key words. If there are important passages then make a note of them - some people like to underline or use a highlighting pen. If this helps then do so - BUT MAKE SURE IT'S YOUR BOOK THAT YOU DO IT TO!
- Keep asking yourself "What does the author mean here?"
- Remember that the author will have structured the material in the same, or similar, ways as you do yours, so you should be able to identify the structure of the material.
- It is probably a good idea to check off the questions you have asked as you go through. Don't try to take copious notes.
- Keep asking:
  Is this an answer to any of my questions?
  What does the author mean here?
  What evidence does he use to substantiate any assertions?

5.6 Recall the material

- At appropriate stages (not at the end of each sentence, unless it's a very long and difficult sentence!), put the material to one side and try to recall what the author has been saying.
- It is difficult to state categorically how big the chunks should be - you will have to decide - it will depend on the difficulty of the material and on your "mood".
- This is probably the most difficult aspect of the approach. It is also the most powerful! It starts in the reading section above.
- DON'T UNDERESTIMATE THIS PART. You could well be spending as much time on this section as on all the others put together.
- You could make an attempt to jot down a few notes at this stage and then in the next stage check out how accurate you were.
- Go through your written list of questions and check if they have been answered. Write down more detailed answers as you recall them.

5.7 Review the material

- Don't jump onto this stage too quickly. Make sure you have recalled what you need. Go through a quick re-run of the previous stages of the approach.
- The temptation is to rush to the bits where you know you've not fully recalled - avoid that temptation. Be systematic. Go through the over-viewing, the skimming and then re-read, altering, adding to the notes as you do so.
- You could extend your notes about the book by writing notes in the following format:

Key words (with relevant page nos):

1   2

3   4

Brief summary of content/Chapter titles:_____

Use(s) to which you have put the material:_____

Context(s):_____

_____

Date(s) you used it:_____

_____

Reason(s) for using used it:_____

_____

How you used it:_____

_____

Relevant pages:_____

_____

Actual quotes:_____

_____

Other possible useful materials referred to in this one:_____

Where the material is:_____

6. What to do with what you've read

Having read the piece most students heave a sigh of relief and turn to the next task. Some time later they are asked to do a similar piece of work and then spend time trying to remember which book it was that had that relevant quote! So, why not keep a systematic record of all that you read?

6.1 An example

1. You have read a book, say Richard Lansdown's "Child development made simple." and you have made your full notes.

2. You review your notes and identify the topics which are relevant to you and to which you may wish to refer again in the future. You then fill in a pro forma something like the one below:

---

*Record Number:*14
Title: Child development made simple
Sub-Title: None
Author(s)/Editor: Lansdown, Richard
Nationality of author: British
Qualifications of Author(s): MA Dip Psych, PhD
Publisher: Heinemann
Address of Publisher: London
Year of this edition: 1984
Other editions: 1983,1982
Catalogue information:
Dewey number: ?
ISBN: 0-434-98599-6
Key words (with relevant page nos):
  1 Heredity. 243ff
  2 Child Development - whole book
  3 Physical development - many references v useful
  4 Cognitive development - many references v useful
  5 Emotional Development - many references v useful
  6 Piaget - best summary so far 106ff
Brief summary of content:
Summarises all major theories of human development.
Use(s) to which you have put the book:
Context(s):
  1. First essay on Human Development Access Course
  2. Essay on child development for Teaching Specialism
Date(s) you used it: 1 Nov. 90. 2 Nov. 90
Reason(s) for using it:
Good overall picture of development and useful for all sub sections of emotional, physical, social development.
How you used it: Good for giving overview and detail of development so gave me a good idea of the plan and shape of both essays.
Relevant pages: Really all of the book
Actual quotes: p34, 37 67
Where the book is: Bookcase in study room at home

You can adapt the record card to meet the needs of your particular interests. I suggest you keep your notes from books on A4 paper and store them with the other records you keep of your notes from lectures, discussions and so on[1] in a box, or filing cabinet. In this case it would go into file number 14 and you should also file the original notes you made of the book in the same file. This is especially useful if the book is borrowed and you therefore may not have access to it in the future.

3. You add the key words into the Key Word Index Book (or card system) with very brief notes:

Heredity: My notes from Lansdown:"Child Development" p234.

Child Development: my notes from Lansdown:"Child Development"- whole book.

Physical development: my notes from Lansdown:"Child Development" - Chapter 7.

Cognitive development: my notes from Lansdown:"Child Development" - many references v useful.

Emotional Development: my notes from Lansdown:"Child Development" - many references v useful.

Piaget: my notes from Lansdown:"Child Development" - best summary 106ff.

For example, below is the page for H.

Keyword	*See File Number*	
Handedness	*7:*	*article by J.McGuiness on effect of handedness on whiskey drinking in Spain.*
Height	*8:*	*notes from J.Tanner's lecture on growth at adolescence*
	6:	*my presentation re genetic/environmental aspects*
	5:	*notes from S.Cohen's book "Dwarfs in Redcar"*
	1:	*p 3 of my notes from intro lecture by B Trenbirth "Height in the Low Countries"*
Heredity	*3:*	*notes from K.Gorman's book "Heredity and Art"*
	6:	*my presentation re genetic and environmental aspects of height*
	9:	*P.Johnson's lecture re genetic tendencies to sloth*
	14:	*my notes from "Child development made simple" by Lansdown, Richard*

If you own the book you could enter the relevant page numbers in the Key Word Index rather than referring to your notes. Obviously you could do both. In the future if you were looking for references to "heredity" in materials which you read you would look in the filing cabinet for files numbered 3,6,9 and 14.

---

[1]. *See Section 16 p.5ff for more detail on keeping records of relevant material.*

6.2 Format for keeping records of books read

The next few pages suggest a format for you to keep records in detail of the books which you read. These records are the ones which would go into your filing system.

RECORD NUMBER: [   ] SECTION ONE   Page 1

Type: (e.g. Basic Text Book, Recommended text book, Government Report, Research Report, Specialist Journal, Newspaper article, TV, Radio):_____

Title:_____

Sub-Title:_____

Author(s)/Editor:_____

Nationality of author:_____

Qualifications of Author(s):_____

Publisher:_____

Year of this edition:_____

Other editions:_____

Catalogue information:_____

Dewey number:_____ISBN:_____

Where it is to be found:_____

Is there a Contents?:_____

How is it divided (Parts/Chapters/sections?)?:_____

Are there Conclusions/Recommendations?:   [ ]

Are there any summaries at appropriate points?:   [ ]

Are there any appendices?:   [ ]

RECORD NUMBER: [   ] SECTION ONE:(Continued)   Page 2
Is there a list of references?:   [ ]

Is there a bibliography?:   [ ]

What type of index or indices?:_____

Is there a Preface?:   [ ]
    What does this say the material's about?:_____

_____

_____

_____

Is there an Introduction?:   [ ]
    What does this say the book's about?:_____

_____

_____

_____

Is there a"blurb"?:   [ ]
    What does this say the book's about?:_____

_____

_____

_____

Does it look as though it will be of use or not?:
USEFUL [ ]   NOT USEFUL[ ]   NOT SURE[ ]

RECORD NUMBER: [   ] SECTION TWO: Page 3

To be filled in if you think the reading will be of use, or if you are not sure.

Read all chapter/section headings.

Note any which are relevant (with page number(s)):_____

_____

_____

Read first and last paragraph of each chapter/section.

Note any which are relevant:_____

_____

_____

_____

Read any summaries of chapters/sections.

Note any which are relevant:_____

_____

_____

_____

Choose two (or more) key words (or synonyms of the key words):What amount of information is there in the book?:

Key Word 1:_____

_____

_____

_____

RECORD NUMBER: [   ] SECTION TWO:(Continued)   Page 4
Key Word 2:_____

_____

_____

_____

_____

Other Key words:

_____

_____

_____

_____

_____

_____

_____

_____

_____

_____

_____

_____

USEFUL [ ]   NOT USEFUL[ ]   NOT SURE[ ]

RECORD NUMBER: [   ] SECTION THREE   Page 5
(To be written only after having used the book)
Use(s) to which you have put the book:

Context(s):_____

_____

_____

_____

_____

Date(s) you used it:_____

Reason(s) for using used it:
How you used it:_____

_____

_____

_____

_____

Relevant pages:_____

Actual quotes:_____

_____

_____

_____

_____

RECORD NUMBER: [   ] SECTION THREE   Page 6

_____

_____

_____

Other possible useful books referred to in this one:_____

_____

_____

_____

_____

Where the book is:_____

_____

_____

Key words (with relevant page nos):

    1_____

    2_____

    3_____

    5_____

    6_____

DON'T FORGET
TO ENTER KEY WORDS
INTO INDEX BOOK!

7. Useful abbreviations

Abbreviation	Foreign meaning	English
abr.		abridged
abs.		absolute(ly)
abstr.		abstract
adj.		adjective
anc.		ancient
anon.		anonymous
app		appendix
Ar.		Arabic
arr.		arranged
art.		article
attrib.		attributed
b.		born
bet.		between
c.	circa	about
c.900 A.D.		about 900 A.D.
cf.	confer	compare
do.	ditto	the same
e.g.	exempli gratia	for example
esp.		especially
et al	et alia	amongst others
et seq.	et sequens	and the following
f.		following
2f.		page 2+following page
ff.		following
2ff.		page 2+following pages
fo.		folio
ibid	ibidem	in the same place. Used to show that the quotation comes from the same source as the previous one
id.	idem	the same
i.e.	id est	that is (It does not mean for example)
ign.	ignotus	unknown
incog.	incognito	unrecognised
inf.	infra	below
k.		1000
l.c.		lower case

loc.cit.	loco citato	same as ibid
Ms.		Manuscript
Mss.		Manuscripts
N.B.	nota bene	Note well
n.d.		not dated (of books)
non seq.	non sequitur	it does not follow
op.	opus	work
op.cit.	opere citato	from the work already referred to.
p.		page
p2		page 2
pp.		pages
pp.2-6		pages 2 to 6
passim		in many places, usually means there are too many references to list.
QED	quod erat demostrandum	that which was to be demonstrated
QEF	quod erat faciendum	that which was to be done
QEI	quod erat inveniendum	that which was to be found
qto.	quarto	folded in four
q.v.	quod vide	which see.
q.v.p.2		see page 2.
Ro.	recto	on the right hand page
RV		Revised version
s.c.	scilicet	namely
sic		thus. Used when there is a mistake or inaccuracy which you wish to retain and you don't want the reader to think you have made a mistake.
sqq.	sequentes	those following
supra		above.
s.v.	sub verbo	under the entry
v.	vide	see
viz	videlicet	namely, that is to say.
Vo.	Verso	on the left hand page

SECTION 18:
PRESENTATIONS AND SEMINARS

1. The rationale

There are three main reasons why you need to acquire the skills involved in presenting information to a group of other people:

1. To have practice at doing research,
2. To have experience of presenting information to a group,
3. To have experience of working with others in an academic context.

1.1 To have practice at doing research

The most fundamental of the skills you need at undergraduate level is that of doing research (i.e. collecting data)[1]. Research at this level is not to do with what YOU think about a subject, but to do with you finding out about a subject by doing some structured investigation yourself (primary research) and by reading what others have done (secondary research):

1. Primary research is first hand investigation done by you, such as interviews, questionnaires, visits, observation etc.
2. Secondary research is what has already been done by others and has been published such as books, statistics, TV/Radio programmes etc.

In order to plan and organise effectively any piece of work for presentation you should ensure that you::

- consult with your Tutor
- consult with experts by letter, phone and/or interview (THIS NEEDS TO BE DONE AS SOON AS POSSIBLE)

and where appropriate:

- plan and use questionnaires/surveys
- visit appropriate sites, making appropriate reports of observations etc.
- do the appropriate reading and summarise and quote the essence of what others have found out.

Note that sometimes you will encounter situations where you will be asked to work in group of 2-3.

1.2 To have experience of presenting information to a group

In almost all University courses students are expected to give what is variously called "seminar paper", or "presentation", or "report". Whatever it is called it means that you are asked to do some research and then present that research to the group of students to whom you belong. Thus it is useful for you to be aware of the skills needed to present your findings effectively orally and visually to a group within a

---

[1]. *More detail about research is in Sections 19 and 20 on essay writing and special studies.*

given time period usually about 20-30 minutes, with say 5-10 minutes in addition for questions from the group, and possibly from the Tutor in charge.
This involves:

> choosing appropriate and imaginative methods of presentation, such as tape, video, slides, OHP's, blackboard, flip charts, role play, handouts, so as to involve the whole group to whom you are making the presentation.
> presenting it effectively with
> > Clarity
> > Effective pacing
> > Variety of tone, pitch, volume
> > "Liveliness"
> > Appropriate "body-language"

1.3 To have experience of working with others in an academic context

If you are working with others then find out if marks are distributed evenly in the team. If they are then there is a responsibility on each member of the group to share evenly and fairly the process of producing the Presentation - who does what, by when etc. If they are not then ascertain the criteria by which the marks are to be allocated.

2. Working out a clear timetable

2.1 Stage 1 deciding on groups

If you have a choice of groups then it would be useful to be geographically near to the other(s) in your group.

2.2 Stage 2 decide on a topic

If you have a choice of topic and unless you are told, the piece of work must be suitable to demonstrate to the Tutor that you have included

> research into books,
> a questionnaire and/or interviews with people,
> letters written to organisational/individual experts appropriate to the topic.
> and any other aspects the Tutor says is important.

Brainstorm to choose and refine the topic.

Eventually define the topic very clearly and then decide what it is that you want your audience to have (i.e. information, skill development, attitude change or whatever) as a result of your presentation.

The size of the topic

Be careful to select a MANAGEABLE SIZE (e.g. Unemployment is too big: Youth unemployment in Sacriston is manageable: John Smith being out of work is too small.)

2.3 Stage 3 topic approach approved by Tutor

You should agree with the Tutor the broad title of the presentation and the broad approach to the work involved. After that it's a good idea to write a summary of the topic no longer than one sheet of A4. This should be submitted to and agreed with the Tutor.

2.4 Stage 4 topic prepared

Your Tutor should be available for consultations in detail re the method of presentation. I advise you, whilst not pestering the Tutor, that you report your progress so that you are sure you are on the right lines.

3. Planning a presentation

3.1 The format

Most investigations take the following format:

investigate what the situation is, usually by looking at a broad picture, then setting the particular piece of research into that context.

find out what the effects are and

look at the implications of your findings for the future.

3.2 An example[2]

If you choose to do Youth Unemployment in Sacriston you will need to:

investigate what the situation is,

i.e. find statistics about unemployment nationally and regionally and then in Sacriston

find out what the effects are

i.e. how does this affect the local community, or even a couple of specific members of the community - perhaps here using a local questionnaire and/or case studies and/or survey.

look at the implications of your findings for the future.

i.e. what are the trends? What are the movements within the community to do something about it? What do locals think will happen? What do experts think will happen? Perhaps also "What can be done?" list of suggestions.

I do not want to inhibit you by giving too much of a straight jacket in the way of guidelines and usually each topic has its own unique structure. The main thing is to talk it through with your Tutor between now and when you make the presentation.

If working in a group you will need to have a clear idea of the allocation of work and the timetable of when work needs to be done.

---

[2]. *For more detail on research methods, see Sections 19 and 20.*

---

4. What should be the structure of a presentation?

4.1 An introduction

This should state the intention of the presentation, give any definitions necessary, make clear the parameters of the topic, and describe the methods you have used in our research. People listening to you like a clear picture of where you are going: headings of the main sections written out on blackboard, flip chart or OHP are very effective.

4.2 Main body

The key ideas should be presented logically and clearly with supporting arguments and evidence drawn from both primary and secondary research. It should be presented in a way which will INVOLVE the listeners.

4.3 A Conclusion

This should summarise the main points, draw out any implication and draw the presentation together.

4.4 Question-time

You should anticipate questions from the listeners and prepare to answer them.

4.5 Bibliography

You should include a list of books etc used.

4.6 Appendices

This is a collection of other material/resources used, actual questionnaire/survey in full. If you have displayed any material then this should be in one of the appendices.

5. How should the material be presented?

5.1 In general

- Get a good, simple, basic "script" worked out first!
- Then use your originality and imagination.
- Consider especially the degree to which the listeners become involved in the presentation.
- Use questions with them.
- Don't let them sit back and nod off! Effective use should be made of the listeners themselves.
- Get them thinking - ask them questions - stimulate them by involving them.
- For example, take in material for the group to examine.

5.2 Clarity

It is not as easy to get complex points over in a verbal presentation as it is in an essay. Your audience cannot easily turn back as they can with the written word. I have always found it useful to give the audience a clear idea of the structure of the presentation before beginning. This should be done simply by saying what the intention of the presentation is, what each part is going to be about, and what you hope they will get out of the presentation. It is sensible to remind them when you are starting each new point. saying something like:

> "Having dealt with X I now want to turn to the Nth aspect of the topic."

or:

> "In the light of what I have said about X, are there any questions from you before we go on to look at Y?",

is useful to let the listeners know where you are up to. Some people have a visual reminder of the plan of the whole presentation and draw it to the listeners' attention at appropriate points.

The structure should be as simple as possible, with clear points made in each part. These points again can be reinforced by visual summaries at appropriate moments, if not throughout, then certainly at the end.

5.3 Effective pacing

One of the mistakes often made in otherwise excellent presentations is the pacing. You should be aware that you can vary the speed of the presentation, sometimes delivering an avalanche of facts and information, followed by a slow thoughtful section which considers the impact and implications of the facts of the previous section.

The important point is to vary the pace of the presentation. If it goes at the same pace, however fast or slow, it becomes monotonous.

5.4 Variety of tone, pitch, volume

The most important audio-visual aids you possess are your voice and your face! You have control over most aspects of these two! The component parts of your voice can be varied. Each one is under your control:

The tone - the pitch - the volume.

The tone can be warm, cold, hectoring, smiling, stern and so on. Make sure that its tone reflects the nature of the particular atmosphere you wish to create at any one time. More importantly, make sure that the tone does vary. Sometimes, just lowering the pitch, or increasing or decreasing the volume is sufficient. Try practising this. Try saying:

> "This is the most important point of the whole presentation."

in a loud voice, and in a whisper. Try saying it loud and fast. Try saying it whispered with lots of pauses between the words.

Your face too can be controlled: it too can look warm, cold, hectoring, smiling, stern and so on. Look in the mirror (if you can bear to!) and try out a few expressions.

If you are presenting in a group then make sure that you distribute the presentation evenly so that there is a variety just because there is a change of person. Think carefully about the basis on which you distribute the script between you.

5.5 "Liveliness"

You will find that liveliness in the voice and face come if you are aware of the variations possible in tone, pitch and volume. Don't attempt to be lively by being fast. Variety is far more important than sheer speed.

Let your enthusiasm for the subject (even if it is long dead!) shine through. Do try to introduce an element of humour too.

Don't forget to smile so that people realise it is meant to be humorous!

5.6 Appropriate "body language"

Don't stare at your script all the time. Make eye contact with your audience. Try to address the four corners of the room and not just your pals.

Use open gestures more than closed ones.

Do try walking about - varying the position of yourself in the room. If possible don't sit. Certainly don't sit all the time.

5.7 A script

You must have a script. NEVER try to go into a presentation and improvise off the top of your head. However...it is very difficult to do many of the above if you are tied to a script which you hold with both hands.

If you can, rehearse your presentation several times, if possible in the actual room you will use.

I like to have the script with me, so that if I do dry up I know it's there and I can always clutch onto it so as not to drown in a sea of nerves, then I can rely on using either cards or OHP's. I write out the main points of the presentation on either postcards or OHP acetate sheets, with a few key sentences to remind me of what I want to say.

The OHP's are useful to the listeners too, in that they give them a visual reminder about what I am talking!

5.8 Handout(s)

Good clear handouts summarising the main points are useful given out at the start or the end of the presentation. I prefer at the end to avoid giving too much away. I don't like the disruption caused by giving them out in mid-presentation unless there is some important purpose served in doing this, otherwise they will read and not listen to you. If you have some complex information you want people to refer to then you are better off putting it on an OHP or flip/wall chart rather than a handout since you are then in control of when people look at it. Give copies out at the end.

5.9 Audio/visual aids

There are many Audio Visual Aids available in Universities and Colleges. Whilst not wanting you to get carried away and forget that the most important aspect of a presentation is really contained in the above points, you can certainly enhance your presentation by the use of any of the following:

*Audio recordings

Because you can record the words effectively in your own home without the stress of an audience, there is a temptation if you are nervous to overuse a recorder and record the whole of the presentation. Do this only as a very last resort. Recordings are never as effective as you talking directly to the audience. You can adjust your pace, your volume and you can respond to the feeling of the people. Furthermore the audience can re-act to you more easily if they feel they can interrupt you. The audio recording IS useful to give atmosphere and character to a presentation, for example, the actual voice of the person being interviewed, some music to establish a mood, sound effects to increase the drama or evoke a setting - these uses are fine and should be explored.

*Video recordings/film

With the recent growth in the use of portable video recorders, (often called camcorders), video has to a very great extent replaced film which was a comparatively cumbersome way of getting pictures into the presentation. Students can often borrow easy to use, flexible and portable equipment to capture their interviews, experiments, illustrative material, even to the point of the presentation being entirely done with the video recorder. Its power is in being able to bring into the group whatever images and sounds you wish to present, in whatever order you want to present them.

Extracts from TV programmes or commercially available videos can also be used.

Overhead Projectors

The OHP, Overhead Projector, is extremely useful in presenting any information to a group. It allows you, as its name suggests, to stand (or sit) facing the group whilst the illustrative material on clear acetate sheets is projected onto a screen or clear wall space behind you. You can prepare the sheets at home, or wherever is convenient beforehand by writing, printing, drawing and/or photocopying onto clear sheets of acetate. It is possible to project these clear, bright, large images which can be prepared beforehand. There are special pens available. Overlays can be made to build up, or to de-construct images. Notes can be written by hand onto the acetate whilst giving the presentation.

I have always found them far more useful than a blackboard or flip-charts, especially as one can prepare them well in advance and keep them easily filed for future use.

Blackboards

One disadvantage of a blackboard is that you have to turn your back to the class to write on them! A further disadvantage is that it is not easy to prepare diagrams etc beforehand and be sure that they will not be rubbed off before you need them! You can't easily take them home to do the night before!

Always practice before you use one! Some need special chalk. Some need special marker pens now!

If you have time to prepare beforehand, or if your only use is to be to note things down during the presentation, then you may find the blackboard useful.

In the absence of anything else then it will do, but it is very cumbersome and often wastes huge amounts of time whilst you scribble away on it.

They are also very dirty things to use!

Wall charts/Flip charts

Wall charts are big pieces of paper displayed on the wall! Flip charts are several big pictures on top of each other, revealed separately. All you need here are large sheets of paper and some marker pens. They can be very effective and can be prepared beforehand. Do check that they will be visible by all the people in the room of the presentation.

*Slides/photographs

These can be useful to illustrate your presentation. Slides demand a comparatively darkened room. Photographs are usually too small to be seen by everyone at the same time[3]. They could be used as a wall display for use before or after the main presentation. But beware giving them out whilst talking: they are a distraction.

Computer

Recently it has become possible to project a computer screen effectively to such a size that it can be seen by a comparatively large group. Alternatively the screen image can be fed into some TV networks. If such a facility is available then you may find it useful to put some of your illustrative material onto the computer, which you can control as you give the lecture. Main points and tables, diagrams and maps etc can be produced and displayed effectively on computers - but do make sure that you are in control of the means of production!

IMPORTANT NOTE: *=Be warned: These have a habit of going wrong!

5.8 In general

In general remember that the important element in your presentation is the script. All the audio-visuals and gimmicks will not substitute for an empty script. On the other hand, a good script can be greatly enhanced by the sensible use of audio-visual tools to illustrate and bring the outside world into the presentation.

---

[3]. *In the olden days there was a very useful machine called an epidiascope which would project images of books, photographs and any three dimensional object onto a screen. There may still be some lurking in Audio-visual departments!*

---

6. A checklist for planning a presentation

You may find the following of use as a guideline to planning a presentation.

Checklist for a presentation (1)
==

Title of Presentation Topic:
Scope of Presentation:

Rough Outline of Presentation:
(Note down the MAIN points you wish to make under each of the following)
Introduction:

Part One:

Part Two:

Part Three:

Conclusion:

Checklist for a presentation (2)

Collecting the secondary data
Who are the experts in the field?

Which books are available to you?

Collecting the primary data
Depending on the type of presentation, you may be asked to show evidence that you have done some primary research and it should have at least a questionnaire and some evidence of you getting in touch with relevant individuals and or organisations on a variety of levels.
THE QUESTIONNAIRE[2]
What you want to find out

Outline of questionnaire:

To whom given

How many

Deadline for completion:

---

[2]*If you are doing a questionnaire see Section 21 for more detail.*

Checklist for a presentation (3)
===

THE INTERVIEWS
What you want to find out:

People whom you intend to interview:

Questions you wish to ask:

Deadline for completion:
If you are doing visits check in Section 20 p.13 for more detail.
THE VISITS
What you want to find out:

Places you intend to visit / observe

Deadline for completion of observations etc

Checklist for a presentation (4)

==

THE LETTERS[5]
Organisations/individuals you intend to write to:

Deadlines for:
        - letters posted,
        - reminders sent out,
        - replies collated.

If you are working in a group then you will need to formalise the distribution of the work.
Allocation of work

---

[5]. *If you are sending letters check in Section 20 page 11 for more detail.*

SECTION 19: ESSAY WRITING

Introduction

Most formal essays require you to demonstrate that you can write an essay that is:

1. Well structured

with a clear statement of intent, definitions, parameters, methodology and rationale,

with clearly defined parts which are relevant and well balanced,

with a clear conclusion, which summarises the main points, and draws out the implications of the work,

2. Well substantiated

with proper use of quotes from and references to appropriate primary and secondary research,

3. Well understood

with accurate interpretation of, analysis of, and evaluation of the research material which you have used,

4. Well presented and set out

with accurate use of spelling, grammar, sentencing and paragraphing,

neat in appearance with consistent setting out techniques,

5. Well written

in a style which is objective, tentative and simple,

6. Rigorous

In all academic work you need to demonstrate an accurate, correct and valid foundation in the subject matter of the topic. It should be:

- synoptic, giving an overall view of the topic as a whole and its relationship to the wider context,
- comprehensive, but selecting the **significant** aspects,
- sensitive, never confusing fact and opinion,
- critical, recognising weaknesses, errors and omissions, and the possibility of alternative descriptions and explanations,
- profound, addressing fundamental principles and presuppositions,
- steady + consistent, based on sound arguments defending the choices made,
- creative, showing that you can appropriately apply the principles you have learnt in different contexts.

You need to adopt a systematic approach to the writing of essays. The method I suggest is not the only way of writing essays, but, in the absence of any guidelines from your Tutors, the approach has many merits. The purpose is to get you started and prevent you from looking at what seems an insurmountable Everest by breaking the task down into separate components.

> **Organise your work so there is no danger of failing to get it in by the deadline. Start as soon as you can.**

1. Choosing the title

1.1 Be decisive

You are usually given a choice of essay titles, not always, but if you are then don't panic! Don't agonise too much about the choice. Remember that there are "swings and round-a-bouts".

1.2 Be thorough

Read through the essay titles and choose one which is clear to you and is of interest to you. You may be lucky and find one immediately. If not then you will have to look in more detail at each question. Go through the process described below. Brainstorm several of the titles before choosing. Don't start gathering data for several essays and then choose, although you could check out the availability of books in the library for more than one of them.

1.3 Choose or eliminate

Your choice may be a positive one: "Oh, I do like that question...it's one I've always wanted to do!", or you may decide by a process of elimination - "Since I can't do any of the others then that's the only one that's left!"

2. Interpreting the title

Define what the question is asking for. Note any "key words" like "criticise" or "describe". These let you know what approach is required. You will need to be aware of the precise meaning of these "key words".

2.1 Key words in essay titles

The following are very common key words in essay titles. They are not by any means the only ones. You should collect all the different types of question which you come across, particularly in your specialism.

Account for	Analyse	Assess	Calculate
Classify	Comment on...	Compare . with ...	Construct
Contrast the...with	Criticise	Define	Demonstrate
Describe	Discuss	Enumerate	Evaluate
Explain	Identify	How far..	To what extent
Indicate	Illustrate	Interpret	Justify
Label	List	Outline	Perform
Predict	Prove	Relate	Review
Show how...	State	Summarise	Trace

2.2 Meaning of key words

The following is a brief description of some of the key words - you should attempt to build up your own "glossary" of key words.

- **Criticise** :DOES NOT MEAN pull to pieces. It means judge the merit of, with reasons and reference to appropriate EVIDENCE, including both favourable and unfavourable comments.
- **Comment** DOES NOT MEAN say anything that comes into your head. It means analyse/assess - again asking for at least two views to be put forward.
- **Compare** DOES NOT MEAN make one out to be better than the other. It means draw attention to the similarities between the two. It also means draw attention to the differences.
- **Justify** means put forward arguments FOR the case presented, perhaps mention arguments against, but you are being asked to be in favour of the statement, even if you personally do not agree.
- **Discuss** DOES NOT MEAN ramble on and on. It means very much the same as Comment (above). Expound the various views which can be taken. There is no need to come down on one side or another unless asked.
- **Assess** DOES NOT MEAN write about your prejudices. It means measure or weigh up "the extent to which" the statement is true. Always give a clear indication of the criteria you are using to do the measuring. There is no need, unless asked, to state your own feelings/views about what you are asked to assess.

Note the different answers required to the following questions, all of which demand a knowledge of the Battle of Hastings, but each of which requires a very different use made of that knowledge in order to answer the question accurately.

Account for the Battle of Hastings.

Analyse the Battle of Hastings.

Assess the effects of the Battle of Hastings

Compare the Battle of Hastings with the Battle of Britain

Construct a model to show the Battle of Hastings

Contrast the Battle of Hastings with the battle of...

Criticise the idea that Battle of Hastings was badly fought by the French.

Define what is meant by the Battle of Hastings.

Describe the Battle of Hastings.

Discuss the Battle of Hastings.

Enumerate the causes of the Battle of Hastings.

Evaluate the Battle of Hastings.

Explain the Battle of Hastings.

How far/to what extent did the Battle of Hastings affect the future of England?

Indicate the place of the Battle of Hastings in our history.

Illustrate the Battle of Hastings.

Interpret the Battle of Hastings.
Justify the Battle of Hastings.
Label this map of the Battle of Hastings.
List the participants in the Battle of Hastings.
Outline the Battle of Hastings.
Perform the basic manoeuvres used in the Battle of Hastings.
Predict the outcome the Battle of Hastings had Harold not been wounded.
Prove the Battle of Hastings took place at Hastings.
Relate the Battle of Hastings to consequent developments of English Language.
Review the Battle of Hastings.
Show how the Battle of Hastings came about.
State the date of the Battle of Hastings.
Summarise the main events leading to the Battle of Hastings.
Trace the causes of the Battle of Hastings
Look carefully through this list and think about the differences that are contained in
the wording of each of the questions.

> **Many marks are lost by writing down all you know about the topic,
> without carefully and precisely answering the question as it is worded.**

3. Brainstorming ideas

Having chosen your essay title, you need to start to generate ideas that will be
useful to include in the essay, bearing in mind the precise wording of the title.
- Think about your topic.
- Jot down any of the the ideas you have. Let your imagination go and write
down anything connected with the ideas generated by the essay title.
- Try to think of the books that may be useful, the authors you think would
be expert in that field, the friends you have who know something about the
topic, the Tutors you need to see, etc, until you are sure that you have
exhausted your own ideas.
- Share the brainstorm list with a friend and see if they can add anything.
Even better, share it with someone who knows the topic very well.

4. Doing a preliminary plan

You should begin to form at least a rough plan of the essay. For a 3000 word essay
Try to get a plan which is simple and follows roughly an outline like the one below.
You will be surprised just how few words this is when it comes to covering the
topic.
Obviously you must adjust your plan to suit the number of words you have at your
disposal.

```
INTRODUCTION (250 words)
PART ONE    (830 words approx.)
    Section 1
    Section 2
    Section 3
PART TWO    (830 words approx.)
    Section 1
    Section 2
    Section 3
PART THREE  (830 words approx.)
    Section 1
    Section 2
    Section 3
CONCLUSION  (250 words)
```

Each part doesn't always have the same number of sections: there are sometimes more, sometimes less. Neither are there always three Parts: it depends on the nature of the topic. Allocate the words to the basic plan: if there are 3000 words and you plan on 250 for the Introduction and 250 for the Conclusion that leaves 2500 to divide between the 3 parts, about 830 to each part, and about 280 for each section.

You will find it useful to have separate sheets of paper for each section of the essay. Clearly label each of them with its title and you can then begin to scribble down relevant ideas, quotations etc on those pieces of paper.

5. Research skills

Remember that at this level of study you will be expected to find out what experts have found from their research. The questioner is NOT usually interested in reading what YOU think from your limited experience. The questioner is looking to see how well you can find out what is known about the subject, not what you know at present. In the light of your research the questioner will then need to know your opinion/view, but it should always be based on substantiated evidence, not just on your narrow experience. This usually means that you need to be seeking several accounts of the topic, rather than one. Obviously in short essays you can't summarise EVERY expert, but you should make sure that you have made reference to the important experts in the topic under consideration. In Higher Education you should remember that no one is interested in your **unsubstantiated** opinion. What I am trying to persuade you to do is to make sure that you have gone and found out what is known about the topic with which you are dealing. You need to identify the experts in the topic you have chosen.

DONT RELY JUST ON YOUR OWN KNOWLEDGE OF THE TOPIC

6. Different types of research

6.1 The range available

There are various ways in which you can substantiate what you say:

Primary research
research you have done yourself.
Secondary Research
research other people have done.

You must establish with the Tutor setting the essay in what proportion they require the above. In comparatively short and simple essays you should concentrate on secondary research. In the longer essays, perhaps presentations and certainly in special studies you should IN ADDITION do some primary research.

Your own experience/anecdotal evidence
You should AVOID using your own experience as the basis of proof. It is not wrong to ILLUSTRATE something from your own experience. But...NEVER try to prove anything from it. For example, it is not sensible to write:

> *"I enjoy fishing, therefore fishing is a popular sport."*

Certainly you CAN use your experience as EXAMPLE:

> *"According to Whitaker's Almanac 1995, over 10,000,000 people in Britain possess fishing licences, a figure which includes myself..."*

You should also avoid what is called "anecdotal" evidence. That is evidence of the type that goes from the particular to the general.

> *"A friend of mine told me that his grandmother had seen a ghost therefore ghosts do exist."*

PLEASE PLEASE PLEASE stick to finding out what the experts have to say about the topic.

6.2 Primary research

This is research/investigation which you carry out yourself, via surveys, questionnaires, observation and so on. A full account of this type of research can be found in the sections on Special Studies and Questionnaires.[1]

6.3 Secondary Research

This is research which others have already done. It is one of the main skills of the under-graduate to investigate what research has already been done on a topic, summarise it, compare and contrast it with other research on the same topic.
Thus...
If you haven't already done so then you MUST at this stage:

---

[1]. *See Sections 20 and 21.*

- Go to the library and ask what books/authors they would recommend on that topic.
- Try to find an "expert" on the subject, some friend/acquaintance who has some knowledge of that topic and ask which books/articles you should read.
- Get a few books on the topic. Use the techniques set out in the "Reading" Section. (i.e. Look at the contents pages to "wrap your mind around" the scope of the book - looking out for where your topic fits in the book. Use the index to help in this as well.)
- LOOK FOR WHAT IS RELEVANT - and make notes. Any REALLY useful sentences jot down verbatim and use as quotations in the essay (ONLY IF THEY ARE REALLY RELEVANT). If it's more than a couple of sentences then just summarise it: that is called a reference.
- Always remember to keep the page number, the author, the title and the publisher and the year of publication of any quotations or references you wish to use.

You need to check with the Tutor setting the assignment just how widely and deeply you need to read around the topic. Don't use one book only. You are usually being asked to find out what research in general says about the topic you've chosen, not just what ONE author/researcher says. (Sometimes the question actually asks you to summarise the research available.)

Accurate interpretation of, analysis of, and evaluation of the research material which you have used.

It is important to emphasise the interpretive, analytic and evaluative skills required with academic work. It is no use just describing the research that has been done. You have to stand back from it and say in what way it illuminates the topic, what significance it has for the topic, what weight can be given to it, and how it relates and compares to other views from other researches.

7. Using the material - how to quote and refer

YOU MUST MAKE CLEAR WHEN USING OTHER PEOPLE'S RESEARCH THAT IT IS NOT YOUR OWN. In other words you must clearly acknowledge your sources. You will need to know how to quote and how to refer.
See Section 25 Setting Out, p.9ff for details of setting out quotations, references and notes.

8. Revising the plan

It may be that in the light of the reading you have done you will want to put more emphasis on one aspect than another, or that you will need to include rather less than you originally thought on a particular part.
Sometimes after reading the first expert you will want to re-write the whole plan!

9. Construction of the essay

9.1 An approach

It is impossible to teach you every way of writing an essay. You will find that every Tutor you have in the future will have a different preference for how you should write them. Some Tutors will have very clear ideas of what they want. Some will know what they don't want.

My personal view is that Tutors OUGHT to be able to state clearly what it is they are looking for in an essay and be able to quantify this in terms of a marking sheet. Not many do!

Never let anyone tell you that you don't need structure, substantiation and good presentation.

There are many ways of structuring essays and doing introductions and conclusions, but, for the time being please try out the following suggestions. When you have become expert in these, then you can try out other, more sophisticated methods and approaches.

9.2 Building the essay

As you collect the data put it into the appropriate sections of the essay. You will then begin to see the shape of the essay grow. There will be gaps. There will be times when you realise that you have too much in one section and you will have to prune. The balance may not be quite right between, say, opposing viewpoints - all these things will emerge as you put the collected data into place.

Don't worry in the early stages about the number of words - you can cut at a later stage, putting illustrative material into the Appendices and making reference to it.

I suggest between 3-5 main "parts" for most essays, each part dealing with a separate aspect. Within each part there should be about 3 major sections.

Eventually you will reach the stage where you'll want to begin to write the connections between the pieces and then to write the introduction and conclusion.

9.3 Introductions

Introductions can be used in many ways. I suggest that you should try to keep them simple. They can be used to perform the following four functions:

> **Introductions**
> 1. A statement of intent.
> 2. Definition of terms.
> 3. Establishing the parameters of the answer by making clear how you interpret the question.
> 4. The rationale (Explaining the reasons why you have chosen to write the essay in the way you do).
> NB. They don't have to come in that order.

A statement of intent

Statements of intent are best following the pattern of:

> *"The intention of this essay is to examine/assess/justify etc*
> *.......Part One deals with .... Part Two tackles .....*

Try to avoid the use of the future tense with the intention. Don't say:

> *"This essay will deal with the major theories which try to*
> *examine the nature of.... Part One will comment on..."*

Say rather:

> *"This essay deals with the major theories which try to*
> *examine the nature of.... Part One comments on..."*

Doing this somehow suggests that you are well in control of the material: that you know what is happening!

Definition of terms

Make clear any specific terms in the title or those which are implied by the title. It is best to say that you are following an acknowledged expert's usage:

> *"Title: "Assess the major changes brought about by the*
> *Thatcher Government since 1979."*
>
> *The term "major changes" is used in the way in which Halford*
> *(1985) suggests:*
>
>> *"A major change is one which affects more than 50% of*
>> *the population in a way which makes their lives*
>> *significantly different in terms of ability to pay for goods*
>> *and services, their right to follow their political or*
>> *religious beliefs..."*
>
> *(Halford, 1985, 345)*

It may be that there are many complex terms used in the essay - in which case include a glossary of terms at the start or at the end and refer the reader to that.

Establishing the parameters

It is also be useful to make a statement about your interpretation of the question/title, making clear the boundaries/parameters of the subject:

> *Title: "Edwina Currie was right!" - Discuss.*
>
> *"This essay is confined to the comments which Edwina Currie*
> *has made on egg production in this country rather than the*
> *many controversial statements she has made on other*
> *subjects."*

or:

> *Title: Describe the physical development of children.*
>
> *"This essay takes development to mean physical growth and*
> *limits the term children to those between the ages of 0 and*
> *the onset of puberty at around the age of 11 or 12."*

The rationale

You need to state why it is you've chosen the essay AND why you've chosen to tackle it in the way you have. Sometimes this is implicit rather than explicit.

"I chose this title since there needs to be some objective clarity shone onto what has become an issue obscured by rhetoric and emotion. I have chosen to examine the matter in the three sections as outlined above because these are the three major contributors to our knowledge of the subject."

When you do a Presentation or Special Study the rationale should include reference to the research methods you have used e.g. questionnaire, interviews, gathering information from Government Departments etc and why you have chosen these particular methods and what you hoped to find out from them. This as well as your reasons for choosing the particular experts you have chosen. Simple essays obviously do not need such reference.

Note: Introductions are rarely written first!

9.4 Conclusions

Conclusions are more difficult. They should do at least two things: summarise what has been said, and bring out the major implications of what has been said.

Summarise what you have said

To some extent this is a repetition of what is said in the introduction - the statement of intent. It is likely that you can put into a sentence the important point from each section of each part. You should try to go further and...

Bring out major implications of what you have said

For example:

"...this essay has described the major changes which have come about as a result of the Thatcher Government from 1979. These were:

1. the move away from nationalised industries and services,

2. the reduction of taxes,

3. etc etc

It seems from the examination of these changes that:

1. they will be difficult to alter: they have taken over ten years to implement,

2. that they have profoundly affected the attitude of the people towards each other, in that ....

3. etc etc..."

10. Do a rough draft

10.1 The shape

The state of the essay by now will be full of crossings out, different types of writing, different pieces of paper and so on.

You will find it useful at this stage try to get a clear idea of the length and the "shape" by constructing a rough draft. This may involve cutting out bits of the essay and pasting them in different places.

Don't worry at this stage about neatness of presentation: that can be done when you have got the basic shape and size right.

Look at the content matter of each part and ensure that it is <u>relevant</u> to the question.

Look at the <u>balance</u> to make sure that you have not written too much on any one particular aspect.

10.2 The style

When you've got the essay in the right order and are fairly happy about the content matter then look at style. You should try to be less "assertive" and more "tentative" - try to provide adequate evidence for any assertions you make. Also use phrases like:

> *"It seems, from the research done by..."*
> *"It appears that..."*

rather than

> *"It's a well known fact..."*
> *"It's obvious that..."*
> *"Everybody knows that..."*

Try in general to avoid speaking directly to the reader (though this is not always possible - nor desirable - but avoid chattiness and slang:

> *"Well, dear reader, I am going to tell you in this essay all what I know about Human Development, OK?"*

Phrase this more like:

> *"This essay surveys 3 different theories of human development."*

It is better to avoid the first person if at all possible. Rather than saying "I" say "The essay...".

You should attempt to evaluate and interpret the material you are presenting, rather than merely leaving it to speak for itself. Point out the differences and similarities the between the various sources upon which you draw. You should also show the relationship(s) between them and the weight which should be given to them. This part of essay writing isn't always easy at first, so don't worry if you find it difficult. You will develop these skills as you become familiar with all the basic elements of essay writing.

11. The Checklist (things to do before final neat version of the essay)

1. STRUCTURE

Get the structure of the essay established and write a clear plan based on accurate analysis of the essay title.   [ ]

The introduction

Make sure you have in your introduction:
- clear statement of intent   [ ]
- clear definition of terms   [ ]
- clear setting of parameters   [ ]
- clear statement of rationale   [ ].

The main body

Make sure that...

the main body of essay is based on your statement of intent   [ ]

that it is clear and relevant (i.e. you have interpreted the question accurately)   [ ]

that it is well balanced (i.e. you have allocated a fair amount of words to each separate section of the essay).   [ ]

The Conclusion

Make sure that...

you have a clear conclusion summarising what has been demonstrated in the body of the essay.   [ ]

the conclusion draws out the implications of what you have found out.   [ ]

2. SUBSTANTIATION

Make sure that...

you have made reference to appropriate experts   [ ]

3. UNDERSTANDING

Make sure that...

you have accurately interpreted, analysed and evaluated the research material which you have used.

4. CLARITY OF EXPRESSION

Have you checked...
- vocabulary - simple, appropriate and clear   [ ]
- Grammar/syntax   [ ]
- Punctuation   [ ]
- Spelling   [ ]

5. RIGOUR

make sure your work:
- gives an overall view of the topic as a whole + its relationship to the wider context,
- selects the **significant** aspects,
- never confuses fact and opinion,
- recognises weaknesses, errors and omissions, and the possibility of alternative descriptions and explanations,
- addresses fundamental principles and presuppositions of the topic,
- has sound arguments defending the choices you have made.

Do make sure that the spelling, punctuation and grammar are accurate. Get a friend to help - or read it backwards!

12. The final draft

This quite a satisfying activity because it is mindless and automatic!
Have a good look through the Section on setting out, Section 25. That tells you how
the whole piece of work should be set out.
There are some things you should leave until this stage is reached:

12.1 The bibliography
See Section 25 Setting Out p.13ff.

12.2 Margins, paragraphs etc
See Section 25 Setting Out p.2.

12.3 Headers and footers
See Section 25 Setting Out p.2.

12.4 Titles for Sections etc
See Section 25 Setting Out p.8f.

12.5 Title page, contents etc
See Section 25 Setting Out p.2ff.

12.6 Numbering paragraphs etc.
See Section 25 Setting Out p.12ff.

Not every Tutor likes essays to be done with headings and sub-headings - others do
- always check.

Binding
See Section 25 Setting Out p.18.

13. Final Check

Always give a final check over the simple things such as:

neatness,	[ ]
clear lay out	[ ]
ease of reading	[ ]
setting out of bibliography	[ ]
setting out of quotes	[ ]
illustrative material made clearly relevant	[ ]
appendices made clearly relevant (if used).	[ ]

ALWAYS COMPLY WITH THE DEADLINES

14. Evaluating your own work

One of the most important developments you can make is being able to evaluate your own work. You should in the long run be able to evaluate the adequacy and sufficiency of your own learning and begin to identify the next stage of your own personal development.

Just looking at this with regard to essay writing, there is the implication that you should have a very clear idea of what the markers are looking for. I do urge you to try to get a clear statement from your Tutor(s) as to what the marking schedule for that particular essay is going to be.

The Marking Schedule overleaf is a useful reminder of what someone marking your work at this stage would be taking for granted.

It is a useful reminder to you of the **basic requirements** of an essay. Do read it through carefully and note what gets marks. Most markers take the schedule overleaf almost for granted and are more concerned with the aspects listed below.

> content matter
> the way in which you
> interpret
> analyse
> evaluate
> the research material which you have used.

This means that you should make sure that the work is:

- **synoptic**, giving an overall view of the topic as a whole and its relationship to the wider context,
- **comprehensive**, but selecting the **significant** aspects,
- **sensitive**, never confusing fact and opinion,
- **critical**, recognising weaknesses, errors and omissions, and the possibility of alternative descriptions and explanations,
- **profound**, addressing fundamental principles and presuppositions,
- **steady+consistent**, based on sound arguments defending the choices made,
- **creative**, showing that you can appropriately apply the principles you have learnt in different contexts.

The schedule overleaf is one which you can use to get a feeling for the basic requirements of an essay. The sort of nuts and bolts that hold the essay together, rather than the styling and engine that's there!

In many instances College, school and University Tutors are reluctant to specify what marking scheme they are using.

You should always ask for one before you start your essay. It is always easier to write an essay when you know for what the Tutor is looking!

Marking Schedule for Essay.

SECTION 1. Structure

[/10]	- clear plan (supplied separately from the essay) based on accurate analysis of title, rubric + key words	
[/20]	- introduction	
	- clear statement of intent	[/ 5]
	- clear definition of terms	[/ 5]
	- clear setting of parameters	[/ 5]
	- clear statement of rationale	[/ 5]
[/25]	- main body of essay based on statement of intent	
	- clear and relevant	[/15]
	- well balanced	[/10]
[/20]	- conclusion	
	- summarising the main points in the essay	[/10]
	- drawing out the implications	[/10]

[/75] = TOTAL FOR SECTION 1

==

SECTION 2. Substantiation by reference to secondary sources

[/25]	- all major points substantiated	
	- reference to appropriate experts	[/15]
	- appropriateness of	[/ 5]
	- use made	[/ 5]

[/25] = TOTAL FOR SECTION 2

==

SECTION 3. Quality of presentation

[/50]	- competence in:	
	- vocabulary: simple, appropriate and clear	[/10]
	- Grammar/syntax	[/10]
	- Punctuation	[/10]
	- Spelling	[/10]
	- General presentation	[/10]
	e.g. neatness, lay out, ease of reading, setting out of bibliography, quotes, illustrative material, and appendices if used.	

[/50] = TOTAL FOR SECTION 3

==

[/150] = OVERALL MARK

==

16. Having a go!

If you would like to have a go at writing an essay and getting some feedback then one of the following titles could be used, or choose a title of your own.

Choose ONE of of the following titles

1. "Give me the child until he is five and I will give you the man" - Comment.
2. "Nature is stronger than nurture" - Discuss.
3. Choose any <u>one</u> of the following aspects of human development and identify and describe the normal stages through which humans develop in that aspect.

   physical,intellectual, emotional, social, or "moral"
4. "Human development is the same in all cultures and all societies." - Critically examine this statement.
5. "Intelligence is what is measured by intelligence tests." - to what extent is this true?
6. What is the importance of language in the development of thought?
7. Adult life is arranged in a series of well defined stages. Discuss.
8. "Boys will be boys." Are gender roles natural or learned?
9. There is no such thing as normal development. Discuss.
10. Compare and contrast the upbringing of children in our culture with that of any one other culture.
11. Identify the important elements in bringing up children. Justify your choice.
12. Explain why individuals achieve maturity at different ages.

The Format

The essay should be no longer than 3000 words - but you may wish to use appendices of supportive, illustrative material which do not count in the 3000. Please provide a plan. This should be no longer than ½A4. This does <u>not</u> count in the 3000 words. Please note that you have a copy of the marking scheme and that you should take that into account when writing the essay.

You will need someone to make comments on:

   your knowledge of content matter and selection of appropriate material, and
   your style.

You will need someone to diagnose and prescribe:

   by pointing to areas where you need to improve,
   by suggesting action to be taken, and
   by identifying areas where you are strong.

You can do the evaluation yourself, indeed it is a very good exercise to do this anyway, but you will probably find it more realistic and satisfying if you get someone else to mark it for you. If you cannot think of anyone to do this, then send it, together with a fee of £5 and a stamped self-addressed envelope, to me via the address at the front of the book and I will return it to you marked and with comments as soon as I possibly can.

SECTION 20: SPECIAL STUDIES

Introduction

In many schools, Colleges and Universities an extended piece of work is required from the student in addition to the essays and other course work. It is called by various names such as a dissertation, extended essay, or special study: I have chosen to call it Special Study, or study, throughout. Often very few guidelines are given to you because you are assumed to have acquired the knowledge and skills to collect and analyse, interpret and evaluate the data, to set out the work correctly, and to be able to organise your time.

With such a piece of work it is vital that you should identify very clearly indeed, precisely what you have to do in order to succeed! Essentially this means you need to answer the following questions:

- What is the aim of the study?
- What are the objectives of the study?
- What do you have to have completed and by when?
- What should it look like when you've finished it?

1. The task

The aim

The aim of the task is usually to present in a given number of words a Special Study of a topic of your own choice or a choice within a given range of topics. The length varies, but is usually longer than the "normal" essay of some 1000-3000 words. 7000 is about the average for such extended pieces of work, but this varies considerably and can be as much as 20,000 words or more for some University Departments.

The time scale also varies. In some Universities you will get as much as 2 or 3 year's notice of the deadlines. In others you can suddenly be presented with this piece of work and given 10 weeks to complete it. I have assumed that you have some 17 weeks in the examples I give here, so you must adjust the time scales accordingly to suit your own particular circumstances.

The objectives

Such pieces of work should demonstrate your abilities in the following areas:

- choosing and making explicit the topic,
- planning the whole project,
- collecting the data/evidence/substantiation,
- organising the data/evidence/substantiation,
- interpreting, analysing and evaluating the data/evidence/substantiation,
- presenting the data/evidence/substantiation.

2. The research skills involved

2.1 Choosing and making explicit the topic
- choosing the topic,
- establishing the parameters/limitations of the study,
- making clear the intention (are you going to examine, justify etc, or what?),
- explaining the methodology (the research techniques used in the study),
- giving the rationale (stating why you are doing it in the way you do),
- defining the terms.

2.2 Planning the whole project
- having a clear written timetable/plan of when to do what and in what order).

2.3 Collecting the data/evidence/substantiation
- choosing and using appropriate "expert(s)" to help identify useful sources,
- selecting appropriate secondary research,
- choosing and implementing appropriate primary research,
   e.g. questionnaire, interviews, visits/observations.

2.4 Organising the data/evidence/substantiation
- being logical, clear and simple.

2.5   Interpreting,   analysing   and   evaluating   the data/evidence/substantiation
- using appropriate statistical and interpretative techniques,
- giving appropriate weight to each piece of evidence,
- saying how it illuminates the topic, what significance it has for the topic,
- showing how each piece relates/compares to other researches,
- coming to tentative conclusions about what you have presented from other people's research and from your own.

This means making sure that the work is:
- synoptic, giving an overall view of the topic as a whole and its relationship to the wider context,
- comprehensive, but selecting the **significant** aspects,
- sensitive, never confusing fact and opinion,
- critical, recognising weaknesses, errors and omissions, and the possibility of alternative descriptions and explanations,
- profound, addressing fundamental principles and presuppositions,
- steady + consistent, based on sound arguments defending the choices made,
- creative, showing that you can appropriately apply the principles you have learnt in different contexts.

2.6 Presenting the material

using appropriate and accurate:
- grammar (including paragraphing),
- spelling,
- neatness/attractiveness,
- illustrative material,

e.g. graphs, diagrams, tables, maps, photographs.

ISLE COLLEGE
LIBRARY

2.7 Knowing when to consult with your Tutor

- formal arrangements,
- realising the difference between pestering and justifiable consultation at times not in the formal structure.

3. The format

It is very important to know at the outset into what framework you have to set the work that you do. What does it have to look like? How many parts? Has there to be a bibliography? And so on. One of the best ways of finding this out is to see what other students have done in previous years. This can be misleading. Tutors change and regulations change, and fashions change. Thus you must not rely on seeing previous work only. The best person to ask is the person, or people, setting the Special Study.

Some Universities have got their own sets of guidelines, but I have found that many do not and many of our former students have complained that having left our course they have had no indication at all of how to set out such pieces of work in their Higher Education Institution. Obviously you need to consult with those setting the work. If you are given no indication to the contrary then use the following guide.

The format of the study should contain the following elements:

3.1 Title page   (not counted in word count)

This should always contain the title, date, your name and address, the course for which the work is submitted and any other administrative detail required by the institution[1].

3.2 Contents page (not counted in word count).

There may also be a need for a separate list of illustrative material if you have used more than three or four diagrams, maps etc.[2]

3.3 Preface   (not counted in word count).

Not essential, but sometimes pleasant to have. It states your thanks to the various people who have helped in the production of the the the work (this is sometimes called "Acknowledgements").

---

[1]. See Section 25 p.5 for sample title page.
[2]. See Section 25 p.6ff for sample contents page etc.

3.4 Introduction[3] (about 500-1000 words).

1. A statement of the intention of the study.
2. Definition of the terms used in the study.
3. Establishing the parameters of the study.
4. The methodology (explaining the research techniques used.)
5. The rationale (explaining the reasons why you have chosen to write the study in the way you do).

NB. They don't have to come in that order.

3.5 Main body

Should consist of at least 3 Parts, no more than 5. Each Part about 6000 divided by the number of Parts. e.g. if 3 Parts then each Part about 2000 words) Each Part can have chapters if you wish.

For example:

Part 1. (Chapters 1 and 2)
"The Background"(about 1000-2000 words).
This is usually setting the topic in a broader context. This would probably have 2 chapters which give the broad background to the topic. You should include a brief description of what research has been done on the topic in the past.

Part 2. (Chapters 3 and 4)
"The Specific Topic in Detail" (about 2000 words)
In Chapters 3 and 4 the research results are presented. In other words you present what you have found out. (It may be that you will find it more convenient to have 3 or 4 Chapters for this part and keep Parts One and Three to 1 chapter each. That is a decision to make in conjunction with your Tutor.)

Part 3. (Chapters 5 and 6)
"The Implications of the Research" (about 2000 words)
In Chapters 5 and 6 you present an analysis of the results. This may be included with earlier chapters depending upon the style of the special study.
This is a key section because it explains the conclusions that can be drawn from the data, the implications of a theory and so on.

3.6 Conclusion(about 500/1000 words)

1. There should be a summary of the main points made in the study.
2. The implications of what you have found out should be stated.
3. Any suggestions for further research should be outlined.

3.7 Bibliography (not counted in word count).

Set out following a consistent system.

---

[3]. For more detail see Introductions and Conclusions p.13ff in this Section.

3.8 Glossary (not counted in word count).

This is not essential unless the study contains specialised words. This may be one of the Appendices, or, if it is a VERY technical and "jargon" ridden study, then it may be better for it to stand alone. It would still not count in the word count. If you use a glossary then point this out in the introduction when you define the terms used.

3.9 Illustrative material

You may use illustrative material. Make sure you number the material and include it in the Contents page, or, if there is a great deal use a separate page immediately following the Contents page and call it List of Tables and Diagrams, or whatever seems appropriate. Each piece is usually labelled as Fig. 1, Fig. 2 etc.

Photographs

Include photographs as near as possible to the relevant text. Try to mount them well and make clear their relevance both in the text and underneath the photograph. At the relevant point in the text state: "See photograph page 44." or "See Photograph opposite." DO NOT USE THEM MERELY TO MAKE IT LOOK PRETTY: use the material by referring to it directly in the text.

Diagrams and tables[4]

Include as near as possible to the relevant text. Use colour and make the relevance absolutely clear.

Maps

Include in the body of the text. Simplify them so that only the relevant information is included and make sure they are clearly relevant and referred to in the text.

Tapes

It is usual to give transcripts of any tapes, audio or video. The transcripts should be in an Appendix. The original tape(s) should be included as appendices and clearly labelled with all the usual detail of name, address, Tutor, title of study, contents etc.

3.10 Appendices (not counted in word count).

Very often the Appendices account for a high proportion of the "bulk" of a special study. They should be used to store material which contains the detailed substantiation of the study. For example, you may have done a questionnaire, sent out 40 letters and received 15 replies, done 3 taped interviews, and read 20 magazine articles. There is no point in cluttering up the main body of the study with the actual answers, photocopies of the articles etc etc. What you do in the main body is to summarise and/or quote directly from these and present the detail separately in the Appendices. For example:

    Appendix One:

    Actual questionnaire: copies of the replies and detailed breakdown of results.

    Appendix Two:

---

[4]. *See Section 21 Questionnaires p.14ff for detail on setting out tables etc.*

Copies of the letter(s) you sent out, with copies of all the replies you have received and a note of who did not reply.

Appendix Three:
If you have done any recorded interviewing then you should include a transcript of the whole interview(s).

Appendix Four:
Photocopies of any relevant magazine articles, you have used.

Appendix Five:
Glossary of terms used, particularly useful if a lot of "jargon" in the study. It can stand alone if longer than a page and placed before the Bibliography.

NOTE: Try to bind appendices with the main text. If this is not possible or appropriate then give the appendices a separate binding and title page with all the usual detail of name, address, Tutor, title of study, contents etc.

3.11 Setting out in general[5]

The study should normally be presented written on A4 paper, single sided. It can be typed/word-processed. It can be hand-written. The pages should be clearly numbered and your name should be on each sheet. Any separate appendices must be handed in clearly labelled with your name and address indicating their relevance to the study. It is very important to check with those setting the work as to the format required. In the absence of any specific instructions from your Tutors follow those set out here and in Section 25 Setting Out.

4. The guidelines

The following suggests how you should set about tackling a Special Study. Obviously there are no hard and fast rules, but the following format has proved very successful with people tackling this sort of work. It gives you a step by step way of setting about the work so that it is not one huge piece of work, but a series of manageable steps.

4.1 The topic

Some people are lucky: they are given the topic and they have no choice! If you have been given a choice then, if you can, you should choose a topic which is of interest to you!

If you are given a free range, either within a given area or just told to choose anything, then give careful thought to the selection and wording of the title.

The process of selecting a topic when you have a free range within a given discipline is helped if you adopt a systematic approach:

Identify the broad area of the topic
Identify precisely the broad area of the topic. Consult with your Tutor to ensure that that broad area is acceptable. At the same time the Tutor may well give assistance

---

[5]. See also Section 25 "Setting Out".

---

with further reading of relevant literature and put you in touch with others interested in that broad area.

The Tutor really is the key person in choosing the area and the specific topic and working closely with the Tutor is essential.

Refine the broad area

Within the broad area you will need to identify a specific aspect which interests you, and which is feasible and realistic for research and which is considered to be worth while researching (usually by your Tutor). There are various sources for exploring the area:

> reading existing published research in books,
>
> reading specialist periodicals and journals,
>
> looking at other people's previous work in similar conditions to your own,
>
> talking with others in the field at all levels.

An example

You might choose to study the broad area of UNEMPLOYMENT. To do so in a limited number of words would be merely skimming the surface of so huge an area. Keep it simple. Keep it manageable. Even "YOUTH UNEMPLOYMENT" is too broad. What is required is something you can study in depth. However, don't choose "JOHN SMITH - UNEMPLOYED YOUTH", it is too specific. You need something between them, something like "YOUTH UNEMPLOYMENT IN SACRISTON", a small community near to where you live. This may well include a part called "Youth Unemployment in Britain", and in another part you may well want to refer to John Smith, amongst several other youths in Sacriston, in order to illustrate the problem.

The topic is then further refined by answering the following type of questions about the subject to start off a brainstorming session:

What...*(e.g. are the levels of unemployment, national and local)*?

Why...*(e.g. has unemployment risen/fallen to these levels)*?

Where...*(e.g. does unemployment hit hardest in this community)*?

Who...*(e.g. are affected?)*?

How...*(e.g. can something be done about it)*?

When...*(e.g. did it all start)*?

etc....etc....

The question list can and should obviously be longer. You will know the answers to some, but not to others. Eventually you will begin to feel that you have a lot of possible avenues for exploration.

Focus

When the topic has been identified you will need to narrow it down, so that you are sure that you are very clear what you are doing with the topic. Beware of just saying "Youth Unemployment in Sacriston". This is not specific, giving no idea of how you are treating it.

The following list might be of use to you in defining your intentions with the topic you choose:

Account for...(e.g. Youth Unemployment in Sacriston)
Analyse ...(e.g. Youth Unemployment in Sacriston)   •
Assess the extent to which ...Calculate ...Classify ...Comment on...Compare
... with ...Contrast the ... with ...Criticise ... .Define ...Describe ...Discuss
...Enumerate ...Evaluate ...Explain ...How far ... to what extent ...Identify
...Indicate ...Illustrate ...Interpret ... Investigate... Justify ...Label ...List
...Outline ...Predict ...Prove ...Relate ...Review ...Show how... ...State
...Summarise ...Trace the development of ...

It may be a combination of several of these, or it may be something different entirely.

Be very clear precisely what you are attempting to do and make sure that you have expressed it in the title.

Refine the title

Titles need not be short and snappy: but you can have a title and then a description. With the YOUTH UNEMPLOYMENT IN SACRISTON - you could have that as the short title and a description which clarifies more precisely the scope:

> *"Youth Unemployment in Sacriston"*
> *An examination of the extent of unemployment of 16-25 year olds in the village and the effect of that unemployment on the young people themselves and on the local community as a whole, with a brief examination of possible solutions.*

It may be that when you start you just have an idea of the topic and then later, after having collected the data, you will at that stage decide what you will do with the data. It is much easier to decide the precise boundaries of the topic **before** you start, otherwise you may find yourself collecting all sorts of irrelevant data.

In other words define your parameters NOW. Do not leave it to sort itself out.

4.2 The research

Remember that at this level of study you will be expected to find out what experts have found from their research. The examiner is NOT interested in reading what YOU think from your limited experience. The examiner is looking to see how well you can find out what is known about the subject, and how you can analyse and evaluate that material. S/he is NOT looking for what YOU know!

This usually means that you need to be seeking several accounts of the topic, rather than one. Obviously in 7000 words you can't summarise EVERY expert, but you should make sure that you have made reference to the important and acknowledged experts in the topic under consideration. Make sure that you include a summary of the available research at some point in the study. It is usual to have a brief overview of this in the early part of the study.

At Higher Education level you should remember that no one is interested in your **unsubstantiated** opinion. Make sure that you have gone and found out what is known about the topic with which you are dealing. You need to identify the experts in the topic you have chosen. DO NOT RELY ON YOUR OWN EXISTING KNOWLEDGE OF THE TOPIC. When you have a clear idea of what knowledge exists already on the topic then you can:

- analyse it,
- evaluate it,
- apply it to the situation you wish to examine,
- plan your own investigative methods,
- come to some tentative conclusions of your own.

Different kinds of research

There are various ways in which you can substantiate what you say:

Secondary research
    research other people have done.

Primary research
    research you have done yourself.

Your own experience/anecdotal evidence
    You should AVOID using your own experience as the basis of proof. It is not wrong to ILLUSTRATE something from your own experience. But...NEVER try to prove anything from it. Certainly you CAN use your experience as EXAMPLE.

    You should also avoid what is called "anecdotal" evidence. That is evidence of the type that goes from the particular to the general.
"A friend of mine told me that his grandmother had seen a ghost therefore ghosts do exist."

PLEASE, PLEASE, PLEASE stick to finding out what the experts have to say about the topic, and to what you find from an accurate and objective questionnaire and (if necessary) other such research techniques as you and your Tutor think appropriate.

4.3 Secondary research

What it is

This is research which others have already done. It is one of the main skills of the under-graduate to investigate what research has already been done on a topic, summarise it, and then compare and contrast it with other research on the same topic.

Finding the relevant books is the first step. If you can consult with Tutors then they should be able to supply a list of the recommended books etc on the topic of your study. However, you can explore the literature available by visiting your library and asking for help there.

Where to find it[6]

Libraries

Most Librarians are only to happy to help. Large towns have reference libraries and these are invaluable in finding such material.

Get a few books on the topic. Use the techniques set out in the Section 17 on reading. In other words, look at the contents pages to "wrap your mind around" the scope of the book - looking out for where your topic fits in the book. Use the index to help in this as well. Follow up references to other books, articles etc.

LOOK FOR WHAT IS RELEVANT - and make notes. Any REALLY useful sentences jot down verbatim and use as a quotation in the study (ONLY IF IT IS REALLY RELEVANT). If it's more than a couple of sentences then just summarise it: that is called a reference.

Always remember to keep the page number, the author, the title and the publisher and the year of publication of any quotations or references you wish to use[7].

When doing a Special Study you will be consulting more than the four or five books you have used in essays.

You are asked to find out what research in general says about the topic you've chosen, not just what ONE author/researcher says. (Usually the summary of existing research comes early in the study.)

Journals and periodicals

Don't forget to look at relevant periodicals and journals. Each discipline seems to have its own clutch of specialised periodicals and journals which contain the latest research, opinions and trends. Well informed studies have reference to these.

---

[6]. See also Section 30 on Libraries.

[7]. See Section 25 p.9 for how to set out quotations and references.

Research directories

There are many books which are useful in finding out what the latest research is on topics. The list in Appendix 2 should help you identify likely sources.

CD discs[8]

Do note that the development of CD discs used to store huge amounts of information, which can be rapidly accessed very simply, is revolutionising research. Gone are the days when students would sit in libraries reading volumes of newspapers searching for references to their topic.

With the CD the student can enter several key words and the computer searches for those words, finds all references to them and identifies which articles are relevant. The articles may then be loaded onto a floppy disk for the student to take away to his own computer!

4.4 Primary research

This is research/investigation which you carry out yourself, via surveys, questionnaires, observation and so on.

The questionnaire

Look through Section 21 on questionnaires. Essentially you need to establish the following basic points:
- What you are going to ask and why.
- Whom you are going to ask.
- How you are going to ask.
- How you will interpret the results.
- How you will present the results.

The interviews

Essentially you need to establish the following basic points:
- What you want to find out.
- People whom you intend to interview.
- Questions you wish to ask.
- Deadlines for conducting, transcribing and completing.

The letters

Make a list of the organisations/individuals to whom you intend to write.

You should be thinking of getting opinion / fact / information about your topic from a wide variety of sources.

Whitaker's Almanac is an excellent source of addresses. Very often one contact will lead to another.

In the initial planning you should try to list the people to whom you wish to write under the following types of heading. Obviously this needs adapting to suit your particular topic.

---

[8]. *See also Section 28 p.2.*

---

1. Organisations.

You should certainly think of getting in touch with organisations at the following levels:

International level.
    e.g. UNESCO/EEC
National level.
    Political/policy
        To the Ministry/Government Department
        To the main political parties
    Organisational
        Head offices of national organisations
Local level
    Political/policy
        Appropriate parts of local government/town hall/county hall
        To local politicians
        Local pressure groups /organisations / individuals

2. Acknowledged academic experts.

These may be published or unpublished international, national, local - you could find them in specialist journals, University Departments. Contact by phone or letter.

3. Letters to local/national newspapers.

These are often useful. Try along lines of:

Your address/date

"*I am a student at -------- doing research into the effects of youth unemployment in Sacriston. If you would like to make any contribution to this research then please contact me:*
name.
address
telephone number."

---

4. Letters to relevant magazines, journals.

You could try asking the editor for advice, or a letter as above inserted in the publication asking for help.

Be warned that there will probably be a considerable time delay with such contacts. You may well have to send a further letter, or even telephone to hurry up the reply!

5. Format of letters.

You should write letters along the following lines:

> _Your address/date_
>
> _"Dear -----,_
>
> _I am a student at---------- and am doing research into -----. I would be very grateful if you could send me any information you may have on -----. As you will understand I have a limited time span to complete this research and would appreciate an early reply. I enclose a stamped addressed envelope for your reply._
>
> _Yours etc"_

It is important to get these off and to keep copies of all those to whom you have written. You should put them into an appendix. Don't worry if you do not get replies on time. It should serve to teach you how long the process of collecting data can be!

REMEMBER THE SOONER THEY ARE SENT THE BETTER.

The visits

Make a list of any places you intend to visit / observe

Deadlines for completion of observations etc

If you do decide to do observations and visits then remember to plan carefully exactly:

- what it is you are going to observe,
- how you are going to observe,
- how you are going to record your observations,
- how you will measure them.

It is not just a matter of going and looking!

Archive material

There is a great deal of data available in archives of various sorts on all levels from international to local, even personal. There are learned societies, museums, private collections. These can be in the form of unpublished documents, artifacts, objects, minutes of meetings, diaries, microfiches.

If you require access to collections of data held privately then a letter from your University may help. Don't hesitate to ask.

4.5 Analysing, interpreting and evaluating the research

It is important to emphasise the evaluative and analytic skills required with a special study. It is no use just describing the research that has been done. You have to stand back from it and say in what way it illuminates the topic, what significance it has for the topic, what weight can be given to it, and how it relates and compares to other views from other researches.

4.6 Academic rigour

In all academic work you need to demonstrate an accurate, correct and valid foundation in the subject matter of the topic. It should be:
- synoptic, giving an overall view of the topic as a whole and its relationship to the wider context,
- comprehensive, but selecting the **significant** aspects,
- sensitive, never confusing fact and opinion,
- critical, recognising weaknesses, errors and omissions, and the possibility of alternative descriptions and explanations,
- profound, addressing fundamental principles and presuppositions,
- steady and consistent, based on sound arguments defending the choices made,
- creative, showing that you can appropriately apply the principles you have learnt in different contexts.

AVOID BEING PURELY DESCRIPTIVE.
ANALYSE, INTERPRET AND EVALUATE
YOUR PRIMARY AND SECONDARY RESEARCH.

---

5. Introductions and conclusions

5.1 Introductions

A statement of intent

In general this should describe the general topic area, the specific topic, why the topic is important, prior research and contributions to be made by that research. Specifically statements of intent are best following the pattern of:

"The intention of this study is to examine/assess/justify etc ......Part One deals with .... Part Two tackles ....."

Try to avoid the use of the future tense with the intention. Don't say:

"This study will deal with the major theories which try to examine the nature of.... In Part 1 I will comment on..."

Say rather:

"This study deals with the major theories which try to examine the nature of....Part 1 comments on..."

Doing this somehow suggests that you are in control of the material!

Definition of terms

Always attempt to make clear any specific terms in the title or those which are implied by the title. It is best to say that you are following an acknowledged expert's usage: something along the lines of:

"Title: "An assessment of the major changes brought about by the Thatcher Government since 1979."
The term "major changes" is used in the way in which Halford (1985) suggests:

> *"A major change is one which affects more than 50% of the population, making their lives significantly different in terms of ability to pay for goods and services, their right to follow their political or religious beliefs..."*

(HALFORD, 1985, 345)

Use a glossary if there are many definitions to be made.

Establishing the parameters

Make clear the boundaries/parameters of the subject:

Title: "Edwina Currie was right!" - An investigation.
"In this study discussion is confined to comments made by Edwina Currie on egg production in this country rather than the controversial statements she has made on other subjects."

You should point out the limitations of the study and key assumptions you've made.

The methodology

This explains what research techniques are used in the study. For example, this might describe the fact that you have done a questionnaire, made a series of visits, a measurement technique, an experiment, and an historical method of analysis.

The rationale

State why you've chosen the topic AND why you've tackled it in the way you have.

"This topic is chosen since there needs to be some objective clarity shone onto what has become an issue obscured by rhetoric and emotion. The matter is examined in the three parts as outlined above. The first gives the broad background of the research which already exists. The three principal sources were ... ... and ... who are acknowledged as the leading researchers in the field of ... Since there is no detailed investigation existing which examines ..... questionnaires were used with...in order to find out.... Visits were made to ... and ... so that specific examples of .... could be systematically observed and analysed. In order to ensure a clear picture of the problem at a local level is given, local politicians, members of the village action group and local industrialists were interviewed. The second part considers the findings of these investigations and the final part looks at the possible ways in which the problems might be resolved by the participants.

Note: Introductions are not necessarily written first!

5.2 Conclusions

Summary

Summarise what you have said. To some extent this is a repetition of what is said in the introduction - the statement of intent.

It is likely that you can put into a sentence the important point from each section of each part.

One method which some students have found useful is to summarise each chapter and include that summary at the end of each chapter, referring the reader to these summaries in the conclusion.

This summary should not be merely descriptive, but should, as stated previously , be evaluative and analytic.

You should try to go further and bring out the implications.

Implications

Bring out the major implications of what has been said, e.g.:

"This study has described the major changes which have come about as a result of the Thatcher Government from 1979.
These were:
1. the move away from nationalised industries and services,
2. the reduction of taxes,
3. etc etc
It seems from the examination that has been done of these changes that:
1. they will be difficult to alter in that they have taken over ten years to implement,
2. that they have profoundly affected the attitude of the people towards each other, in that ....
3. etc etc"

Enlightenment

It is useful to note any change in your perception of the topic along the lines of (here the use of "I" is obviously permitted):

"When I started this piece of research I expected ....however, as a result of the work I have done I have found that....."

Further research

You should also suggest areas for further research into the topic:

"I feel that I would like now to examine more closely several further aspects of the topic, namely....., because...."

or:

"The work I have done raises several questions which need further research. These questions are:....."

6. The style

6.1 The shape

When you get to the rough draft stage, the state of the study will be full of crossings out, different types of writing, different pieces of paper and so on. I find it useful at this stage to try to get a clear idea of the length and the "shape" by constructing a rough draft. This may involve cutting out bits of the study and pasting them in different places. Don't worry at this stage about neatness of presentation: that can be done when you have got the basic shape and size right.

Look carefully at the content matter of each part and ensure that it is relevant to the question.

Look at the balance to make sure that you have not written too much on any one particular aspect.

6.2 The "voice"

Be tentative

When you've got the study in the right order and you are fairly happy about the content matter then listen to how it sounds. If it is strident and "know-it-all" then try the following.

> You should try to be less "assertive" and more "tentative" - always provide adequate evidence for any assertions you make.
>
> Use phrases like:
>
> *"It seems, from the research done by..."*
>
> *"It appears that..."*

rather than

> *"It's a well known fact..."*
>
> *"It's obvious that..."*
>
> *"Everybody knows that..."*

Be objective

Try in general to avoid speaking directly to the reader (though this is not always possible, nor desirable) - but avoid chattiness and slang:

> *"Well, dear reader, I am going to tell you in this study all what I know about Human Development, OK?"*

Phrase this more like:

> *"This study surveys 3 different theories of human development."*

It is better to avoid the first person if at all possible. Rather than saying "I" say "The study...".

Be simple
There is a rather complicated way to find out your "FOG INDEX" which involves the following formula:
- FOG INDEX= 0.4(Average sentence length + percentage of words more than two syllables in length)

Try this with a couple of pages of your text, especially one you think might be a bit "obscure". If the number you get is greater than 12 then you are in serious danger of fogging your readers to the point of losing them!

Although you don't have to do the fog index, try reading your study aloud to someone and watch out for that glazed look! Always beware of being complicated when being simple is much more effective.

Be reflective
It is important to emphasise the evaluative and analytic skills required with a special study. Thus the style should be reflective. That is you should stand back from it and say:
- in what way the research illuminates the topic,
- what significance it has for the topic,
- what weight can be given to it,
- how it relates and compares to other views from other researches.

AVOID BEING PURELY DESCRIPTIVE. ANALYSE, INTERPRET AND EVALUATE YOUR PRIMARY AND SECONDARY RESEARCH.

6.3 Some general points

Length
The study should be as near as possible to the given words in length. You do not get extra marks for putting in more words than specified. Part of the discipline of a Special Study is to stay within the number of words set. Equally you should not be much short of the words specified. Much of the detailed supportive evidence should be in the appendices. You should refer to that supportive material, and use short extracts only in the main text.

Originality
The study must be your own original work. There have been cases of plagiarism (passing off other people's work as your own) which have resulted in students being barred from taking further part in academic life. Be careful that you acknowledge all your sources. Tutors are usually very experienced in such matters and can identify work which is not original.

Confidentiality
You must show regard for confidentiality and safeguard the anonymity of any
people whom you use in your study and, unless they give you explicit and written
permission, you must NOT use the real names. This also applies to institutions.

7. Getting organised

7.1 Deadlines

You are usually given deadlines by those setting the piece of work, but you should
in any case give yourself some definite deadlines for completing the major aspects
of the study. It is important to have these deadlines clearly set out for yourself, so
that they are incorporated into your year planner, term by term, week by week, day
by day filofax/diary[9]! The worst thing you can do is to leave the work until a few
days before the final deadline.
The example below could serve as a model. Obviously you need to adapt it to the
nature of the work which you are doing and to the time you have available. The
example below assumes about 17 weeks from start to finish.

An overall view of when things have to be done by!
DEADLINE 1: Topic and scope.   By end of Week 1.
DEADLINE 2: Methods.   By end of Week 2.
DEADLINE 3: Action Plan.   By end of Week 3.
DEADLINE 4: Detailed Plan.   By end of Week 4.
DEADLINE 5: Rough Draft.   By 2 weeks before:
FINAL DEADLINE: By final deadline!

DEADLINE ONE: Topic and scope
By one week after being given the task: you should produce a written statement of
the topic you have chosen and an indication of the scope of the aspect of the topic
you intend to explore. Use the pro forma at the back of this Section[10].

Title:Youth Unemployment in Sacriston.
Scope:To examine the extent of youth unemployment in that
village and see how it has affected the community in general
and young people (16-25 year olds) in particular in terms of
occupation, income and "life-style". I also want to examine the
things being done to help these unemployed people.

---

[9]. _See Section 16 p.5ff._
[10]. _See page 26 of this Section._

DEADLINE TWO: Methodology

By 2 weeks after the start: you should produce a written statement of the methods of research which you are going to use. You could use or adapt the pro forma at back of this Section[11].

Methodology

Title: Youth Unemployment in Sacriston.

Proposed methodology

Primary research:

Questionnaire to members of youth club.

  questions include some to try to find out:

    how old/male/female/school

    at school/unemployed/employed?

    how long unemployed

    attitudes to being unemployed/unemployment

    who can help you?

    their opinions re future.

  40 questionnaires to be given out

Visits to schools to interview:

  Careers teacher(s)

  teachers of leavers' classes.

  head teacher(s)

Visit to Youth Club to interview:

  Youth Leader(s)/Members

A case study of two young unemployed teenagers

Interviews with parents

Interviews with local GP's to illustrate the medical effects.

Search of local newspapers to trace development of youth unemployment in the village.

Letters to appropriate newspapers/journals

Letters/interviews with politicians national/local

Secondary Research:

Reading of statistics of unemployment, theories of unemployment

---

[11]. *See page 27 of this Section.*

DEADLINE THREE: ACTION PLAN. By Week 3.

NAME:

TOPIC:

You may use this pro forma or produce another which shows the overall plan of what you are going to do and when you hope you will have done it. There may be other aspects you wish to include.

Week Number and date															
Deadlines															
Topic chosen															
" focused															
Overall plan															
Lit search															
list															
select															
read/note															
Letters															
written															
sent out															
written up															
interpreted															
Interviews															
set up															
done															
interpreted															
set out															
Questionnaire															
written															
sent out															
collated															
interpreted															
set out															
Illustrative															
planned															
done															
set out															
1st draft															
Final draft															

It is essential to work out a time-table for yourself with such a complex piece of work which depends on so many different pieces of activity coming together and being organised by a specific date. I have suggested a list of items which should be planned well ahead. You should give yourself specific dates by which each activity is completed. There may be other aspects you wish to include. You may use the pro forma on page 28 of this Section, or produce another based on the same principle which shows the overall plan of what you are going to do and when you hope you will have done it.

DEADLINE FOUR: Detailed plan.

By 4 weeks after the start.

Plan of study: With Part/Chapter Titles - rough summary of each chapter. Include wordage. Indicate what will be your probable appendices. Use the pro forma at back of this document[12].

DEADLINE FIVE: Rough draft

At least two weeks before the final deadline.

This gives you a chance to ask if everything is going OK - you can check with your Tutor as you go along but use this as a date to aim at for being in a position to set about tackling the final draft of the material. You should aim to have this done before the actual deadline.

FINAL DEADLINE:

When you are given a final deadline please remember that that is what it is! Please regard this is the last date for submission. There will then be no difficulty in getting all things marked etc etc.

If you are in desperate straits then some Universities MAY be able to have an extension. This is NOT recommended and will NOT be available except in exceptional circumstances such as illness.

The extension will have to be negotiated with the University and the External Examiner. In cases of illness a doctor's note/letter is essential and must be produced for the External Examiner.

Keep a copy of the Study as they do sometimes go astray.

7.2 Working with Tutors

If you are doing a Special Study then it must be assumed that you will have to begin to take on more responsibility for your own work, for example in terms of making decisions about when to consult with your Tutor.

Schools, Colleges and Universities usually set aside time for students to consult with staff about their progress with the study. It is vital that you take advantage of this. If you take your work along regularly you will be able to receive feedback about your progress and if you are on the right lines. It is far better to do this early and regularly than to leave it and put off seeing the Tutor(s).

---

[12]. *See page 28 of this Section.*

- If you are making mistakes then it is far better that your Tutor should spot this early and give you the chance to put it right.
- If you do not consult then you are taking a very great risk.
- If the Tutors do not give a formal opportunity for consultation then ask as early as possible to consult and check that your work is on the right lines.

Your University should not use any material from your special study in any way without first asking your explicit and written permission.

They should attempt to ensure that you have your original copy returned as soon as possible.

It is often useful to offer a photocopy of your study to your Tutor, since they are always of use to help future students.

8. Evaluating your own work

8.1 Checking the basics

Obviously it isn't possible for me to deal with how your Tutor(s) will mark the piece of work. You can at least ensure a good start, and that you won't lose marks for silly things like spelling if you evaluate your piece of work, or get someone else to do so by following the scheme set out on page 25. As with essays, you will need someone to make comments on:

- your knowledge of content matter and selection of appropriate material, and your style.

You will need someone to diagnose and prescribe

- by pointing to areas where you need to improve,
- by suggesting action to be taken, and
- by identifying areas where you are strong.

As with essays I must point out that the marking scheme on the next page is a useful reminder to you of the **basic requirements** of an essay.

Do read it through carefully and note what gets marks.

8.2 Demonstrating your understanding

Most markers take the schedule almost for granted and are more concerned with the aspects listed below.

YOUR UNDERSTANDING, AS SHOWN BY
THE WAY IN WHICH YOU
INTERPRET
ANALYSE and
EVALUATE
the research material which you have used.

8.3 Academic rigour

At Higher Education level your Tutors will be looking for evidence that you can examine a topic effectively in academic terms. This is given more marks than the other aspects which I have dealt with above. But remember that without those nuts and bolts, the engine will fall to pieces!

Do not worry too much, when you first start your study, about the final conclusions. If you follow the patterns indicated above they will emerge as you build up your understanding of the research, done by others and yourself, on the topic. I must emphasise that you should constantly be questioning that research made by other researchers, asking always if the evidence they produce to substantiate their assertions is credible, sufficient and relevant. As you evaluate the research, including your own, you will come to your own judgement about which aspects make more sense than others, and you will accordingly give more weight to those. This active process will inevitably move you to begin to formulate your own opinions about the topic. When you present your own conclusions make sure that **your** study really does substantiate what **you** are asserting. Be logical: that way you will persuade. It may be that you find it hard to come to definite exclusive conclusions. In which case say so, pointing out why. Is it lack of evidence? Is it because the evidence is contradictory? Be specific.

> ## You should make sure that the work is:
> ## SYNOPTIC, COMPREHENSIVE, SENSITIVE,
> ## CRITICAL, PROFOUND,
> ## STEADY AND CONSISTENT,
> ## CREATIVE, WELL STRUCTURED,
> ## WELL SUBSTANTIATED, WELL ARGUED
> ## AND WELL PRESENTED.

8.4 A marking scheme

The schedule overleaf is one which you can use to get a feeling for the basic requirements of an essay, the sort of nuts and bolts that hold the essay together, rather than the styling and engine that's there! You can do the evaluation yourself, indeed it is a very good exercise to do this anyway, but you will probably find it more realistic and satisfying if you get someone else to mark it for you.

If you cannot think of anyone to do this, then send it, together with a fee of £5 for every 1000 words of the study and a stamped self-addressed label for returning the package, to me via the address at the front of the book and I will return it to you marked and with comments as soon as I possibly can.

```
SUGGESTED MARKING SCHEDULE FOR A SPECIAL STUDY
SECTION ONE: STRUCTURE
Introduction:
   - making clear your intention                        [   / 5]
   - defining your parameters                           [   / 5]
   - defining your terms                                [   / 5]
   - explaining methodology                             [   / 5]
   - giving the rationale of the study                  [   / 5]
Main body
   - key ideas presented logically                      [  /10]
   - clear structure within each part                   [  /10]
   - relevance of each part made clear                  [  /10]
   - balance between the parts                          [  /10]
Conclusion
   - summarising main points                            [  /10]
   - implications of the study                          [  /10]
   - changes in your perception                         [   / 5]
   - suggestions for further research                   [   / 5]
Bibliography
   - set out using Harvard system                       [  /10]
Appendices
   - material/resources used,
   - actual questionnaire/survey in full,
     transcripts, cassettes etc etc.                    [  /20]
                               Total Section 1=[  /125]
SECTION TWO:SUBSTANTIATION
Use of primary sources
   - questionnaire/survey
   - letters/contacts
     other (e.g./interviews/observation/visit(s)        [  /45]
Use of secondary sources
   - reference to appropriate experts                   [  /45]
                               Total Section 2=[  /90]
SECTION THREE: OVERALL PRESENTATION
   - Grammar (including punctuation)                    [   / 5]
   - Spelling                                           [   / 5]
   - Neatness + "The Look"                              [   / 5]
   - Illustrative material                              [  /10]
                               Total Section 3=[  /25]
SECTION FOUR: STYLE
   - "Tentativeness"                                    [  /10]
   - Objectivity                                        [  /10]
   - Simplicity                                         [  /10]
                               Total Section 4=[  /30]
SECTION FIVE: COMPLYING WITH DEADLINES
   - ONE  : Topic + scope      by Week  1               [   / 5]
   - TWO  : Methods.           by Week  2               [   / 5]
   - THREE: Action Plan.       by Week  3               [   / 5]
   - FOUR : Plan.              by Week  4               [   / 5]
   - FIVE : Rough Draft.       by Week 13               [   / 5]
   - FINAL DEADLINE:           by Week 17               [   / 5]
                               Total Section 5=[  /30]
PERCENTAGE= [    ]             TOTAL MARK=[  /300]
```

DEADLINE ONE: Topic and scope.   By Week 1.

===

NAME:

TOPIC:

SCOPE:

TUTOR COMMENTS:(If applicable)

===

TUTOR   :
STUDENT   :
DATE AGREED:

===

DEADLINE TWO: METHODOLOGY. By Week 2.

===

NAME:

TOPIC:

PROPOSED METHODOLOGY:
(Include Primary and Secondary research)

ISLE COLLEGE
LIBRARY

TUTOR COMMENTS:(If applicable)

===

TUTOR   :
STUDENT   :
DATE AGREED:

===

DEADLINE THREE: ACTION PLAN. By Week 3.

NAME:

TOPIC:

You may use this pro forma or produce another which shows the overall plan of what you are going to do and when you hope you will have done it. There may be other aspects you wish to include.

Week Number and date																
Deadlines **Topic chosen** **" focused** **Overall plan** **Lit search** list select read/note **Letters** written sent out written up interpreted **Interviews** set up done interpreted set out **Questionnaire** written sent out collated interpreted set out **Illustrative** planned done set out **1stdraft** **Final draft**																

DEADLINE FOUR: Plan. By Week 4.

NAME:

TUTOR:

TOPIC:

PLAN:
Introduction:(Words:)

Chapters/Sections with titles and brief summary

Conclusion (Words:)

Probable Appendices

TUTOR COMMENT:(If applicable)

TUTOR :
STUDENT:
DATE AGREED:

A CHECKLIST.

===

NAME:

TOPIC:

I have set out SOME of the aspects of a Special Study. They are not in any order of importance. There may well be others which you need to include.

Week Number and date																	
Title Page Contents page Preface Introduction Part I Chapter 1 Chapter 2 Part II Chapter 3 Chapter 4 Part III Chapter 5 Chapter 6 Conclusion Bibliography																	

SECTION 21: QUESTIONNAIRES
Introduction

Questionnaires and interviews are important tools for anyone doing primary research.

A questionnaire consists of a carefully worked out series of questions written down and given to a number of selected people in order to indicate the likely response of a larger group of people of whom this group is a representative selection.
Sometimes the questionnaire is given aurally to the interviewee either in person or by telephone, and the responses are written down by the questioner. More usually the questionnaire is distributed to the interviewees (e.g. by hand individually and/or in groups, or by post), with a request that they complete the questionnaire and return it to the questioner when the questions are answered. The results are then collated.

An interview is a situation where the questioner talks with one or more people with a view to ascertaining their views on a particular topic by asking questions in a less formal way, allowing the interviewee to respond at length. The questions are thought out carefully beforehand, but may well be altered in the light of the responses given. This is not the case with questionnaires. Interview situations are recorded either by hand or, more effectively, by a video or sound recorder. The objective may be to seek the views of one person and/or group of people in order to present those views in support of a particular part of the research, or to compare/contrast those views with those of other people and/or groups.

Many of the points made about the nature of questioning obviously apply to both questionnaires and interviews. However, there is a big difference between the two situations.
Questionnaires are useful ways of gathering structured data. Much thought should go into the design of the questionnaire.

> 1. What are you going to ask?
>
> 2. Whom are you going to ask?
>
> 3. How are you going to ask it?
>
> 4. How will you interpret the responses?
>
> 5. How will you present the results?

1. What are you going to ask?

1.1 Question Content

The purpose may be to learn:
> what the people know (facts),
> what they think, expect, feel, or prefer (beliefs and attitudes), or
> what they have done (behaviours).

These distinctions are useful, but there may be other areas which you wish to explore.

So, for each aspect of the topic decide if it is:

```
            factual              [   ]
            attitudinal          [   ]
            behavioural          [   ]
            other     specify precisely.
```

**ALWAYS BE SPECIFIC ABOUT PRECISELY
WHAT IT IS THAT YOU ARE TRYING TO EXPLORE.**

1.2 Questions aimed at facts

Factual questions about who the person is are essential to any questionnaire. In any survey you need to know whom you are asking so you need to ask such questions as are significant to reveal the "type" of person. Usual categories are:

```
            age
            gender
            marital status
            occupation
            class (Registrar General's categories')
            where live
            income
```

There may be others depending upon what you consider to be significant. For example, if it is a survey of use of left handed screw-drivers then the individual's "handedness" becomes important.

These factual questions appear to be the simplest BUT...

There is always the chance that the person asked about their income, (if they don't just say "Mind your own business"!) may want to impress you with by exaggerating

---

. See Section 23 on Class.

income, or may think you are from the Inland Revenue, and reduce income accordingly!

It is possible to use indirect methods of ascertaining wealth/class, by asking such questions as how many cars do you have? What newspapers do you read?

There are dangers in asking questions which are apparently simple and factual. They always need very careful wording, since many people interpret the question in different ways. For example, if you asked people:

"What proportion of your day is devoted to eating?"

Some will assume that that is a 24 hour day, others a 12 hour day, others the hours they are awake. Some may not fully understand the word "proportion" and then how would you like to work out what proportion of 24 hours is 17 minutes? Further complications arise with this question when one considers the different eating habits people have on different days of the week and different times of the year. The question will be interpreted in many different ways and produce answers which are based on those different interpretations. With such factual questions you are far better being very precise and limiting the range of answers so that people don't have complex maths involved. For example:

yesterday did you eat:		Please tick how long		
		less than 10 minutes	10-20mins	20+mins
breakfast	[ ]	[ ]	[ ]	[ ]
lunch	[ ]	[ ]	[ ]	[ ]
tea	[ ]	[ ]	[ ]	[ ]
dinner	[ ]	[ ]	[ ]	[ ]
supper	[ ]	[ ]	[ ]	[ ]
other(please specify)				
	[ ]	[ ]	[ ]	[ ]

1.3 Questions aimed at attitudes

Direct

These can be direct:

Are you in favour of abortion?
Tick which of the following best describes your feelings:
against   [ ]
in favour   [ ]
etc

Indirect

Or they can be indirect. In this case you could describe a situation involving characters taking different attitudes and ask which character the respondent felt most sympathy for.

A girl of 13 (A) finds she is pregnant. She wants to have an abortion. Her boyfriend (B), aged 16, says he wants her to have the baby and he will marry her when he legally can do so. Her parents agree with him. His parents agree with her. With whom do you agree, A or B?

Multiple choice questions

These can be given as in the following:

Which of the following comes nearest to your views on abortion?
A: I agree strongly with a woman's right to do what she wants with her own body.
B: I believe that the unborn child has the right to live.
C: etc etc.

The main problem here is that you really do have to have many views expressed for people to chose, and even then you may not be able to encompass all of the views possible!

If you are asking for people's opinions, e.g. about Access to HE Courses, and you find that some people don't know about them, then rather than fill them in with information in the questionnaire and then ask their opinion you are better off recording the fact that that person has not heard of them and that after explanation they did have such and such an opinion. This is a different kind of opinion to the one held by someone who has heard of them and has had a chance to form their opinion before responding to your questionnaire.

Hypothetical questions

These are questions which are based on wording such as:

If there were a general election tomorrow, what would you vote?

CONSERVATIVE	[ ]
LABOUR	[ ]
LIBERAL DEMOCRAT	[ ]
OTHER(Please specify)	[ ]

These questions are frequently used in the well known opinion polls.

1.4 Questions aimed at behaviour

These questions are very like the factual questions: they seem to be easy, but when you have done a couple of questionnaires you will realise that there are many problems associated with them, many of which are directly connected with the way in which you word the actual questions. Again you have to trust that people are being honest, and that they can recall what they they did and when they did it. The problems are usually associated with time.

Time problems

There are several techniques for helping people to be accurate with their memory of when an event happened and enable you to measure and compare different replies.

Bounded recall:

Rather than asking:"Do you play golf often?", ask: "How many times have you played golf in the last 3 months?"

Averaging.

Because people have problems when asked to tell you the amount of time they spend on an activity, for example, watching TV, you might be able to allow them to become more accurate by asking the question in a wording such as follows:

The next few questions are about *watching TV*
First, how much time, if any, did you *watch TV* YESTERDAY?
> Was that amount of time typical of the time you spend *watching TV* on WEEKDAYS during the past week or so?
> (If No) What WAS the typical amount of time you spent *watching TV* on WEEKDAYS over the past week or so?

A similar, but separate, question can then be asked about weekENDS, because people tend to have different habits during a weekend. This avoids mathematical and memory problems! You will find that it is easier for them to be given answers which they can tick as in the example given above on factual questions:

Yesterday did you *watch TV*:	Please state how long
less than 10 mins	[ ]
10-20 mins	[ ]
20-30 mins	[ ]
30-60 mins	[ ]
1- 2 hours	[ ]
2- 3 hours	[ ]
3- 4 hours	[ ]
5- 6 hours	[ ]
Other (Please Specify)	[ ]

<u>Using reminders.</u>
It is difficult to rely on people's memories too much, and it useful to give landmarks:
"Since you came on the Access Course, has anyone beaten you up?"
Events or major holidays, such as New Year's Day, can anchor the timing of other events.

2. Whom are you going to ask?

2.1 The criteria for an acceptable sample

    appropriate and representative,
    large enough,
    giving a high response rate.

2.2 Appropriate/representative.

The group you choose must be appropriate and representative. You might hand out questionnaires to 20 of your friends and acquaintances and achieve a near-perfect response rate - but the results would not be meaningful (except as a description of that particular set of people) because they do not constitute a representative sample of any larger population.

Consider carefully whom you should ask: if you are trying to find out about the attitudes of town's people to fox-hunting then there is little point in asking country people about their attitudes, unless you are interested in comparing the two groups.

Equally if you are trying to find out what people in general think of fox-hunting, then you will have to find a way of sampling "people in general". It is no use asking a couple of friends and relatives and three people down the pub!

Note that you can fool yourself into thinking you have been objective in choosing your sample, but remember that if you have no control over who returns the completed questionnaire then there will be an element of self selection from those who choose to answer. Those who don't answer may well have significantly different views to those who do reply. You should always say :

> how you have chosen the people you have used in your questionnaire,
> how many you chose,
> how many replied,
> how many did not.

People will then be able to weigh the significance of the results of your questionnaire. Thus it is important that you give some thought to the selection of the group you ask. Make sure that it fulfils the three criteria above.

2.3 Consider what sample you are making

If you take a sample of the larger group whose opinion you are trying to find then you can take a random sample - a small proportion of the whole group taken literally at random. You need to know as much as you can about the make-up of the larger group from which you take the small random sample and you need to check to see if it IS representative. For example, has your sample the right proportions of genders, age, income?

2.4 Size of the sample

The size of the sample must be reasonable enough to ensure that it can be representative. It is difficult to give a figure for this. Many of the leading polling companies ask about 1000 selected people in their opinion polls about voting intentions. This is a very small sample indeed of the whole of the voting public in Britain, but great care is taken to ensure that the 1000 represent accurately as many aspects of the total votal population of Britain as is possible. You should check with your Tutor just how many people need to be asked to give a satisfactory result for your purposes. In general a MINIMUM of 30 has been my recommendation for questionnaires for comparatively simple investigations. If your questionnaire is meant as a real investigative tool then you will certainly need to ask many more people than 30.

You must always state how many you have asked, how many, in number, have responded: do NOT give results only in percentages, though percentages are used once you have established actual numbers.

2.5 How many reply?

People don't always reply to your questionnaire. You need to have as many as possible replying. This is the percentage of people who actually return your questionnaire. This is often used as a measure of how seriously the information gathered can be taken. If only 2% of your sample reply then not a great deal of weight can be given to the information as being representative of the whole sample, let alone the whole group! The best rate of response is obtained when you take the questionnaires out and go through the questions with the person. Distributed or mailed questionnaires have the lowest response rate. Telephone questionnaires are expensive, but do have a good response rate. You can usually depend on a good response from groups of people who meet together regularly, especially students, if you can deliver and collect the questionnaires personally. Another expensive way of increasing replies is to offer a freepost address. Your institution may allow you to take advantage of their freepost address. It's always worth asking. There are expensive things you can do to try to increase response rate such as telephoning reminders, sending reminder letters, or calling on people. They cost money and/or time. I have found that giving the questionnaire out personally is by far the most effective but also time-consuming!

2.6 Using your colleagues

As mentioned above, sometimes just giving the questionnaire to a group of students can be appropriate if it is their opinions etc you seek. It is possible in such circumstances to get a 100% response. If you use students remember that they are not necessarily representative of any group other than students of that particular course. You CANNOT use them to represent "Public Opinion", nor really even "student opinion", unless you have checked very carefully that the group is a truly representative sample of all students.

2.7 Should you be there?

There seems to be an advantage if you are there while the people fill in the questionnaire, but it is really time-consuming to sit with 30+ separate individuals filling in the answers to a questionnaire. You should be able to get a simple and clearly written questionnaire which does not require you to be there to explain it. An advantage of being there is that you are there to collect it when they have finished and it wont get lost or forgotten! What you should NOT do is to be there for some people and not for others. That is because it is imperative that those filling in the questionnaire do so in broadly the same conditions as others. I do not advise telephone questionnaires unless someone else is paying the bill: they are expensive and could well be seen as intrusion if you are doing it ujust as an academic exercise.

3. How are you going to ask it?

3.1 Confidentiality

You must make clear to the people that their replies are completely confidential: try not to have anything on the questionnaire which will enable you to identify who has filled it in (e.g. no name/address question, though it may be important to know where the person lives in some questionnaires). This confidentiality can encourage people to be truthful.

3.2 Wording in general.

Be careful not to offend anyone by aggressive wording, or by letting the person realise your own viewpoint. For example, "I am trying to find out why some stupid people want to kill foxes." The way in which questions are asked seriously affects the replies you get. For example, suppose you ask: "Do you think the College should not allow students to make speeches against democracy?" as opposed to: "Do you think the College should forbid students to make speeches against democracy?". Curiously, many more people are willing to "not allow" such speeches than are willing to "forbid" them. The wording of any questionnaire using such words as ban, debar, disallow, exclude, prohibit, proscribe, restrict, control, forbid, banish, outlaw and the like, must be very carefully thought through.

It is obvious from this that it is possible to envisage ways of manipulating the replies of your questionnaire!

3.2 Open or closed questions?

Open Questions

These are questions which allow the respondent to respond in any way they wish:

    e.g.:"How do you feel about The Prime Minister?"

Closed questions

These are questions which limit the response of the respondent:

    e.g.:"Do you like the Prime Minister?"

this includes tick box questions, which are very useful if time is short. e.g.:

Tick the box which is closest to your feelings about the Prime Minister:	
Disapprove	[ ]
Approve	[ ]
Other	[ ] - please specify

Note that you must make sure that the options cover most of the feelings possible, or provide an "Other - please specify" option.

The main advantage of closed questions is that you can count the replies more easily!

An area in which open questions has been shown to be better than closed ones is the measurement of sensitive or disapproved behaviour.

If you are asking about sensitive areas such as drinking or sexual activity you could ask, as has been suggested above, with various categories for people to choose:

never,	[ ]
once a year or less,	[ ]
every few months,	[ ]
once a month,	[ ]
every few weeks,	[ ]
once a week,	[ ]
several times a week,	[ ]
daily	[ ]

If you ask an open question with nothing other than :

    "How frequently do you...?"

the tendency is that people give a higher estimate on the open form of question than on the closed form of question. On the other hand some people exaggerate because that is what they they think you would like them to say, or sometimes because they think that you will be shocked by what they say!

Offering a No Opinion Option

With a closed question where you are offering alternatives including a "don't know" option you will find that many more people offer this option than will refuse to fill in the question when the "don't know" option is not offered!

3.4 Length of questions?

It is difficult to give a general rule, but remember that the people you ask to fill in your questionnaire probably have something else to do with their time and that the shorter the time taken to fill it in the better. Always try to be as simple and as clear and as short as you possibly can. You must balance these factors out. Err on the side of clarity rather than brevity!

3.5 Avoidable confusions in wording

Avoid ambiguity

"Do you think that men drink more than young people?"

Does this separate the alternatives properly?

"What do you think of the Prime Minister's policy on Tax?"

Worded like this there are two factors involved: the personality of the Prime Minister and the policy of the government. Further the question is vague about which tax is being talked about.

Avoid double negatives

These can be very confusing:

"Do you agree or disagree that children should not smoke?"

Avoid complex language

Too often we get caught out by assuming that people are going to understand the words and phrases that we use every day. Such things as initials for European Common Market, jargon and short-hand that you use because you are very familiar with the subject, all these should be avoided.

Order of questions

It is usual to put the factual questions first, followed by any behavioural ones, before the attitudinal. There is no real need for this to be the case, except that that is what people seem to expect!

IMPORTANT!

ALWAYS TRY OUT YOUR QUESTIONNAIRE ON A SMALL SAMPLE OF PEOPLE BEFORE YOU GIVE IT TO THE FULL SAMPLE. NOTE ANY DIFFICULTIES THEY HAVE ABOUT YOUR QUESTIONNAIRE AND BE PREPARED TO RE-WORD THE QUESTIONS IN THE LIGHT OF THEIR RESPONSES.

---

4. How will you interpret the results?

4.1 Tick boxes

If you are attempting to measure fact, opinion or behaviour then the question should always be phrased so that the responses can be counted in some way. For example:

Do you approve of fox-hunting? YES   [   ] NO   [   ] DON'T KNOW   [   ]

4.2 Scales

These are useful to measure intensity of feeling and, used with tick boxes, are much easier to count. Quite a wide degree of opinion and intensity of opinion can be measured using a variety of scales, for example:

On a scale of 1-4:			
4	3	2	1
Very	Moderately	Somewhat	Not at all

Some questionnaires use a sort of scale which is explained along the lines of:

On a scale of 0-10, where, 0 is unfavourable and cool 5 is neutral 10 is favourable and warm. Please tick a box below to indicate where would you rate X?" [0] [1] [2] [3] [4] [5] [6] [7] [8] [9] [10]

Odd numbers in a scale tend to produce more people expressing a middle view than even numbers in a scale. Thus if you are interested in finding out general trends towards or away from a particular item, then use even numbers in the scale.

In the example above the statement could be made:

```
Examinations are an essential part of learning
    STRONGLY AGREE          [ ]
    AGREE                   [ ]
    DON'T KNOW              [ ]
    DISAGREE                [ ]
    STRONGLY DISAGREE       [ ]
```

Here there are 5 options - 2 agreeing and 2 disagreeing with one on middle ground. If you wish to push your respondees onto one side or the other then don't offer the middle alternative.

```
Examinations are an essential part of learning
    STRONGLY AGREE          [ ]
    AGREE                   [ ]
    DISAGREE                [ ]
    STRONGLY DISAGREE       [ ]
```

It is much easier to count tick boxes than to interpret lots of individual replies to open ended questions. Open-ended questions are very difficult to quantify because you have purposely given people the opportunity to express their views in whatever way they want. You have to be very careful how you summarise them and you may very well not get the patterns emerging which can so easily be observed and counted in closed questions.

4.3 How reliable is it?

You must be wary of accepting your own findings as PROVING without caveat what people seem to be, believe and do! In other words you must state that:

"From the evidence of the questionnaire x% of those questions state
that they....etc"

rather than:

"From the evidence of the questionnaire x% of those questioned
do.....etc"

Use bigger surveys as a yardstick

It is always useful to compare your comparatively small investigation with larger surveys that have been done with more resources than you have. Check your library for such relevant surveys. Government departments often have statistical information which can be useful.

5. How will you present the results?

5.1 Some basic rules

Always state:

how many questionnaires sent out.   [Total numbers=100%]

how many replies   [As percentage of how many sent out]

The latter may then be regarded as the 100% - so one says x% of those replying.
For example:

---

200 sent out. 80 reply.

Thus 40% reply.

Of those replying

10 are in work	= 12.50%
20 are on Government Schemes	= 23.00%
50 are out of work	= 64.50%

Percentages are always more understandable than numbers. Use both where possible. At least an elementary knowledge of statistics is essential.

Percentages can be worked out with a calculator, if you don't have one then the following may help:

If the total number of replies is 160 and the number saying YES is 32 then the formula to find out the percentage is:

Formula for percentages

100 divided by TOTAL REPLIES (T), then multiply that by the NUMBER (N) SAYING YES:

or you could put it as:

$$\frac{100}{T} \times N$$

In this example:

$$\frac{100}{160} \times 32$$

which is 20%

I have found it useful when doing a lot of such calculations to work out before beginning what percentage each number is and keep referring to that list rather than calculating the sum each time. In the above example I would work out what 1 out of 160 is a percentage, then 2, then 3 etc.

Being able to present your findings clearly is extremely important. Always try to present the actual replies and "raw data" in an appendix as proof that the survey has been done. You then need to have a clear breakdown of the results usually set out in tables indicating the numbers and percentages. This data can then be turned into appropriate tables, diagrams, graphs etc.[2]

5.2 Using tables

The simplest way to present your findings is in the form of a table:

Table to show results of survey on opinions about fox-hunting.

Against	For	DontKnow	Total
62.5%	21.9%	15.6%	100.0%

This is fine and gets across the information simply and without bias. It is usual to present information in a more graphic form.

The examples which follow have been produced on a computer, but a ruler, pencil, protractor, compasses and perhaps some coloured pencils or pens are really all you need to produce acceptable bar charts, line graphs and pie charts.

Use your imagination, but try always to present the information in the simplest form possible. Never try to put too much in one diagram.

5.3 Bar Charts

5.3.1 Vertical bar charts

- Bar charts are called that because bars of varying lengths are used to symbolise the values in the table.
- Simple bar charts have 2 elements: an X and a Y axis. The x axis goes across and the Y axis is the vertical element, where they cross is usually 0. Numbers are usually counted on the Y axis.
- Bars are drawn upwards from the base line to represent the amounts measured on the vertical axis.
- The height or length of each bar is proportional to the data. The bars are of a uniform width.
- Each axis is labelled and the diagram accurately titled. Any information to explain shading or colouring of the graph should be displayed clearly (these are referred to as the "legend").

These are the simple elements of a vertical bar chart.

---

[2]. *There is a lot of information which is useful in the collation, interpretation and presentation of material in Section 22 on statistics.*

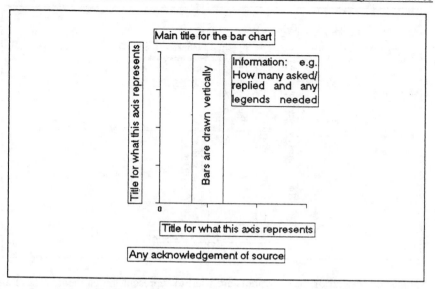

If the numbers are on the horizontal axis (X and Y axes are swapped over) and the bars drawn from the left hand line, then you have a horizontal bar chart.

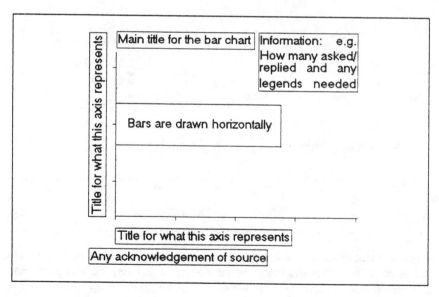

If there are any minus values then the 0 line is moved so that the minus values can be seen:

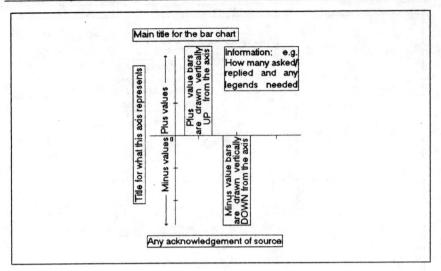

Sometimes instead of bars, symbols are used to represent the elements. These are called pictograms.

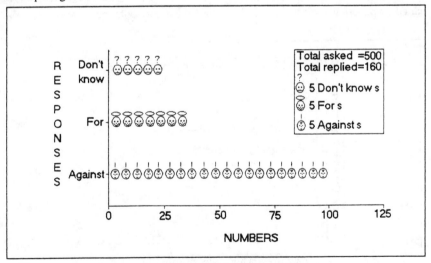

If you do them by hand, use a template to ensure they look alike and are the same size as each other. Pictograms can be misleading in that they are less easily made accurate. Sometimes too, there are messages sent by the drawings which affect the objectivity of the information. The advantages of simple bar charts are that they are comparatively easy to draw and fairly accurate. When you are comparing sizes they usually do better than other forms such as pie charts (see below).

The information about opinions on fox-hunting could be represented in simple vertical bar graph form:

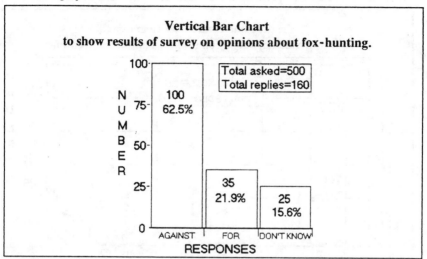

Shading can be used to make clearer the different elements of the graph.

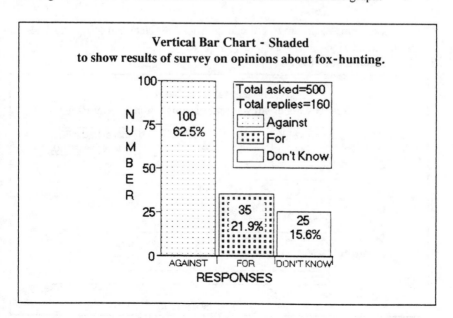

If shading is used then you should state clearly which shading represents which elements in the graph. This is called the "legend". Shading can get in the way of reading the numbers. Flat colour washes are probably better to differentiate. Sometimes the bars used to represent the values are drawn in 3 dimensions.

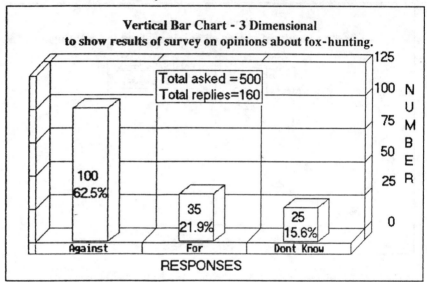

This is more complex to draw, but can be effective. Note that too many lines can interfere with clarity.

5.3.2 Horizontal bar charts

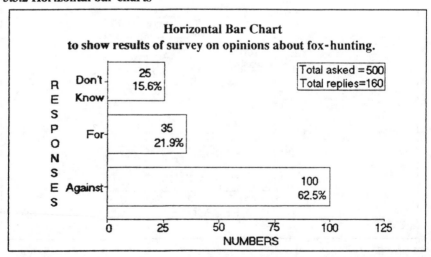

The above is a horizontal bar graph without shading. Shading can be used to make clearer the different elements of the graph.

Note again that:

1. The length of each bar is proportional to the data.
2. The bars are of a uniform width.
3. Each axis is labelled and the diagram has an accurate title.

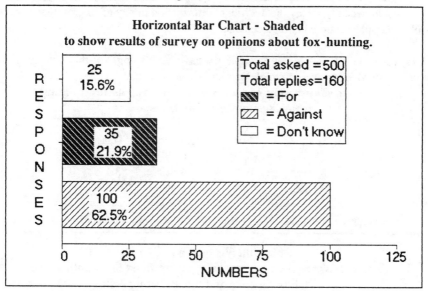

Horizontal Bar Chart - Shaded
to show results of survey on opinions about fox-hunting.

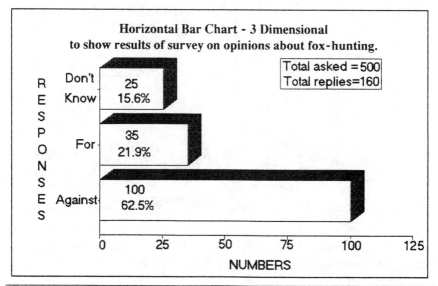

Horizontal Bar Chart - 3 Dimensional
to show results of survey on opinions about fox-hunting.

The choice of which to use, vertical or horizontal, depends really on how easily the columns fit into the space. Large differences between the numbers tend to suit vertical and low differences horizontal.

5.3.3 Other types of bar chart

The simple bar chart often fails to give sufficient information. For example, if you had other factors involved in the survey on fox hunting such as male/female then you would need to display the additional information in any of the following ways: split, multiple, sectional and percentage.

Below are the figures for the example we have been using, but this time showing the way in which male and female opinion was represented.

Table to show results of survey on opinions about fox-hunting
(showing male and female responses)

	Against	For	DontKnow	Total
Male	25.4%	15.7%	6.2%	46.9%
Female	37.5%	6.2%	9.4%	53.1%
Total	62.5%	21.9%	15.6%	100.0%

The problem is to find a way of showing differences between male/female opinion.

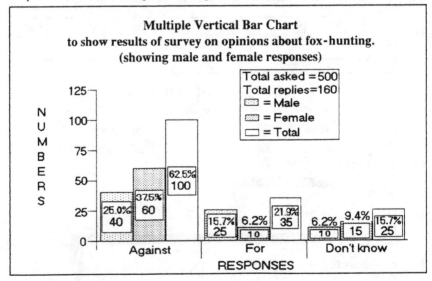

This is one method of presenting the information so that you can see easily how the total is divided into different components. Use it to emphasise the component figures rather than the totals. It isn't very useful beyond three or four components.

You need to shade or colour the different elements. Note also there isn't room to show the individual percentages within the bars on the lower values, so it is permissible to place these values outside the bar.

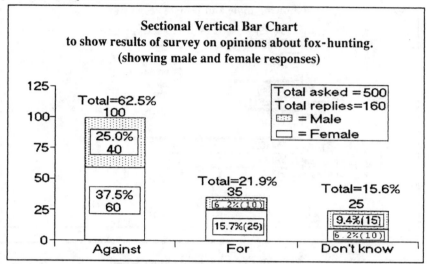

This consists of single bars sub-divided into parts. This method is used where both the overall totals and the sub-totals are to be emphasized. You don't need a bar for the total: the sum of the component parts is the total!

The above charts can also be presented as horizontal charts.

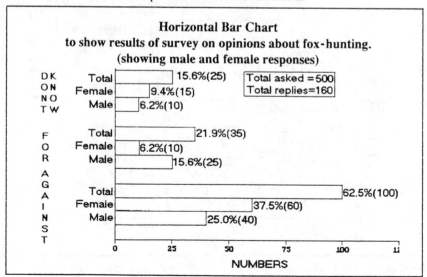

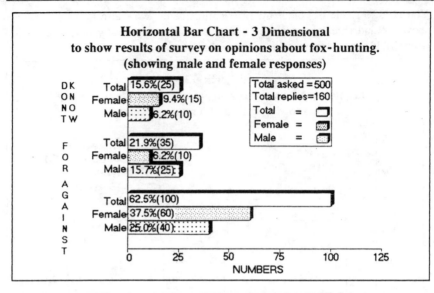

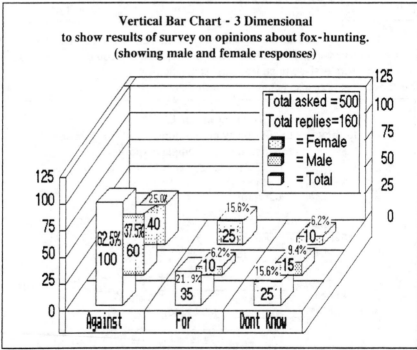

Here the number of lines on the chart is beginning to confuse the issue!

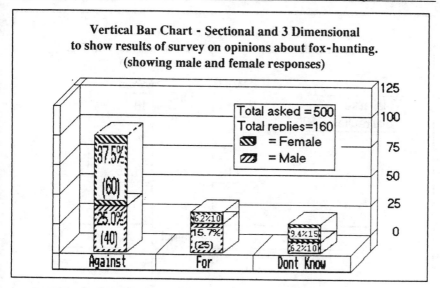

Note there is no need to have separate parts for the total since it is implicit.

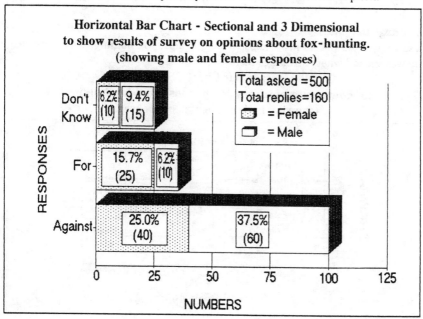

These 3D charts are not easy to draw, but look attractive, especially if coloured.

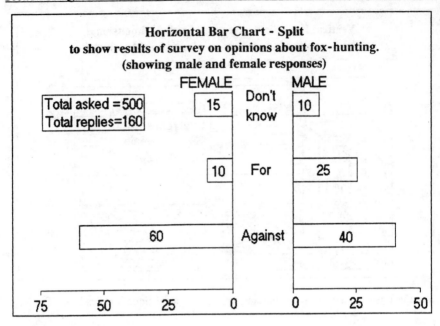

Horizontal Bar Chart - Split
to show results of survey on opinions about fox-hunting.
(showing male and female responses)

Percentage bar chart

These answer the question: Of those voting against fox-hunting, what percentage were women and what percentage men?

Percentage Bar Chart - Sectional
to show results of survey on opinions about fox-hunting.
(showing male and female responses)

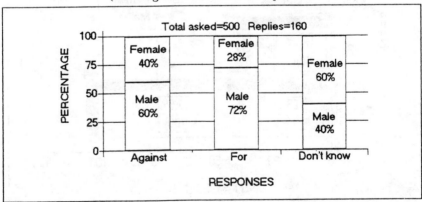

In this case bars are the same length and component parts are represented by percentage of that length, allowing comparisons between the relative components.

Further complications

Note carefully here that what is being presented is the percentage of the women and men who actually replied. It is slightly misleading throughout the above examples because 10 fewer men replied than women. Thus it appears that only 37.5% of women are against fox hunting in this survey, but, if the sample of women is representative of the whole of group of women one could do further calculations and state that the percentage of the 85 women voting against fox hunting is 70.6%.

	Against	For	Dont Know	Total
Male	25.4%(40)	15.7%(25)	6.2%(10)	46.9%(75)
Female	37.5%(60)	6.2%(10)	9.4%(15)	53.1%(85)
Total	62.5%(100)	21.9%(35)	15.6%(25)	100.0%(160)

Compare these with the figures adjusted to represent percentages of those voting:

	Against	For	Dont Know	Total
Male	53.2%(40)	32.2%(25)	13.3%(10)	100.0%(75)
Female	70.6%(60)	11.7%(10)	17.7%(15)	100.0%(85)
Total	62.5%(100)	21.9%(35)	15.6%(25)	100.0%(160)

5.3.4 Line Graphs

The line graph is good for showing progressive trends either upward, or downward. The emphasis is on movement rather than differences between.

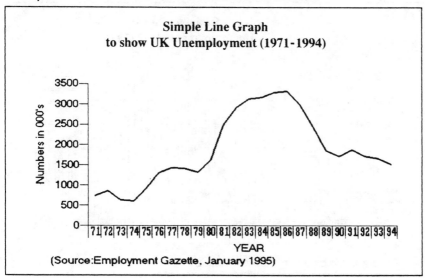

**Simple Line Graph
to show UK Unemployment (1971-1994)**

(Source:Employment Gazette, January 1995)

Note that there is an acknowledgement of the source of the graph's statistics. This is essential, otherwise it will be assumed that you've made them up! A grid can be added to make reading off the figures easier, but this sometimes produces clutter.

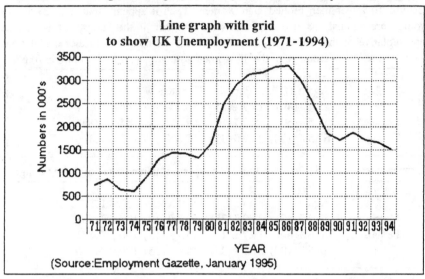

The same figures can be used in a bar graph. The decision is aesthetic rather than mathematical! Choose which ever is going to put over your idea most effectively.

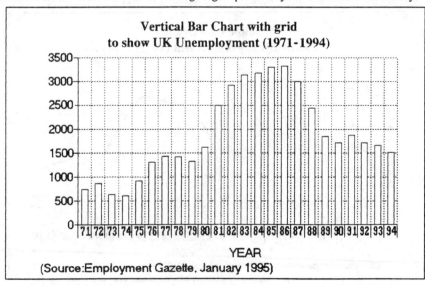

This one has a grid, which I think clutters the picture. The one below is simpler and uses "sticks" to represent the numbers. This is certainly simpler

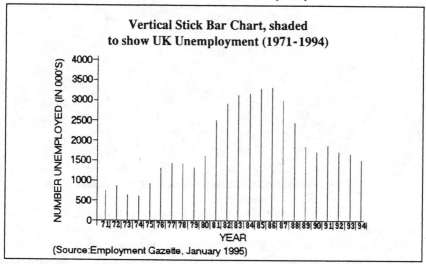

**Vertical Stick Bar Chart, shaded
to show UK Unemployment (1971-1994)**

(Source:Employment Gazette, January 1995)

Stick charts are not often used as bars probably look more pleasing than the sticks. If there are several lines to be represented in a line graph then shading can help to differentiate.

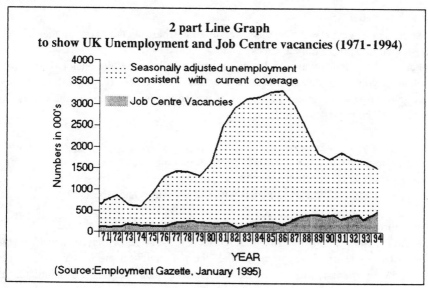

**2 part Line Graph
to show UK Unemployment and Job Centre vacancies (1971-1994)**

Seasonally adjusted unemployment consistent with current coverage

Job Centre Vacancies

(Source:Employment Gazette, January 1995)

Here the two elements are shaded differently to emphasise the differentiation.

If many different lines are required then different styles of lines are used.

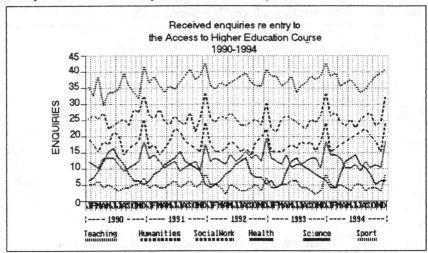

The line graph is often useful for reading off information which is implied by the original statistics, especially if there is a grid. Use it for when you wish to show progression, regression or significant patterns produced by the figures (as in the case above where is is possible to identify the peaks and troughs of enquiries).

5.4 Pie Charts

The results of a survey can be displayed in a Pie Chart. As the name implies a circle is divided into proportionate slices.

There are all sorts of ways of depicting them. I have seen 3 dimensional ones with colour. If you watch any of the news programmes on television you will see almost every night new and interesting ways of presenting information via pie charts. As with all of the previous examples:

    - use you imagination.
    - do not try to cram too much information onto one chart,
    - try to keep the chart as simple as possible,
    - try not to clutter up the chart with lots of figures and labels.

Calculating the pie slices

The information about the fox-hunting survey could be displayed simply in the form of a pie chart. As its name implies the pie chart is a pie (circle) with slices (sectors) representing the various elements. The sector angles are calculated as follows:

Formula for constructing a pie chart

Sector angle = $\dfrac{\text{Number in sector x 360}}{\text{Total replying}}$

In the case of those voting against fox-hunting where the number is 100 and the total is 160 the formula would give:

$$= \frac{100 \times 360}{160} = 225°$$

In the case of those voting for fox-hunting where the number is 35 and the total is 160 the formula would give:

$$= \frac{35 \times 360}{160} = 78.75°$$

In the case of those who "Don't Know" about fox-hunting where the number is 100 and the total is 25 the formula would give:

$$= \frac{25 \times 360}{160} = 56.25°$$

All you need now are compasses and a protractor:

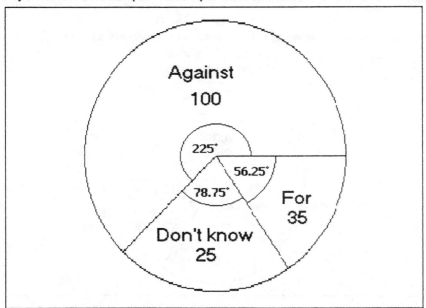

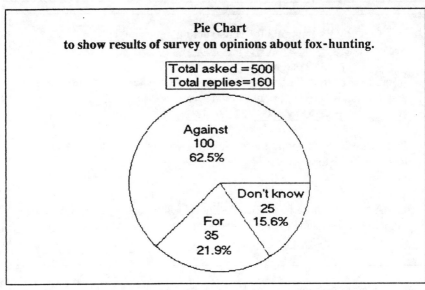

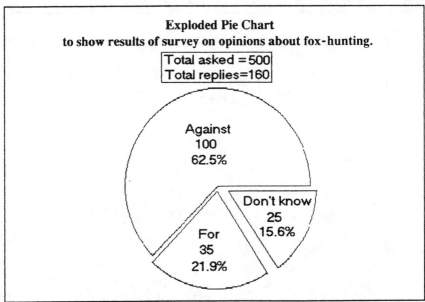

Here the slices have been pulled out from the pie. This could be done with any of the pies which follow. It is useful when there are long labels to attach to the slices. Sometimes slices are pulled out to indicate negative values. If you do this then make it very clear that they are negative values by labelling them as such.

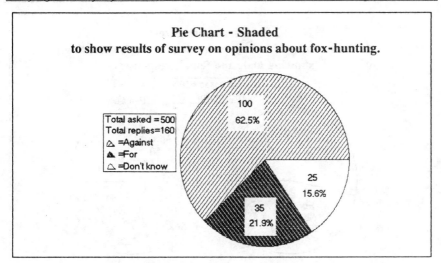

Pie Chart - Shaded
to show results of survey on opinions about fox-hunting.

Total asked = 500
Total replies=160
△ =Against
▲ =For
△ =Don't know

100
62.5%

25
15.6%

35
21.9%

Colouring is perhaps more effective.

There comes a point when the pie chart is not clear, because there are too many slices. For example, if we used it to display the male and female variations of opinion:

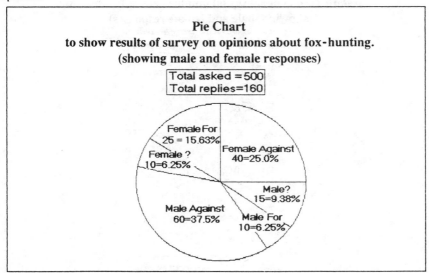

Pie Chart
to show results of survey on opinions about fox-hunting.
(showing male and female responses)

Total asked = 500
Total replies=160

Female For
25 = 15.63%

Female ?
10=6.25%

Female Against
40=25.0%

Male?
15=9.38%

Male Against
60=37.5%

Male For
10=6.25%

Here the number of slices and amount wording clutter the message.

Pies can be used to compare amounts by using separate pies. In this first example the pies are the same size as each other.

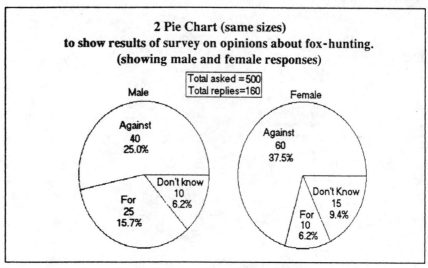

The **one below** shows the comparative sizes of each element.

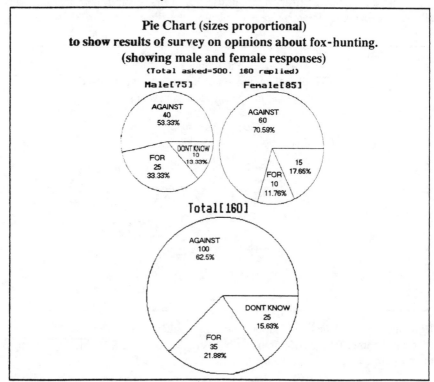

It is possible to include pie charts with other diagrams to give fairly complex information in a very simple way. For example, in order to get over quickly comparative amounts of fish being caught around Britain.

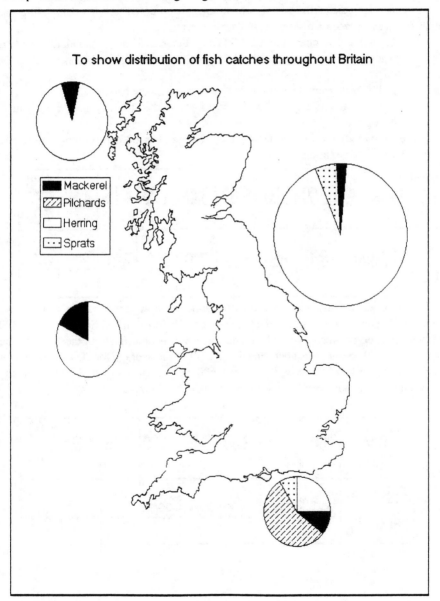

To show distribution of fish catches throughout Britain

Mackerel
Pilchards
Herring
Sprats

5.5 Histograms

When you have to present data which is more complex because it has further factors involved then the histogram may be of use. A histogram consists of a series of rectangles, the AREAS of which are proportional to the data. Note the differences between a histogram and a bar chart.

1. In the bar chart the LENGTH of the bar is proportional to the data, whereas in the histogram the AREA of each rectangle is proportional to the data.

2. The histogram does not have spaces between the bars.

3. The bar chart bars are all the same width, this may not be so with a histogram.

For example: the following table gives the number of competitors finishing a marathon in given time intervals.

Time	2.00	3.00	3.30	3.45	4.00	4.15	4.30	5.00 - 7.00
Finishers	300	850	600	700	800	550	500	600

To construct the histogram we have to work out how many people would have finished in an hour for each of the times given. Obviously in the first box where 300 have finished between two o'clock and three 300 people finish in the hour. In the next box 850 people finish between 3 and 3.30 so the average for the hour would be twice that i.e.1700. In box 3 we have 600 people finishing in 15 minutes, the average for the hour would be 4 times that, which is 2400, and so on.

Time in hours	2.00	3.00	3.30	3.45	4.00	4.15	4.30	5.00 7.00
Finishers per hour	300	1700	2400	2800	3200	2200	1000	300

Thus the histogram is constructed from these figures. Remember it is the AREA of the boxes which is giving the significant information

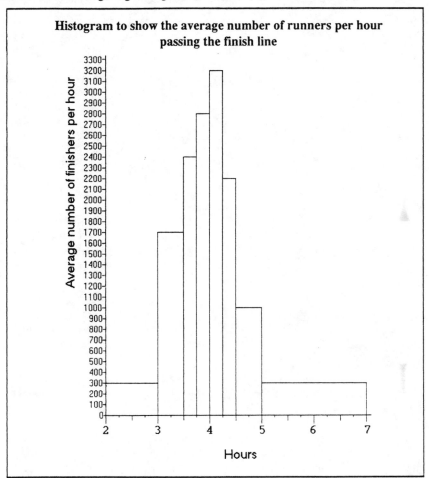

Histogram to show the average number of runners per hour passing the finish line

5.6 Some final points

There are always niggling little decisions to be made with graphs and charts. Should the numbers be bigger than the writing?! Should the numbers go mid-way against the dash that marks their position or on the same level?! Should there be a vertical grid? A horizontal grid? Should you use colour or shading or just labels? Should the labels be in boxes? And so on.

The main rule is keep things as simple as possible and be consistent in terms of lettering, size, shading, colouring and positioning.

SECTION 22: STATISTICS

Introduction

This is by no means a comprehensive introduction to statistics, which is a branch of mathematics and a study in its own right. I have merely attempted to list here a very few of the topics which have been useful to students in:

1. presenting information gathered from their questionnaires.
2. understanding statistics which are presented in other people's work.

There are many books on the market which take the student further in this fascinating, but complex area. If you are interested in going further then see the list of recommended books in Appendix II.

This section deals with:

1. Averages
   - Mean
   - Mode
   - Median
   - Midrange
2. Variance
   - Range
   - Variance and Standard Deviation
3. Some symbols and what they mean
   - Mathematical/statistical/other

1. Averages

When you are conducting a survey, or when you read someone else's set of statistics, you are usually looking to find out what the main tendency is, what the norm is, or by how much something deviates from the norm.

Thus it is important when reporting results of questionnaires and when reading and interpreting information presented by others to have some knowledge of what is meant by "average", since most people think of the term as applying to the sort of cricket averages we see in sports pages where each score is added up and then divided by the number of scores.

However, there are several kinds of processes which produce an "average". Further there are many problems associated with calculating by how much something deviates from that central norm, tendency or average.

First then, let's look at the four main types of "average" which statisticians use:

1. the mean,
2. the mode,
3. the median,
4. the midrange.

1.1 The mean

The arithmetic mean is the "average" mentioned above. It's the sort you see in cricket batting/bowling averages.

Batsman X had 5 innings and scored

Innings Number:	1	2	3	4	5	TOTAL
Runs scored:	20	10	0	0	0	30

To find his average we add up his total runs and divide by the number of completed innings.

Thus:

the total is 30,
the total number of completed innings is 5
The average is 30÷5=6
The mean, then in this case, is 6.

To calculate the mean from any set of values:

add up the values and divide by the number of values.

mean =   Sum of the values
            Number of the values

So far so good!

Perhaps unfortunately mathematicians use symbols to express this more quickly in what they call formulas.

It is just another way of saying what we've just said above.

The formula used in statistics to calculate the mean is:

$$\bar{x} = \frac{\sum x}{n}$$

where

$\bar{x}$ represents the mean,
$\sum$ represents sum of,
x represents the single value
n represents the number of values.

For example: Calculate the mean of the following values:

2, 5, 7, 3, 3

The sum of the values is 2+5+7+3+3=20

The number of values is 5

The mean of the values is 20 divided by 5, which is 4.

Using the formula

$$\bar{x}\text{(the mean)} = \frac{\sum x\text{(the sum of 2,5,7,3,3)}20}{n\text{ (the number of values) }5} = 4$$

You don't have to use the formula, you can just remember it in the way I set it out above, but you may well come across some of the symbols in your reading and if you don't understand them there, you can always come back to this section and check up just what they mean! I'm afraid there are several other symbols that we will encounter but I will introduce them to you carefully and gradually! They are in fact quite useful as long as you don't try and remember them all at once. Over the time you will be reading and using them in your own work. I am sure you'll get as used to them as you have to the symbols we use for numbers and letters.

The mean is the most commonly used of all the averages. It is the most usual way to find out what the "average" is. In other words what the "central tendency" is.

1.2 The mode

Another method which is used to describe what the "average" is the mode. The mode is the value that occurs most frequently in a list of values. There may be more than one mode. To find the mode choose the value with greatest frequency.

For example: 3,1,7,1,12,**6,6**,10,**6,6**,3,2,9,5,**6,6,6**,7,2,11,**6,6**,9

The most frequent value is 6

thus the mode is 6.

There is no formula to worry about! You just have to count up how often each number occurs.

A useful way of doing this when you have got a huge amount of numbers, say from a questionnaire where there have been 43 replies, is to use a tally chart. This is set out below and is a simple way of counting the frequency a value occurs in a given list:

For example, suppose the responses to a question were as follows:

1,3,5,7,3,8,9,7,3,2,6,9,8,7,5,1,6,7,4,3,8,0,9,4,3,2,4,7,8,9,4,4,2,6,6,4,4,4,1,7,8,4,4

Construct a chart with each of the possible answers on the left, in this case numbers from 0-10, put a tick to keep a tally of how often that value crops up in the centre column, and then add up the ticks and enter the number of occurrences under the frequency column.

Number	Tally	Frequency(f)
0	✓	1
1	✓ ✓ ✓	3
2	✓ ✓ ✓	3
3	✓ ✓ ✓ ✓ ✓	5
4	✓ ✓ ✓ ✓ ✓ ✓ ✓ ✓ ✓ ✓	10
5	✓ ✓ ✓	3
6	✓ ✓ ✓	3
7	✓ ✓ ✓ ✓ ✓ ✓	6
8	✓ ✓ ✓ ✓ ✓	5
9	✓ ✓ ✓ ✓	4

In this list the mode is 4, because that value cropped up most times.

Incidentally the total of these values is 215, the number of values is 43, thus the mean is 215÷43, which is 5.

Did you notice that I had sneaked in another symbol, by the way? f means frequency.

1.3 The median

The median is the number which is in the middle. To find it out you have to

1. arrange the values in order size,

2. find the one which is equidistant from highest and lowest (i.e. the one in the middle).

For example, calculate the median of the following values:

        2, 5, 7, 3, 3

Arrange the values in order of size

        2, 3, 3, 5, 7

The number 3 is the value in the middle, and therefore the median is 3.

If there are two numbers in middle, then the median is the mean of those two.

For example, calculate the mean of the following values:

        2, 5, 7, 8, 3, 3

Arranged in order of size

        2, 3, 3, 5, 7, 8

The numbers 3 and 5 are the values in the middle. The sum of 3 and 5 is 8, the mean of 8 is 4, thus the mean of the list above is 4.

The formula used to calculate the median in statistics is:
The median with an odd number of values is:

the $\left(\dfrac{n+1}{2}\right)$ th number in the series.

where n = the number of values.

For example, calculate the mean of the following values:
2, 3, 3, 5, 6, 7, 8
There are 7 values, thus the median will be the n(7)+1 divided by 2, which is the 4th number in the series, which is the number 5.

The median with an even number of values is:
the $\left(\dfrac{n}{2}\right)$ th number plus the next, divided by 2

Where n=the number of values.

For example, calculate the mean of the following values:
2, 3, 3, 5, 7, 8, 9, 10
The number of values is 8, thus the median will be:
n(8) divided by 2, which is the 4th number in the series which is 5: this is added to the next number which is a 7. The total is 12 and the median is 12 divided by 2, which is 6.

With our big example above the problem, as usual, is one of the time taken to sort out the list of values into order without making a mistake!

1,3,5,7,3,8,9,7,3,2,6,9,8,7,5,1,6,7,4,3,8,0,9,4,3,2,4,7,8,9,4,4,2,6,6,4,4,4,1,7,8,4,4

However, if you look at the tally list, you will see there is a simpler way of doing it. There are:

1 zero, 3 ones, 5 twos, 10 fours, 3 fives, 3 sixes, 6 sevens, 5 eights and 4 nines.

0 1 1 1 2 2 2 2 2 4 4 4 4 4 4 4 4 4 4 5 5 5 6 6 6 7 7 7 7 7 7 8 8 8 8 8 9 9 9 9

The mid point is the (43÷2)+1=21+1=22nd number. If you count along to the 22nd number you will find out what the median is. It is 5.

A further note about calculating the median
You may find it interesting to go a little further with this example. Suppose we missed out the zero to make an even number with 42 values instead of 43:

1 1 1 2 2 2 2 2 4 4 4 4 4 4 4 4 4 5 5 5 6 6 6 7 7 7 7 7 7 8 8 8 8 8 9 9 9 9

If we now calculate the median's position it is between the 22nd and 23rd numbers, both of which are sixes. This is interesting since there are in fact 3 sixes at this point of the central tendency, the median. The middle point lies between 1st and 2nd of the 3 sixes.
Statisticians like to be exact!

They say that we must accept that these values of 6 that we see in front of us in the list have an actual range of value of 5.50 to 6.50 and that the value 6 is the mid point of that range.

Thus in the list as we have it we have 3 sixes. These 3 values cover the range 5.50-6.50, so each 6 covers an interval of .33. Thus the first six starts at 5.50, up to 5.83, the second at 5.83 up to 6.16, the third at 6.16 up to 6.50. Thus the actual central point between the 1st and 2nd six is between 5.50 and 6.16 which is 5.83!

1.4 The midrange
This is a simple average where the top and bottom numbers are added together and and divided by 2.

For example: calculate the mid range of the following values:
2, 3, 3, 4, 5, 7, 8.

The lowest value is	2
The highest value is	8
The sum is	10
The midrange is (10/2)	5

In our long example from above the highest number is 10 and the lowest is zero. Thus $(10+0) \div 2 = 5$

1.5 Which to use

This depends entirely on the spread of values and which is best going to describe the central tendency.

When the list of values is symmetrical and there is only one set of numbers that predominate, then probably the mean, the mode and the media will be very similar.

If there is more than one mode, i.e. there are at least two values which occur with the same frequency, then even if the values are symmetrical the mode will obviously differ (since there are at least two of them!).

If the values in the list are not symmetrical then the values of all three will inevitably differ.

If there are extreme values in the list then again there will be big differences between the three.

You must remember that the purpose of these averages is to describe usefully what the central tendency is and really they are useful only for lists of values where symmetry and single mode occur.

It is possible to deal with the problem of extreme scores by either omitting the extreme scores, (which is in fact falsifying the figures!), or by taking the square root or logarithm of the values and using those values to calculate the mean/median/mode.

2. Variance

The above "averages" can give information about the average value of lists of numbers. They give no idea of how the numbers are spread around the "average". For that you need measures of dispersion.

2.1 The range

This is simply the difference between the highest and lowest numbers you have in your list.

For example:

What is the range of the following values?

1,7,5,6,9,24,1021,34,79,102

The lowest number is 1, the highest is 1021.

The range is 1021-1=1020.

2.2 Variance and Standard Deviation

The variance of a list of values is defined as each value subtracted from the mean, squared, added together and divided by the total sum of values minus 1! This is an attempt to say just how much each of the values differ from the mean.

The formula is this:

Variance   = $\dfrac{\text{The sum of (mean - each value)}^2}{\text{Number of values - 1}}$

For example:
44556789
The mean is (4+4+5+5+6+7+8+9)=48÷8=6

Raw Value	Mean - Raw value			Square
4	6 - 4	=	2	4
4	6 - 4	=	2	4
5	6 - 5	=	1	1
5	6 - 5	=	1	1
6	6 - 6	=	0	0
7	6 - 7	=	-1	1
8	6 - 8	=	-2	4
9	6 - 9	=	-3	9
Sum of (mean - each value)^2		=		24

The variance is **worked out by dividing this value by the number of list values less 1. Thus the variance = 24÷7=3.4 This answer is in squared units, rather than in the units of the original value. Thus to get the answer back to the original value you must find the square root of 3.4 which is 1.8 and this is the standard deviation.** That is the average amount by which each item deviates from the mean.

2.3 Standard deviation

Standard deviation is the average of deviation around the mean. The standard deviation is useful when we want to compare the differences between groups and within groups.

If group A of students have a mean score of 67% for a piece of work and a standard deviation of 6.3 that indicates that about two thirds of them are within 6.3% of the 67%. In group B the mean is again 67%, but the standard deviation is calculated to be 32, which indicates that there is far more variation from the mean than Group A.

3. Some symbols and what they mean

I set out here a few of the more common symbols used in mathematics and statistics, some of which you will know, others you will get to know as you meet them in the text books. I have also included a few used in other disciplines.

≅	= equal to or nearly equal to isomorphic to
≈	= approximately equal to
≠	= is not equal to
∓	= minus or plus
±	= plus or minus
÷	= divided by
/	= divided by
*	= asterisk, can be multiplied by
+	= plus
%	= per cent
‰	= out of 1000
×	= multiplied by
∏	= product
√	= root
°	= degree(s)
∞	= infinity
∑	= the sum of
f	= frequency
∝	= proportional to
∥	= parallel to
⊥	= perpendicular to
∡	= marked angle
∠	= angle

a→b	= a implies b
a=b	= a exactly equals b
a≈b	= a approximately equals b
a≡b	= a is identical to b. This occurs only in formulas.
a≠b	= a does not equal b
a>b	= a is greater than b
a<b	= a is less than b
a≥b	= a is equal to or greater than b
a≤b	= a is equal to or less than b

| ∫ | = integral sign |
| ∮ | = Contour integral clockwise |

| ⌠
⌡ | = large integral sign |

| ∴ | = therefore |
| ∵ | = because |

(	= open parenthesis
)	= close parenthesis
[	= open bracket
]	= close bracket
{	= open curly bracket
}	= close curly bracket

∧	= Vector product
∨	= Sum of two sets
∅	= Null or empty set
\	= Set difference
⊂	= proper subset, strict inclusion
⊃	= proper superset, contains
⊆	= reflex subset, inclusion
⊇	= reflex superset, does not contain
⊄	= Not contained in

| ⊢ | = syntactical entailment |
| ⊨ | = semantic entailment |

§	= Section
¶	= Paragraph
...	= triple dot
?	= question mark without dot
!	= Exclamation mark, also used as factorial sign
¡	= Upside down exclamation mark
!!	= double exclamation mark
¿	= Upside down question mark
:	= colon
@	= at sign
&	= ampersand, used for and
\	= backward slash
†	= dagger (used in notes along with asterisk)
®	= Registered Trademark
TM	= Registered Trademark
©	= Copyright
℅	= Care of

∈	= element
|	= modulus
∇	= gradient

∀	= Universal
∩	= intersection
∪	= union
∋	= such that
∃	= there exists
∧	= logical and
∨	= logical or
¬	= logical not

♀	= Venus
♂	= Mars

SECTION 23: CLASS
1. Defining social class

Most people know what they mean by social class! If you ask anyone which class they belong to they will give you an answer. The main factors people use to decide seem to based on such things as:
- way of life,
- family background,
- job,
- money
- education,

but others have been used too:
- the way a person speaks,
- where they live,
- the friends they have,
- the school they went to,
- how they spend their money,

ISLE COLLEGE
LIBRARY

and so on. It is very difficult for everyone to agree on what makes up the criteria for this measure of social class.
- For official statistics in Britain we tend to use occupation as defined by the Registrar General.
- In America the trend is to education or income.

When you read anything about class, make sure you know how the writer is defining social class. What criteria is being used to classify the people? A great deal of confusion is created when this term is not clearly defined.

1.1 Definitions by Karl Marx and Max Weber

Two sociologists, Marx and Weber classified the populations of society into classes based on their relationship to the means of production. It is important to be aware that they use social class in a very different way to the way described above.

Marx

Karl Marx pointed out that there were differences in the way that people were divided in any society. He believed that the way one could classify them was in their relationship to the economy. He said that the group which controlled and owned the means of producing food and goods was the most powerful class.

In 1847, with Friedrich Engels, he wrote Communist Manifesto in which he traced the way in which this pattern could be seen. The ownership of property gave one group control over others. This was true of ancient civilisations built on slavery, feudal society where the the owning classes exploited the labour of the villeins and serfs, and was also true of his society of his day. He maintained that everything depended upon the ownership of capital (wealth) - it shaped religion, government, and the family. The owners were the aristocracy and the bourgeoisie, who owned and controlled the land and the factories (means of production) in the capitalist system, and they dominated the wage-earners (the proletariat or working class) who had only their brains and/or their labour to sell and worked for the bourgeoisie. Marx said that eventually the working classes would rise up and overthrow the other classes and begin to own the means of production themselves.

Max Weber

This sociologist, who lived some 50 years later, pointed out that really many of the people in a capitalist society were quite happy. He did not think that the shop owners and the middle classes would throw in their lot with the workers and overthrow the system. And the workers themselves didn't necessarily want to get rid of the system if it treated them fairly. They didn't own the means of production, but they had the vote and they had their trades union which protected their rights and their wages and they didn't really want the responsibility of owning and risking their capital.

These definitions can be used to describe people in our society, but the most commonly used classification system is the Registrar General's.

1.2 Overview of the Registrar General's classification system

The Registrar General, who is in charge of the government's statistical department, divides the population into five classes based upon occupation, with a subdivision of Class 3 into manual and non-manual workers.

Registrar General's classification system

> Registrar General's classification system
>
> A =   Upper middle class.
>
> B =   Middle class.
>
> C1=   Lower middle class.
> C2=   Skilled working class.
>
> D =   Working semi-skilled & unskilled manual class.
>
> E =   Lowest level of subsistence State pensioners etc.

Registrar General's Classification of people in Great Britain

Registrar General's Classification of people in Britain						
Class	A	B	C1	C2	D	E
Males	7%	19%	18%	36%	15%	4%
Females	6%	18%	25%	29%	18%	5%
Totals	3%	12%	22%	32%	23%	9%

2. Registrar General's classification system

2.1 Brief descriptions of each of the "classes"

'A' HOUSEHOLDS-UPPER MIDDLE CLASS
About 3% of the total. The head of the household is a successful business or professional man, senior civil servant or has considerable private means.

'B' HOUSEHOLDS-MIDDLE CLASS
About 12% of the total. In general the heads of 'B' Grade households will be quite senior people but not at the very top of their profession or business. They are quite well-off, but their style of life is generally respectable rather than rich or luxurious. Non-earners will be living on private pensions or on fairly modest private means.

'C1' HOUSEHOLDS-LOWER MIDDLE CLASS
About 22% of total. In general it is made up of the families of small tradespeople and non-manual workers who carry out less important administrative, supervisory and clerical jobs, i.e. what are sometimes called "white-collar" workers.

'C2' HOUSEHOLDS-THE SKILLED WORKING CLASS
About 32% of total. Grade C2 consists in the main of skilled manual workers and their families. When in doubt as to whether the head of the household is skilled or unskilled, check whether he has served an apprenticeship. This may be a guide, though not all skilled workers have served an apprenticeship.

'D' HOUSEHOLDS-UNSKILLED WORKING CLASS
About 23% of total. Grade D consists entirely of manual workers, generally semi-skilled.

'E' HOUSEHOLDS-LOWEST LEVELS OF SUBSISTENCE
About 9% of total - but growing as the population gets older and lives longer. Grade E consists of old age pensioners, widows and their families, casual workers and those who, through sickness or unemployment, are dependent on social security schemes, or have very small private means. Individual income of the head of the household (disregarding additions such as supplementary benefits) will be little, if any, above the basic flat-rate social security benefit.

3. Details of the Registrar General's classification system

3.1 'A' HOUSEHOLDS-UPPER MIDDLE CLASS

About 3% of the total. The head of the household is a successful business or professional man, senior civil servant or has considerable private means. A young man in some of these occupations who has not fully established himself may still be found in Grade 'B', though he eventually should reach Grade 'A'.

In country or suburban areas, 'A' grade households usually live in large detached houses or in expensive flats. In towns, they may live in expensive flats or town houses in the better parts of the town. Some examples, which are by no means exhaustive, are given below.

Examples of occupations of the head of the household

Professional or semi-professional

Church of England dignitaries (bishop and above) and those of other denominations.

Physician, surgeon, specialist.

Established doctor, dentist (if a principal or partner in a large practice).

Established solicitor, barrister (own practice or partner in a large practice).

Matron of a large teaching hospital.

Headmaster of a public or grammar school or of any large school or college (i.e. 750 pupils or more).

Architect, chartered accountant, surveyor, actuary-fully qualified and principal or partner in a large practice. Also if working as a very senior (at or near board level) executive in a very large (200+) organisation.

Senior civil servant, e.g. Permanent Secretary, Deputy Secretary, Under Secretary, Assistant Secretary, Principal.

Local Government chief officers.

Senior Local Government Officer (e.g. Town Clerk, Treasurer, County Planning Officer, Borough Surveyor).

University Professor.

Editor of a newspaper or magazine, senior journalist on national or very large provincial publications.

Commercial airline pilot (captain or first officer).

Captain of large merchant vessel (5,000 tons or more and/or 25+ crew).

Senior professional executives, i.e. professionally qualified people working as very senior executives or administrators (at or near board level in very large (200+) establishments) - e.g. Chief Engineer, Company Surveyor, Company Secretary, Chief Accountant, Curator, Artistic Director, Chief Designer, etc.

Librarian, qualified, in charge of a really major library.

Business and Industry

Senior Buyers for leading wholesale or retail establishments.

Self-employed owners of businesses with 25 or more employees.

Self-employed farmers with 10 or more employees.

Board (i.e. Directors) or near board level Managers in large organisations (i.e. with 200 or more employees).

Managers in sole charge of branches or outlying establishments with 200 or more employees at the branch (e.g. factory managers, managers of very large retail establishments, depots, hotel, etc).

Stock broker or jobber (principal or partner in the firm).

Insurance underwriter.

Advertising, research, public relations executives (and others offering professional or semi-professional services in specialised agencies) if at board level or principals or partners in agencies or practices with 25 or more employees.

Bank branch managers, managers of branch of other financial institutions (e.g. building societies, insurance company, finance house) with 25 or more employees at the branch.

Police and Fire Brigade

Superintendent, Chief Constable.

CID Superintendent and Chief Superintendent.

Chief Fire Officer.

Armed Forces

Army-Lieut. Col. and above.

Navy-Commander and above.

RAF-Wing Commander and above.

None-earners

People living in comfort on investments or private income.

Retired people where the head of the household before retirement would have been 'A' grade.

3.2 'B' HOUSEHOLDS - MIDDLE CLASS

About 12% of the total. In general the heads of 'B' Grade households will be quite senior people but not at the very top of their profession or business. They are quite well-off, but their style of life is generally respectable rather than rich or luxurious. Non-earners will be living on private pensions or on fairly modest private means.

Examples of occupations of the head of the household

Professional and semi-professional

Vicars, rectors, parsons, parish priests and ministers, clergymen above these ranks but below Bishop.

Head-teachers of secondary, primary or preparatory schools with fewer than 750 pupils, qualified teachers aged 28 and over in public, secondary or grammar schools.

Civil Servant - higher and senior and chief executive officers, executive officers.

Recently qualified assistant principal.

Local government-senior officers (9 grades).

University Lecturers, readers, technical college lecturers.

Established journalist for provincial and local papers, trade and technical publications, less senior journalist for national press.

Matron of a smaller hospital (non-teaching), sister/tutor in large hospital or teaching hospital.

Qualified pharmacist.

Qualified accountants, surveyors, architects, solicitors, etc. who do not have their own practice but are employed as executives not senior enough to be graded 'A'.

Newly qualified professional men of all sorts who have not yet established themselves (i.e. less than 3 years from qualification).

Librarian, qualified, in charge of a library or branch library.

Business and Industry

Self-employed owners of business with 5-24 employees in skilled or non-manual trades (e.g. shopkeepers, plumbing contractors, electrical contractors, etc.)

Self-employed farmers with 2-9 employees.

Managers of large farms, stewards, bailiffs, etc.

Bank clerks with special responsibilities (e.g. Chief clerk, teller, etc.)

Insurance clerk with professional qualifications and/or special responsibilities in large branch or head office.

Manager of a retail or wholesale establishment with 25-199 employees at the establishment.

Some relatively senior managers or executives in commerce and industry.

General Foreman, Clerk of Works, i.e. with other foreman under him.

Chief buyers for wholesale or retail establishments.

Area Sales Managers or senior representatives (especially if technically/professionally qualified).

Executives with professional or technical qualifications who are not senior enough to be graded 'A' e.g. department managers.

Technicians with degree or equivalent qualifications, especially in high-technology industries such as electronics, computers, aircraft, chemicals, nuclear energy etc.

Police and Fire Brigade

Chief Inspector, Inspector.

Assistant Chief Officer.

Divisional Officer.

Officer.

Armed Forces

Army-Captain, Major.

Navy-Lieutenant-Commander.

RAF-Flight Lieutenant, Squadron Leader.

Non-Earners

People with private income living in a less luxurious way than Grade 'A' people. Retired people who,before retirement would have been 'B' grade.

3.3 'C1' HOUSEHOLDS - LOWER MIDDLE CLASS

About 22% of total. In general it is made up of the families of small tradespeople and non-manual workers who carry out less important administrative, supervisory and clerical jobs, i.e. what are sometimes called "white-collar" workers.

Examples of occupations of the head of the household

Professional and semi-professional

Curates in the Church of England, ministers of "fringe" free churches, monks and nuns of any denomination, except those with special responsibilities.

Teachers, other than those graded 'B'.

Student nurses, staff nurses, sisters in smaller hospitals, Midwife, Dispenser, Radiographer.

Bank clerk, insurance clerk with no special qualification or responsibilities.

Insurance agent (door-to-door collector).

Civil Servant-clerical grades.

Local government-clerical, junior administrative, professional and technical grades. Articled clerk.

Library assistant (not fully qualified).

Student (on grant).

Business and Industry

Self-employed owners of small business (with 1-4 employees) in non-manual or skilled trades, e.g. shopkeepers, electrical contractors, builders, etc.

Self-employed farmers with only one employee.

Manager of a retail or wholesale establishment with 1-24 employees.

Some relatively junior managers in industry and commerce.

Clerks, typists, office machine operators, punch operators.

Telephonists, telegraphists.

Buyers (except very senior buyers).

Representatives, salesmen (except those grade 'B').

Technicians/Engineers, etc. with professional/technical qualifications below degree standard.

Foreman in charge of 25 or more employees, mainly supervisory work (other than a few very senior foreman coded 'B').

Draughtsman.

Driving Instructor.

Police and Fire Brigade

Station Sergeant, Sergeant, Detective Sergeant.

Station Officer and Sub-Station Officer, Leading Fireman.

Armed Forces

Army-Sergeant, Sergeant Major, Warrant Officer, 2nd Lieutenant, Lieutenant.

Navy-Petty Officer, Chief Petty Officer, Sub-Lieutenant.

RAF-Sergeant, Flight Sergeant, Warrant Officer, Pilot Officer, Flying Officer.

Non-Earners

Retired people who, before retirement, would have been C1 grade and have pensions other than state pensions or have private means of a very modest nature.

3.4 'C2' HOUSEHOLDS - THE SKILLED WORKING CLASS

About 32% of total. Grade C2 consists in the main of skilled manual workers and their families. When in doubt as to whether the head of the household is skilled or unskilled, check whether he has served an apprenticeship, this may be a guide, though not all skilled workers have served an apprenticeship.

Examples of occupations of the head of the household

General

Foreman (responsible for up to 24 employees), Deputy (mining) Charge Hand, Overlooker, Overseer, whose work is mainly manual (these may be found in nearly all trades and industries - including farming and agriculture).

Agriculture

Agricultural workers with special skills or responsibilities, e.g. head cowman, shepherd (chief).

Building Industry (including Construction and Wood-workers)

Most adult male skilled workers or craftsmen including: Bricklayer, Carpenter, Plasterer, Glazier, Plumber, Painter.

Coal Mining

Skilled underground workers including: Coal Cutters, Filler, Getter, Hewer, Miner, Putter.

Manufacturing

Metal Manufacturing, Shipbuilding and Repairing, Engineering, Furnace, Forge, Foundry and Rolling Mills.

Most adult male workers including: Furnace-men, (except coal, gas, and coke ovens), Moulder, Smelter, Blacksmith, Coppersmith.

Plater, Riveter, Shipwright.

Fitter, Grinder, Millwright, Setter, Tool-maker, Turner.

Vehicle Builder, Welder.

Electrical Fitter, Electrician, Lineman.
Skilled Labourer (docks and Admiralty only).

Rubber
Most adult skilled workers.

Textiles, Clothing and Leather
Skilled workers in rayon or nylon production.
Skilled Knitters (hosiery or other knitted goods).
Weaver, Bleacher, Dryer, Drawer-in.
Boot and Shoemaker.
Cutter and Fitter - Tailoring.

Furniture and Upholstery
Most adult male skilled workers including the following:
Carpenter, Joiner, Cabinet Maker.

Paper and Printing Trades
Most adult male skilled workers, including:
Machine Man, Finisher (paper and board manufacturer).
Compositor, Linotype Operator, Typesetter, Electrotyper, Stereotyper, Process Engraver.

Transport
A few only of the better paid workers such as:
All heavy and long distance Vehicle drivers, Engine Driver and Fireman.
Bus Drivers, Bus Inspectors, Signalmen, Train Drivers, Shunters.
Passenger and Goods Guards.
AA Patrolman, Ambulance Drivers.
Post Office Sorters and high grade Postmen.
Stevedore.

Distributor trades
Proprietors and Managers of small shops with no employees.
Shop Assistants with responsibilities.

Glass and Ceramics
Most adult workers including:
Formers, Finishers and Decorators, Furnace-men and Kilnsmen.

Electrical and Electronics
Including Radio and radar Mechanics, Telephone Installers and Linesmen, Electrical and Electronic Fitters.

Agriculture - Farming, Forestry and Fishing
Skilled and specialised workers.

Food and Drink
Baker, Pastry-cook, Brewer, Maltster.

Police and Fire Brigade
Prison Officer, Constable, Fireman, CID Detective Constable.

Security Officers.

Miscellaneous

Self-employed unskilled manual workers with 1-4 employees, e.g. Chimney Sweep, Window Cleaner, Taxi Driver (London).

Self-employed skilled manual workers with no employees.

Coach Builder, Plumber.

Dental Mechanic and Technician.

Armed Forces

Army-Lance Corporal, Corporal.

Navy-AB Seaman. Leading Seaman.

RAF-Aircraftsman, Leading and Senior.

Non-earners

Retired people who before retirement would have been in C2 grade and have pensions other than State Pensions or have private means.

'D' HOUSEHOLDS - UNSKILLED WORKING CLASS

bout 23% of total. Grade D consists entirely of manual workers, generally semi-skilled.

Examples of occupations of the head of the household

General

Most semi-skilled and unskilled workers.

Labourers and mates of the occupation included in C2 grade.

All apprentices to skilled trades.

Agriculture-Farming, Forestry and Fishing

The majority of male agricultural workers, other than those with special skills or responsibilities including:

Tractor or other agricultural machine Driver, Ditcher, Hedger, Farm Labourer.

Forestry Worker, Timber Man.

Fisherman.

Gardeners and self-employed Marked Gardeners with no employees.

Coal Mining and Quarrying

Surface workers except those with special responsibilities.

Unskilled underground workers.

Textiles and Clothing Manufacturer

Most manual workers including the following:

Woolstorer, Blender, Carder, Comber, Spinner, Doubler, Twister, Textile Printer.

Machinist (clothing manufacturer).

Food, Drink and Tobacco

The majority of adult workers, including the following:

Dough mixer, Oven man.

Bottler, Opener.

Stripper, Cutter (Tobacco).

Transport

Bus conductor, Railway Porter including leading Porter.

Ticket Collector (Railway).

Cleaner.

Traffic Warden.

Distributor Trades

Shop assistant without special training or responsibility.

Gas, Coke and Chemical

Most adult workers including Furnace-men and chemical production process workers.

Plastics

Most adult workers.

Glass and Ceramics

Production process workers.

Electrical and Electronics

Assemblers.

Miscellaneous

Caretaker, Warehouseman, Park Keeper, Storekeeper, Postman, Works Policeman, Domestic Servant, Woman Factory Worker, Waitress, Laundry Worker.

All good delivery including milk and bread roundsmen.

Meter Readers.

Self-employed unskilled manual workers with no employees e.g. Window Cleaner, Chimney Sweep, Taxi Driver (provinces).

Armed Forces

Army-Private or equivalent.

Navy-Ordinary Seaman.

RAF-Aircraftsman.

Non-Earners

Retired people who before retirement would have been in D grade and have pensions other State Pensions, or have other private means.

'E' AT LOWEST LEVEL OF SUBSISTENCE

About 9% of total - but growing as the population gets older and lives longer. Grade E consists of Old Age Pensioners, Widows and their families, casual workers and those who, through sickness or unemployment, are dependent on social security schemes, or have very small private means.

Individual income of the head of the household (disregarding additions such as supplementary benefits) will be little, if any, above the basic flat-rate social security benefit.

Examples of occupations of the head of the household

Earners

Casual Labourers.

Part-time clerical and other workers.

None-Earners

Old Age Pensioners.

Widow (with State Widow's Pension).

Those dependent on sickness, unemployment and supplementary benefits for over 2 months who are without benefits related to earnings.

Private means, private pension, disability pension compensation, etc. amounting to little, if any, above the basic flat-rate social security benefit.

Only those informants will be graded as E whose head of the household is E and where no other member of the family is in fact the Chief Wage Earner.

4. Social grade of occupations under industries in the Registrar General's classification

Social Grade

I Farmers, Forester, Fishermen

D	Agricultural workers, unskilled
C2	Skilled agricultural workers
D	Agricultural machinery drivers
D	Gardeners) with
D	Foresters) no
D	Woodmen) qualifications
D	Fishermen (employed)
C1	Agricultural workers-junior technically qualified
B	Grieve (Scotland only) farm manager, bailiff, steward (of large farms or estates)

II Miners and Quarrymen

C2	Coal mine-face workers (skilled)
D	Coal mine-face workers (unskilled
C2	Coal mine-underground workers (skilled)
D	Coal mine-underground workers (unskilled)
D	Coal miners (majority of workers above ground)

III Gas, Coke, and Chemicals Makers

D	Furnace-men, coal, gas and coke ovens
D	Chemical production process workers

IV Glass and Ceramics Makers

C2	Ceramic formers
C2	Glass formers, finishers and decorators
C2	Furnace-men, Kilnmen, glass and ceramic
C2	Ceramics' decorators and finishers
C2	Ceramics' decorators doing hand painting
D	Glass and ceramics production process workers

V Furnace, Forge, Foundry, Rolling Mill Workers

C2	Furnacemen-metal
C2	Rolling, tube mill operators, metal drawers
C2	Moulders and coremakers (foundry)
C2	Smiths, Forgemen
D	Metal making and treating workers
D	Fettlers
D	Metal dressers

V1 Electrical and Electronic Workers

C2	Radio and radar mechanics
C2	Installers and repairmen, telephone
C2	Linesmen, cable jointers
C2	Electricians
C2	Electrical and electronic fitters
D	Assemblers (electric and electronic)
C2	Electrical engineers (manual)
D	Mates to above workers

VII Engineering and Allied Trades Workers

C2	Sheet metal workers
C2	Constructional engineers, riggers
C2	Metal plate workers, riveters
C2	Gas, electric welders, cutters, braziers
C2	Machine tool setters, setter-operators
D	Machine tool operators
C2	Took makers, tool room fitters
C2	Fitters, machine erectors, etc
C2	Engineers (manual)
C2	Electro-platers, dip platers and related workers
C2	Plumbers, lead burners, pipe fitters
D	Press workers and stampers
C2	Metal workers (skilled)
C2	Watch and chronometer makers and repairers
C2	Precision instrument makers and repairers

C2	Goldsmiths, silversmiths, jewellery makers
C2	Coach, carriage, wagon builders and repairers
D	Other metal making, working, jewellery and electrical production process workers (unskilled)

VIII Woodworkers

C2	Carpenters and joiners
C2	Cabinet makers
C2	Sawyers
C2	Wood working machinists
C2	Coopers
C2	Hoop makers
C2	Benders
C2	Pattern makers
C2	Woodworkers
D	Mates to above workers

IX Leather Workers

C2	Tanners, leather, fur dressers, fellmongers
C2	Shoemakers
C2	She repairers
C2	Cutters, lasters, sewers, footwear and related workers
C2	Leather product makers
D	Mates to above workers

X Textile Workers

D	Fibre preparers
D	Spinners, doublers, winders, reelers
C2	Warpers, sizers
C2	Drawers-in
C2	Weavers
D	Weavers-jute, flax, hemp (Scotland only)
C2	Knitters
C2	Bleachers and finishers of textiles
C2	Dyers of textiles
C2	Textile fabrics and related product makers and examiners
D	Textile fabrics etc, production process workers
D	Winders and reelers
C2	Rope, twine and net makers

XI Clothing Workers

C2	Tailors-cutters and fitters
D	Sewers and embroiderers, textile and light leather products

XII Food, Drink and Tobacco Workers

C2	Bakers and pastry cooks
C2	Butchers and meat cutters
C2	Brewers, wine makers and related workers
D	Food processors
D	Tobacco preparers and product makers

XIII Paper and Printing Workers

C2	Makers of paper and paperboard
C2	Paper products makers
C2	Compositors
C2	Printing press operators
C2	Printers (so described)
C2	Printing workers
D	Mates to above workers

XIV Makers of Other Products

C2	Workers in rubber
D	Workers in plastics
C2	Craftsmen
D	Other production process workers
D	Mates to above workers

XV Construction Workers

C2	Bricklayers, tile setters
C2	Masons, stone cutters, slate workers
C2	Plasterers, cement finishers, terrazzo workers
D	Mates to above workers

XVI Painters and Decorators

D	Aerographers, paint sprayers
C2	Painters, decorators
D	Mates to above workers

XVII Drivers of Stationary Engines, Cranes, etc

D	Boiler firemen
C2	Crane and hoist operators, slingers
C2	Operators of earth moving and other construction machinery
D	Stationary engine, material handling plant operators, oilers and greasers

XVIII Labourers

D	Railway lengthmen
D	Labourers and unskilled workers
D	Chemical and allied trades

D	Engineering and allied trades
D	Founders in engineering and allied trades
D	Textiles
D	Coke ovens and gas works
D	Glass and ceramics
D	Building and contracting
D	All other Labourers

XIX Transport and Communications Workers

B	Deck, engineering officers and pilots, ship
D	Deck and engine room rating, barge and boatman
A	Aircraft pilots, navigators and flight engineers
C2	Drivers, motormen, firemen, railway engine
C2	Railway guards (passenger and goods)
C2	Drivers of buses, coaches, trams
C2	Drivers of road goods vehicles-heavy or long distance
D	Drivers of road goods vehicle-local and light
C2	Shunters, pointmen
C1	Telephone operators
C1	Telegraph and radio operators
D	Postmen
C2	Sorters and higher grade postmen
D	Messengers
D	Bus and tram conductors
D	Porters, railway
D	Ticket collectors, railway
C2	Bus Inspector
C2	Stevedores
D	Dock labourers
C2	Skilled labourers (Docks & Admiralty only)
D	Lorry drivers' mates, van guards
D	Unskilled workers in transport and communication occupations

XX Warehousemen, Storekeepers, Packers, Bottlers

D	Warehousemen, storekeepers
D	Assistant warehousemen, assistant storekeepers
D	Packers, labellers and related workers

XXI Clerical Workers

C1	Typists
C1	Shorthand writers, secretaries
C1	Clerks, cashiers, office machine operators

XXII Sales Workers

C1	Salesmen, representatives (unless professionally qualified)
C1	Shop assistants with qualifications and training
C2	Shop assistants with special responsibilities
D	Shop assistant without special responsibilities
D	Roundsmen (bread, milk, laundry, soft drinks)
D	Street vendors, hawkers

XXIII Service, Sport and Recreation Workers

C2	Security Guards
D	Barmen, barmaids, Housekeepers
D	Stewards
D	Waiters, counter hands
C2	Cooks
D	Kitchen hands
D	Maids, valets and related service workers
D	Caretakers, office keepers
D	Chimney sweeps (employed)
D	Charwomen, officer cleaners, Window cleaners (employed)
C2	Hairdressers, beauticians if apprenticeship served
D	Hairdressers, beauticians if serving apprenticeship
D	Hospital or ward orderlies
D	Launderers, dry cleaners and pressers
C2	Ambulance men

ISLE COLLEGE LIBRARY

XXIV Administrators and Managers

A	Ministers of the Crown, MP's, senior Government Officials
A	Local Authority senior officers

XXV Professional, Technical Workers, Artists

A	Medical practitioners (qualified with own practice.)
B	Junior medical practitioners (recently qualified)
A	Dental practitioner (qualified with own practice)
B	Junior practitioners

A, B, C1

Authors, journalists and related workers, stage managers, actors, entertainers, musicians. Painters, sculptors and related creative artists. The grade of these and similar cases, e.g. sportsmen obviously depends on their success and your grading must depend upon this.

6. Classifications used by Market Research Companies

The following information is gathered usually only at the very end of the interview. The exception is on quota surveys when they sometimes need to establish quota details (age and social class) before proceeding with the interview. A questionnaire without a complete classification cannot be used. Here is what they have to ask:

1. Name and Address

Full name and initials and postal address (including post code and County) in BLOCK CAPITALS as we may need to contact the informants again.

2. Telephone Number

Print the exchange name too. (We verify interviews by telephone as well as by post).

3. Age

If informant refuses to give exact age, then ask into which age group he/she fits. Should the age still be refused (very rarely does this happen) then write E (for estimated) beside the code they have circled.

4 Marital Status

Single includes widowed, divorced or separated informants.

5. Working Status

Full time is 30 hours or more a week at paid work.
Part time is less than 30 hours but 8 hours or over paid work.
Non-working is less than 8 hours paid work over week.

6. Household

A household consists of either 1 person living alone or a group of persons. It is essentially a group of people who live together and whose food and other household expenses are managed as one unit. Includes lodger is she/he takes at least one meal a day with the family. People who are not normally at home but there only on holiday (students, relatives) are not counted as being in the household.

7. Housewife

This person is responsible for the household arrangements, i.e. cooking, cleaning, shopping etc. she may not do the household chores herself but is responsible for seeing they are done. Other woman is an adult woman living in the household who is not responsible for the household arrangements.

8. Head of Household

This person will either own the accommodation or be responsible for the rent, or, if the accommodation is rent free, the person who is responsible for the household having it rent free. If this person is a married woman whose husband is a member of the household, then the husband is counted as "head of household".

9. Chief Wage Earner

This person is the senior working member of the household, normally the oldest related male of 21 years of age and over in full time employment. If there is no male of 21 years and over then the oldest related female of 21 and over in full time employment is taken. Non-related persons living in the household cannot count as chief wage earner.

10. Children

These are people in household aged 15 years and under.

11. Social Class

Except in exceptional cases the grading of informants is based exclusively on the occupation information. In the majority of cases the grading is based on the occupation of the head of household. The exceptions are:

a)   If the head of household is not in full time employment or is sick (for a period of more than 6 months) or is retired, widowed or a pensioner (with an income of less than the basic flat-rate weekly pension obtaining at the time of the interview), then the occupation of the chief wage earner determines the status of the household and therefore informants living in it.

b)   Lodgers, boarders and resident domestic servants are graded on the basis of their own occupation.

SOCIAL CLASS IS BASED ON CLASS OCCUPATION OF HEAD OF HOUSEHOLD.

Guide to Social Class for Market Researchers(1993)

NON-MANUAL

A.   Upper Middle. Higher managerial, admin or professional.

B.   Middle. Intermediate managerial admin or professional.

C1.   Lower Middle. Junior Managerial, admin or professional, supervisory. clerical.

MANUAL

C2   Skilled working. Skilled manual.

D   Working. Semi and unskilled manual

E   Lowest level of subsistence. State pensioners etc. where no other member of the household is the chief wage earner.

---

7. Some caricatures!

To amuse ourselves my students and I made up a survey of an imaginary village. There is truly nothing in the survey which wasn't actually said at some time within my earshot. I do not put it forward as anything other than amusement and would not want it to be quoted as authoritative research! It was done by listening very selectively to people in the pub!

WHAT THE A'S SAY

about themselves, the A HOUSEHOLDS - UPPER MIDDLE CLASS
"OUR SOCIAL EQUALS"
"THE BETTER CLASS OF PERSON"

about B HOUSEHOLDS - MIDDLE CLASS
"NOT QUITE OUR EQUALS"
"SOCIAL CLIMBERS"   "THEY TRY TO BEHAVE LIKE GENTLEMEN"

about C1 HOUSEHOLDS - LOWER MIDDLE CLASS
"NEITHER HERE NOR THERE"
"THEY ARE MORE INTELLIGENT THAN THE NORMAL RUN OF PEOPLE"
"WELL EDUCATED AND VERY HANDY WHEN YOU HAVE ABOUT A DOZEN VILLAGE ORGANISATIONS TO SEE TO"

about C2 HOUSEHOLDS - SKILLED WORKING CLASS
"SOCIAL CLIMBERS"
"CAN BE VERY BORING AND DULL AT PARTIES WHEN ONE HAS TO SPEAK TO THEM!"

about D HOUSEHOLDS - UNSKILLED WORKING CLASS
"VILLAGERS AND FARMERS DECENT SORTS"
"THE GOOD OLD COUNTRY FOLK"

about E HOUSEHOLDS - LOWEST LEVEL OF SUBSISTENCE
"QUITE CHARMING"
"I OFTEN DONATE SOMETHING TO THEM"

WHAT THE B'S SAY

about A HOUSEHOLDS - UPPER MIDDLE CLASS

"THE ARISTOCRACY HAVE MORE BREEDING THAN SENSE"
"THE ONES WITH MONEY ALL TALK LIKE THE BBC AND THINK
THEY OWN THE PLACE"

about themselves, the B HOUSEHOLDS - MIDDLE CLASS

"WE ARE AMBITIOUS GO-AHEAD PEOPLE"
"I SEE US AS THE PEOPLE WHO MAKE BRITAIN GREAT"
"WE ARE THE PEOPLE WHO GET HERE BY MERIT AND BRAIN
AND HARD WORK"

about C1 HOUSEHOLDS - LOWER MIDDLE CLASS

"THEY TRY THEIR BEST, BUT THEY HAVEN'T REALLY GOT
WHAT IT TAKES"

about C2 HOUSEHOLDS - SKILLED WORKING CLASS

"FARMERS AND TRADES PEOPLE - GOOD SORTS IF YOU KEEP
THEM IN THEIR PLACE AND DON'T GIVE THEM ANY ROPE"

about D HOUSEHOLDS - UNSKILLED WORKING CLASS

"FARM WORKERS AND VILLAGERS - YOU NEED THEM I
SUPPOSE"
"VERY DULL AND ILL-EDUCATED"
"I CAN NEVER FIND ANYTHING TO TALK TO THEM ABOUT
EXCEPT FOOTBALL, RACING AND MONEY"

about E HOUSEHOLDS - LOWEST LEVEL OF SUBSISTENCE
"MOST OF THEM ARE BETTER OFF THAN THEY LET ON"
"VERY DIRTY MOST OF THEM" "THE IMMORAL ELEMENT IN
THE VILLAGE" "IF THEY WANTED TO WORK THEY COULD -
LOOK AT ME: I CAME FROM NOTHING" "THE WORST OF THE
LOWER ORDERS"

WHAT THE C1'S SAY

about A HOUSEHOLDS - UPPER MIDDLE CLASS

"THE USUAL WELL OFF PEOPLE YOU FIND IN THE COUNTRYSIDE MOSTLY"
"RETIRED PEOPLE LOT OF NOUVEAU RICHE AMONGST THEM"

about About B HOUSEHOLDS - MIDDLE CLASS

"MONEY MAKERS VERY AMBITIOUS SET OF PEOPLE BUT THEY JUST HAVEN'T MADE IT"

about themselves, the C1 HOUSEHOLDS - LOWER MIDDLE CLASS

"WE ARE IN BETWEEN REALLY - ITS PROBABLY THE BEST PLACE TO BE"
"I DON'T REALLY LIKE OUR LOT - I'M REALLY IN THE CLASS ABOVE!"

about C2 HOUSEHOLDS - SKILLED WORKING CLASS
"THE KIND THAT DON'T MIX WITH US - THEY ARE USUALLY SOCIAL CLIMBERS"
"I USED TO BE ONE OF THEM - Y'KNOW, VOTED LABOUR AND ALL THAT - BUT NOW I VOTE LIBERAL DEMOCRAT - I HOPE SOON IT'LL BE TORY"
"THEY ARE ALWAYS HOB NOBBING WITH THE UPPER SET"

about D HOUSEHOLDS - UNSKILLED WORKING CLASS

"THEY ARE ALRIGHT BUT YOU HAVE TO WATCH THEM OR THEY'LL DO YOU"
"I WOULDN'T ACTUALLY LIKE THEM AS NEIGHBOURS - BUT I SUPPOSE THAT'S WHY WE'VE GOT COUNCIL ESTATES"

about E HOUSEHOLDS

"VERY UNFORTUNATE"

WHAT THE C2'S SAY

about A HOUSEHOLDS - UPPER MIDDLE CLASS

"THE SORT OF PEOPLE YOU CAN REALLY RESPECT AND LOOK UP TO"
"THE BETTER CLASS OF PERSON"

about B HOUSEHOLDS - MIDDLE CLASS

"THEY LIKE TO THINK THEY ARE IN THE TOP LOT - BUT THEY AREN'T AND YOU CAN TELL"

about C1 HOUSEHOLDS - LOWER MIDDLE CLASS

"SCHOOL TEACHERS AND THAT LOT"
"I THINK FOLK MAKE TOO MUCH FUSS OF THEM"
"A LOT OF TOFFEE NOSED KNOW-ALLS"
"MAINLY TOWNIES AND PINKOES"

about themselves, C2 HOUSEHOLDS - SKILLED WORKING CLASS

"DECENT PEOPLE WHO TRY TO GET ON"
"KEEP THEMSELVES TO THEMSELVES"

about D HOUSEHOLDS - UNSKILLED WORKING CLASS

"ORDINARY HONEST FOLK"
"JUST HAVEN'T HAD THE LUCK THEY DESERVE"
"NO SIDE ON THEM - SALT OF THE EARTH"

about E HOUSEHOLDS - LOWEST LEVEL OF SUBSISTENCE

"THEY DON'T TRY TO HELP THEMSELVES"
"DON'T TALK TO ME ABOUT THE UNEMPLOYED - IT'S THEM AS HAS DRAGGED THIS COUNTRY DOWN ON ITS KNEES"

WHAT THE D'S SAY

about A HOUSEHOLDS - UPPER MIDDLE CLASS

"PEOPLE WHO ARE VERY MUCH BETTER THAN WE ARE"
"GOOD LUCK TO 'EM: THEY KEEP THE COUNTRY GOING"

about About B HOUSEHOLDS - MIDDLE CLASS

"PEOPLE WHO HAVE PLENTY OF MONEY AND PLENTY OF CHEEK AND WHO DESERVE TO GET ON IN THIS WORLD"
"THEY HAVEN'T GOT THE BREEDING AND THE MANNERS OF THE REAL CLASS PERSON - YOU CAN TELL, JUST BY LISTENING TO THEIR VOICES"

about C1 HOUSEHOLDS - LOWER MIDDLE CLASS
"PONCY SCHOOL TEACHERS AND THE LIKE"
"I DON'T HOLD WITH THEM - THEY DON'T KNOW NO PRACTICAL COMMON SENSE THINGS - THEY GOT TOO MUCH BRAIN FOR THEIR OWN GOOD"

about C2 HOUSEHOLDS - SKILLED WORKING CLASS
"THEY USED TO BE LIKE US, BUT THEY GOT AIRS AND GRACES"
"MOST OF THEM ARE UNEMPLOYED NOW - SO THEY AREN'T NO BETTER THAN US!"

about themselves, D HOUSEHOLDS - UNSKILLED WORKING CLASS

"ORDINARY HONEST FOLK WHO JUST WANT TO GET BY AND BE RESPECTABLE"
"WE DON'T SAY MUCH BUT WE KNOW. WE KNOW HOW TO GET BY AND HOW TO BEHAVE AND WHAT'S GOOD AND WHAT'S BAD"

about E HOUSEHOLDS
"THEY DON'T GIVE A DAMN AND SCROUNGE OFF OUR TAXES"

WHAT THE E'S SAY

about A HOUSEHOLDS - UPPER MIDDLE CLASS

"POSH FOLK IN THE BIG HOUSES - THEY'RE ALRIGHT MOST OF EM"
"THEY WAS BORN INTO IT AND GOOD LUCK TO THEM"

about B HOUSEHOLDS - MIDDLE CLASS
"BLOODY SNOBS"

about C1 HOUSEHOLDS - LOWER MIDDLE CLASS
"LOAD OF BARRACK ROOM BLOODY LAWYERS"

about C2 HOUSEHOLDS - SKILLED WORKING CLASS
"LOAD OF *********************"

about D HOUSEHOLDS - UNSKILLED WORKING CLASS
"JUST LIKE US, BUT SOME OF THEM IS HIGH AND MIGHTY"

about themselves, E HOUSEHOLDS - LOWEST LEVEL OF SUBSISTENCE
"DECENT FOLK"
"FOLKS THAT LIKE TO DO WHAT THEY WANTS TO DO"

SECTION 24: CULTURE

Introduction

I believe strongly that any educated person ought be able to answer the questions:
- 1. What's going on?
- and
- 2. What's been going on?

By that I mean you should have a knowledge of the people and events that are significant at the present time and the cultural heritage of our civilisation i.e. the people who have contributed to it.

1. What is it to be human?

Humans have:
- PERCEPTIONS

    We have the capacity to perceive via our 5 senses:
    - hearing
    - seeing
    - tasting
    - touching
    - smelling

    and we develop an ability to discriminate ever more finely between the inputs to our senses: we can see light and dark and colours in between.

Humans have:
- FEELINGS/EMOTIONS

    We feel about our perceptions.

Humans have:
- THOUGHTS

    We have the capacity to reflect on what we have perceived and felt, and to discriminate ever more finely between these thoughts.

Humans have:
- COMMUNICATION

    We have the capacity to communicate these reflections to other humans.

Most humans attempt to do this. Artists, who perhaps are better perceivers, (or are they better communicators?), attempt to communicate to others: "This is the way it seems to me."

It is interesting to examine how other humans who have existed in this space if not in this time have re-acted to it. Thus we have need to examine those who have perceived, felt, thought and communicated.

WRITERS - historians - novelists - dramatists - poets - journalists.
VISUAL ARTISTS - painters - sculptors - film makers - photographers
COMPOSERS - classical - pop
SCIENTISTS - biologists - chemists - physicists
PHILOSOPHERS - ancient and modern
POLITICIANS - of left - right - green
are all worth examination by anyone interested in finding out how others have
perceived, felt and thought about our existence.

WRITERS "factual" writers historians, who look at the way in which things have
changed since man first began to leave interpretable signs of his existence.
"Fictional" writers who tell us how it seems to them that people and people and
people and societies and things interact. Some in the theatre, TV, film, some in
novels, short stories, some in poetry.
SCIENTISTS have perceived the world and attempted to explain it in terms of the
nature of physical universe, the animals, the plants, in biology, etc.
PHILOSOPHERS have attempted to explain the nature of the universe and human
life and everything! MODERN PHILOSOPHERS have given us a tool for
analysing language which is what we use to communicate our thoughts about our
perceptions.
POLITICIANS have said "This is the way it is: THIS is the way it OUGHT to be."
They believe it is possible to affect the way in which the society we live in is
structured through politics and/or religion.

It is useful for us as humans to acknowledge our own nature and perspective in time
and space, and to begin to look over the "culture" which we have available to us.
An exercise such as listing chronologically all the people we know of who have
made a contribution to our knowledge and experience of the world can help give us
a perspective on the events in all these areas, as well as giving us insight into the
ways in which ideas interact and into our own selves...
WE ARE NOT ALONE. NO MAN IS AN ISLAND!
If you are intending to go into any further study, especially at HE level then you
will need to be aware of the people who are considered as important contributors to
our civilisation. That is the civilisation of our Western World. I am not saying any
more than that this list is a starter for you to be able to identify some of the
important contributors in the spheres of Literature, Philosophy, Visual Arts, Music,
Science and Politics. I am sure I have missed out some very significant and
important people: you can always add them. You may find the list useful when
studying a particular age, or a particular person just to be able to see those who
were contemporaries. The dates given are the birth dates. I have also put in the
rulers of England/Britain in italics: their date indicates the start of their reign.

Date	Literature	Philosophy	Visual	Music	Science	Politics
1	Ovid	Christ				
300		Buddhism				
521				Boethus		
570		Mohammed				
600				Gregorian		
742				Chants		Cha'emagne
827						*Egbert*
838						*Ethelwulf*
858						*Ethelbald*
860						*Ethelbert*
865						*Ethelred I*
871						*Alfred*
899						*Edward*
924						*Athelstan*
939						*Edmund*
946						*Edred*
955						*Edwy*
959						*Edgar*
975						*Edward*
978						*Ethelred II*
1000	Beowolf					
1016						*Edmund*
						Canute
1027	OKhayyam					
1035						*Harold I*
1040						*Hardicanute*
1042						*Edward*
1066						*HaroldI I*
						William I
1087						*William II*
1100						*Henry I*
1110	Miracle					
1135	Plays					*Stephen*
1154						*Henry II*
1162						G Khan
1182		St Francis				
1189						*Richard I*
1199						*John*

Date	Literature	Philosophy	Visual	Music	Science	Politics
1200				Carmina		
1214				Burana	R Bacon	
1216						Kublai Khan
						Henry III
1225		Aquinas		Summer is		
1254				y comin in	M Polo	
1265	Dante					
1272						Edward I
1305	Gotfried		Giotto			
1306			Lorenzetti			
1307						Edward II
1327						Edward III
1328		J Wycliffe				
1340	Chaucer					
1348	Boccaccio					
1369				Dunstable		
1377						Richard ii
1381						Wat Tyler
1387			F Angelico			
1390			van Eyck			
1397			Uccello			
1399						Henry IV
1400					Gutenberg	
1401			Masaccio			
1412						Joan of Arc
1413						Henry V
1420			PFrancesca		Henry the	
1422					Navigator	Henry VI
1430			Bellini			
1431			Mantegna			
1422					Caxton	
1444			Botticelli			
1450			H Bosch			
1451					Columbus	
1452			L da Vinci			
1461						Edward IV
1465			Holbein			
1469			the Elder		V da Gama	
1471			Durer			

Date	Literature	Philosophy	Visual	Music	Science	Politics
1475			M'angelo			
1477			Titian			
1478		T More				
1473		Wolsey			Copernicus	
1480					Magellan	
1483		Luther	Raphael			*Edward IV*
						Richard III
1485					Cortes	*Henry VII*
1489		Cranmer				
1494	Rabelais		Correggio			
1496	Machiavelli					
1495				J Tavener		
1497			Holbien			
1503	T Wyatt	Nostr'amus	(Younger)			
1505		John Knox		T Tallis		
1506		F Xavier				
1509		Calvin				*Henry VIII*
1510	Everyman					
1514					Rheticus	
1518			Tintoretto			
			Palladio			
1520			Brueghel			
1525			the Elder	Palestrina		
1533	Montaigne					
1541			El Greco			
1543				W Byrd		
1544	Tasso					
1546					T Brahe	
1547	Cervantes					*Edward VI*
1553						*Mary I*
1554		Hooker			W Raleigh	
1557				Gabrielli		
				T Morley		
1558	Greene,					*Elizabeth I*
	Kydd,					
	Peele					
1561		F Bacon				
1562				John Bull		
1563					Mercator	

Date	Literature	Philosophy	Visual	Music	Science	Politics
1564	Shakespeare	Bruegel		Galileo		
	Marlowe	(Younger)			Vesalius	
1570	Dekker					G Fawkes
1571			B Cellini		Kepler	
				Praetorius		
1572	J Donne					
	B Johnson					
1573			I Jones			
			Caravaggio			
1577			Rubens			
1579	J Fletcher					
	Spenser					
1580	Middleton		F Hals			
1582	Fletcher					
1584	Beaumont					
1585						Richlieu
1587				Monteverdi		
1586	Sydney					
1588		T Hobbes				
1591	R Herrick					
1593	I Walton		Poussin			
1594		Hooker				
1596		Descartes				
1598	Carew		Brueghel			
1599		Cromwell	Van Dyke			
			Velasquez			
1600	Calderon		Claude			
1601					Fermat	
1603					Tasman	*James I*
1606			Rembrandt			
1608	Milton				Torricelli	
1612	S Butler					
1617			Murillo		Napier	
1619					Harvey	
1622	Moliere					
1625						*Charles I*
1627					Boyle	
1628	J Bunyan					

Date	Literature	Philosophy	Visual	Music	Science	Politics
1629					Hugyens	
1631	J Dryden					
1632		J Locke	Vermeer			
		Spinoza	C Wren			
1633	G Herbert					
	Pepys					
1635					Hooke	
1639	Racine					
1640	Whych'ley					
1642					I Newton	
1646		Leibniz				
						Commonwealth
1652	Ottway					
	N Tate					
1652				Correlli		
1656					Halley	
1659				Purcell		
				Scarlatti		
1660						*Charles II*
1661	Defoe					
1664			Vanbrugh			
1667	Swift					
1670	Congreve					
1672	Addison					
	Steele					
1675				Vivaldi		
1676					Walpole	
1678	Farquhar					
1681				Telemann		
1683				Rameau		
1684			Watteau			
1685	J Gay	Berkeley		J S Bach		*James II*
				Handel		*William III*
				Scarlatti(D)		*Mary II*
1686					Fahrenheit	
1688	Pope					
1694		Voltaire				
1696			Tiepolo			

Date	Literature	Philosophy	Visual	Music	Science	Politics
1697			Canaletto Hogarth			
1701					Celsius	
1702						*Anne*
1703		J Wesley				
1707	Fielding Goldoni					
1709	S Johnson					
1710				Boyce Pergolesi Arne		
1711		D Hume			Lomonosov	
1712		Rousseau				
1713	Sterne	Diderot				
1714				CPE Bach Gluck		*George I*
1716	T Gray					
1717	Walpole					
1721	Smollett					
1723			Reynolds		A Smith	
1724		Kant	Stubbs			
1728	Goldsmith				J Cooke J Hutton	
1726			Hepplewhite			
1727			Gainsborough			*George II*
1728			Adam			
1729	Burke					
1730			Wedgewood			
1731	Cowper				E Darwin	
1732				Haydn		Washington
1735				J C Bach		
1736					J Watt	
1737	T Paine					
1739				Dittersdorf		
1740	Boswell					
1743				Boccherini	J Banks	Toussaint
1745					Volta(Volt)	
1746		Pestalozzi	Goya			
1748		Bentham	David			

Date	Literature	Philosophy	Visual	Music	Science	Politics
1749	Goethe			Cimarosa	Jenner	
1750				Salieri		
1751	Sheridan		Sheraton			
1752	Chatterton		Nash			
1755				Mozart		Marie
1756			Raeburn			Antoinette
1757	W Blake					
1758						Robespierre
						Nelson
1759	Burns					Wilberforce
	Schiller					Pitt
1760						*George III*
1762	Cobbett					
1766		Malthus				
1769					Brunel	Napoleon
1770	Wordsworth	Hegel		Beethoven		
1771	Scott	R Owen				
1772	Coleridge	Schlegel				
1774	Southey					
1775	J Austen		Turner		Ampere	
1776			Constable			
1777					Gauss	
1778	C Lamb				H Davy	
					Gay-Lussac	
1780		E Fry				
1781					Stephenson	
1782		Froebel				
1783	Stendhal			Paganini		
1784				Spohr		Palmerston
1785	DeQuincey					
	Grimm					
	Peacock					
1786				Weber		
1788	Byron	Schop'hauer				Peel
	Ruckert					
1787					Ohm	
1789	F Cooper					
1791					Morse	
1792	Shelley			Rossini	Babbage	

Date	Literature	Philosophy	Visual	Music	Science	Politics
1792					Herschel	
1795	Keats	T Arnold		Albeniz		
		T Carlyle				
1796			Corot			
1797				Donizetti		
				Schubert		
1799	Balzac		Delacroix			
1801		Newman		Bellini		
		Shaftsbury				
1802	Dumas	Macaulay			Wheatstone	
	Hugo					
1803	Merime	Emerson		Berlioz	Doppler	
1804				Glinka		Disraeli
				J Strauss		
1805	HCAnd'son			Boccherini		
1806	EBrowning					
		JS Mill				
1807	Longfellow					
1809	Gogol	C Darwin		Mendels-		Gladstone
	E A Poe			sohn		Lincoln
	Tennyson					
1810	Ade Musset			Chopin		
	B Stowe			Schumman		
1811				Liszt	Bunsen	
	Thackeray					
1812	Browning					
	Dickens					
	E Lear					
1813		Kirkegaard		Verdi	Livingstone	
				Wagner	Bessemer	
1814			Millet			
1815	Trollope					
1816	C Bronte					
1817			Watts			
1818	Turgenev	Marx		Gounod	Joul	
1819	G Eliot	Ruskin		Offenbach		
	W Whitman					
	H Melville					
1820						George IV

Date	Literature	Philosophy	Visual	Music	Science	Politics
1820	Baudelaire Dostoevsky Flaubert	Engels	Tenniel		Night'gale	
1822				Franck	Mendel Pasteur Schliemann	
1824	A Dumas			Bruckner Smetena		
1825				Strauss		
1827			H Hunt		Lister	
1828	Ibsen Meredith Tolstoy Verne		GRossetti			
1829			Millais			
1830	EDickenson C Rossetti		Leighton Pissarro			
		E Davies				
1832	M Alcott Bjornson L Carroll		Manet			
1833			B Jones		Nobel	
				Brahms		
1834	W Morris		Degas GdMaurier Whistler		Daimler	
1835	M Twain S Butler			Saint-Saens		
1836	WS Gilbert			Delibes		
1837	Swinburne			Balakirev Walteufel	McAdam	*Victoria*
1838				Bizet Bruch	Mach	
1839			Cézanne	Tch'kovsky Mo'sorgsky		
1840	Hardy		Monet		J Dunlop	
1840	Zola		P Renoir Rodin		Holland	

Date	Literature	Philosophy	Visual	Music	Science	Politics
1841	Hudson	OWHolmes		Chabrier		
1842		W James		Dvorak		
				Massenet		
				Sullivan		
1843				Grieg		
1844	R Bridges			RKosarkov		
	M Hopkins					
		Nietzsche				
1845				Faure	Roentgen	
1845				Widor		
1847					Boole	
					Edison	
					Bell	
1848			Gauguin	Parry		Balfour
1849	Str'dberg				Pavlov	
1850	Stevenson					
1853			Van Gogh			
1854				Janacek	Eastman	
				Sousa		
1855	Pinero	Freud				
1856	Haggard		JSSargent		JThompson	
	GB Shaw					
	Wilde					
1857	Conrad	B-Powell		Elgar		
1858		B Webb		Leon'allo		E Pankhurst
				Puccini	Huxley	
				E Smyth		
1859	Houseman	J Dewey	Seurat		Curie	
	JKJerome					
	C Doyle					
					H Ellis	
	K Grahame					
		S Webb				
1857					Hertz	
1860	JM Barrie			Mahler		
				Wolf		
				Suppe		
			Sickert			
	Chekhov					

Date	Literature	Philosophy	Visual	Music	Science	Politics
1861		R Steiner Whitehead R Tagore				
1862	Maeterlink Hauptmann			Debussy Delius German	Lumiere	
1863	D'Annunzio	Santayana	Munch L Pissarro	Mascagni		L George
1864			T-Lautrec		C Pathe H Ford	
1864				R Strauss		
1865	Kipling			Dukas Glazunov		
	Yeats			Sibelius Nielson		
1866	HG Wells Benavente		Kandinsky	Busoni		Baldwin
1867	A Bennett Pirandello		Rousseau Bonnard		MdmCurrie Faraday	
1867	Galsworthy					
1868	Gorki			Bantock	RF Scott	
1869	Gide Leacock		Matisse FL-Wright	H Wood		Cham'laine Ghandi
1870		Adler				Lenin
	H Belloc	Montessori				
1871	Proust JM Synge	Lenin			Rutherford O Wright	Rasputin
1872	Beerbohm	B Russell			Bleriot	
			Beardsley Modrian	VWilliams		
1873	de la Mare		Rach'ninov	De Forest		
				WC Handy		
1874	Chest'ton R Frost Maugham G Stein Colette			Holst Schonberg C Ives	Marconi	
						Churchill
		Thorndyke				

Date	Literature	Philosophy	Visual	Music	Science	Politics
1875	J Buchan			Ravel	Schweitzer	
		Jung	DWGriffith			
	T Mann					
	Rilke					
	R Burrows					
1876	J London			de Falla		
	Trevelyan			W-Ferrari		
	S Anderson					
1877	H Hesse			Dohnanyi		
1878	Masefield		Munnings			
1878			A John			
1879	EM Forster		Daumier		Einstein	
			P Klee	Respighi		Beveridge
1880	L Strachey		Epstein	Bloch		
		H Keller		Beecham		
1881	E M Dell		Picasso	Bartock	Fleming	Kerensky
	Wodehouse			V-Lobos		E Bevin
			CBdeMille			
1882	V Woolf		Braque	Stravinsky	Goddard	
	J Joyce		Gill		Bugatti	
	Drink'ter					
	Giraudoux					
	AA Milne					
1883	C McKenzie		Utrillo	Webern		Attlee
		JM Keynes				Mussolini
	Kafka	O y Gasset				
1884	Runyon		Modigliani			H Truman
	Duhamel					Roosevelt
	S O'Casey					
1885	Lawrence		A Berg			
	E Pound			Varèse		
	S Lewis					
1886			Kokoschka			
1887	E Sitwell		Chagall	Borodin	J Huxley	ChKaishek
			Corbusier		B Wallis	
			P Nash			

Date	Literature	Philosophy	Visual	Music	Science	Politics
1888	TS Eliot			I Berlin		
	E O'Neill				J L Baird	
	M Anderson					
1889	C Chaplin				Sikorsky	
1889	J Cocteau					Nehru
		Heidegger			Hubble	
		Wittg'tein				Hitler
1890				Martinu		de Gaulle
			Man Ray			Eisenhower
						HoChiMinh
1891	Pasternak		David Low	Bliss		
	A Christie		Max Ernst	Prokofiev		
1892	P S Buck					Franco
	O Sitwell					
	C-Burnett					
	JRR Tolkien					
1893	D Sayers		Grosz	Milhaud		M'T'tung
	W Owen		J Miro	C Porter		
			Gropius			
1894	A Huxley			B Smith	Kinsey	MacMillan
	Thurber					Krushchev
	JB Priestley					
1895	Hammerstein			Hindermith		
	R Graves			Hart		
1896	Firbank					
	R Sherwood					
	Sassoon					
	Fitzgerald					
1897	Faulkner					A Eden
						A Bevan
1898	Brecht			Gershwin		Chou En-lai
	Hemingway			Magritte		
			H Moore			
			Eisenstein			
1899	N Coward			Poulenc	Muller	
	Lorca			Kurt Weill		
	Nabokov			Copeland		
			H Bogart			

Date	Literature	Philosophy	Visual	Music	Science	Politics
1899				Ellington		
			Hitchcock			
1900	Betjamin			Armstrong		
1901		M Mead	Disney		Heisenberg	*Edward VII*
				Rubbra	Fermi	
1902	Steinbeck			Walton		
	O Nash				Lindberg	
				Barber		
1903	E Waugh		J Piper		Oppe'eimer	
			Sutherland			
			Hepworth			
1904	Isherwood		Klimt	B Crosby		Kosygin
	G Greene		S Dali			
			Beaton	G Miller		
1904			Brant			
1905	CP Snow			Tippett		Hamm'jold
	Sartre					
1906	S Beckett			Shost'vich		Brezhnev
	Odets					
1907	WH Auden		B Spence			
	A Moravia		L Olivier			
	C Fry					
1908				Messiaen		L Johnson
			C-Bresson		Bronovski	
1909	S Beauvoir		B Goodman			
	I Fleming					
1909	S Spender					
1910	J Anouilh		Bacon	M Waters		*George V*
	Genet	AJ Ayer			F Hoyle	
1911						R Reagan
1912	Ionesco				WvonBraun	
	P White					Callaghan
1913	A Wilson			Britten	B Lovell	W Brandt
	A Camus					R Nixon
						G Ford
1914	T Williams			B Holiday		
	D Thomas					
1915	A Miller				Townes	H Wilson

Date	Literature	Philosophy	Visual	Music	Science	Politics
1916				E Piaf		E Heath
						Mitterand
1917				F Sinatra		JF Kennedy
				D Gillespie		
				T Monk		
1918	Solz'tzin			Bernstein		Nasser
				Fitzgerald		N Mandela
1919		B Graham			Hounsfield	
1920			J Pollock			
				C Parker		
1921						A Dubcek
1922	K Amis				C Barnard	
	Kerouac			C Mingus		
1923	Behan					
1924	J Baldwin					G Bush
						J Carter
1925				P Boulez		M Thatcher
				BB King	BFSkinner	J Delors
				Theodarakus		
1926				W Henze		Idi Amin
			M Munroe			
				C Berry		
				M Davis		
1927						F Castro
1928	N Mailer			Stockh'en	JWatson	
						Buthelezi
1929	J Osborne			Bacharach		M L King
						Bob Hawke
1930	H Pinter			O Coleman		H Kohl
				Sondheim		
1931			B Riley			Gorbachev
						B Yeltsin
1933	J Orton					
1934	W Soyinka		B Bardot		Gagarin	
1936				E Presley		de Klerke
						Edward VIII
						George VI

Date	Literature	Philosophy	Visual	Music	Science	Politics
1938		R Baxter!	D Bailey			
1937	T Stoppard	Terechcova				Hussein
1939	Ayckbourn					J Smith
1940			A Warhol			
				P Spector		
				J Lennon		
				S Robinson		
1941				B Dylan		Gaddafi
1942				McCartney	S Hawking	
				J Hendrix		N Kinnock
				L Reed		
				P Simon		
1943	M Leigh			M Jagger		J Major
						L Walesa
1944				D Ross		M Robinson
1945				E Clapton		
				B Marley		
				V Morrison		
1945				Niel Young		
1947				David Bowie		
1952						*Elizabeth II*
1953						T Blair
1958				M Jackson		
				Madonna		

Some books to read
The following books are useful works of reference if you wish to seek out more information.

Introduction to Contemporary History	Barraclough	Penguin
Penguin History of the USA	Brogan	Penguin
The Civilisation of Rennaisance in Italy	Burckhardt	Penguin
The Penguin History of Greece	Burn	Penguin
Encyclopaedia of ancient civilisations	Cotterell	Penguin
Norse Myths	Crossley Holland	Penguin
The rebirth of History	Glenny	Penguin
Cartoon History of the Universe	Gonick	Penguin
Myths of Ancient Greece & Rome	Penguin	Penguin
The Penguin History of the world	Roberts	Penguin
World Since 1945	Vadney	Penguin
Dictionary of English and European History	Williams	Penguin
Who's Who in the Ancient World		Penguin
Dictionary of Historical Slang		Penguin
Encyclopaedia of dates and events		Hodder & Staughton
Timetables of History (latest edition)		**Thames Hudson**

The latter is an excellent publication, giving a much more detailed overview than the one here. It includes historical and political events, literature and theatre, religion, philosophy and learning, visual arts, music, science, technology and growth, and daily life.

SECTION 25: SETTING OUT

Introduction

This section deals with how you should present your work. These guidelines do not represent any general regulations throughout Higher Education, but, in the absence of any other guidelines, use these since they do represent "good practice". The guidelines refer to most written work, especially essays and special studies/dissertations and the like. **You must obviously use your common sense when applying the guidelines to a specific piece of work.**

1. Presentation in general

1.1 Typing or writing

IF AND ONLY IF YOU CAN EASILY get the work typed then do so. THIS IS NOT ESSENTIAL. However, please be very clear that at HE level you will be required usually to get Special Study/dissertation work typed/word-processed, and sometimes you must have it bound too. There are many advantages in obtaining a word processor for your written work.

If you do use handwriting then make your handwriting as clear and neat as possible. When hand writing always try to be legible. This usually means:

- using the same style throughout,
- suiting the size of the letters to the width of the lines,
- keeping the same slope throughout especially with the single line letters like l h k t and the ones with tails like q y p g (i.e. straight up, or sloping to the left or right),
- keeping all round letters like o a q p d b clearly round and closed,
- keeping any loops you use closed.

If your handwriting is bad then try using a fountain pen - or changing from the type of pen you have got used to.

In general use black or blue ink. You can use other colours for decoration.

1.2 Paper type

The work should be presented in A4 format, written on one side of the paper only.

- Do not write on both sides of the paper. (There are times when this is permissible (e.g. when there is a diagram or map which is necessary for the proper understanding of the text, and is best placed opposite the text) - but in general try to avoid it.)
- If you are handwriting the work then use wide lined paper.
- If typing then use plain paper.
- In general use white paper, though other colours can be used as separators, or for effect.

2. Margins and paragraphs etc

2.1 Margins

- Leave 1" margins on BOTH left and right.
- Draw a line for both margins.

2.2 Paragraphs

- Block paragraphs (do not indent).
- Leave an empty line between paragraphs.

2.3 Spaces

- Leave 1 space after a comma, a full stop, colon, semi-colon, exclamation mark and question mark.

2.4 White space

There are advantages in "white space", that is each page not having a great deal of writing on it. This is achieved by:

- leaving a line between paragraphs,
- indenting quotations,
- leaving space between headers/footers and the body of the page.

2.5 Headers and footers

It is useful, but not essential, to have a "header/footer" system (as on the pages of this book).

Headers

Usually the header, at the top of the page, is the same throughout the piece of work, giving the overall title and your name on the right hand side.

Footers

Usually the footer, at the foot of the page, carries the information which varies. The page number, on the right, for ease of reading, and the title of the Part or Chapter, or which appendix it is.

3. Title pages etc

It should clearly indicate:

- the title of work, what it is (e.g. essay, a special study), who is submitting it (your name), how you can be contacted (address), for what course it is submitted, who has asked for it (Tutor), how many words were used, for what institution, what date it was submitted.

See sample title page p 5.

3.1 Contents page

A contents page is essential <u>only</u> in a large piece of work (over 4000 words), but if you think the reader would find contents useful then you can use it for shorter pieces. (See following pages.)

SAMPLE TITLE PAGE

A critical examination of the statement:

"Human development is the same in all cultures

and all societies"

An Essay

Submitted by
A.Smith
27, Sacriston Close
Sacriston
Co Durham
DH3 5TH

As part of the
College Certificate
for Access to Higher Education

Tutor: Norah Cohen

Total words used: 2,932 + Appendices

New College Durham
Spring Term 1993

SAMPLE CONTENTS PAGE FOR AN ESSAY

Contents

Introduction.
Part 1: Who I am.
　　The facts
　　A geographic perspective
　　An historic perspective
　　My skills and achievements
Part 2: How I got here.
　　The family in which I grew up
　　My education
　　The important events in my life
　　The influence of society on me
Part 3: Where I am now.
　　My beliefs, opinions and prejudices!
　　My relationships
Part 4: Where I am going.
　　My ambitions
　　My plan of action
Conclusion.

Bibliography.

Appendix 1: My family tree
Appendix 2: Extracts from diaries
Appendix 3: Photographs
Appendix 4: Documents

(Note that with an essay up to 3000 words there is probably no need to give page numbers.)

SAMPLE TITLE PAGE FOR A SPECIAL STUDY.

Youth Unemployment in Sacriston

"An examination of the extent of unemployment of 16-25 year olds in the village and the effect of that unemployment on the young people themselves and on the local community as a whole, with a brief examination of possible solutions."

A Special Study
Submitted by
A.Smith
27, Sacriston Close
Sacriston
Co Durham
DH3 5TH

As part of the
Access to Higher Education Course
1992-1993

Tutor: Norah Cohen
Total words used: 6,932 + Appendices

New College Durham
Summer Term 1993

SAMPLE CONTENTS PAGE FOR A SPECIAL STUDY.

Contents

             Contents - Page i

SAMPLE LIST OF ILLUSTRATIVE MATERIAL FOR SPECIAL STUDY

3.2 Titles for chapters etc

Any titles for parts, chapters, sections and paragraphs etc (if used) should begin at left hand margin (some people prefer main titles centred). Which ever you choose BE CONSISTENT. They should stand out and there should be a hierarchical way of marking them.

The system I have used for this book is

SECTIONS in capitals, bold and 24 points high.

Sub-sections in lower case, bold and 18 points high.

Sub-sub-sections in lower case and 14 point high[1].

3.3 Preface

A preface is certainly not essential, but sometimes pleasant to have, especially in a long piece of work where many people have helped you. It states your thanks to these people who have helped in the production of the the work. It is sometimes called "Acknowledgments". This not essential in a piece of work of less than 4000 words.

4. Illustrative material

Your essays and other pieces of work do not have to be all writing. The inclusion of photographs, maps, diagrams, tables and so on are often essential to the efficient transmission of what you have to say. NEVER include material to which you do not refer. ALWAYS make clear the relevance of any material you include. DO NOT assume that the reader will know what the relevance is. You should always put a separate list of the illustrative material in the Contents.

4.1 Photographs

Include photographs, if relevant, in the body of the text. Try to mount them well and make clear their relevance both in the text and underneath the photograph as well. At the relevant point in the text state:

See photograph page 44.

DO NOT USE THEM MERELY TO MAKE IT LOOK PRETTY.

4.2 Diagrams and tables[2]

Very often tables, diagrams, graphs, pie-charts and the like will be able to make your point far better than words can do. Include them in the body of the text if they are clear and simple. If there are many of them and you need to extract the important sections then place them in an appendix and extract only the relevant parts in the text. If possible use colour and make the relevance absolutely clear.

It is usual to number diagrams etc as Fig.1 Fig.2 etc. and refer to them as such in the text.

---

[1]. *The original manuscruipt was then reduced from A4 to A5.*

[2]. *See also Section 21 p.13ff on tables and graphs etc.*

4.3 Maps

Simplify them so that only the relevant information is included and make sure they are are clearly relevant and referred to in the text. Include maps in the body of the text, or if there are many of them, put them in an appendix and make clear their position when you refer to them.

4.4 Video and audio tapes

It is usual to have a transcript of both audio and video tapes as well as including the original tapes. Always make clear in the main text what relevance the tape has to the topic.

5. Quotations

5.1 Simple quotations

When you wish to quote (i.e. use the ACTUAL WORDS from a source other than yourself) then you should:
- indent AGAIN on both margins,
- surround the actual words with "" marks,
- state clearly beneath the quote:
    from whom you are quoting,
    from which book,
    (Note that the title is enclosed in "" marks and is usually underlined)
    which year it was published,
    which page it is on,
- then go back to normal margins.

Like this:

>"Quotations are very simple to do in your essays because you have had my help in the instructions to the first essay which you wrote."
>(R.J.Baxter, "Second Essay", New College Publications, 1987, Page 3)

This makes the quotes look neat and clear.

There is a shorter way of identifying the source where the initials of the author, the title, the publisher and the word Page are omitted, thus:

>"These quotations are very simple to do in your essays because you have had my help in the instructions to the first essay which you wrote."
>(Baxter, 1987, 3)

This shortening of the information can be used because the full details are available in the bibliography or list of references. See 9.4 below.

5.2 Incomplete quotations

Where you wish to use an incomplete extract from a quotation you must indicate that it is not complete, thus (see previous example):

> *"...quotations are very simple to do...because you have had my help in the instructions to the first essay..."*
> *(Baxter, 1987, 3)*

The dots are used to indicate that there have been words missed out.

5.3 Some abbreviations

Ibid

If a book or other reference occurs frequently then it is possible to use the following:

> *"This is a method of saving time."*
> *(Ibid. 7)*

Ibid. means "the same", and it is used when you are quoting from the same source as the previous quotation. The only addition it needs is the page number.

op.cit.

If you are quoting from an already quoted book but from one which you have used before the previous quote then you can say

> *"There are other Latin phrases which are useful"*
> *(Dalton, op.cit.126)*

Op.cit. means "already cited". Here you must include the name of the author and the page number.

loc.sit.

Another one is loc.sit. which means a quotation which is from the same passage as an already quoted work:

> *"As in this example from my work at New College."*
> *(Baxter, loc.sit. 4)*

Which means the same passage, but a different page

> *"Or as in this example"*
> *(Baxter, loc.sit.)*

Which means the same passage and the same page.

When you collect your quotations from your reading then always make a note of the page, date of publication etc: it will save a very long time searching later!

6. References

If you find that what the person has said is useful but is far too long winded for you to use the actual words then you may say, as Baxter says, that it is important for quotes and references to be properly set out in essays (R.J.BAXTER, "Second Essay", New College Publications, 1987, Page 3). Notice that there are no quotation marks ("") because you are not using his specific words, merely referring to the gist of what he says.

Never give the impression that <u>you</u> have done the research when in fact it is done by someone else. This is especially true in Higher Education where one of the most heinous of crimes is that of the plagiarist. You can be sure that if the book is relevant then your Tutor will know it and recognise it as not your work, but that of the "expert". Thus NEVER fail to acknowledge your sources.

Further, it is self evident that when the examiner reads a passage which is a summary of a expert's work such as:

> *"After small amounts of learning early in the life of the individual, every instance of learning is a function of the already learned organisation of the subject: that is all early learning is organised by transfer...the learning of abstract complex meaningful materials and the solution of problems by reason are to a great extent the function of transfer..."*

then it will be immediately apparent, because of the skilled and experienced use of words in a very specialised sense, that it is not the work of a student. All that is needed is an acknowledgement that states:

> *"McGeoch's work shows that after small amounts of learning early in the life of the individual, every instance of learning is a function of the already learned organisation of ...etc"*

I repeat: ALWAYS ACKNOWLEDGE YOUR SOURCES.

7. Other ways of dealing with quotations and references

Some Tutors prefer each quotation or reference to be followed only by a number and then the numbers are listed together at the end of the book or section and the details of the sources are given there. In the example below the text is given first and then the list of sources which is placed either at the end of the section or the end of the work.

Baxter[1] points out that all references should be placed as near as possible to the text, whereas Cohen says:

> *"...sources of quotations and references are best placed in one list at the end of each section, or even at the end of the whole work, thus leaving the text clear from the clutter of sources."[2]*

Thus the problem is to some extent unresolved. The view taken by Black[3] is that it really doesn't matter at all!

> *List of sources of quotations and references.*
> (1) *Baxter,R.J.,"Second Essay"*, New College Publications, 1987, p. 7.
> (2) *Cohen,N.,"Clearing the Mess"*, ASJ Publications, 1995, p. 1.
> (3) *Black,M.,"Witchcraft and Grammar"*, Wo Publications, 1995, p 100.
> etc...

You should check with your Tutor(s) as to which method, if any, is prefered.

8. Notes

There are occasions where an author wishes to make a comment or qualify something which is not really part of the main "thrust" of what s/he is saying. It is usual to number the note and place the comment at the bottom of the page. Another method is to use an asterisk (*) or another symbol such as (+) and again make the note at the foot of the page. Sometimes the notes are collected at the end of the chapter or the whole work. I prefer to see the note at the foot of the page rather than having to search for it on another page.[3]

9. Numbering

9.1 Numbering of sections, paragraphs etc

Sometimes it is useful to number the different parts of an essay or a study. For example the sample contents quoted above could be numbered as follows:

> 1. The extent of the problem in Sacriston   *Page 3*
>   1.1. The National Picture
>   1.1.1 Unemployment in Britain 1900-1988
>   1.1.2 Recent demographic changes in Britain
>   1.2. Sacriston's Youth Unemployment
>   1.2.1 Unemployment 1950-1970
>   1.2.2 Unemployment 1971-present day
> 2. The effect on specific individuals   *Page 8*
>   2.1. Johnny
>   2.1.1 Financial
>   2.1.2 Social
>   2.1.3 Self esteem
>   2.2. Mandy
>   2.2.1 Financial

---

[3]. *As in this particular case.*

This is not essential in essays, but is VERY useful in longer pieces of work.

9.2 Numbering pages

Number all pages from title page (page 1) to finish but do not include the appendices (If there are any). They should be numbered consecutively within the Appendix. i.e. a twenty page Appendix I would be numbered from 1 to 20. A 2 page Appendix II would be numbered from 1 to 2. I must admit I have had problems with this book. I decided to number each section separately, because the problem of re-numbering each page when I added, or took away a page from the whole was very time-consuming. It is permissible to use Roman numerals for the title page, the contents page(s) and the preface and then start the normal numbering from the start of the text proper, usually with the Introduction.

Place page numbers on bottom right of the page if the piece of work is single sided. If the piece is double sided then it is useful to put the page number on the right for odd numbers, and on the left for even numbers. Put your name on the top right of every page - just in case a page comes adrift.

10. Bibliographies

10.1 What they are

A bibliography is the list of books, pamphlets etc which you have used to write your essay. It includes all the books you have used, even if you decided that that book wasn't quotable or referable, if it contributed to your general understanding of the topic then it should be in the bibliography. It is normally in alphabetic order by author. It is placed at the end of the essay and does not count in the word count. Other sources such as Radio or TV programmes from which you have quoted or to which you have referred should be included. There may be unpublished material. Any reference you have made to evidence in whatever format, apart from your own primary research needs to be listed in the bibliography.

10.2 How to set them out

The order in which the information is presented should be consistent. The usual way (sometimes called the Harvard system) is to give:

Books

1. Author(s), *(surname first followed by initials, e.g. BAXTER, R.J.)*
2. Year of publication, *(usually in brackets),*
3. Title *(usually in quotation marks and/or underlined, and/or in italics),*
4. Edition *(if other than the first),*
5. Publisher,
and if required
6. Chapter and page numbers *(e.g. Ch.6.,pp.6-78)*

Examples:

WALKER, C.W., (1987), "A Walker on the Pennine Way.", Pendyke Publications.

WALKER, C.W., *(Author's name, initials following surname)* 1987,*(Year of publication),* "A Walker on the Pennine Way." *(Title of book - sometimes in italics),* Pendyke Publications *(Publisher).*

BERGER, L. Ed, (1968), "Rising above it all", 2nd Edt, Pelican.

BERGER, L. Ed, *(Ed indicates this is the editor of the book)*1968, *Year of publication),* "Rising above it all" *(Title of book.(Sometimes in italics),* 2nd Edt *(2nd Edition - this can be important in that the first edition or the 3rd don't have specific material you are required to read).* Pelican *(Publisher).*

FLETCHER, G. et al, (1995), "Schools on Trial", O.U.P. *("et al" means "and others"- there were too many other authors to mention).*

Periodicals, journals, articles

1. Author(s), *(surname first followed by initials, e.g. BAXTER, R.J.)*
2. Year of publication, *(usually in brackets),*
3. Title *(usually in quotation marks and/or underlined, and/or in italics).*
4. (IN) title of periodical etc *(usually underlined),*
5. Volume number,
6. Part or issue number *(usually in brackets),*
7. Date of publication, (usually in brackets),
8. Page numbers *(e.g. Ch.6.,pp.6-78).*

Example:

GRENNAN, P., (1995), "The Male Animal" in "Nature", 6 (3), February 1995, pp 23-46.

Parts of books etc

Sometimes you quote or refer to an author who is in a book edited by someone else. In this case the title would read thus:

COHEN, N., (1995), "Overhead Projectors in Counselling" in BERGER, L. Ed., "Rising above it all", 2nd Edt, Pelican, pp 134-199.

Government publications

1. Country of origin,
2. Originating body/committee/department, *(usually underlined)*,
3. Title *(usually in quotation marks and/or underlined, and/or in italics)*,
4. Edition,
5. Publisher,
6. Date,
7. Series title, *(if any)*,
8. Identifying code mark *(if any)*.

and if required

9. Chapter and page numbers *(e.g. Ch.6.,pp.6-78)*.

Examples:

Great Britain, Report of the Review Group on the Youth Service in England, (1982), "Experience and Participation", London, HMSO.

Great Britain, *(Country of publication)*, Report of the Review Group on the Youth Service in England *(Originating body)*, (1982) *(Year of publication)*, *"Experience and Participation"* *(Title)*, London *(Place of publication)*, HMSO *(Publisher)*.

Theses

1. Author(s), *(surname first followed by initials, e.g. BAXTER, R.J.)*
2. Date of publication, *(usually in brackets)*,
3. Title *(usually in quotation marks and/or underlined, and/or in italics)*,
4. Qualification for which work submitted *(e.g. PhD)*,
5. Name of institution awarding qualification.

Example:

ROEBUCK, A., 1979, "Goodbye Socialism", Thesis for Ph.D., University of London.

There are variations on the above:

FLETCHER, G. et al, 1985, "Schools on Trial", Milton Keynes, O.U.P.

("et al" means "and others" - there were too many other authors to mention.)

Radio/TV programmes and Video/audio tapes
1. Author(s), *(surname first followed by initials, e.g. BAXTER, R.J.)*
2. Date of broadcast, or recording *(usually in brackets)*,
3. Title of extract *(quotation marks and/or underlined, and/or in italics)*,
4. Title of programme *(e.g."Panorama")'*
5. Name of source *(e.g. BBC2)*.

Example:

NEWELL, P., (28 October 1988), "Practice What You Preach", "Panorama Special", BBC1

BENN, A., (07.07.89), "Any Questions", BBC Radio 4.

10.3 An example

On the next page is an example of a bibliography set out according to to the system described above.

If you do vary from this system then, as usual with setting out clearly, be consistent and use the same format throughout. It can be very confusing if you alter the order of the way the author, title date, publisher etc are set out.

Always check with your Tutor(s) as to what system is recommended. It can become very tedious and time consuming if you have to set out the whole bibliography again.

10.4 Other methods of setting out references etc

I MUST point out that this is not the only method of setting out references, quotations and books used. For example, some Tutors prefer to see the list of references and quotations placed separately to the list of books which have been used in the study. See 7 above.

Do check with your Tutor what system is prefered.

SAMPLE BIBLIOGRAPHY

Bibliography

Books

BAXTER, R.J., (1987), "Second Essay", New College Publications.

BERG, L. Ed, (1968), "Risinghill: Death of a Comprehensive School", Middlesex, Pelican.

(Ed means that BERG is the editor of this book)

BULL, J., Autumn (1984), "Students into Governors: When and How?", in "Forum for the discussion of New Trends in Education", 27, 19-21

FLETCHER, G. et al, (1985), "Schools on Trial", Keynes, O.U.P.

FOX, R.D., (1986), "Cleveland's Unemployed - A Summary Report", Cleveland County Council Research and Intelligence Unit. (Appendix 1)

Great Britain, Report of the Review Group on the Youth Service in England, (1982), "Experience and Participation", London, HMSO.

Great Britain, Department of Education and Science, (1978), "Special Educational Needs", (The Warnock Report), HMSO.

HALFORD, J.H., in METCALF, D., (1985), "Schools in Trouble", London, Tryst Publishing

Articles

SAWOIN, D.B., (1977), "What do you do after you say hallo? - Observing, coding and analysing parent-infant interactions.", in "Behaviour and research methods and instrumentation", Vol 9, 5, pp 425-428, New York, Seminar Press.

WALKER, C.W., (1987), "A Walker on the Pennine Way.", Pendyke.

TV Programmes

BENN, A., (07.07.89), "Any Questions", BBC Radio 4.NEWELL, P., 28 October (1988), "Practice What You Preach", Panorama Special, BBC1 TV

Radio Programmes

11. Glossary of terms used

This is particularly useful if there is a lot of "jargon" in the study. It can be a separate section called Glossary of Terms, or one of the Appendices. There is no need to use one if the language is simple.

12. Appendices

Appendices are NOT included in the word count.

Very often the Appendices account for a high proportion of the "bulk" of a piece of work. Appendices should be used to store material which contains the detailed substantiation of the study.

For example, in a special study you may have done a questionnaire, sent out 40 letters and received 15 replies, done 3 taped interviews, and read 20 magazine articles. There is no point in cluttering up the main body of the study with the actual answers, photocopies of the articles etc etc. What you do in the main body is to summarise and or quote directly from these. The main body has the essence of these things. Thus, for example, you could include as:

Appendix One: The actual questionnaire: copies of replies + detailed results breakdown of the results.

Appendix Two: Copies of the letter(s) you sent out, with copies of all the replies you have received and a note of who did not reply.

Appendix Three: If you have done any recorded interviewing then you should include a transcript of the whole interview(s).

Appendix Four: Photocopies of any relevant magazine articles.

Appendices should be "bound" in some way together and presented separately from the study itself.

13. Binding

Always make sure that the final draft is bound together in some way - there are many cheap binders available. If you cannot afford these then at the very least staple the pages together in the top left hand corner. With larger pieces of work it may be that you will have to bind the appendices separately from the main body of the work. Try to make sure that your name and the title of the work is visible on the spine and front of the binding.

14. Some books on setting out

These are advanced books really about publishing, but are worth a browse if you come across them in a library. The Myra style guide is very good for formal dissertations.

"Copy Editing - The Cambridge Handbook"   Judith Butler   CUP
"Hart's Rules for Compositors"   OUP
"Myra Style Book and Style Sheet" Modern Humanities Research Assoc
"Rules of printed English" Herbert Rees   Darton Longman & Todd

SECTION 26:EXAMINATIONS

Introduction

Examinations still take a major role in the education system. They come in different types. They last for different lengths of time. They are marked in different ways. You may well have to face any one, or some, or all of the types of question set out below in your return to learning. DON'T PANIC! Again, be systematic!

1. Well in advance (like at the start of the course!!)

1.1 Assessment procedures

- Confirm the **assessment procedures** of your course.

> YOU MUST BE CLEAR FROM THE START OF YOUR COURSE HOW YOU WILL BE ASSESSED. THERE'S NOT MUCH POINT IN MERRILY WORKING AWAY AT COURSE WORK IF EXAMINATIONS COUNT FOR EVERYTHING & COURSE WORK COUNTS FOR NOTHING!

1.2 Format

- Confirm the **format** of all your examinations.
    Try to get copies of past examination papers.
    Find out what sort of questions you will be asked (see 2 below), and how long you will have in which to answer the questions.

1.3 Conditions

- Confirm the **conditions** under which you will take the exam.
    Find out what the rules are (see sample of rules 7 below), so that you'll know if you are allowed to go out to the toilet, take in any food, or drink or sweets or mascots or tools etc etc.[1]

1.4 Dates

- Confirm the **dates** of all your examinations.
- Put down the actual exam dates & your deadlines for completing the various stages of revision leading up to that date.
- Identify clashes (if of examinations then inform authorities at once).
- Identify revised deadlines.
- Make a revision plan.
- Incorporate everything into your diary/filofax.

---

[1]. *I can remember invigilating an examination where one young man brought in with him what appeared to be a full English breakfast, together with several cans of fizzy drinks!! We had to ask him to take it outside as the appetizing aroma was distracting everyone around him!*

1.5 Practising the exam

It may sound strange but the one thing which students find really difficult is sitting for three hours and writing. The difficulties are:
- sitting for that length of time,
- writing for that length of time.

We just aren't used to it! Some people don't do much writing with pens now, being used to key-boards.

If you haven't sat a three hour exam and that's what you have to do, then you really should give yourself a trial run well before the exam itself. Check just how much you can write in three hours. If you find it is less than 6 A4 sheets then I suggest you need to find ways of improving your speed. Check with your Tutor(s) what a "normal" amount is in the examination. If you cannot reach that amount then try to identify what it is that is making you slow. Is it physical or mental?

2. Different types of examination formats

2.1 Essay type answers

- In most Arts courses and in some Science and Technology courses, this is the usual type of examination. They vary in length but are usually around 3 hours.
- The examiner expects a response in essay style[2], though there **may** not be quite such a demand for accurate quotations.
- You need to check with your Tutors as to the style of essay response which is acceptable.

2.2 Short answer questions

- Here you are expected to give a comparatively brief answer to a question. The length of the answer is sometimes:

     given in numbers of words or sentences, or

     you are just left a given number of lines, or

     the length is implicit in the answer (e.g. Name 3 French generals).

- Try to save time in these by answering the question and no more, for example, if asked for 3 French generals, don't give 4.

2.3 Objective tests

- These are called objective in that the questions provoke answers which are clearly either right or wrong (or some identifiable point in between). They do not have the possible subjective bias of the marker.

2.4 Practical

- In this situation the candidate is asked to perform or make something under specific observed conditions.

---

[2]. *See Section 19:"Writing Essays"*.

2.5 Multiple choice questions

- Here several alternative answers are given to the question and the student ticks what s/he thinks is the correct answer.
- Try to get practice with questions of a similar nature to those you will get in the examination. Practice will help you to speed up your response to them.
- In answering them, go through the questions first marking the answer to those about which you are sure. Leave the more difficult ones until you have done those you do know. Spend more time with the dubious questions.

2.6 Oral

- Though this is usual as part of language assessment, the technique is used in other subjects too.
- They are sometimes called "Vivas". One or more Tutors question the candidate and measure his/her responses.

2.7 Seen questions

All of the above can be either seen or unseen (or a mixture).
- You research questions given to you before the examination.
- The examiners expect a higher standard.

2.8 Unseen questions

- You do not know what the questions will be.
- They are difficult to revise for because there is the element of gambling, spotting the question(!).
- Always attend lectures since many hints seem to be dropped by lecturers as to the questions that will be set this year!
- Never rely on "spotting the question", i.e. gambling with your revision time for a specific question to crop up.
- Try to do an all round revision throughout the year so that it's not left until, the last moment.

3. Revision for examinations

3.1 "Ongoing revision"

I know you know about this! And if you don't then you should read the Section on getting organised for learning, Section 16. It is something which you need to take seriously. If you put off your revision until the last minute then you will not have enough time to stay in control of yourself and the situation. More importantly the quality of learning which takes place with revision done only near to the examination is not that which takes place using the system described in Section 16. **Your revision needs to start from your first week in the course.**
You need to establish a ritual again, a regular pattern. Remember that 15 minutes each day is better than 2 hours one day a week.

Make the session active - force yourself to write out re-caps/summaries of what you are supposed to have learned in your 15 minutes. Check that it has been learned. Clarify for yourself anything that hasn't gone in.

Many of my students in the past have founded "self-help groups", students who have similar revision areas and who have divided amongst themselves the work of summarising some of the material to be learned to save others time.

3.2 Specific revision

A weekly timetable

Plan a weekly timetable which includes all subjects, the difficult and the disliked, as well as those with which you feel comfortable! If you are studying several subjects then keep a pattern going so that one does not dominate to the detriment of others. Make sure this is built into your existing timetable[3] and isn't something separate.

- Allow time for:
>   breaks,
>   eating,
>   sleeping,
>   recreation,
>   relaxation,
>   family,
>   academic work.

Be aware that you have to compromise. There is nothing worse than missing a whole day's revision and panicking because you are a slave to your timetable! Build in chunks of time which can be used as fall-back times, just in case the hangover really is too bad all day!

Optimise your best time

You may already know if you are a morning, afternoon or evening person, but I'm sure you will find out when your peak concentration is. Use this. BUT...Avoid late night revision immediately before the exam: you can get into a bad sleep pattern, and destroy yourself for the day of the exam.[4]

3.3 Revision techniques

Make it relevant

Many people think that just by sitting and reading a book they are revising. It is important that you don't waste your time by fooling yourself that you are revising material just because it is vaguely connected with your subject. You must be positive and ensure that what you do is actually relevant to the exam that you are going to sit. Check the syllabus and the previous exam papers, talk with other students and particularly your Tutor(s) and get clear what you need to be able to do

---

[3]. *See Section 16 p.20ff.*
[4]. *See Section 16 p.9.*

---

in the exam that will ensure that you pass. Then revise and practice those elements which are essential to that.

Make it active by making it structured and meaningful to you as you learn
Re-arrange and summarise material. Make notes of your revision material, using any sort of notes that you find useful. The types of notes can range from linear notes, patterned notes and diagram notes.

Useful for rote-learning, that is learning lists and formula etc by heart, are key words, memory triggers such as images, stories, mnemonics.

Make essay plans for typical questions, perhaps from old papers.

Some people like to work with others, friends and or family, or with a self-help group to exchange information and to give each other support, perhaps testing and encouraging each other.

Be imaginative about your revision. I've known people hang up checklists in the loo, have cards above the cooker, put material to memorize on cassettes and jog with Walkmans!

Using a tape recorder
Some people like to record lots of bits and pieces they wish to learn onto cassettes and listen to them while they do the ironing, or drive the car, or have a bath etc.

Reward achievements!
Try not to make your rewards too frequent and too easily earned or you will end up with that hangover again! Be sensible about it. It does work.

Check Section 16 for more detail on getting organised for learning.

4. How to prepare mentally for examinations

4.1 Identifying your fears

It is worth while trying to find out exactly what it is about exams that frightens you. Try writing down a list of what frightens you about them. Some you may well find to be things you can actually do something about - such as "I'm frightened I might arrive late." I'm sure you can find ways to minimise that risk.

Others are more difficult: "I'm frightened because EVERYTHING, my whole life and future, depends on the outcome of the exam, and everyone will laugh at me if I do badly."

In this case the only thing you can do to overcome your fear is to make sure that you study systematically and wisely for the period preceding the examination, so that, with advice from your Tutor, you have revised the subject matter which is relevant and necessary for the examination. Also that you have practised writing some examination answers under examination conditions before the actual examination itself so that you are familiar with the conditions under which you will answer the questions in the examination itself.

4.2 Relaxing

There is no doubt that the worst aspect of examinations is "nerves", the feeling of butterflies, inability to sleep the night before, that feeling of something dreadful about to happen every time you wake! It can get to the point where it is intolerable. There are very few people who do not suffer from these feelings. So what is the solution?

I'm afraid there isn't one! I can suggest some things which may alleviate the problem, but I don't think there is a "cure-all" that is effective and not harmful!

Relaxing and following a relaxation programme which suits you is probably the best way to tackle this.

There are several relaxing tapes, which can be purchased, which work on the basis of getting you to relax the muscles in your body and to focus on calming music and/or voice.

Relaxing before starting work

See Section 16 p.28ff.

Tension and performance

It is possible to reduce the stress and tension produced by examination nerves, but don't panic if they still intrude. As I said above, most people experience them. You would not be normal if you didn't have some butterflies. I can remember hearing several actors saying how that even after many years of experience of going on stage they were still physically sick before a performance. When I was lecturing I would experience similar feelings even after 30 years! In fact, unless I did feel nervous, I would worry! I think we need an element of tension and adrenaline going so that we are operating on a slightly higher level than normal. So regard this as normal.

Panic attacks in examinations

The best advice I can give is:
- Stop writing.
- Close your eyes.
- Take 6 slow, deep breaths.

Remember the brain needs its oxygen to operate properly.

Focusing

When doing revision for exams you must have noticed that it is possible to read whole paragraphs of books and realise that you haven't taken in a thing!

The ability to focus or concentrate on the task in hand is not easy[5]. You can improve your ability to do it by making your task more active, so that, for example, you make a habit of making a note of the main points of a section of a book.

Have a look at Section 17 on reading where I suggest using a record card for your reading of books.

---

[5]. *See p.10 Section 16.*

---

5. Examination techniques

All these can be thought about and prepared weeks before the examination itself. Have a plan of campaign and stick to it.

5.1 Before the exam

- The night before get ready **everything** you need for the following day, so you aren't rushing around trying to find pens and rubbers at the last moment.
- Arrive in plenty of time, at least 15 minutes before the official start. This will allow you to allow for the unexpected! You will be able "settle down" and check, for example, that your desk and/or chair don't wobble and are the right size for you. If they aren't then bring this immediately to the attention of the person in charge of the examination (usually called "the invigilator").
- You can then use your focussing and relaxation techniques.

5.2 Timing the examination

NB. The following points are based on exams asking for essay type answers, although much of what is said is applicable to other types of examination questions. Before you enter the examination room you should have already worked out how much time you will spend:

- reading the question paper (the rubric),
- selecting the questions to do (assuming there is a choice),
- deciding in what order to do the answers,
- planning the answers,
- writing each section/question,
- reading and correcting at the end.

DO NOT RUSH INTO THE FIRST QUESTION YOU CAN ANSWER AND SPEND ALL THE TIME YOU HAVE DOING THAT ONE QUESTION. Answering 2 questions where you are supposed to answer three reduces optimum marks by a third - the most you can get is 66%. So NEVER come out of an exam without having attempted all the answers you are asked to answer.

If you have three hours and three questions to answer there really isn't much point spending two hours on one question and leaving only an hour for the other two. Be savage and divide up the time relatively evenly.

Reading the rubric

The "rubric" is the set of instructions given in the examination paper. You really would be surprised how often people don't read the instructions given at the start of an examination. "Answer 1 question from each section" actually does mean that! One way to be sure is to have a good look at previous examination papers and get familiar with what you are likely to be asked in terms of the rubric.

Selecting the question(s)

If you have to answer all questions then there's no problem with this. But if you have any choice then it really is worthwhile planning to spend at least a few minutes reflecting on the questions after you have read them. Looking carefully at the wording and selecting calmly the one(s) which you do know something about. Be careful of doing a Thatcher: answering a question you wish you'd been asked but weren't! Some people like to eliminate those they cannot answer, some like to be more positive and identify the ones they can and then select from those.

Deciding in what order to do the answers

Again you have a choice: some people like to do the one(s) they are really good at first and leave the less easy one(s) til the end. Others prefer to do the difficult one(s) first and leave the easier one(s) until last. Be aware of the choice and make it before you get into the examination room!

Planning the answers

Plan your answer before writing it! It helps clarify your thinking and gives a clear structure to your answer. A quick plan BASED ON THE WORDING OF THE QUESTION[5] can save you from just regurgitating all you know about the topic without making it relevant to the question as it is worded.

Writing each section/question

If you have followed previous advice and found out how much you can write legibly and neatly in a given time under exam conditions, then you will know how much you will be able to write on the particular question in the time you have available. Thus you will be aware of how much detail you can give. This is not the easiest of exam techniques. The more you practice this, the easier it becomes.

Reading and correcting at the end

You would be surprised at what missing out the word "not" can do to the meaning of a whole essay! Time spent checking for:
  - factual errors,
  - "typographical" errors,
  - omissions in what you have written,
is time well spent. If many marks are given to spelling and grammar then check these too, as well as errors of fact, or omission. There's not much you can do about style at the last minute of an exam!

What to do if you are running out of time

Be strict about your timetable. If you haven't finished your first answer in the time you've allocated, then move on to the second one and come back to complete the first in any spare time at the end of the examination. If you do find you haven't time to complete the question in essay format, use note form - write something like:

"Running out of time: answer continues in note form..."

NEVER LEAVE BEFORE THE END

[5]. See pages 3-4 of Section 19:"Writing Essays".

6. Learn from each examination

I used to ask students to fill in this questionnaire as a learning experience for them after the completion of their examination. You may well find it a useful aid to reflecting on the experience and being then better able to cope with it next time.

6.1 Examination questionnaire
How did you feel?
Before
During
After
What problems did you have?

In what order did you do the questions and why?

What plan/strategy did you have before you started the exam?

Did you stick to it?

Did anything distract you? If so then what was it?

Were you dressed OK.? Hot/Cold.

Were you stiff (uncomfortable) what?

Did you get writing cramp? What did you do about it?

How was your writing to look at?

Did you need food or drink?

Did you need the loo? Nervous to ask?

Did you need rubber /handkerchief/pen/pencils/tippex?

Did you make full use of time?

How did you cope with time pressure?

What did you learn about yourself and exams?

6.2 Reactions to examinations

Below are some comments from former students from the questionnaire above. You will find it useful to read through then to re-assure yourself that others have been through exams with similar feelings to yourself **and have come out the other side!**

How did you feel: Before: *"Apprehensive but curious to find out after 30 years how it would be."*

"A little nervous - if I'd not known the content I'd have been worse."

"Alive."

"Very Anxious."

"Nervous."

"OK til I met the rest of the group."

"Exhilarated."

"Looking forward to getting it over and done with."

"Very nervous."

"OK."

How did you feel: During: *" Fear of forgetting the facts - had fit of shakes lasting 15 minutes."*

"A little more relaxed - worried about time."

"Frustrated."

"Still anxious."

"Very nervous."

"OK."

"Frightened and so serious I found it hard to think."

"Exhilarated."

"Very anxious at the way time was flying."

"Worried constantly about time that I may not finish."

How did you feel: After: *"Elation and annoyance."*

"Very relaxed."

"Relieved."

"Exhilarated."

"Very down-everyone else saying how they felt happy when I didn't really feel happy."

"OK."

Problems: *"Memory recall."*

"None."

"Nervous."

"Very cold - dissatisfied with my answers."

"Writers cramp and mental block."

"Time."

"Too much to say-too little time to say it."

"nerves caused me to take a while to get started also well revised things went out of my head because 9 was nervous and shaking."
Plan:"Not arrive early so as to avoid others' nerves."
"No."
"Deep breaths."
"Deep breathing a couple of minutes before/during exam."
"Very calm because 9 had practised my answers and timed myself."
"9f 9'd started on essay one 9 would have spent too much time on it."
Distractions:"The noise of sweets and straws."
"People going off to the loo."
"People walking out."
"no."
"Mark's bottom." (!)
"Lady in front not well."
Dress:"Cold."
"Cold at first."
"stiff:tension and the cold."
"stiff with cold."
"Very cold."
"Feet were cold."
"9 was freezing."
"Bit cold."
"No."

ISLE COLLEGE
LIBRARY

Writing cramp:"Yes - worse cos of tension -wrist and middle finger."
"Aching pains in thumbs and palms."
"No."
"A little."
"Yes."
"Hand cramp-total seizure of right hand."
"Desk too low chair uncomfortable."
"Hands were freezing."
Writing quality: Spidery - awful as if someone else had done it."
"Scruffy."
"OK."
"OK not perfect."
"Very poor."
"Dreadful."
"OK but not on Section 2 lines too narrow."
"9 was not happy with it - it appeared untidy."
Food/drink: "No - didn't use things taken in."
"No."

"Not enough time."

"Mints/Mints mouth got dry."

"Drink to stop coughing."

"Can of coke."

Rubbers etc: "I forgot rubber and wished I hadn't."

"Tippex. I over used the Tippex."

"I needed a coloured pen."

"I didn't have a handkerchief, and was very uncomfortable sniffing."

Full use of time: "Yes. I really forced myself to stay."

"Yes but could have done better."

"Time pressure: badly - panic at speed of hands on clock."

"Was enough time."

"Not too bad."

"Badly."

"Very badly."

"Yes but could have done better."

"Scribbled frantically."

"I had practised the time limits, as Ray had said, and it really did pay dividends!"

"Finished with 2 mins to go."

Learned: "I thought I was well prepared but didn't realise how much nerves would affect me. I need more preparation mental and otherwise."

"A great deal: that every minute must be used to full advantage and that nothing is impossible."

"HMMMM!"

"To try and stay calm."

"I needed more time."

"Timing."

"Not as bad as I'd thought - but wish I could do it again-panic made me start off badly."

"Too slow. Wish I'd done course essays long hand rather than Word Processed."

"Enjoyable if you know your stuff - but realised I must learn to write more quickly."

"That I panic more than I'd anticipated. Nerves prevented me from getting a good start, yet I had planned what I was going to do and I revised thoroughly - I was still nervous."

"I was less intimidated as I knew what was on the paper. Pressure in exams comes from not knowing what the question will be - have I revised all the wrong information?"

7. Examination regulations

I print below some of the instructions given to invigilators for exams. **Not all examination regulations are the same as these and you should always try and get a copy of the regulations that apply to your examination.**

7.1 Conduct of Examinations

Before the start of the examination the invigilator must read to the candidates the examination rules concerned with specific examination(s) taking place in the room. The papers should then be given out face downwards and the candidates instructed not to read them until directed to do so. When all papers have been distributed, the Chief Invigilator should indicate that the examination may now begin and all examinations will commence at the same time.

Candidates are allowed to enter the examination room up to half an hour after the start time of the examination. Any candidate turning up after the half hour period should be sent to see the Examinations Officer.

Candidates must stay in the examination room at least one hour from the start of the examination. Candidates should be allowed to leave the room after this period if they have finished the examination and not allowed to return. No candidate should be allowed to leave the examination room during the last 15 minutes.

In the case of illness or a candidate wishing to visit the toilet the candidate must be accompanied by an invigilator.

Except where answers are to be written on part of the examination paper itself, candidates are not allowed to work on any paper other than that supplied by the invigilator, or to write, or make marks of any kind, on the timetables, calculators, mathematical tables or drawing materials allowed at the examination.

Candidates are not to be issued with scrap paper.

No persons other than the invigilators shall be permitted to enter the room during the period of examination, with the exception of the Examination Officer or his/her nominee, or an officer of the Examining Board. No spare question papers must be removed from the room during the time of the examination. These may be obtained from the Examinations Officer after s/he has received the finished scripts.

Invigilators are reminded that they are expected to give their entire attention to the work of the invigilator and engaging in any occupation other than invigilating during the examination is incompatible with the proper discharge of their duties. They should patrol the examination room at regular intervals taking the opportunity to ensure that candidates have entered the required details on their answer books/answer sheets correctly and are filling in objective type answer sheets in pencil and in the correct way. Invigilators are not to be involved in unnecessary conversations and are to patrol in such a way that candidates are disturbed as little as possible. Invigilators should not bring to the examination room any papers and/or books other than those which relate to the examination.

While strict supervision of candidates must be maintained at all times during the course of examinations care should be taken that, in the exercise of such supervision, candidates are not hindered in their examination work. No food or beverages are to be brought into the examination room. Smoking by either candidate or invigilators is strictly forbidden.

The invigilator must not give any information to the candidates as to the meaning of examination questions, nor should any misprint or defect in the papers be interpreted except when special instructions have been issued by the Examinations Officer. If a candidate disputes the accuracy of any question the Examination Officer should be consulted immediately.

Should candidates wish to ask a question or require additional stationery they should attract the attention of an invigilator by raising a hand and the invigilator should then go to the candidate. However, no explanation of the meaning of an examination question can be given.

A candidate who leaves the room during any period of examination shall not normally be readmitted during the examination. In exceptional circumstances, however, (illness, etc.), where permission has been given to leave the room, the candidate may be readmitted to the examination provided s/he has been in the care of another invigilator, or person authorised by the invigilator, during the entire period of absence.

Where a candidate is found violating the rules laid down for the conduct of the examinations, such as having any unauthorised books or notes in his/her possession, obtaining aid from or giving aid to another candidate etc. the invigilator should warn the candidate that the alleged violation is being reported to the Examinations Officer and that his/her examination work may be disqualified. If the candidate has been detected with any book or note(s) in his/her possession, the book or note(s) should be impounded immediately. The candidate should be allowed to continue the examination. A report including seating plan should be forwarded to the examinations officer for transmission to the Examining Board.

A candidate must be expelled from the examination room if his/her behaviour is such as to jeopardise the successful conduct of the examination. In such a case, the candidate's work should be taken up immediately by the invigilator, who should pass it to the Examinations Officer with a full special report, following the procedure detailed in the preceding paragraph.

The invigilator should prepare a written report giving details of any breach of the rules or unusual occurrence during the examination for the Examination Officer.

A candidate who has finished his/her work before the time appointed for the conclusion of the examination may be permitted to leave the room after attracting the attention of the invigilator by raising his/her hand and having his/her script collected, but s/he may not return after leaving.

SECTION 27
PUNCTUATION AND GRAMMAR
1. Some notes on punctuation

The following is an attempt to bring together information on the basics of punctuation. Punctuation marks must be used to help to avoid confusion and ambiguity and should be consistently used. I suggest that the simpler the better.

1.1 The full stop

Used at the end of all sentences which are not questions or exclamations. The next word should normally begin with a capital letter.

BUT...what is a sentence?

Sentences are very difficult to define, especially if you have little knowledge of what is a phrase, a clause, and a noun and a verb.

The simplest way of explaining it is that given in the Oxford English Dictionary:

> "...such a portion of utterance as extends from one full stop to another."

But what can you put between them? Sir Ernest Gowers in "The Complete Plain Words" suggests there are only two things to remember:

> "They should be short and they should have unity of thought."

A sentence is a complete unit of sense which can stand on its own. It may consist of only one word, as in "Hallo."

There is the other method of saying that punctuation marks pauses. Broadly a comma marks a count of one, a semi-colon of two, a colon of three and a full stop of four. My own view is that this is a dangerous and confusing way of approaching the problem. You will end up with far more colons and semi-colons than you need.

Used after abbreviations

If a full stop making an abbreviation comes at the end of a sentence, it also serves as the closing full stop:

> "The students liked lectures, exams, taking notes etc."

but:

> "The students liked learning activities (lectures, exams, taking notes etc.)."

I have noticed that there is a move away from using full stops after abbreviations. Superfluous punctuation marks, such as the commas at the end of address lines, seem to be disappearing too. This may well be a trend set by business, where speed is important. I would advise you to be consistent in your use.

When a sentence concludes with a quotation which itself ends with a full stop, question mark, or exclamation mark, no further full stop is needed.

> "He shouted, 'We have ways of making you love lectures!' But the students still slept."

But if the quotation is a short statement, and the introducing sentence has much greater weight, the full stop is put outside the quotation marks:

"There was a notice on the wall that said, 'Do not disturb'."

Full stops omitted sometimes in titles

If you look through this book, you will find that there are occasions where the full stop is not used in titles of section headings and so on. This is to avoid clutter.

1.2 The comma

The least emphatic separating mark of punctuation, used:

Between adjectives which each qualify a noun in the same way

"He is a studious, hard-working person."

But when one adjective qualifies another, no comma is used:

"She is a dark blue Tory." Otherwise she would be dark and blue!

To separate items in a list of more than two items

"Men, women and children are all welcome."

"Men, women or children can come to the dance."

"Here is a list of men, women and children on the boat."

"Red, white and blue are the colours of a flag."

To mark the beginning and end of a parenthetical word or phrase

"I am sure, however, that it will not happen."

"Fred, who is bald, complained of the cold."

After a participial or verbless clause, a salutation, or a vocative

"Having had (←participial clause) breakfast, I went for a walk."

"The lecture over (←verbless clause), the students filed out."

"The lecture being over (←participial clause), the students filed out."

"Mrs Smith (←salutation), how good to see you!"

"Oh Great God (←vocative), hear me!"

To separate a phrase or subordinate clause from the main clause so as to avoid misunderstanding

"In the valley below, the village looks very small."

"In the valley below the village it looks very small."

"He didn't go to church, because he was playing golf."

"In 1982, 1918 seemed a long time ago."

"The whole purpose of the lecture, which had been prepared before the advent of modern technology, was to bring to the students, who had been born after the coming of the computer, a fact of which the lecturer was consciously aware, a sense of history."

Following words introducing a quotation

"They answered, 'Here we are.'"

In letters

Following:

Dear Sir,
Dear John, etc.,
and after:
Yours sincerely, etc.
* No comma is needed between month and year in dates:
"In December 1999."
or between number and road in addresses:
"12 Acacia Avenue"
Modern usage seems to have got rid of the commas at the end of address lines:
Ray Baxter
11 Sycamore Road
Redcar
North Yorkshire
DL11 7TJ
Though it would not be wrong to include them:
Ray Baxter,
11 Sycamore Road,
Redcar,
North Yorkshire,
DL11 7TJ

1.3 The colon

To introduce a list of items (a dash should not be added)
"These students should see Ray: J. Smith, J. Brown, P. Thompson."
To introduce a quotation or an example
To introduce a quotation or an example:
"As I have done in this case!"
To link two clauses which are grammatically complete, the second of which marks a step forward, from introduction to main theme, from cause to effect, or from premise to conclusion.
"To write an essay with poor punctuation is terrible: to do that is dreadful."
It would be OK to use a full stop instead and I personally prefer it. I think you do not need to use colons where a full stop will do:
"To write an essay with poor punctuation is terrible. To do that is dreadful."
It can be used after such expressions as:
"for example:" "namely:" "the following:" "to resume:" "to sum up:"
My own preference is for a comma in these cases.

1.4 The semicolon

My advice is to beware of semi-colons! I don't think I've used one in the book! I probably should have done so! But I have got away without using one (except, of course in this particular part of this particular section!)

It is used to separate those parts of a sentence between which there is a more distinct break than would call for a comma, but which are too closely connected to be made into separate sentences. Typically these will be clauses of similar importance and grammatical construction:

> To err is human; to forgive, divine.

But I feel that here you could well use a comma and still impart the same message.

1.5 The apostrophe

Possessive case

The apostrophe is used to denote possession:

Ray's book.	James's book.	The dog's lead.

means:

The book of Ray.	The book of James.	The lead of the dog.

The problem comes in knowing where to place the apostrophe and if one should add a letter s.

The simplest rule I have found is as follows:

1. Convert the expression back into an "of/of the" sentence.

2. If the word following the "of/of the" ends in any letter other than a letter s, then use apostrophe s ('s) to denote possession.

> For example:
>
> | | |
> |---|---|
> | The problems of the man. | The man's problems. |
> | The problems of the men. | The men's problems. |

3. If the word following the "of/of the" ends in the letter s AND if the syllable expressing possession IS pronounced, then use apostrophe s ('s).

> For example:
>
> | | |
> |---|---|
> | The books of James. | James's books. |

4. If the word following the "of/of the" ends in the letter s AND if the syllable expressing possession is NOT pronounced, then use just the apostrophe.

> For example:
>
> | | |
> |---|---|
> | The books of his sons. | His sons' books. |

5. The question of whether the word following the "of" is singular or plural is irrelevant.

6. Do NOT alter the word following the "of/of the" by inserting any apostrophe within it.

Some awkward apostrophe uses

Expressions such as:

a fortnight's holiday	two weeks' holiday
a pound's worth	two pounds' worth
your money's worth	

contain possessives and should have apostrophes correctly placed.

In:

"I am going to the butcher's, grocer's."
there is a possessive implied because of the omission of the word "shop" or "place".
The same is used in:
"I am going to Brown's, Green's, etc",
the implication being the shop of Brown, the house of Green,
so that properly an apostrophe is called for.
Where a business calls itself "Browns", "Greens", etc, without an apostrophe, as in
"Binns"or "Barclays Bank", no apostrophe is necessary.
It should be used in expressions such as:
In a year's time.
which implies "in the time of a year."
The apostrophe must not be used
With the plural non-possessive -s:
e.g. AFTERNOON TEA'S is wrong.
With the possessive of pronouns: hers, its, ours, theirs, yours,; the possessive of
who is whose.
* it's = it is; who's = who is.
* There are no such words as her's, our's, their's, your's.
The apostrophe is used to mark an omission
e'er, we'll, he's, '69.
Sometimes written, but unnecessary, in a number of curtailed words:
bus, cello, flu, phone, plane (not 'bus, etc.)

1.6 The quotation marks

Double quotation marks are as follows:
" "
or:
" "

They are used to mark off words that are quotations from another source, e.g. what
someone's actual words were, the title of a book, an extract from an article.
Single quotation marks are:

Double quotation marks can used for a first quotation, single for a quotation within
this, double again for a further quotation inside that - or the other way round.
Whichever you choose, be consistent.
The closing quotation mark should come before all punctuation marks unless these
form part of the quotation itself:
"Did Nelson really say, 'Kiss me, Hardy.'?"
but:
"Then she asked, 'What is your name?'"
The comma at the end of a quotation, when words such as *he said* follow, is

regarded as equivalent to the final full stop of the speaker's words, and is kept inside the quotation:

"That is nonsense," he said.

The commas on either side of *he said*, etc., when these words interrupt the quotation, should be outside the quotation marks:

"That", he said, "is nonsense."

But the first comma goes inside the quotation marks if it is part of the actual words spoken even if there were no interruption:

"That, my dear fellow," he said, "is nonsense."

Quotation marks are used when citing titles of articles in magazines, chapters of books, poems not published separately, and songs.

* Not used with indirect speech (that is when the actual words are not used):

He said that he was coming tomorrow.

1.7 The question mark
Follows every question which expects a separate answer. The next word should begin with a capital letter

*Not used after indirect questions:

He asked me why I was there.

May be placed after a word, etc., whose accuracy is doubted

"T. Tallis 1505(?)-85.

or:

"T. Tallis 1505?-85.

1.8 The exclamation mark
Used after an exclamatory word, phrase, or sentence

It usually counts as the concluding full stop. It may also be used within square brackets, after a quotation, to express the editor's amusement, dissent, or surprise:

"Ray Baxter's work was said to be excellent [!]."

To express amusement, or exaggeration or sarcasm, 2 or more exclamation marks can be used, but this is not usual in formal work.

"Ray Baxter's book is first class!!!"

This could be from an advertising blurb, or in a sarcastic comment!

1.9 Parentheses
Enclose:

Interpolations and remarks made by the writer of the text himself

"Mr. X (as I shall call him) now spoke."

An authority, definition, explanation, reference, or translation

John came in and said, "Je ne sais pas." (I do not know.)

Though here I would personally prefer the square brackets if the translation is not actually spoken by John, but added by the writer:

John came in and said, "Je ne sais pas." [I do not know.]

Reference letters or figures (which do not then need a full stop)

(1), (a).

1.10 Square brackets

Enclose comments, corrections, explanations, interpolations, notes, or translations, which were not in the original text, but have been added by subsequent authors, editors, or others

My right honourable friend [John Smith] is mistaken.

Used within round brackets

Alma Mahler married Gustav (the composer [1841-1912]) when she was...

1.11 Punctuating brackets

Another difficulty with brackets of all kinds is where to put the full stop. The rule I have used is that if the brackets can be contained within the sentence which preceded it then the full stop of that sentence follows the final bracket:

Joan was still in bed (a fact which did not surprise anyone).

and not:

Joan was still in bed. (A fact which did not surprise anyone.)

and definitely not:

Joan was still in bed (a fact which did not surprise anyone.)

1.12 Capital or small letters

Compass points

Use capitals:

When abbreviated:

N N E for north-north-east.

When denoting a region:

unemployment in the North.

When part of a geographical name with recognized status:

Northern Ireland, East Africa, Western Australia.

In the game of Bridge.

Otherwise use small initials:

facing the south, the wind was south, south-bound, a south-easter.

Political parties, denominations, and organisations

The general rule is: using a capital letter makes the word or words specific to that particular party, denomination or organisation. A Christian Scientist is a person who belongs to a particular sect, whereas a Christian scientist is a Christian who happens to be a scientist.

Capitals are used with names of political parties such as Conservative, Socialist, Liberal, but not when the words are used as wider adjectives as in:

"He was a very conservative person, keeping himself to himself."

"Many of his friends held more liberal views about hanging and disagreed with him strongly when he became public executioner."

Similarly words like Roman Catholic, Orthodox, Congregational take capital letters when referring specifically to the particular sects, but do not have them when they are used as normal adjectives with broader meaning:

He had catholic taste in music and liked Mahler and Madonna.

His orthodox views about congregational singing were not accepted by his radical friends who preferred singing alone.

Words derived from proper names

The general rule is when the connection with the proper name is indirect, in that the person is not actually referred to, but is something completely different then use a small initial letter:

boycott, jersey, mackintosh, quisling, herculean, platonic, quixotic

When the connection is more direct, use a capital:

Christians, Platonic (philosophy), Remberandtesque, Roman, Anglicise, Christianise, Russify.

Nationalities

All words of nationality take a capital letter. Adjectives of nationality usually retain the capital even when used in transferred senses:

Dutch courage, go Dutch, Russian salad, Turkish delight.

Exceptions are (sometimes!) arabic (numerical), roman (numeral).

Brand names

All brand names take a capital letter:

Canon, Kleenex.

The name of a product or process

Registered trade marks should be given a capital,

Dolbey, Tandy.

2. Some help with spelling

2.1 Adjectives and adverbs adding -ly

-ly is added to words (mainly nouns and adjectives) to form adjectives and adverbs:

earth, earthly   part, partly   sad, sadly

With certain words one of the following spelling changes may be required

- If the word ends in double ll, add only -y:

full, fully   shrill, shrilly

- If the word ends in consonant +le, change the *e* to a *y*:

able, ably   single, singly   terrible, terribly.

* Exception: supple, suppley (to distinguish it from "supply").

- If the word ends in consonant + y, change y to i and add -ly:

day, daily   happy, happily.

* Exceptions: shy, shyly sly, slyly spry, spryly wry, wryly.

- If the word ends in unstressed -ey, change ey to i and add -ly:

matey, matily.

- If the word has more than one syllable and ends in -ic, add -ally, even if there is no corresponding adjective in -ical:

basic, basically   scientific, scientifically.

* Exception: public, publicly

- Final e is exceptionally changed to i before -ly in daily, gaily (greyly, coyly are regular).

2.2 Often confused words

Two, too and to

two = 2, too = a great deal, to = all other uses.

There, their

"there" points (opposite of "here" - a "t" in front of here).

"their" is possessive (like the "heir" to the throne - the throne belongs to him?).

Where, were

"where" points (like "here"- a "w" in front of "here").

"were" is a verb - past tense of "are".

effect, affect

effect is a noun. You cannot say "The affect of anything", because affect is a verb.

dependent, dependant

Either can be used for the noun meaning someone depending on another. -ent is used for the adjective.

The ONLY time "its" has an apostrophe is when it's short for it is.

oral, aural

"oral" means or the mouth.

"aural" means of the ear.

2.3 Words that are often spelt incorrectly

"a lot" is often wrongly spelt "alot".
"develop" is often wrongly spelt "develope".
"infinite" is often wrongly spelt "infinate".
"definite" is often wrongly spelt "definate".
"acquire" is often wrongly spelt "aquire".

3. The split infinitive

The split infinitive is the name given to the separation of "to" from the infinitive by means of an adverb (or sometimes an adverbial phrase). The most famous example is that from "Star Treck":

"To boldly go..."

Here the word boldly comes between the word "to" and the infinitive "go".
It should be either:

"Boldly to go..."

or:

"To go boldly..."

Recently the rule is often broken. You will hear it often in News Bulletins. I would say that the rule has now become a recommendation rather than a rule. In formal written work I would avoid it at all costs! In ordinary conversation it probably doesn't really matter. If it leads to clumsiness then you can allow the split.

"It fails completely to carry conviction."

Either means:

"It totally fails..",

in which case "completely" should precede "fails",

"It completely fails to carry conviction."

or it means:

"It fails to carry complete conviction."

in which case that should be written.

4. Nouns

Words used to denote a person, place, or thing.

4.1 Proper noun

A name used to designate an individual person, animal, town, ship, etc.

4.2 Noun phrase

A phrase functioning within the sentence as a noun:

The one over there is mine.

4.3 Collective noun

A singular noun denoting many individuals.

army, people, crowd, collection

4.4 Pronoun

A word used instead of a noun to indicate (without naming) a person or thing already known or indefinite,

I, you, he, she, it, they, us, we, anyone, something, etc.

4.5 Case of nouns

The case of a noun or pro-noun in a sentence can be described as subjective, objective, or possessive depending on its relationship to other words in the sentence.

With the pronouns to do with oneself you would use:

"I" for the subject of the sentence:

"*I* came up the road."

"me" for the object of the sentence

"He hit *me* with a fist."

"my" for the possessive

"That's *my* book."

With the pronouns to do with "him" you would use:

"He" for the subject of the sentence:

"*He* came up the road."

"him" for the object of the sentence

"She gave *him* an apple."

"his" for the possessive

"That's *his* book."

With the pronouns to do with "it" you would use:

"it" for the subject of the sentence:

"*It* came up the road."

"it" for the object of the sentence

"He hit *it* with a fist."

"its" for the possessive

"That's *its* book."

With the pronouns to do with "they" you would use:

"they" for the subject of the sentence:

"*They* came up the road."

"them" for the object of the sentence

"She gave *them* an apple."

"their" for the possessive

"That's *their* book."

4.6 Apposition

A noun or phrase supplying further information about another which is placed next to it: "William, the Conqueror", "Ray, a lecturer."

5. Verbs

Verbs are doing words. They are the words that tell us what is happening technically the part of speech that predicates. Verbs have tenses and moods!

5.1 Transitive verb

A verb that takes a direct object,

> I *said* nothing.
> I *like* oranges.

5.2 Intransitive verb

A verb that does not take a direct object.

> She *fell*.

Some verbs are both. Some verbs are just transitive. Some verbs are intransitive.

5.3 Auxiliary verb

A verb used in forming tenses, moods, and voices of other verbs:

> Simon *had* come from the shop in Durham.
> Norah *will* sell the old car.
> Joe *might* travel by bus.

5.4 Moods of verbs

The indicative mood

This is our normal everyday use of verbs and indicates what is, or seems to be, the case.

The subjunctive mood

This mood indicates what is imagined, wished, or possible:

> I might walk with the dog.
> I might have walked with the dog.
> I insist that it be finished.
> I may come in.

5.5 Uses of verbs

Active use

Where the subject is also the source of the action of the verb,

> We saw him.

Passive use

Here the subject receives the action of the verb.

> He was seen by us.

The active is usually preferred, but there are times when it is easier to use the passive:

> Jan was struck from behind.

is easier than:

> Someone struck Jan from behind.

5.6 Parts of verbs

The infinitive

This is the basic form of a verb that does not indicate a particular tense or number or person:

the to- infinitive, used with a preceding "to":

I want *to know*.

the bare infinitive, without preceding "to":

Help me *pack*.

The perfect infinitive

He seems *to have finished* now.

The gerund

The part of the verb which can be used like a noun, ending in -ing,

What is the use of my *scolding* him?

The participle

The part of a verb used like an adjective and also used to form compound verb forms: the present participle ends in -ing, the past participle of regular verbs in -ed.

While *doing* her work she had *kept* the baby *amused*.

The imperative

The mood of a verb expressing command,

Come here!

5.7 The tenses

Tenses tell us about "when" the action of the verb happens.

Present

Expresses action now going on or habitually performed in past and future:

He *walks* with the dog.

Present continuous

Expresses action which is continuing to happen:

He *is walking* with the dog.

It *is raining*.

Past

Expresses past action or state:

He *walked* with the dog

I *arrived* yesterday.

I *was* pink when it happened.

Perfect

Expresses completed action or action viewed in relation to the present:

He *has walked* with the dog.

I *have finished* now.

Past imperfect

Expresses continued action in the past:

He *was walking* with the dog.

Pluperfect

Expresses action already completed prior to the time of speaking:

He *had walked* with the dog.

James *had arrived.*

Thomas *had started* the meal.

Rebecca *had been* very good that day.

Mary *had had* a terrible day at school.

Future tense

Expresses action yet to happen:

He *will walk* the with the dog.

I *shall see* you tomorrow.

Future in the past

Expresses action about an event that was yet to happen at a time prior to the time of speaking:

He said he *would walk* with the dog.

Past in the future

He *will have walked* with the dog.

6. Other types of word

6.1 Adjective

A word that describes a noun or pronoun:

the *purple* book	(attributive = in front of noun).
the tree was *old*	(predicative = following verb).
the chairman *elect*	(postpositive = after noun).

6.2 Adverb

A word that modifies an adjective, verb, or another adverb, saying something about place, time, circumstance, manner, cause, degree, etc:

here, now, accordingly, gently, because, gradually.

Watch the positions of adverbs. the position affects the meaning considerably.

Consider the alterations in meaning in the following sentences:

Only he came into the room.

He only came into the room.

He came only into the room.

He came into the only room.

He came into the room only.

Comparative/superlative adjectives/adverbs

The form of an adjective or adverb expressing a higher degree of a quality:

Adjective/Adverb	Comparative	Superlative
good	better	best
bravely	more bravely	most bravely
bad	worse	worst
fast	faster	fastest
badly	worse	worst

6.3 Article

a/an is the indefinite article.
the is the definite article.

6.4 Conjunction

A word which links two or more other words, phrases, clauses or sentences, such as:

and, but, yet, because, or, when.

6.5 Preposition

A word governing a noun or pronoun, expressing the relation of the latter to other words. They are words such as:

at, on, under, with, to, by, up, etc.

In general a preposition is a bad thing to end a sentence with! In formal work it is best avoided, though sometimes it can make the sentence sound clumsy as in the example:

Up with which I will not put!

7. Clauses and phrases

Part of a sentence which includes a subject and verb:

"*He*(←subject) *came*(←verb) into the room."

7.1 Main clause

The principal clause of a sentence.

7.2 Subordinate clauses

A clause dependent on the main clause and functioning like a noun, adjective, or adverb within the sentence,

Alan said *that Daphne had gone.*

7.3 Phrases

A group of words without a main verb (predicate), functioning like an adjective, adverb, or noun:

He came *into the room.*

"into the room" is a phrase.

8. Singular and plural

Singular   = a single person or thing.

Plural   = more than one.

8.1 The main verb in a sentence must agree in number with the subject of the sentence

"The effect of such laws, on so many nations, who were spread over many many continents, are enormous."

is wrong because the verb "are" is plural (referring to more than one) and the subject, "The effect", is singular (referring to only one).

Confusion often arises about sentences such as:

"The army are in charge."

and:

"The army is in charge."

The general rule is that if the noun (the army) is regarded as a collective noun then it is singular and the first sentence is wrong. The second is correct. Further you can have more than one army, therefore it is not correct to use army as a plural noun. This would also apply to words such as "the government".

9. Figures of speech

9.1 Alliteration

Where there is a repetition of the same sound at the start of most of the words:

The white wise women of the wild western windy woodland.

9.2 Antithesis

Where ideas which contrast strongly with each other are juxtaposed:

Better to love a little than hate a lot.

9.3 Apostrophe

Where the writer suddenly breaks off and addresses someone, sometimes someone not even present, or an imaginary person, or an abstraction:

Look where she comes...oh, ye Gods, defend me from her charms...there, amongst the trees.

9.4 Assonance

A repetition of similar vowel sounds:

Along the wrong, long, oblong song of the gong.

9.5 Bathos (anti-climax)

Going from the sublime to the ridiculous:

He climbed great Hymalayan mountains and put the dog out every night.

9.6 Climax

Letting the ideas build one on top of the other, each gaining greater power than the previous:

> The bottom of the valley was quiet. On the slopes the noise became apparent. As he neared the top the avalanche of sound drowned out everything else, and at the summit the tumult crushed his senses completely.

9.7 Epigram

A concise and witty saying. Coleridge says:

> "What is an epigram? A dwarfish whole:
> Its body brevity and wit its soul."

9.8 Euphemism

Where a gentle pleasant image is substituted for an unpleasant reality:

> He has passed over, gone to the great pavilion in the sky, is pushing up the daisies etc, when speaking of someone's death.

9.10 Hypallage (transferred epithet)

An adverb or adjective is separated from the word to which it belongs:

> The man gave a smiling farewell.

here the man is smiling, but the adjective smiling is transferred to the farewell.

9.11 Hyperbole

Deliberate exaggeration:

> "All the perfumes of Arabia would not sweeten this little hand."

9.12 Innuendo

The writer implies something by stating something else. For example:

> The women were scantily dressed: Eric approved.

implies that Eric's interest is sexual, without that being said.

9.13 Irony

The writer here says almost the opposite of what is meant:

> I am sure that you know how honest a man he is!

This said of a dishonest character.

Dramatic irony is where the audience knows something which allows them to understand further meaning in remarks made by one of the characters, whilst others on stage, not aware of what the audience know, cannot understand.

9.14 Litotes

Usually expressing a positive characteristic by use of a negative:

> "This is no easy job." means that the job is hard.

9.15 Malapropism

A misuse of words - usually intended to be humorous.

> That's totally irreverent [instead of irrelevant], Vicar."

9.16 Meiosis

Deliberate use of understatement in order to point to the enormity of the described:

This is **some** meal!

9.17 Metaphor

The writer does not only liken something to something else, as in a simile, but says it actually is the other thing:

The window of your eyes lets me see your soul.

Here the image is of the eyes actually being a window through which the observer actually sees a soul. Literally that would not be possible.

Beware of mixed metaphors where inadvertent humour can creep in:

The road snaked through the pass and then arrowed to the town.

This is barely acceptable, since a snake does not quite function as an arrow.

9.18 Metonymy

This is where something is substituted for something else as in the expression:

The prisoner addressed the bench.

which actually means that the prisoner addressed the people sitting at the bench, the magistrate.

9.19 Onomatopœia

Where the words sound like, or echo what they intending to describe:

bang, crash etc

but more subtly:

Dirty British coaster with a salt caked smoke stack
Butting through the Channel in the mad March days.

9.20 Oxymoron

Where words with opposite meanings are juxtaposed:

bitter-sweet, sweet and sour.

9.21 Paradox

Where at first sight the words seem contradictory:

If you drive on the left, you'll be right.

9.22 Pathetic fallacy

Where things in nature are assumed to have human feelings:

The flowers wept their dew.

9.23 Personification

Where inanimate objects are given human characteristics:

The sun lifts himself up in the sky.

9.24 Puns

Where double meanings are purposely used:

Hardy by name and nature.

9.25 Simile
Where something is said or implied to be like something else:
> The road was like a ribbon in the moonlight.

9.26 Zeugma
Where an image is used literally and metaphorically:
> He was tied up with a rope and his own feelings.

# 10. Antonym/synonym/homonym/acronym
Antonym = A word meaning the opposite of another.
Synonym = A word of the same or almost the same meaning as another.
Homonym = A word which sounds the same as another.
Acronym = A word formed from the initial letters of other words:
> QANGO   Quasi autonomous non-governmental organisation

11. Consonants and vowels
A consonant is a letter which isn't a vowel (the vowels are a,e,i,o,u).

12. Direct object, indirect object, subject and main verb
He sent a present to Philip.

"He"	= the subject	of the sentence.
"sent"	= the main verb	of the sentence.
"a present"	= the direct object	of the sentence.
"Philip"	= the indirect object	of the sentence.

13. Some books to read

On Learning to Read	Bettelheim/Zelan	Penguin
Collin's Dictionary of Spelling & Word Division		Collins
Penguin Students' Grammar of English	Bosewitch	Penguin
Penguin English Grammar A-Z for advanced students	Broughton	Penguin
Grammatical Man	Campbell	Penguin
Penguin Basic Grammar of English	O'Driscoll	Penguin
Penguin Basic Grammar Exercises	O'Driscoll	Penguin
Grammar	Palmer	Penguin
Spell it Right	Industrial Society Press	
Pocket Guide to Written English	Industrial Society Press	
Report Writing	Industrial Society Press	
Write On	Lodge	Penguin
Effective Writing	Murphy and Snell	Pitman
Complete Plain Words	Gowers	Penguin
Plain English	Roberts	Penguin

Practical English Usage	Michael Swan	Oxford
Clear English	Summers	Penguin
Usage and Abusage	Partridge	Penguin
Who Cares About English usage?	Crystal	Penguin
Le Mot Juste	Ehrlich	Penguin
Beyond Words		Hart Davis
A Communicative Grammar of English	Leech and Svartvic	Longman
Language and Learning	Britton	Penguin
Introducing Applied Linguistics	Corder	Penguin
New Horizons in Linguistics 1	Lyons	Penguin
New Horizons in Linguistics 2	Lyons	Penguin
Sociolinguistics	Pride/Holmes	Penguin
Linguistics	Crystal	Penguin
State of the Language	Howard	Penguin
English Language	Crystal	Penguin
Our Language	Potter	Penguin
Collin's English Dictionary		Collins
English Learners Dictionary	Hill/Cameron	Penguin
Collins Pocket English Dictionary		Collins
Collins Concise English Dictionary		Collins
Chambers 20th Century (latest edition)	Ed.Senton	Chambers
Chambers Pocket 20th Century Dictionary		Chambers
Wordmaster Dictionary	Manser/Turton	Penguin
Penguin Spelling Dictionary	Market House	Penguin
Collins Paperback Thesaurus		Collins
New Collins Thesaurus (latest edition)	Ed. McLeod	Collins
Roget's Thesaurus		Penguin
Rhyming Dictionary	Fergusson	Penguin
Dictionary of Slang	Partridge	Kegan
Dictionary of Abbreviations	Paxton John	Penguin
Dictionary of Challenging words	Schur	Penguin
Result of Chomsky's Revolution	Smith/Wilson	Penguin
Sociolinguistics	Trudgill	Penguin
Dictionary of Curious and Interesting Words	Wells	Penguin
Dictionary of English Idioms		Penguin
Dictionary of Literary Terms		Penguin
Dictionary of Troublesome Words		Penguin
Modern Guide to Synonyms and Related Words		Penguin
Brewers Dictionary of Phrases and Fable		Cassell

SECTION 28: COMPUTERS

Introduction

Whatever your attitude to computers I have to say that you will need to become familiar with them. Many university courses in the near future may well become what is sometimes called "paperless". That is to say you will have to produce examinations and course-work directly onto computers.

More importantly the computer provides several extremely useful tools for the student for creating and storing all written work, notes and essays. This tool is called a word-processor. A further tool available is a data base which allows you to store and retrieve information extremely efficiently.

In this Section I concentrate on the use of the computer as a tool for you the student, not for you the person who may or may not be interested in all the other things which computers can now do. I have therefore ignored the uses of the computer as an entertainment centre for music and films and games, as a communications medium, linking in to what is called the Internet, and as an educational aid[1].

1. As a tool for the student

1.1 Writing essays

Essentially a word processor allows you to type your work as you would with a typewriter. There are advantages:

- The typing does not go direct to the paper. It goes to the screen and is displayed there. You can correct mistakes before you ask the computer to print out the completed document.

- You can move text around the document on the screen. If you decide that the last paragraph is better placed elsewhere, you can move it to that place. If, having done that you don't like it, then you can move it back!

- You can save your final draft and then re-load it later.

- You can "import" sections of other documents you have written into the document you are working on, which means that if you have already written something relevant you don't have to re-type it out laboriously. With the use of a few keystrokes you can copy it directly into the document you are working on.

- Most word processors will check your spelling for you! Some will even have a go at grammar!

---

[1]. *Although as a student you should be aware of what the Internet can mean to all areas of communication, and of the educational packages available which may help you. See 4. below.*

- They encourage creativity. A few brainstormed sentences on a scrap of paper can often remain like that. On a word processor they can be expanded and moved about quickly and simply.

- The main advantage I find is that unlike with a type script you don't think "Oh God, another mistake, I'll have to re-type the whole of that page!". You can alter the mistake simply and the computer automatically re-sets all the words for you. Curiously this fact makes you more likely to work away at a piece of work until it is as good as you can make it!

- The quality and variety of print available is excellent and far above that offered by conventional typewriters. Most word-processors now have a range of sizeable fonts (type-styles) which means you can use a wide range of styles and effects.

1.2 Storing information in an ordered way

The other main tool I like with a computer is what is called a data base. I keep several on my computer. One of them keeps all the names and addresses of friends, relatives, shops, contacts, restaurants. I use it for addressing envelopes. I use it to find telephone numbers. I can also print out a copy of it and keep it in my filofax.

A data base is an electronic filing cabinet with lots of advantages.

- Each "card" is automatically filed in order (e.g. by surname).

- They can be re-filed at the stroke of a key, to another order (e.g. by first name).

- You can ask the computer to find a particular piece of text (e.g. 11 Sycamore Road, if that's all you can remember of a particular address).

- The example I've used is addresses, but I also have one for all the cassettes, CD's and discs that I have, indexed by title, composer and so on.

- I also use it, when doing research, to hold lists of useful books, quotations, references. Finding appropriate references becomes much simpler.

2. How easy are computers?

Well, I must admit that I do find I cannot use paper and pen now to produce books, lectures, handouts etc. I started my life in education seeing the typewriter and the "Banda", which was a spirit duplicator, as being the most efficient way of producing these things. In the mid 1970's I purchased a Tandy TRS80 with 16k of memory and began using a a word processing package called Scripsit. Since then I have gone on to more complex and sophisticated computers and word processing packages. I now use a computer which is called a "PC" and a word processing package called LOCOScript.

So, it's very easy for me to say that they are easy. I've used them a long time. I do believe that the time spent learning how to use them is time well spent. I have met quite a bit of unfounded prejudice against them.

Apart from using your own computer you will find that libraries and many educational establishments are increasingly using computers for the storage and retrieval of information.

The advent of the CD ROM means that huge amounts of information can be stored AND RETRIEVED very quickly and efficiently. I remember using the "Times "CD ROM, just to find out what it could do I typed in the word Lamont, and the word Threshers and was presented almost instantaneously with a list of 7 articles which mentioned those two words. To have found the articles myself would have meant wading through many 100's of editions of "The Times".

3. Buying a computer

3.1 Some technical points

There are different types of computers on the market and many magazines to help to confuse you. It is difficult to choose which is going to suit you.

The specifications of computers are changing so rapidly that what I write now as being the most up to date will be out of date within a very short time.

At the risk of putting you off reading any further let me say at once that you do need some patience in order to make sure that you have wrapped your mind around this business of computers. Remember that you will need to be able to use one because it is an invaluable tool for you the students. So bear with me whilst I tell you what you need to know in order to equip you with the knowledge to be able to make a wise choice when you come to buy one.

I am going to structure my comments in the following way: I am going to tell you about each of the following factors:

Types   : The different types of computers available.
Style   : desktop, portable, notebook, laptop.
Processor   : what a "chip" does.
Memory (RAM)   : why your computer needs Random Access Memory.
Hard disc   : why your computer needs some capacity to store things.
Disc drive   : why you need to load in information from small discs.
Operating system : what it is and which is best
Monitor   : what different sorts there are
Printer   : why you need it and what different sorts there are.
Word-processor   : which type is best for you.

3.2 Types

There are PC's (personal computers)

which are based on the standards set by a firm called IBM. These are the most widely available, the cheapest and have much support and advice available.

There are PCW's (personal computer word-processors)

which are made exclusively by Amstrad. These are cheap but very slow and inefficient compared to PC's. (Having said that I used one very happily for 10 years and resisted the lure of the PC! I have seen them advertised for as little as £200 to include the printer and all the operating software. If all you want is a word-processor then there isn't much wrong with them except they are very slow compared with the PC's.)

There are Apple-Macs (Apple Mackintosh computers)

which are similar to PC's cost about the same but do not have as much software (programmes) available for them as PC's. The most recent models are compatible with PC programmes, but are in the range of £2000+. Prices will inevitably fall as new models supersede old ones very rapidly in the world of computers.

There are Acorns - (Originally made for the BBC)

The Archimedes Acorn is one type which is growing in popularity in education, particularly in schools. These computers are often available with a special card which allows you to run programmes made for the PC's as well as programmes made for the Archimedes. They are expensive £900+.

I do not know a great deal about computers other than the ones I have used (PCW's and PC's). I have found PC's adequate for my purpose of writing. I am therefore limiting my comments to what are called PC's.

3.3 Style

Desktop

The most popular is the desktop because it is the style that has been around longest! They are quite heavy and not easily moved. They plug into the mains supply and take up quite a bit of space on a desk.

Portable, notebook, laptop

Recently there has been an increase in the number of and popularity of the portable computers. They are called variously portable, notebook and laptop. They are designed primarily for business people on the move and are very light. They have as much memory and disc space as you can afford to buy.

They can be in colour or mono. They are ideal for a student in that you can carry them around with you. Their disadvantage is usually the screen, which is not as bright as the desktop because it is a liquid crystal display rather than a luminous tube display. They run off batteries or mains. They are coming down in price and are around £500-£1500+ new. Not many are available second hand yet.

3.4 Processors (Speed measured in MHz's)

When computers first came to be widely available they were built around a silicone chip called a Z-80. The first for the PC was the 8088, then the 8086 (some of the latter are still available and are very cheap because they are much slower than the later chips).

On the piece of silicone complex circuits were built which could perform complex mathematical operations very quickly. The chips have developed from then into more and more sophisticated pieces of electronics which are capable of doing the calculations faster and faster.

The first one worth looking at from the point of view of you wanting a good word-processing operation on your computer is the 286 processor. There are 386 and 486 and now 586 processors. The higher the number the faster it is. You will be OK with a 386 and a bit irritated by the 286 because it is slower and will not run your word-processing package as swiftly as the 386 or 486 or 586. You pay more for more speed, which is measured in megahertz (MHz).

You get an indication of how fast a computer is by looking at the specifications for: the number of the processor: which started for PC's with 8088:

Chip name	Speed (MHz)
8088	4-10
8086	4-10
286	12-20
386SX	16-25
386DX	16-25
486SX	20-50
486DX	20-50+
586	Intel Pentium 60/75/90/100MHz)

3.5 Memory (Size measured in megabytes or MB's)

About memory

Memory is measured in bytes, kilobytes and megabytes.

1 byte = amount of space in the computers memory to store 1 single letter.

1 kilobyte = amount of space required to store 1024 single letters.

1 megabyte = amount of space required to store 102400 single letters

Random Access Memory or RAM

This is the part of the computer which is used to run the programmes. Most machines come with at least 1 megabyte (1MB) of RAM. This can be expanded i.e. you can get 1 MB at first and if you feel you need extra memory then you can add it on at a later stage when you have some spare cash(*!!)[2].

Recently that the standard amount has moved up to 4MB[3]. The size increase is due to an increase in the demand for memory from the programmes which are created

---

[2]. _You can pay up to £40 per megabyte of RAM!_

[3]. _I am told that the newest version of Windows will need even more and that 16MB may become standard._

---

for the computers. A computer operates faster if it is operating electronically rather than mechanically. Huge amounts of data can be stored and retrieved from discs, but in order to get it from the disc there has to be a mechanical reading of the data whilst the disc spins and the information is read. Once in the computer's RAM no further mechanical reading is required, so programmes operate considerably faster if they are operating within the RAM.

If you are running just a word-processing package and a database then 1 MB will probably do.

But if you are going to use the computer for the kids to play games on (or even play them yourself as a reward for being a good student!!) then you will need to start looking to get more memory.

3.6 Hard disc (Size measured in MB's)

Computers can store data on the hard disc. This is stored magnetically rather like a cassette tape stores music. The information is recorded onto and read from the disc mechanically. PC's are supplied with hard discs varying from 20-500+ megabytes of storage capacity.

The larger the disc the more expensive the computer. Always buy more than you think you'll need!!

3.7 Disc drive (Size measured in bytes and MB's)

There are several types:

5½" disc drive	can store up to 1.2 megabytes.
3½" disc drive	can store up to 1.4 megabytes.
CD disc drive	can store up to 600 megabytes!

These are used for temporary storage of data so that you can move information between machines. The most common and strongest are the 3½" discs. Recently there is the CD disc which can store much more information, but at present it stores only information recorded on it in the factory and the user can only retrieve information. However, this will change soon when recordable discs appear. These could be capable of recording up to 600 megabytes.

3.8 Operating system

DOS

Every PC has an operating system. Disc Operating System, referred to as "DOS", is by far the most common and is usually supplied with your PC when you purchase it. There are variations of DOS, the most popular and frequently used is MS-DOS, which is the original version developed by Microsoft.

If you are buying second hand then I advise you to check that the version of DOS supplied is 3.0 or above. My own preference is for DOS 5 or 6.

The disc operating system is, in my opinion, very poorly documented and is not very friendly. You really will have to seek advice about how to optimise your system using the operating system.

DON'T BE PUT OFF. If all you want is a good word-processor then you will hardly know that DOS exists. You will be able to switch on, input the name of your word-processor and it will come up on the screen.

Windows

Windows is the name of a system of controlling the computer which has proved very popular. It is not actually an operating system since it needs DOS to run, but it makes DOS more manageable. It allows you to manipulate files, run several programmes at once and is in general very friendly and easier to use than DOS. However, it does take up a lot of memory and I don't really see the need for it. I have removed it from my own computer as I think it slows things up and is just a fancy sort of window dressing. However, many programmes are now designed to run only if Windows is present.

With a bit of effort it is certainly possible to use DOS effectively to control your computer. I use a very simple menu system that allows me to type "1" and the computer loads the word processor. If I type "2" it loads the drawing programme and so on[4].

3.9 Display

The display system has two elements: **circuitry** in the computer to produce the signals for the **monitor**. The first choice is monochrome or colour. Quite honestly you can word-process easily with just black and white. But, there aren't many mono monitors available now and colour dominates the market. You could well pick up a very cheap mono system second-hand. I have seen them for £300 including a printer, but they are increasingly fewer available. There are many types of circuitry. The only ones worth considering for your purposes are the following:

VGA - (Video Graphic Array) The most commonly available, colour or mono.

SVGA - (Super VGA) Higher resolution than VGA, not all programmes run on it. Get a monitor which is compatible with the circuitry. Size is usually about 14".

3.10 Printer

Basic types

Dot matrix - 9 dot the cheapest and least effective print.

Dot matrix - 24 dot slightly more expensive and better quality print.

Daisywheel - noisy and not as available or as popular and disappearing.

Bubblejet - high quality printing but more expensive to run than a dot matrix.

Laser - most expensive to buy and to run, but very high quality print.

All of them (except the daisywheel) give better quality and much more variation than a typewriter or electronic typewriter.

---

[4]. *If you are interested in finding out how to produce a menu for your PC using batch files, and/or if you want to know how to do CONFIG.SYS and AUTOEXEC.BAT files then do write to me sending £10 and a sae and I'll send you full information including a disc with samples on.*

Colour printers are now available from under £200, but they are not necessary for our purposes. The simplest 9 pin dot matrix will suffice for starters. 24 pin dot-matrix next. These are cheaper than the others to run because they use an endless inked ribbon which seems to go on and on for ever, admittedly getting fainter, but I have used generous, messy sprayings of WD40 and seen a dead ribbon revived! That you cannot do with Bubblejet cartridges - once they have emptied, they have emptied! You can buy re-fills, but the print quality is definitely less good with the re-fill. If price is important then stick to the dot-matrix.

3.11 Selecting a word-processing package

All the above information is to do with the machinery, often called the hardware. The computer can be used to run a variety of programmes, which are called software. These programmes include games, business control programmes, data bases and word processors. It is the word processor which is of relevance to you. People tend to drift into the one supplied with their PC. Which is sensible because you then don't have to spend extra money on purchasing a different one! I use LOCOScript because it came with the PCW and I then got the LOCOScript software for the PC when I bought the PC. What was supplied with the PC was Microsoft Works, which has a package of tools, a word-processor, a spread sheet, a chart maker, a data base and a communications package. Because I was so used to LOCOScript I've never bothered to use it! The only piece of advice I would give is that the What You See Is What You Get (WYSIWYG) word-processors are more convenient than others which do not show on the screen what you get on the paper[5]

The major brands of word-processor for the PC are: WordPerfect, Wordstar and Word. Word for Windows and WordPerfect for Windows are also available. It is what you get used to that will be your favourite!

3.12 Recommendations

Buying a computer is fraught with confusion. If you know someone who owns one then approach them and ask their advice. It is very dangerous to recommend specific models because they come and go rapidly and are replaced with other models which are not always improvements! Have a look in the computer magazines and see what they are recommending. Better still go to the computer department of your School, College or University and ask what they recommend you buy for you the student.

---

[5]. *WYSIWYG word processors show on the screen as you enter the words etc, exactly what you will get on the paper when it is printed. Others do not, so there is a mismatch between what is viewed on the screen and what comes out on the paper. Some word-processors offer you the option of previewing what it will look like on the paper.*

Having said that, I set out below some guidelines for you which may be of use when it comes to your decision making about what computer to buy. You will have to be prepared to spend at least several hundred pounds.

For the wealthy!

If you have £1500-£2000 to spare then you will be able to buy a comprehensive system comprising a fast processor, a CD-ROM drive, speakers, a colour monitor, a modem (for communications), facilities for recording TV pictures, playing CD music and film discs and have software programmes for word-processing and so-on. I must emphasise that if all you want is a tool for you the student then you do not need to spend that amount. However, there is no doubt that if you can afford it then such a computer would be a useful machine in many other areas of your life. If you are spending this much then look for the following features as a minimum:

Type	: PC
Style	: Desktop or laptop
Processor	: Intel Pentium 100
Memory (RAM)	: at least 16 megabyte
Hard disc	: at least 200 megabytes
Disc drives	: 3.5" floppy disc drive and CD ROM drive
Operating system	: DOS 5.3 or above.
Monitor	: 14" colour SVGA or VGA
Printer	: Bubblejet
Word-processor	: Whatever comes free (preferably with WYSIWYG)!

For the less wealthy
The most basic set-up for a PC that I would recommend is as follows:

Type	: PC
Style	: Desktop or laptop
Processor	: 386
Memory (RAM)	: at least 1 megabyte
Hard disc	: at least 20 megabytes
Disc drive	: 3.5" floppy disc drive
Operating system	: DOS 5.3 or above.
Monitor	: 14" colour SVGA or VGA
Printer	: 9 pin dot-matrix
Word-processor	: Whatever comes free (preferably with WYSIWYG)!

I have seen these offered second hand for under £500, with printer. New they range from about £500 for the computer plus £100 for the printer, but prices drop as new models appear. When the 286 chip was superseded by the 386, 286 dropped in price and the same happened to the 386 when the 486 was recently introduced. There are bargains to be found in the many computer magazines.

For the poor!

If you are finding money difficult then look for the very cheapest second hand Amstrad PCW. The new models have Bubblejet printers and are around £500. The best of the older models is the 8516. The 8256 has very limited memory. Avoid the 9256 and the 9512 since they have a noisy daisywheel printer which limits the type styles of print that you can use.

Try to get one with as much memory as possible. I have seen some second hand Amstrad PCW's for as little as £100 which includes software and a 9pin dot matrix printer. They have the drawbacks of being slow and having no hard disc, but, as I said before, I produced more than acceptable handouts and so on.

However, I have never regretted moving to a PC and if you can get one second hand then I would say it is a better buy in the long run than a PCW.

3.13 After-sales support

There are problems with buying second hand since you will have no guarantee that it will work and no back-up after-sales service. If you are buying a new computer then make sure you find out what support is available. This is usually by phone, so check it out carefully. Ring the number and see how long it takes for a reply! Find out too how long support lasts. Check too the price of the phone-calls. The warranty is also a danger! Make sure that it is at least two years, and preferably 3 years at no extra cost.

Other significant uses of the computer

4.1. Educational uses of the computer

Already on the market are CD's which contain huge amounts of structured and easily accessible information. There are dictionaries, encyclopaedias, 3D atlases and reference books which enable the user to find references to specific topics much more quickly than by using the book versions. Many of them are now supplied with sound and moving pictures so that you can see and hear President Kennedy, or the Victoria Falls! Microsoft's Encarta has 26,000 entries and over 8 hours of sound and 100 video clips.

You can get 100's of pictures, called "clip art", which can be used to illustrate your written work. You can buy a "scanner", which enables you to convert any illustrative material into a picture which your computer can "understand" and therefore enables you to manipulate the picture, make it smaller, bigger, stretch it, shrink it, remove sections, add others, redraw, re-touch, give it different textures and print it.

There are teaching programmes in every subject there is, even swimming! You can take on the role of MacBeth whilst internationally famous actors supply the bit parts!

The good programmes monitor your progress and select the appropriate next step, or practice of mistakes, making the lessons individually structured to improve your specific weaknesses. It has been shown that users of one of the Maths programmes made some 20 months progress in just 6 months!

4.2 The Internet

Although not yet of direct use to you as a student in writing essays and storing information, the development of the Internet is one of the most significant developments in the world of computers and communications. By using a computer and a piece of equipment called a modem, which enables your computer to communicate with other computers via a telephone line, you can link into the Internet, an international global network of computers. Worldwide there are over 20 million users, ranging from individuals to huge government departments, universities, large corporations, non-profit making organisations and millions of private users. You can send and receive electronic mail through it, access information on any subject you care to name, load the information into your computer and even socialise world wide. There is a cost, that of the computer, the modem, the telephone usage, and some extra software and usually a fee to belong to some of the information services available. The development of this network is incredibly fast and already many commercial enterprises are using it to sell all sorts of goods. You can also access films, music and books, all of which can be loaded from the Internet onto your computer.

SECTION 29: PHILOSOPHY

Introduction

It is my belief that every student in Higher Education would benefit from a study of the discipline of philosophy. Not so much the old fashioned attempts by humans to find out "what it's all about", but from the attempts of more modern thinkers, such as Wittgenstein, A.J.Ayer and John Wilson, to look at the basic questions we must ask ourselves about "What do we mean by...?" and "How do we know that such and such a thing is 'true'?".

1. What is philosophy?

"Philosophy is the search for knowledge or certainty."

and:

"Philosophy is a second order subject concerned with analysing the meaning of concepts and language."

Popular uses:

1. Well man, it's like this...I mean, well my philosophy of life is...
2. The philosophy of Christ.
3. The philosophy of the Labour Party.
4. The philosophy of the social worker.

In each of these uses of the word there are three things in common:

1. Each describes the sum total of values, attitudes and beliefs.
2. Each functions as a guide to action, e.g. what one ought to do as a result of being in the Labour Party and holding those values, attitudes and beliefs.
3. Each attempts to get to grips with what are considered as serious and important issues.

Thus if someone says "My philosophy of life is to seek happiness.", then we can learn about their:

values/attitudes/beliefs,

the principles upon which that person would act to secure his/her happiness,

the order of priorities the person may have.

Technical uses

The academic usage of the word philosophy is to do with the study of several areas of human experience. The philosopher, in this sense, examines the nature of these areas and the kinds of evidence required to verify their basic assumptions.

1. Metaphysics

"meta" means beyond. Thus meta-physics is examining what lies beyond the physical world. It is concerned with reality - what is real? What is the nature of reality and existence? It enquires into the most fundamental of scientific assumptions, such as:

Is the material world the only real world?

Is there a reality beyond the world of the senses?

Does God exist?

Must every event have a cause?

Must the sum total of all the matter of the universe be constant?

The main criticism levelled against this branch is that it is very difficult to verify any of its conclusions. What sort of evidence is acceptable to prove such questions?

2. Epistemology

This is the central branch of philosophy. It examines the nature of knowledge. It addresses such questions as:

What is knowledge?

What are the different kinds of knowledge?

How is knowledge different to belief?

How is knowledge acquired?

What is the nature of the sorts of things we can be said to "know"?

3. Logic

This branch is concerned with the nature of arguments:

How do we put argument together?

What are the specific forms of argument?

How can one test the validity/fallaciousness of an argument?

e.g. If all elephants are animals and I am an animal then I am an elephant.

It is important in all branches since all are concerned with reasoned argument.

4. Ethics

This branch is concerned with the study of morality. The nature and justification of action in as far as it is good/bad and/or right/wrong. It is mainly concerned with trying to arrive at the basis of morality - what is it to call an action "good", "right", and one we "ought to do"? The two main questions are:

How do we judge what is good/bad right wrong?

Is there any objective standard by which we judge actions?

5. Aesthetics

A branch essentially concerned with the Arts. It asks these type of questions:

What is the nature of a work of art?

What distinguishes a work of art from other forms of knowledge?

What is meant by saying art is concerned with expression/feelings?

Is a critic justified in saying that art has a high moral purpose?

On what grounds, if any, can one art form be better that another?

6. Philosophy of mind

This branch is mainly concerned with the nature of the human mind. It asks such questions as what is the nature of:

needs, drives, motivation, learning, training, education, personality, character?

7. Political/social philosophy

This branch examines the nature of society and politics and asks such questions as:

What sort of attitude, if any, should the citizen adopt to the state?

What does the state owe to the individual?

What kind of society should we be attempting to create?

2. The tools which philosophy provides

As can be seen from the above, philosophy is a tool which can be used to examine the nature of different aspects of our experience. That is what is meant by it being a second order discipline. It is not necessarily useful in itself, but it is useful to use as a tool to analyse and criticise other disciplines.

Linguistic analysis

The most important aspects of this are:

1. identifying the type of statement being dealt with.

2. asking:

What does the particular statement MEAN? Or what is it intending to communicate?

What sort of evidence would support the statement? Or how can we discover if the statement is true or not?

If you are substantiating your assertions in your essays and special studies by reference to other researchers, and/or if you are using your own research as evidence then you are entering into this aspect of philosophy. I recommend you read A.J.Ayer's brilliant book "The Problem of Knowledge" which deals with this such questions as how we know, and what constitutes sufficient evidence in order to believe that something is true. Implicit in much of what he says is the notion that in order to investigate any topic from any discipline you must seek out sufficient appropriate evidence to support a belief in any assertions to be made. These assertions themselves can be open to re-revision in the light of new evidence, or a change of interpretation of existing evidence. To me this is at the root of being a student, (indeed being a human being), for it is important that we retain the ability to change our minds in the light of new evidence. This aspect of philosophy is of great important for any student of any subject.

Equally useful is John Wilson's book "Language and the Pursuit of Truth".

Different types of statement

- Imperatives and attitude - statements
- Empirical statements

- Analytic statements
- Value statements
- Metaphysical statements

Imperatives and attitude - statements

Imperatives give commands:

Be quiet

Pay attention

Attitude statements express the speakers feelings:

I hate study skills.

I'm afraid of my Tutor.

Neither of these two types are concerned with stating facts about the outside world. They are neither true nor false. They tell us how an individual FEELS about the world, but not about the nature of the world itself.

What does the attitude statement MEAN?

Or what is it intending to communicate?

simply an expression of feeling?

What sort of evidence would support the statement?

Or how can we discover if the statement is true or not?

We could test if X hates study skills by

asking X,

observing X.

Empirical statements

Thess are essentially a descriptive statement. It gives information about the outside world:

It is raining outside.

There are 48 people in the room

I am now speaking.

The distinguishing feature is that they can be verified by tests conducted in terms of our sense experience.

What does the empirical statement MEAN?

Or what is it intending to communicate?

That there is moist precipitation beyond the confines of the house.

What sort of evidence would support the statement?

Or how can we discover if the statement is true or not?

By going outside and using our senses.

Only if a statement is verifiable by experiment is it empirical.

Analytic statements

All straight three sided shapes are triangles.

Quadrupeds have four legs.

2+2=4.

All men are human.

A yard is three feet.

These do not give us information about the world, or about our sense experiences at all. Their verification is not to be found in experience. You have to look into the statements themselves. We do not need to check these statements against anything except themselves.

Their distinguishing feature is that they can be verified only in the terms governing the statement. Consider the following:

All men are human beings.

All men are equal.

Are these both analytic statements?

Men are human beings - but is equality implied by "All men"? The later is a value statement.

Value statements

These are prescriptive statements:

It is with statements in this area that accurate agreement about what the words mean, or how they are being used is vital. What one person means by "good" is not always what another person means by "good"

You deserve a <u>good</u> wife.

Huh, <u>you've</u> turned out to be a <u>good</u> wife.

He'll make someone a <u>good</u> wife.

In each case the word good means something different.

Look at the following examples:

John is a good student.

Does this mean that John gets an average of 90%, or that John doesn't ask questions and gets his work in on time and is neither outstanding nor mediocre!

Democracy is a good system.

Here we need to know what is meant by "democracy" and what is meant by "good". Does the statement mean that a political arrangement whereby each person may vote regularly for a representative in the legislature of a country is one which is desirable. That is only one possible meaning: other possible interpretations exist.

With value statements you must ask:

- What does the value statement MEAN?

- Or what is it that the person who uttered it intends to communicate?

- What criteria are being used to measure words like "good", "bad", "acceptable" and so on?

- What sort of evidence is needed to support the statement?

- How can we discover if the statement is true or not?

These are difficult to verify. We need to consider what are the relevant criteria for judging a value statement true/false.

EVERY VALUE JUDGEMENT NEEDS REASONED ARGUMENT TO SUPPORT IT.

Metaphysical statements
Already touched on. They are statements such as:
   God exists.
   There is life after death.
What does the metaphysical statement MEAN?
Or what is it intending to communicate?
   There is considerable doubt as to whether they mean anything.
What sort of evidence would support the statement?
Or how can we discover if the statement is true or not?
This is the problem with metaphysical statements - how can they be verified? They
are certainly not like any of the other types of statement we have dealt with.

3. Some books to read about philosophy

The Problem of Knowledge	A.J.Ayer	Penguin
Language and the pursuit of truth	J.Wilson	
Real Philosophy	Applebaum/Needleman	Penguin
Theories of Life	Arthur	Penguin
Central questions of Philosophy	A.J.Ayer	Penguin
Language, Truth and Logic	A.J.Ayer	Penguin
Ludwig Wittgenstein	A.J.Ayer	Penguin
Descartes' Dream	Davis	Penguin
Learning to Philosophize	Emmett	Penguin
Dictionary of Religions	Hinnells	Penguin
Logic	Hodges	Penguin
Philosophy As It Is	Honderich/Burnyeat	Penguin
Sleepwalkers	Koestler	Penguin
Divided Self	Laing	Penguin
Wittgenstein	Lenny	Penguin
Ethics - Inventing Right and Wrong	Mackie	Penguin
Existentialism	Macquarrie	Penguin
What Philosophy Is	O'Hear	Penguin
Hundred years of philosophy	Passport	Penguin
Theories of existence	Sprigge	Penguin
Gurdjieff - An approach to his ideas	Waldberg	Penguin
Critical thinking		Midcrest
Fontana dictionary of modern thought		Collins

SECTION 30: USING THE LIBRARY

Introduction

Libraries are vital to your life as a student. As is pointed out in Section 16 on reading, you should join as many as you can and do not rely solely on the University or College library. At a time when resources are limited and student numbers are rising the search for relevant books is not always easy.

Try to get a list of the books you will need for the term, or even the year, from your Tutors as soon as you possibly can. If you can afford to buy them then do so. Many students leaving the course, or leaving the year may be able to sell you their books considerably cheaper than you can buy them. But your major sources of information in book and electronic form are the libraries. You will need to know how to find them and use them!

1. Finding them

There is usually a library for the whole of the University or College. In many Universities there are other libraries too within departments or faculties. They are sometimes called resource centres. The town or city will also have a central library as well as branch libraries. There may also be specialist libraries. Look in the Yellow Pages under libraries and check on all of them.

- Get to know the different sections, e.g. the reference section as well as the lending section.

- Get to know the opening times and holidays.

- Get to know the regulations about borrowing. Public Libraries do give you such rights, but many University libraries restrict book borrowing, and some do not allow books out and are for reference only.

- Enquire about any inter-library loan schemes which may be available so that you can ask one library to acquire from another library a book for you which is not at present available.

2. Working in a library

A library can be an excellent place to work. There are fewer interruptions, people are encouraged to be quiet. You have access to a huge resource of books.

3. Classification systems

Trying to find the relevant books is not easy. You should get familiar with the way in which the library organises its books. You also need to know which books will tell you where you get information on your topic! See Appendix II

3.1 Non-fiction
Most libraries have the following catalogues:
- the author catalogue, which lists alphabetically all the books in the library by the author's surname.

- the classified catalogue, which lists all the books in the library according to subject matter.

- the subject index, which shows which classification mark or number labels a particular topic.
    Until recently these were stored in some sort of filing cabinet on cards. This is changing, and you will find the information stored in some libraries on a microfiche system. In this system the information is photographically reduced and stored on small plastic films which are viewed through a magnifying screen. Other libraries store their catalogues on computers which allow a great flexibility of cross-referencing,

- You need to get to know your way around these systems in order to identify books which may be of use to you.

- Most libraries use the Dewey Decimal Classification system to arrange their books on the shelves. It was invented by an American librarian in 1873 by Melville Dewey. Each book is catalogued and placed on the shelves according to the system set out below. Most libraries display the numbers and the subject names on notices attached to the shelves.

3.2 Magazines, journals, periodicals and newspapers
Don't ignore this extremely valuable source. Libraries usually keep copies of these going back a considerable period of time. They are usually kept separately in specialised indexes. Rules vary on access. If in doubt consult the librarian.

3.3 Fiction
Note that works of fiction are not included in the system and are arranged on the shelves usually in alphabetic order by author.

4. The Dewey classification system

000   GENERALITIES

010	Bibliography
020	Library and Information Sciences
030	General Encyclopaedic works
040	
050	General serials and their indexes
060	General organisations and & museology
070	News media, journalism, publishing
080	General collections
090	Manuscripts and rare books

100   PHILOSOPHY AND PSYCHOLOGY

110	Metaphysics
120	Epistemology, causation, humankind
130	Paranormal phenomena
140	Specific philosophical schools
150	Psychology
160	Logic
170	Ethics
180	Ancient, medieval, Oriental philosophy
190	

200   RELIGION

210	Natural theology
220	Bible
230	Christian theology
240	Christian moral & devotional theology
250	Christian orders and local church
260	Christian social theology
270	Christian church history
280	Christian denominations and sects
290	Other and comparative religions

300		**SOCIAL SCIENCES**
	310	General statistics
	320	Political science
	330	Economics
	340	Law
	350	Public administration
	360	Social services, association
	370	Education
	380	Commerce, communication, transport
	390	Customs, etiquette, folklore
400		**LANGUAGES**
	410	Linguistics
	420	English and Old English
	430	Germanic Languages
	440	Romance languages
	450	Italian, Romanian, Rhaeto-Romanic
	460	Spanish and Portuguese
	470	Italic Languages
	480	Hellenic languages
	490	Other languages
500		**NATURAL SCIENCES/MATHEMATICS**
	510	Mathematics
	520	Astronomy and allied sciences
	530	Physics
	540	Chemistry and allied sciences
	550	Earth sciences
	560	Palaeontology, Paleozoologu
	570	Life sciences
	580	Botanical sciences
	590	Zoological sciences
600		**TECHNOLOGY(APPLIED SCIENCES)**
	610	Medical sciences, medicine
	620	Engineering and allied operations
	630	Agriculture
	640	Home economics and family living
	650	Management and auxiliary services
	660	Chemical engineering
	670	Manufacturing
	680	Manufacture for specific uses
	690	Buildings

700		THE ARTS
	710	Civic & landscape art
	720	Architecture
	730	Plastic arts, sculpture
	740	Drawing and decorative arts
	750	Painting and paintings
	760	Graphic arts, printmaking and prints
	770	Photography and photographs
	780	Music
	790	Recreational and performing arts
800		**LITERATURE**
	810	American literature in English
	820	English and Old English literature
	830	Literatures of Germanic languages
	840	Literatures of Romance languages
	850	Italian, Romanian, Rhaeto-Romanic
	860	Literatures of Spanish and Portuguese
	870	Literatures of Italic and Latin
	880	Hellenic literatures
	890	Literatures of other languages
900		**GEOGRAPHY AND HISTORY**
	910	Geography and travel
	920	Biography, genealogy, insignia
	930	History of the ancient world
	940	General history of Europe
	950	General history of Asia, Far East
	960	General history of Africa
	970	General history of North America
	980	General history of South America
	990	General history of other areas

5. Ways books etc are described

Reading lists are fairly straightforward, but sometimes the way in which the books are set out can be a bit confusing. Most Universities and Colleges follow the Harvard system of setting out the names of references, though there are several other methods of setting out. However, this is the most usual and is acceptable in most institutions. Check with your Tutor(s). The system usually follows the following pattern.

5.1 Books

Author(s), date of publication (usually in brackets), title (usually either in quotation marks, underlined, and or in italics), edition (if other than the first), publisher, and if required chapter and page numbers.
Look at the following examples.

WILLIAMS, D., (1987), "Exchanges in Counselling", Pendyke Publications.

WILLIAMS, D.,	Author's name, initials following surname.
1987,	Year of publication.
"Exchanges in Counselling"	Title of book (sometimes in italics).
Pendyke Publications.	Publisher.

CONSTANCE, C. Ed,1968, "Rising above it all", 2nd Edt, Pelican.

CONSTANCE, C. Ed,	Ed indicates this is the editor of the book.
1968,	Year of publication.
"Rising above it all",	Title.
2nd Edt	2nd Edition - this can be important in that the first edition or the 3rd doesn't have specific material you are are required to read.
Pelican	Publisher.

CONNELL, P. et al, 1995, "Thinking about it", O.U.P.
("et al" means "and others"- there were too many other authors to mention.)

5.2 Parts of books

Sometimes you are asked to read a specific author who is in a book edited by someone else. In this case the title would read thus:

COHEN, N., (1995), "Overhead Projectors in Counselling" in CONSTANCE, C. Ed., "Rising above it all", 2nd Edt, Pelican, pp 134-199.

5.3 Government publications

Country of origin, originating body/committee/department (usually underlined), title, edition, publisher, date, series title (if any), identifying code mark (if any).

Great Britain, Report of the Review Group on the Youth Service in England, 1982, "Experience and Participation", London, HMSO.

Great Britain,	Country of publication
Report of the Review Group	
on the Youth Service in England,	Originating body
1982,	Year of publication
"Experience and Participation",	Title
London,	Place of publication
HMSO.	Publisher

5.4 Periodicals, journals, articles

Author, date of publication, title, (IN) title of periodical etc (usually underlined), volume number, part or issue number (usually in brackets), date of publication, page numbers.

GRENNAN, P., (1995), "The Male Animal - a personal view" in "Nature", 6 (3), February 1995, pp 23-46.

5.5 Theses

Author, date of publication, title, qualification for which work submitted, name of institution awarding qualification.

ROEBUCK, A., 1979, "Goodbye Socialism", Thesis for Ph.D., University of London.

5.6 Finding specific books

Find the titles in the author index to find the titles and note the Dewey numbers. You should then be able to find the shelves where those numbers are stored. If in doubt ask the librarian.

5.7 For essay topic etc

Obviously there are times when you aren't given a list of specific books, but have to select books which are going to illuminate a particular topic.

Use your previous knowledge of the library to find the shelves which contain the books which are relevant to your topic.

Having found the right places in the library for your search how do you choose the book(s) which will be of relevance to your work? Do not choose the first book that

---

comes to hand with a reference to the topic you need. Follow a systematic plan of checking on the relevance of the book. Some are too easy, some too difficult. Do not trust the title of the work as a guide, look at the summaries, introduction, contents and index.

Take advice from your Tutor(s)

Look at the book carefully by checking the contents pages and the index to see if key phrases or words you are looking for are mentioned.
Check the bibliographies of the books that you do find potentially useful and see if they recommend any other books which seem relevant.

If you are checking journals etc then don't forget that there is probably an annual index which may save hours of searching through individual contents/indexes!
BE REALISTIC - don't try to read more books than you have time to read! Make sure the ones you do choose are relevant and up to date[1].

---

[1]. *See also Section 17 on reading in general.*

SECTION 31: LECTURES

Introduction

The main thing about lectures is to go to them (even if you find them tedious and boring)! It is absolutely vital that you go to them! The relevance of what is said may not at first be obvious and students are notorious for talking bad about lecturers! I suppose it's because I'm one of them that I say such things, but I do believe that you are very foolish if you miss any lectures at all. The lecturers often set the examination papers and very often like to see some of what they have said in the answers!

Techniques for dealing with lectures

Becoming actively involved

- BEFORE going to the lecture, preferably the night before, ask yourself what you expect the lecture to be about.
- Write down some aspects you think it might address.
- If it is not the first lecture in the series, look over your notes from the previous lecture and try to predict where the coming lecture will go.

Most lectures have a structure similar to that which we have looked at in the Sections on essay writing and special studies. There is an introduction, a middle set of parts and a conclusion.

Some lecturers give this structure at the start of the lecture which makes it much easier for you to follow what is going to happen. Some give it out at the end. Don't let that stop you taking notes. The more you establish the ritual of taking notes at every lecture you go to, the more likely you are to be able to remember what was said, and certainly you will be able to compile a useful set of notes which make revision much easier than if you rely on your hazy memory for the revision.

Taking notes

Get a note book, or an A4 pad, or paper and a good pen or pencil with a rubber (which I prefer for taking notes at a lecture, since you can rub bits out). Get into the habit of using the same equipment for taking notes. Establish a ritual of writing down:
- the title of the lecture,
- the date,
- the lecturer's name, and,
- any important references to books etc which the lecturer gives.

Then:
- Try to listen out for and **note the main points of the lecture** as it progresses. Put them down and underline them.

- Underneath that try to jot down a summary of what is said about each main point.
- You can ignore examples and illustrations.

It is not wise to attempt to take down the lecture verbatim by some clever sort of shorthand, because:

- you are still left with the problem of sorting out the main points from the detail, and,
- whilst taking the notes you are often missing the next important point.

What I consider to be a "good" lecturer does indicate the broad headings and often gives an outline so you can easily follow the structure.

Recording lectures

I had a student once who taped every lecture he went to. He complained of two things at the end of the course: 1. he had spent a fortune of cassettes, 2. he was still only half way through listening to them all! I suppose it can be useful for the very complex and opaque lecture which goes at speed and is difficult to disentangle, but I am not advocating the use of recorders. They only postpone the problem.

Reviewing the lecture

On an evening it is essential to re-read the notes and re-write them in a neat and clear way. This can be a co-operative venture, checking your notes with those of a friend, or done on your own.

Keeping a formal record of your notes

You should also keep them in such a way so that you can easily identify the key topics within that particular set of notes. **Incorporate them into your filing system, by putting the notes into your filing cabinet (or whatever), AFTER you have noted in your Key Word Index Book (or card system) the key words to indicate what topics are dealt with in that lecture.**[1] As I point out in Section 16, this way of incorporating and linking your learning experiences is essential and very powerful in helping you to structure and cross reference your learning.

The value of lectures

Whatever method you adopt for taking notes remember that lectures are a part of the whole experience of your learning. They are not something tagged on to the course, they are very much the centre of the course. Try to make yourself ask the lecturer questions which genuinely puzzle you. If you are critical of the lecturer then make your comments away from the lecture hall. If you do have to miss a lecture it is polite to send a note to the lecturer excusing yourself and promising to get the notes from it from a friend.

---

[1]. *See Section 16 p 5ff.*

CONCLUSION

Over the past few years whilst I was setting up an Access to Higher Education Course I have learnt not to worry about teaching and how to do it! The most important thing a "teacher" can do is to worry about how the students learn!

I saw it as my job to act as a facilitator, a starter of engines, a giver of information when asked, but essentially someone who says to the student:

> "You have the skills, you need to be asking questions and searching for the answers. I can help you to search in the right places, but essentially you need to learn how to learn!"

I think that too often we see the teacher as the person who gives the knowledge, who gives the answer, who tells us what to do. Not enough emphasis has been given to the capacity of the student to learn. My belief is that this capacity is often blocked by "teaching" because the student has become accustomed to wait for the answer, the direction, the teacher's truth.

What I would encourage you to do is to become more free of the teacher. I do not mean rebel and go to lectures with placards! I mean be aware of your academic aims. You should be asking yourself the question:

> "What should I be able to do as a result of this learning experience?"

every time you go to a lecture, attend a tutorial, read a book and so on. BEFORE you actually start on the experience. Very often if you know what it is you are supposed to be able to do at the end of that experience, the experience becomes more illuminating and more "absorbable" by yourself.

There is an importance in you being realistically able to say that you are in control of your own learning. That stage comes when you are aware of, because you have actually listed them, all objectives of your learning. Once you are aware of what you want to be able to do, in terms of your learning, then the process of achieving those objectives becomes almost mechanical.

I hope that this book will give you some of the information you need to be able to develop an attitude towards learning which will free you of some of the tensions and some of the misguided notions of what it is to be a student.

Above all I hope that the book has been able to give you some of the information you need in order to develop three qualities which I believe to be necessary in any human being:

- academic rigour, springing from your yearning to enquire and investigate thoroughly, always questioning never accepting, and never asserting without substantiating, and always being able to change your opinion in the light of new evidence,

- a sense of your own worth, so that never again will you feel the inferior of anyone,

- an empathy with, a compassion and respect for, our fellow human beings, so that in an increasingly competitive and market driven society, you will use the skills and knowledge that you acquire in the world of Higher Education, and the sort of effort that you have put into gaining your qualification, not to push others out of the way, but to work together to bring about a more aware, better educated, healthier and happier world.

I hope that you fare well. Farewell!

Ray Baxter

Aldbrough St John

May 1995

APPENDIX I
COMMENTS FROM FORMER STUDENTS

Male student David aged 30, who went on to New College Durham to study A level French & German says:
Study hard it's worth while in the end.

Female student Yvonne aged 35, who went on to Durham to study BA. Anthropology says:
When Ray tells you that FE/HE is like a drug - he is right: you become hooked. It's hard work. It's frustrating, but, above all, it's fun. Good Luck.

Female student Elizabeth aged 38, who went on to Sunderland to study BA. Combined Arts says:
Part-time study is the very best way if you are a single parent (like me) and you can afford the fees and books. It's expensive! Also find out all you can before starting about HE course available and future employment prospects in the area.
Find out as much as you can before you begin your course as to what the subject covers - i.e. if you are really interest in it! It takes lots of commitment. Get a good back up system going prior to HE for family emergencies. Exams do get much harder but are less frightening the more you take! If I can "hang on in there" after five weeks of absence, 3 burglaries in 6 weeks, and a divorce, anyone can!

Female student Moira aged 38, who went on to Sunderland to study BA. Combined Arts says:
Stick in - it's well worth all the trials, tribulations and the tears!

Female student Sheila aged 37, who went on to Sunderland to study BA. Combined Studies says:
Be prepared for lower essay marks at University and don't rely on the format you have been given. Organising your time is vital: be prepared to adapt. Don't panic - enjoy every minute. A degree course is hard work but stimulating and enjoyable, well worth the effort.

Female student Jean aged 47, who went on to Northumbria to study BA. Criminal Justice says:
Good Luck, You have to believe in yourself.

Male student Harry aged 65, who went on to York to study BA. Economics says:

Tell your students to do lots of practice on taking notes in Lectures - and inform them that the onus on learning is on THEM and not on the lecturers or Tutors. Best of luck - it can be done.

Male student Iain aged 25, who went on to Northumbria to study BA. English & History says:

Don't worry - you have been well prepared by Ray's course - and if you can cope with the pressures of that, you can deal with HE! At least you can write presentable and readable essays.

Female student Kathleen aged 35, who went on to Bretton Hall to study BA. English & Related Studies says:

Oh to be back with those on Access,
Caring tutors - faithful friends.
They sent us forth equipped with knowledge
Into an unsuspecting land.
You take your place with grace and splendour.
It makes no difference what your gender.
You leave your tutors, friends and family.
Oh, how you'll wish you'd joined the army!

Female student Sylvia aged 28, who went on to Bretton Hall to study BA. English & Related Studies says:

Ray's course is the best pre-degree course you can do. It puts you light years ahead of the other students especially those who only have A levels. Make the most of it; use the tutor and don't be afraid to make mistakes. When choosing a degree course, go for the one you can really sink your teeth into: motivation is all.

Ray's work on study skills is above all else a challenge. Personally, I feel I paid a very high price to be privy to its benefits. Every area of my personal life was radically altered. Although this was often painful and the more painful to watch the 'damage' wreaked on my child and partner, I feel I have been offered a salvation of sorts. The gains, to my self-esteem, to my sense of academic worth, to my ability to assert myself - are immeasurable. I wrote to a friend, 'this course has totally changed my life'.

The real challenge is, of course, to retain this invaluable sense of self throughout the summer, and beyond.

I feel almost purified by the course! As though many aspects of my life were pared down to accommodate its rigours, and I am left cleansed!

Autonomy is a very valuable asset, especially to women (I feel), and autonomy appears to be hard to learn yet simple to teach; my child benefits immensely from my improved autonomy.

It has played havoc with my equilibrium, but the chaos was fruitful. I am left with a feeling of overwhelming gratitude to you all."

Female student, Joan, who went to Durham to study Teaching.
Personally I found stimulation in discovering others (students actually better than myself. Learned to listen more, talk less, respect and like others less able as well as more able. Discovered faults in myself I'd often suspected but denied. Found I can't play 'mother' all the time and do justice to the Course so must at times actually be more selfish. Found that money matters more than I considered it did. Reinforced my belief that with 'youngsters' such as those I've mixed with recently we really could be about to find a 'Brave new world' to be peopled by such as these.

Female student Pauline aged 39, who went on to Durham to study BA. English Literature says:
You must be determined to succeed. Doubts are fatal. Make sure that domestic arrangements are as watertight as possible.

Female student Fiona aged 35, who went on to Durham to study BA. English Literature says:
Stop saying "yes but what if"! I have found that I can do all that is required of me if I just concentrate on the one thing right in front of me rather than projecting about the next endless number of things - and if I do just that then I also enjoy the one thing so much more because I'm not wishing to get on to something else. My degree course is enjoyable, fascinating, exciting etc etc: so can yours be!

Male student Nicholas Michael aged 51, who went on to Newcastle
to study BA. French & East Asian Studies says:
When (not if!) you:
(a) feel that you can't cope with the workload
(b) wonder why on earth you ever decided to go to university/college
(c) become really depressed
(d) are frightened that you are going to fail
(e) begin to envy the "carefree life" of the man sweeping the street
(f) feel like giving it all up
DON'T WORRY!
All these feelings are perfectly normal and natural. I haven't met any student, young or old, who doesn't have some or all of these feelings at some time or another.
1st: Don't panic or think that it's only you who feels that way, remember you weren't given a place because you have such a winning smile. You were given it

because the selectors recognised that you have ability. So you must also recognise this.

2nd: PERSEVERE.

Keep at it! Of course there will be times when you feel overwhelmed and wonder what on earth you are doing, but don't despair. Think positively. Mature students have a tendency to magnify negative feedback and minimise positive feedback, thus sustaining their low sense of learning competence.

Female student Anna Thérèse aged 31, who went on to Sunderland to study BA. Historical Studies says:
Try to enjoy the course. Keep going. Find out what the tutor want, don't be frightened to ask.

Female student Susan aged 30, who went on to Sunderland to study BA. Historical Studies says:
Keep working. Yes, it's hard work but worth while. Ray's course prepares you well for the rigours of university, especially in essay preparation. Go for what you want. The achievement is worth the sleepless nights and the writer's cramp. Good Luck!

Harriet aged 61 who went on to Newcastle to study History says:
Wish I had known earlier about Access. At the start of the course lack of confidence. Would I hold back younger students - would I be able to bridge the generation gap? But I did - or they did.

Male student Kieth aged 28, who went on to Durham to study BA. History says:
I'm in my second term of my third year, and I've stopped thinking, "Am I good enough?" Now I just think of how high my degree is going to be.. and I don't have 'A' levels..only Ray's course.

Female student Catherine aged 56, who went on to Newcastle to study BA. History says:
Dig in! The best is yet to come both with your 'special study' (which can be fascinating in you're of a nosy disposition and enjoy meeting and 'interrogating' people) and when you get to university, which is brill./fab./great/super/smashing/hellish/wunderbar and bloody hard work. So dig in there!
Always get your essays in on time- it's like borrowing when you're already in debt.

Male student Robin aged 24, who went on to University College Stockton to study BA. Human Sciences says:

You will get there and the Ray's course is vital when you reach University.

Male student Paul aged 30, who went on to Durham to study BA. Philosophy says: Take it easy because you will get through. Don't take it as seriously as I did, because as long as you plan and get through the work you'll find how easy it is when at HE. It's a lot less tense/intense than Ray's course. However, there's still a lot of hard work to do and pressure but of a different nature.

Male student Adrian aged 26, who went on to Sunderland to study BA. Psychology & Philosophy and is now doing a P.Hd at Aberdeen says:
Do not panic, higher education isn't all writing and work, it is also a great deal of fun.

Dear Ray,
I hope that you and the other Access Staff are in good health and that the course itself is running smoothly...In hindsight I'd advise any student not too sure of their numbers to take only one of these rather than divide their time between both, with Statistics being a more useful option for those going on to a psychology course as it tends to be compulsory. Funnily enough I've had no problems whatsoever with Statistics this year, although this could be due to it being more interesting when related to psychological experiments rather than the average size of oranges "Mr Greengrocer" expects to find in a crate of fruit.

Initially I enrolled on a joint scheme of Science degree comprising psychology, computer science, Geology, Physics and Chemistry. However I soon realised that, although an interesting course, Geology was taking up too much of my time (most weekends Students are expected to go on field trip to Yorkshire and weird Scottish Islands) and so was interfering with my main interest in Psychology. Added to this was the point that the computer course was a badly organized mess prompting the decision to change over in the 6th week to a combined arts degree comprising a lot more Psychology as well as Philosophy and Sociology.

As for as my advice for students goes I would urge them to get preliminary booklists before going onto their HE course as a little background reading really does pay off later. They should also be quick to get their grant forms off to County Hall as my grant didn't arrive until a month into the first term.

Above all I'd advise students not to worry about going on to their degree course as the workload is not as bad as they may believe (at least in the first year). Finally I'd advise them to keep their essays, notes and handouts from Ray's course as these are useful to refer back to.

Male student David aged 36, who went on to Sunderland to study BA. Psychology & Sociology says:

Try to glean as much information from students taking the same subject(s) at the same educational establishments so that most things, although new to your experience, will not come as a surprise.

Male student Timothy aged 20, who went on to Manchester Metropolitan University to study BA. Social Science says:

Stick it out - it can be done, and the time goes incredibly fast - before you know it you've finished your exams and you're waiting to go to University, and be careful to hang on to the various bits and pieces you collect on the course, they can come in handy.

Female student Joyce aged 34, who went on to Sunderland to study BA. Social Science says:

Plan your study, make timetables etc. But if you have any problems or worries ask your tutor they are there to help.

I'm proof that Ray's course is successful - anyone can be successful at HE with careful planning - I learned how to learn and how to study. I was also able to combine study with a family life.

Female student Tracy aged 22, who went on to Durham to study BA. Sociology & Social Policy says:

HE is no easy ride. It's very important to look ahead when writing essays, or all the library books will have gone. You are basically given very little guidance, and are therefore left to your own devices. Be prepared to write at least one essay each week, but it's usually two, and you have the added pressure of writing seminar papers at the same time!

Male student Daryn aged 24, who went on to Bangor to study BA. Sport, Health & Physical Education says:

Stick in! You will love it!

Female student Maureen aged 56, who went on to Durham to study BA. Theology says:

Well, if you don't know how to write a critical essay yet, get as much help as you can from graduate on the staff. To read sections of 3-4 books/articles and then come to your own conclusion is an elusive skill. It is only just coming together for me - half way through 2nd year, and I'm not wooden!

What I would want to pass on to today's students is pertinent to those who like me, may begin with little or no confidence in their ability to 'make it'.

I doubted and I would be able to cope with Ray's course. In fact I did, with reasonable marks around mid 60-70s. I doubted and I would get a place at Durham University. I got one!

I doubted I would ever pass the Greek Collection - I passed.

I doubted very much if I would pass Prelims. I passed; though had to resit one paper.

I doubted if I would survive this term with one essay a week plus seminar preparation. I survived just! Have 2 essays to complete during the vacation, so required an official extension.

The pressures are not imaginary, but there are people willing to help.

Surprisingly I find I get on remarkably well with a number of the young ones. I thought the huge age gap would be a handicap, but not so. There are some very nice young people in the course with me.

With the Govt. insistence on greater in takes of undergraduates, but no funding for more teaching staff, all are under pressure; the tutors trying to stretch themselves too far, and marking essays gets behind. We often have lectures several weeks after we've done the essay topic. Not ideal, but with excellent bibliographies, and using your academic tutor, it can be done. The important thing is not to panic! Though the feeling is common!

I have discovered that any subject can be reduced (for exam purposes) to 10 points which are easy to memorise.

Female student Georgina aged 45, who went on to Durham to study BA. Theology & Ministry says:
You can do it! Trust in Ray et al! And yourself, of course!

Female student Margaret aged 33, who went on to Ripon and York St John to study BA.(QTS) says:
Keep going. Don't give up. It gets much easier. Believe in yourself.

Female student Jacqueline aged 35, who went on to Durham to study B.Ed. says:
Advice to those wanting to go on to HE? DON'T! Seriously, do it, but be prepared to work hard. Prepare yourself and your family well before hand and remember you will need their support as much as they will need yours. Advice for those who are going on? Pass! And there are at least two meanings to this word!

Male student Alan aged 26, who went on to Durham to study B.Ed. says:
Go for it! Enjoy it! Time management is very important. Always remember there is life outside HE. Good Luck!

Female student Judith aged 26, who went on to Durham to study B.Ed. says:

I chose finally to study at Durham because it was easier for me to get to, my friends were all going there too and whether I liked it or not an honours degree from "Durham" does carry more prestige! I have been and still am very happy there on the whole. Most of the lecturers are very supportive and understanding, and welcome mature students as they are more dedicated, committed and sensible than their younger colleagues and are prepared to do the work. The education department is especially keen on mature students I have found, and will go to just about any lengths to help us.

The last thing I would say is to have faith in Ray's course and in all the skills that you acquire from it. I haven't done anything so far that I didn't do first on the course. None of my essays have been any harder or any longer than those on the course, nor have the presentations, special studies or research been that much different. I still follow Ray's guidelines for writing essays etc and they are often much better than those of the younger students straight from school. The library procedure is basically the same, and the tips on tackling reading are certainly worth practising and remembering.

When I began my studies at Durham I felt extremely inferior and inadequate. I was sure that I would not last very long, that they would ask me to leave, but they didn't. In fact I realised after a while that I was going to be OK, and as long as I was prepared to do the work I would get there, and if I did have a problem there was someone who would do whatever they could to help me if I asked them to. After a while I realised the department IS ON MY SIDE, and they also want me to succeed. So, even though it's very hard at times, it is important to believe in yourself, because you can do it.

Female student Penelope aged 33, who went on to Durham to study B.Ed. says:
Ray's research and essay writing skills will prove invaluable at institutions of HE. At this time of the year everyone is under pressure and feeling very stressed but just hang on in there, push on and you'll succeed. Believe me, after learning these skills you'll cope with anything HE throws at you! Good luck everyone.

Female student Eileen aged 37, who went on to Durham to study B.Ed. says:
Grit your teeth. It's worth all of the stress and pain. University is easier than Ray's course. Don't worry it is a lot less stressful than getting there!. Choose subjects that you know you're interested in. Attend mature students conferences at the beginning of term and see how many other wrinklies there are (quite a few). One of the greatest advantages for me is the opportunity I have been given to work in America,

---

all expenses paid during the summer break for B.U.N.A.C. Thanks again for this opportunity.

Female student Harriet aged 37, who went on to Durham to study B.Ed. says:
As a basic grounding for entry into Higher/Further Education I don't think you can beat Ray's Course. It reintroduces topics re reference books, reading things up, and the discipline to put a piece of work together. Just as well!

Female student Linda aged 35, who went on to Durham to study B.Ed. says:
To the student...
1. Apply for more than one course at the outset.
Several people have tried to change once "in" and this does appear to be possible - but very difficult. Be sure of the course you want to take.

2. Durham University is now very "mature student friendly"
 I have had positive feedback from all my departments, in this respect, especially Anthropology.

3. Do make every attempt to learn Word Processing before entry to HE. Virtually everything is expected in this format now and you will not have time to learn later.

The skills learned on Ray's course which I have found most useful are: Library and research skills, time management, note-taking, notes on reading, Latin terms and presentation skills. The latter has been especially useful for presenting papers to tutorials.
Thank you once again for all your help and keep up the good work,

---

Female student Christine aged 40, who went on to Durham to study B.Ed. says:
Keep calm. Try not to worry. Take each day as it comes. It does improve. Adjustments are made, problems solved.

Female student Elspeth aged 29, who went on to Lancaster to study B.Sc. Ecology says:
Don't be put off, by the fact that you are outnumbered by 18 and 19 year olds, or lecturers who claim to be experts on everything. The latter is almost certainly not true, and in the former case they not necessarily any cleverer, more intelligent, or even more suited to the course than you are. They've merely had more opportunity, and not necessarily made full use of it.

Female student Nicola aged 31, who went on to Newcastle to study B.Sc. Midwifery says:

Stick at it.!! Is worth it in the end. Ray's course is a second chance not to be wasted.

I feel that Ray's study skills, prepared us well especially the research areas, as our course and future profession is based on research.

Female student Angela aged 31, who went on to Sunderland to study B.Sc. Psychology & Sociology & Philosophy says:

Learn how to speed read. There is so much I could say - However, the first that comes to mind when I was in your position last year is DON'T PANIC! YUK. Use your tutors: talk to them not just of academia but personal. Try and keep an open mind and be prepared to change, not only your points of view but your life completely. Do some of these things now and it won't hurt so much later. Reading has become my life and as I could not read until I was 19 years old I am enjoying my expansion as a person. For me there was no easy way. I tended to make things more complicated than they should have and suffer the consequences of certain actions I could have avoided. Plan your time and be productive: if the essay is not going anywhere ask someone to help. Read Ray's handouts on special studies: there's lots in that that will give you insight later in HE. Ray's course gave me competence, staying power, insight and enlightenment. The sense I could be "someone" and was in control of my own life and that education is not a collection of facts and data but experience and mental reality. Can you tell I love philosophy! ABOVE ALL ENJOY YOURSELF IN THE WORLD OF LEARNING - IT'S WONDERFUL!

Female student Susan aged 23, who went on to De Montfort University to study B.Sc. Speech & Language Therapy says:

Entering in to Higher Education as a mature student was the best move I've ever made. The work is hard but lots of fun. Don't let people tell you how you will find it impossible - be prepared to work hard and you will find everything goes well. Good Luck!

Female student Christina Carole aged 36, who went on to study Dip SW says:

If you really want to do a course then make sure you stick in, apply early and don't become complacent about your chances of getting in to university.

Female student Patricia aged 36, who went on to New College Durham to study Dip SW says:

Still studying! On placement (final one) in Washington. Don't give up! The rewards of coming through Ray's course and succeeding in the areas I am interested

---

in (in higher education) have had effects in all areas of my life. I feel like a completely different person, and it's brilliant!! Thanks to everyone.

Female student Tina aged 38, who went on to New College Durham to study Dip SW says:
Make sure you have mastered the art of time management. For anyone who is starting the Dip SW course in September: enjoy your summer holidays, because you will need all the energy you can muster for the coming year. Good luck to everyone starting new courses in September.

Female student June aged 44, went on to New College to study Dip SW says:
Ignore any self doubt, keep going despite the urge to give up. Keep telling yourself "I can do it!" Good luck!

Female student Christine aged 28, who went on to New College Durham to study Dip SW says:
Keep on going. When you pass the course all the agony and mental suffering is well worth while.

Female student Wendy aged 35, who went on to New College Durham to study Dip SW says:
Go for it, if I can do it anyone can.

Male student Martin aged 22, who went on to Ruskin College Oxford to study Diploma in Social Studies says:
How are you doing! I'm doing fine. Sorry I've been so long to write, but I've been snowed under with work. Last term my tutorial subject was economics and this term it's political ideas. I'm also doing German and a public speaking course. As far as clubs and societies are concerned I'm a member of the Oxford Union and the Ruskin Art Society. I'm due to start my mock exams at the end of this term so will have to start revising. Well, that's all for now.

Male student Julian aged 24, who went on to Birmingham (Westhill College) to study Diploma Youth & Community says:
Ray, your course has been an excellent introduction into higher education. I fully appreciate it only now. I have been receiving really good marks in my essays which I would not have achieved without the help I got from your course. Thank you for all your help. I hope to visit you when I return in the summer! All the hard work is worth it. I am nearly finished my course and well on the way to getting my diploma and hopefully doing a job that I will enjoy doing. Ray, your course gave me the skills and confidence to do that. Without it I'd still be unemployed and frustrated!

Female student Brenda aged 42, who went on to Durham University to study Diploma Youth & Community says:
Keep options open and make sure you do what you want to. DON'T LOSE HANDOUTS.

Female student Linda aged 29, who went on to New College Durham to study HND Business & Finance (Accountancy) says:
Stick with it!! It is well worth the effort. The first week is strange but after that things settle down. Being a mature student can be useful as the tutors are very understanding of any problems you may have.

Male student Mark aged 21, who went on to Suffolk College to study HND Business Studies Leisure says:
I've been meaning to reply to your invitation to the "Life after Access" meeting since I received it, but I have been extremely busy since returning from Christmas. The first 4 weeks were our mid term exams which were followed by 10 assignments over the next 5 weeks. I managed to achieve merits in most of my exams but I referred 2 which I passed on the re-sit. They were difficult exams and I was pleased with the results considering the referral rate for most exams was 50%. I would like to point out that Ray's course, to me, was an excellent way of oiling my dormant brain in order to prepare for an HE course. I do not think I could have lasted more than a week here without the foundation of the course. On entering Suffolk College on my first day I was greeted with a smile and an assignment!! That is how it has continued to this day, only the 1 assignment has now become 10 over 5 weeks.

Female student Yvonne aged 26, who went on to Teesside to study LL.B. Law says:
Stick in and persevere as the hard work pays off in the end!

Female student Celia Ann aged 38, who went on to study a BA at home says:
Don't give up! Try to form a clear view of where you would like to be in say 10/12 years time (or longer) and aim for this.

Female student Suzanne aged 31, who went on to study a BA at home says:
Think positive and it will give you confidence, within the course and in social life to. Keep your tutor up to date with each piece of work and you can't go wrong. Don't get competitive with others in your group (it doesn't work)!

APPENDIX II
USEFUL BOOKS

Basic books which you will need to have

Chambers New Compact Dictionary
Collins Pocket Dictionary of the English Language"
The Pocket Oxford Dictionary

The rest of these books you do not need to purchase - but they are useful

Chamber 20th Century Dictionary
Collins' Concise Dictionary of the English Language
The Concise Oxford Dictionary
Longman Modern English Dictionary

You should have a

Thesaurus - various publishers including Penguin and Longmans

Useful to have

You need access to recent editions of:

Whitaker's Almanack
Pears Cyclopaedia
MacMillan Encyclopaedia

Books on study skills worth borrowing from a library

There are several books on study skills on the market. Worth looking at are:

Exams Without Anxiety	Acres	Deanhouse
Make the most of Your Memory	Ansell, G	Nat Ext College
Study Skills for Adults Returning to School	Apps, JW	Mcgraw Hill
Your Memory	Baddeley	Penguin
A Guide to Study	Baker EI	BACIE
Students Must Write	Barrass	Methuen
STUDY!	Barrass, R	Champman & Hall
The Complete Public Speaker	Brandreth	Sheldon Press
Use Your Head	Buzan	BBC
Student's Guide to Success	Cassie & Constantine	Macmillan
Working on Number, Reading, Writing	COIC	COIC
Returners	Dobie	
High Speed Way to Increase Learning Power	Dudley	Thorsons
Mastering Study Skills	Freeman, R	MacMillan
Teaching Students to Learn	Gibbs	OUP
Learning to Study	Gibbs	NEC

Learning to Study	Gibbs	NEC
A Guide to Rapid Reading	Grummitt	Industrial Soc
Teaching Study Skills	Hamblin	Blackwell
How to Study Effectively	Harman and Freeman	NEC
Learning to Learn	Heaton and Mitchell	Better Books
Management of a Student Reseach Project	Howard and Sharp	Gower
Residential Teachers Manual	ILEA	ILEA
Access Study Skills	ILEA	ILEA Resources
Help Yourself to Learn	ILEA	ILEA Resources
Neighbourhood Action	ILEA	ILEA Resources
Clear Thinking	Inglis and Lewis	NEC
A Student's Guide to Efficient Study	James, D	Pergamon
It's Never Too Late	Joan Perkin	Impact Books
Learning Together and Alone	Johnson and Johnson	PrenticeHall
Patterns of Fact	Kennedy and Hunston	
Read Better, Read Faster	Leeun, E & H de	Penguin
Report Writing	Lewis & Inglis	NEC
Women Returners	Linda Stoker	Bloomsbury
Studying for a Degree in the Humanities	Dunleavy	MacMillan
A Guide to Learning Independently	Marshal Rowland	Open University
The Experience of Learning	Marton	Scot Academic
Help yourself to study	Millard & Tabberer	Longman
Study Skills	Philip Hill	Pan Study Aids
Learning in Action - Activities for group development		R.Kirk
Writing Essays in Social Science	Rouse	NEC
Studying	Sullivan	NEC
Reading and Understanding	Sullivan	NEC
Introducing Study Skills	Tabberer & Allman	NFERNelson
Straight and Crooked thinking	Thouness	
Finding Facts Fast	Todd/Loder	Penguin
Report Writing	Wainwright	Man Update
Learning to Learn in HE	Wright	Croom Helm
Facts		ASE
Rapid Reading	Industrial Society Press	
Decision Taking	Industrial Society Press	
How to Study effectively	Industrial Society Press	
Effective Use of Time	Industrial Society Press	

Useful books to have available

but by no means essential to buy.
Readers Digest Atlas of the World (latest edition)
Readers Digest Atlas of Great Britain (latest edition)
The Times Atlas of the World

Dictionary of Modern Quotations	Cohen	Penguin
Dictionary of Quotations	Cohen	Penguin
Dictionary of Modern Humerous Quotations	Mecalf	Penguin
Oxford Companion to English Literature		Oxford UP
MacMillan Dictionary of Biography		MacMillan
The Oxford Dictionary for Writers and Editors		Clarendon
Timetables of History (latest edition)		Thames Hudson
Dictionary of Proverbs	Fergusson	Penguin
Oxford Companion to the Theatre		Oxford UP
Encyclopaedia of Popular Music	Clarke	Penguin
Dictionary of Music	Jacobs	Penguin
Dictionary of Musical Performers	Jacobs	Penguin
New Dictionary of Music		Penguin
Oxford Companion to Music		Oxford UP

Books you might find useful about the education system

For Higher Education schemes in Europe.

"Erasmus-The UK Guide" £8.80 +£1.10(p&p) contains a compendium of ERASMUS/LINGUA Action II programmes as UK Universities. From ISCO Publications, 12A Princess Way, Camberley, Surrey, GU15 3SP, 01206 21188

"ERASMUS Directory of programmes", lists over 1500 inter-university co-operation programmes. From HMSO Books

"Higher Education the European Community", a directory of courses and institutions in 12 European countries, published by Kogan Paul.

"International Guide to Qualifications in Europe", compiled by the National Academic Recognition Information Centre of the British Council, published by Mansell.

"Insight", a magazine published by the Employment Department, Information Branch, Room E801, Moorfoot, Sheffield, S1 4PQ, 01742 594 487.

"Studying in Europe", £8.99, covers courses, institutions and locations, CRAC, published by Hobsons Publishing, 01403 710 851.

Money

"Student Grants and Loans, a brief guide for higher education students", a free guide from Department of education Publications Centre, PO Box 2193, london E15 2EU, 0180 533 2000

"Students Grants in Scotland- a guide to under-graduate allowances", obtainable from: Scottish Office Education Department,Gyleview House,3 Redheughs Rigg, South Gyle, Edinburgh, EH12 9HH, 0131 244 5823,

"Grants and Loans to Students", available from Department of Education for Northern Ireland, Rathgael House, Balloo Road, Bangor, Co Down, BT19 7PR, 01247 270077.

A Welsh language booklet of grants and loans: Welsh Office Training, Enterprise and Education Department, 3rd floor, Companies House, Crown Way, Cardiff CF4 3UT, 01222 388 588.

"Money to Study", a guide £11.95, EGAS and National Union of Students and UKCOSA, write to EGAS, c/o Family Welfare Association, 501-505 Kingsland Road, Dalston, London E8 4AU, 0170 254 6251.

Choosing courses in universities

UCAS Handbook.

"University and Colleges Entrance: The Official Guide" (make sure it is for the current or the coming year of entry). It is expensive to buy, £12.00 in bookshops, + postage and packing of £3.00 (UK) from Sheed and Ward Ltd, 14 Coopers Row, London EC3 2BH.

APPENDIX III
BOOKS TO HELP WITH RESEARCH

Book list

These are not books to purchase. they are books which you may find helpful when researching a particular topic.

NB. Many of these publications are available soon on CD discs which can be accessed in libraries. These cut down search time, e.g. many years of the "The Times" can be scanned on CD in a few seconds, whereas reading through would take many hours.

Benn's Media Directory, Benn's Business Information Services Ltd, Kent (yearly)

Biography Index, H W Wilson Co, New York (quarterly).

Britain, (yearly)

British Books in Print, J Whitaker & Sons Ltd, London (yearly)

British Education Index, University of Leeds, Brotherton Library,　Leeds (quarterly)

British Humanities Index, Library Association, London (quarterly)

Chronological and Occupational Index to the Dictionary of National Biography, Oxford University Press, Oxford

Clover Information Index, Clover Publications, Bedfordshire (quarterly)

Concise Dictionary of National Biography, Oxford University Press, Oxford

Cumulative Book Index

Current Biography, H W Wilson, Co., New York (yearly)

Current British Directories, CBD Research Ltd., Kent (latest edition 1988)

Current European Directories, GBD Research Ltd., Kent, 1981

Current Index to Journals in Education, Oryx Press, Phoenix, Arizona (monthly)

Currently Technology Index, Library Association Publishing Ltd., London (monthly)

Dictionary of American Biography, American Council of Learned Societies

Dictionary of National Biography, Oxford University Press, Oxford (updated every decade)

Directory of British Associations and Associations in Ireland, Henderson, G P and Henderson, S P A (Eds), CBD Research Ltd., Kent (Latest edition 1990)

Directory of British Associations, Beckenham, CBD Research Ltd.

Directory of British Oral History Collections, Oral History Society, 1981

Directory of European Associations, CBD Research Ltd., Kent, 1986

Education Yearbook, Longman Group Ltd

Guide to Reference Material, Library Association, London

Hansard's Parliamentary Debates: House of Commons and House of Lords, HMSO

Hollis Press and Public Relations Annual, Hollis Directories, Sunbury-on-Thames, Middlesex, 1989

Index to Theses Accepted for Higher Degrees by the Universities of Great Britain and Ireland and the Council for National Academic Awards, ASLIB, London (twice yearly)

International Books in Print, Bowker, New York, 1989

International Who's Who, 1989-90, Europa Publications Limited, London (53rd edition)

International Yearbook and Statesman's Who Who, Macmillan, London, 1988

Keesing's Contemporary Archives

O'Dwyer's Directory of Corporate Communications, New York

O'Dwyer's Directory of Public Relations Firms, New York

Pears Cyclopaedia, Pelham Books, London (yearly)

Popular Medical Index, Mede Publishing (quarterly)

Readers' Guide to Periodical Literature, Wilson, New York

Research Index - Finance, Business surveys Ltd (fortnightly)

RILA - (Repertoire International de la Literature de l'Art), Bibliographic service of the J Paul Getty Trust (semi-annually)

Sectional Lists, HMSO

The Times Index, Reading Research Publications

Trade Associations and Professional Bodies in the United Kingdom, 10th edition, Gale Research International Andover, Kent

Ulrich's International Periodicals Directory: a Classified Guide to Current Periodicals, Foreign and Domestic, 1989 edition, Bowker, London, New York.

Walford's Guide to Reference Material, Walford, A J (Ed) London, Library Association

Whitaker's Almanac, 1990, J Whitaker & Sons Ltd, London (122nd edition)

Who Was Who (7 volumes to 1980), A & C Black, London

Who's Who in America (44th revised edition), Marquis, Chicago, 1986

Willing's Press Guide: A Comprehensive Index and Handbook of the Press of the United Kingdom and Great Britain, Thomas Skinner Directories, East Grinstead (yearly)

More detail on some of the more useful books.

Aslib Directory of Information Sources in the United Kingdom.

Used in Reference Libraries by the Librarians. It lists different types of libraries and sources of information in the UK.

Volume 1: about 3,300 entries on science, teaching and commerce.

Volume 2: about 4,100 entries on sources of information in social sciences, medicine and the humanities.

Walford's Guide to Reference Material.
This lists and describes available reference books. It is published by the Library Association . For American literature **Reference Books: A brief Guide** (published by Enoch Pratt Free Library).

British Humanities Index.
The British Humanities Index, issued quarterly by the Library Association, is the best single source from which to find references to recent and past periodical articles, which you can then read in libraries. It is cross-referenced under author and subject headings. It is widely available in public and college libraries both in the UK and abroad. The British Humanities Index helps one find the answers to three kinds of questions:
*   What articles on a given subject were published in periodicals of general circulation in a specific period?
*   What articles by a certain writer were published in that time?
*   Exactly where (which periodical and issue) can one find an article where one has a partial reference, but not a full citation?

Periodicals Indexes.
For comprehensive research in periodical articles the **British Humanities Index** is insufficient, because it is largely concerned with magazines and newspapers of general circulation and covers relatively few specialised periodicals.

Antiques and Collector's Index.
This quarterly index is based on comprehensive coverage of about twenty periodicals devoted to antiques and various kinds of collecting hobbies, plus other articles in this subject-field assembled from the editor's scanning of more than a hundred additional periodicals.

Britain
Statistical information about Britain. Published yearly.

British Education Index (BEI).
BEI is published quarterly with an annual cumulative volume and covers over 200 British and international periodicals of permanent educational interest.   The information provided for an article includes the title, the author(s), the number of pages, the issues's numbers, or date, and the title of the periodical in which it was published.

Clover Information Index.
Nearly a hundred periodicals in the hobby, recreation, popular science and travel fields are covered in the Clover Information Index, which is issued quarterly.

Cumulative Book Index
Lists all books published in a given year.

Current Index to Journals in Education (CIJE)
CIJE is published monthly by the Oryx Press, USA, with semi-annual cumulative issues in March and September of each year.

Current Technology Index.

The Current Technology Index covers more than 300 British periodicals in all branches of engineering and chemical technology, including the various manufacturing processes based on them.

Indexes to Legal Periodicals.

Because all sorts of issues of human concern are continually the subject of litigation and of court rulings, articles in the law journals discussing them can be most useful to a wide range of researchers - not merely lawyers.

Current Law Index.

A monthly published in California by Information Access Company, with periodic cumulations. It indexes more than 700 law periodicals in the UK, the US and other countries.

Current Law.

a monthly publication consisting largely of abstracts of the most recent rulings in Britain, but also with citations of the latest articles on the same subjects that have appeared in British and in foreign law journals. The publisher, Sweet and Maxwell Ltd, issues a yearly cumulation title Current Law Yearbook.

Index to Legal Periodicals.

a monthly published in New York by the H W Wilson Company, covering articles in UK and Commonwealth law journals as well as American Journals.

Keesing's Contemporary Archives

Weekly resume of current events in politics, economics and social sciences. It is taken mainly from government publications and newspapers.

Popular Medical Index.

This helps one find articles and books on health and medical subjects, in both specialised and lay sources.

Research Index - Finance.

Issued fortnightly, each edition of the Research Index is a comprehensive reference to articles and news items of financial interest appearing in more than a hundred periodicals and the national newspapers during the previous two weeks.

Repertoire International de la Literature de l'Art. (RILA)

Published semi-annually since 1975, RILA is a massive, detailed guide to worldwide literature on western art in all media from late antiquity (fourth century) to the present.

Statesman's Year Book

An annual review of the national life of all countries, with special emphasis on government, industry, population, education etc.

INDEX

The first number indicates the section, the second the page number of that section.

ISLE COLLEGE
LIBRARY